TIME AND COMMUNITY

TIME AND COMMUNITY

J. Neil Alexander
Editor

In Honor of
Thomas Julian Talley

The Pastoral Press
Washington, D.C.

Acknowledgments

The fugues *Thomas, Julian,* and *Talley.* Copyright © 1990 by David J. Hurd. The hymn tune *Talley.* Copyright © 1983 by GIA Publications, Inc. All rights reserved.

Library of Congress Cataloging-in-Publication Data

Time and community : in honor of Thomas J. Talley / J. Neil Alexander, editor.
    p. cm. -- (NPM studies in church music and liturgy)
    ISBN 0-912405-66-X
    1. Liturgics. 2. Time--Religious aspects--Christianity.
    3. Church year. 4. Talley, Thomas J. I. Talley, Thomas J.
    II. Alexander, J. Neil, 1954- . III. Series.
    BV176.T564 1990   90-31782
    264'.009--dc20   CIP

ISBN 0-912405-66-X

The Pastoral Press
225 Sheridan Street, N.W.
Washington, D.C. 20011
(202) 723-1254

The Pastoral Press is the publications division of the National Association of Pastoral Musicians, a membership organization of musicians and clergy dedicated to fostering the art of musical liturgy.

PRINTED IN THE UNITED STATES OF AMERICA

Thomas Julian Talley

Contents

Introduction

THE ESSAYS IN THIS VOLUME HONOR THE LIFE AND WORK OF THOMAS JULIAN Talley, his distinguished career as a liturgiologist and teacher, his faithfulness as a priest of the church. The essayists represent six countries and several religious traditions. Included among the contributors are several of Professor Talley's own teachers, several of his pupils, and a number of distinguished colleagues. The list of contributors alone attests to the high regard with which Professor Talley is held by the international community of scientific liturgiology.

The book has been shaped both by the general interests of Professor Talley and the particular current interests of each contributor. As a result, one group of the essays concerns various aspects of liturgical time, a sub-field of liturgiology to which Professor Talley has made enduring contributions. Other essays are concerned with topics in the early history of the liturgy, another sub-field to which Professor Talley has vigorously contributed. Several writers have contributed essays in liturgical theology. Theological essays in honor of one known in the scholarly community primarily as an historian may seem odd to some, but those who know Professor Talley well will attest to his extraordinary theological and pastoral discernment; an attestation that while true, will be found by him to be highly embarrassing. The final essay is musical. It honors the contribution that Professor Talley has made over the years as a musician and composer, and as an indefatigable champion of distinguished church music.

It is of the nature of an introduction to a *Festschrift* for the general editor to make at least a few observations of a personal nature. I have known Professor Talley for a far shorter span of time than many of the contributors to this volume. Yet, in the nearly ten years since we first met, I have come to know him increasingly well as a teacher and mentor, priest, colleague, and friend. As a teacher, Talley is a taskmaster, particularly with graduate students. "It is never enough to know the right answer," he would tell us. One must know the history of the question-- from its genesis, through every stage of its development, to the emergence of all the possible answers, and on to the best response *for today*, knowing full well that tomorrow's research may render useless today's results. But never did Talley send us to the library to do the work that was his to do. One always got the impression that he had been there first, blazing a clear, if at times untidy, path through the sources.

Few are those who have known him as a teacher who have not also known him as a priest. Students in The General Seminary usually have at least a year to get to know Father Talley in the chapel before they must face Professor Talley in the classroom. That's good! For the first few months, the two seem like quite different people. Inevitably, however, the students begin to see that marvellous integration of priest and professor that so many of his colleagues have come to envy. His priestly ministrations are deeply embedded in a profound knowledge of the tradition; his teaching is saturated with a priestly love both for his students and for the church his students are sent to serve.

To have Tom Talley as a colleague is to know one of the joys of academic life. His correspondence with fellow liturgiologists around the world is nothing short of exhausting. He is not bashful about writing to a scholar half-a-world-away to get the latest reading on an obscure manuscript buried in a remote monastic scriptorium. He is just as likely to be found making copies of the treasures of the Saint Mark's Library at The General Seminary and sending those copies to a distant corner of the globe to assist a scholar there, together, of course, with a carefully prepared letter calling attention to all the nooks and crannies of the text in question that must not be overlooked.

To honor him as a teacher, scholar, priest, and colleague, would be incomplete if we failed to honor Tom as friend. Among the writers and readers of this volume, few will have escaped the deep love and profound care that Tom shows for his friends. He is always busy, but never too busy. The hospitality of his home is as comfortable as an old shoe. His culinary prowess never ceases to astonish. His coffee pot and ice-maker are on twenty-four hour alert.

Through the centuries many giants have been small in stature. Thomas Talley is no exception. As his immediate successor in the liturgics chair at The General Seminary, I am significantly larger than Talley in almost every physical dimension. My feet, for example, are at least a third larger than his. One thing seems abundantly clear: I may sit in his chair, but I will *never* fill his shoes!

Finally, it is a good and joyful thing to acknowledge with sincere gratitude those persons without whom this volume would have been impossible. Virgil Funk and Lawrence Johnson of The Pastoral Press agreed to undertake the publication of the volume and patiently endured my never ending pursuit of the details. Aidan Kavanagh, O.S.B. and Robert Taft, S.J. enthusiastically endorsed the project from the beginning and offered valuable insights during the formative stages. The writers willingly agreed to give their time and expertise to the preparation of the essays and graciously endured my nagging about deadlines. James Fenhagen, Dean of The General Seminary, provided significant financial support that facilitated the completion of the work in a variety of ways. Gordon Lathrop of the Lutheran Theological Seminary at Philadelphia, and David Green of The General Seminary, translated two of the essays with style and efficiency. Deborah Dunn and King McGlaughon of The General Seminary devoted long hours to typing, editing, and verifying the texts. Thomas J. Talley gave us himself.

J. Neil Alexander
Chelsea Square
New York City

Lent 1989

LITURGICAL TIME

1

The Jewish Lectionary, the Great Sabbath, and the Lenten Calendar: Liturgical Links between Christians and Jews in the First Three Christian Centuries

Lawrence A. Hoffman

IN 1987 THE NORTH AMERICAN ACADEMY OF LITURGY HONORED PROFESSOR Talley with its coveted *Berakah* Award, an annual offering by which liturgists designate one of their own as specially deserving of praise. Talley's wisdom for the occasion included this bit of insight, borne of the many years in which he cultivated the scholarly landscape that marks the interface between territory where he felt completely at home, and neighboring ground where other differently trained scholars tilled the soil.

> ... if we must draw on other disciplines, we will probably find ourselves studying things we hadn't counted on... Other experts in other fields of study are more than willing to be of help, [to] lead us toward the necessary knowledge of things we didn't think we would need to know to understand our [own] liturgical traditions.[1]

Speaking for Christian liturgy, Talley listed "rabbinic studies, classical studies, art history, musicology, archaeology, [and] chronology," among the "things we didn't think we would have to know." He thus recognized that the men and women of antiquity whose liturgical existence we seek to reconstruct somehow managed their lives without regard for the arbitrary academic boundaries that mark modern disciplines. The departmental turf of higher education simply does not correlate with anything beyond its own office floor plan. Our understandable hesitancy about staking out claims in other people's territory should be tempered by Talley's judgment that, like it or not, scholarship requires cooperative endeavor if it is to advance.

What goes for Christian liturgy goes for Jewish as well. What follows, then, is an example of what Talley had in mind. It would never have come about, were I not encouraged by him to extend myself into fields adjacent to my own. I am indebted to Tom Talley, then, for encouraging this study; and to other colleagues who helped along the way, among whom I must single out two. John Baldovin proved himself both friend and mentor, by taking me patiently through literature I had only dimly heard of; and Michael Signer, whose academic wisdom and ardent spirituality always enrich me, offered his usually sterling advice as this article was being composed.

I begin with a long-recognized example of Christian sources shedding light on Judaism: the origins of *Shabbat Hagadol* (The Great Sabbath). I then move to a discussion of the reverse: an as yet unrecognized example whereby rabbinic texts may shed light on Christianity: its Lenten calendar. And finally, I return to references to the Great Sabbath in the Acts of the Christian Martyrs, with a suggestion as to how the term "Great Sabbath" is used there.

The Great Sabbath

The Jewish lectionary for Sabbaths and holy days contains a Pentateuchal (*Torah*) and a prophetic (*Haftarah*) reading. Scholars are undecided as to when either of them came full-blown into being.[2] We know, however, that some sort of *Torah* cycle was in effect by the first century, in at least a (so-called) triennial version—it was really variable, taking three to four years to complete—and in some places, possibly also an annual system, both being *lectio continua*. Special calendrical occasions commanded their own readings, which took priority over the normal lection of a Sabbath on which they fell, with the result that the normal reading would be postponed in such a case. A fixed *Haftarah* cycle developed later, possibly out of the eventual piecing together of several independent smaller lectionary lists. Unlike the Pentateuchal reading, the Prophets were never read *seriatim*, and to this day there are different traditions as to which

Haftarah accompanies some of the *Torah* readings. The question of whether by the first century any specific prophetic readings were assigned to particular Sabbaths depends largely on one's reading of Luke 4:17.[3] At any rate, our purposes require only the recognition that both *Torah* and *Haftarah* readings were in effect by the second century, with the result that particular Sabbaths could be named after either of the readings found thereon.

Rabbinic literature normally names individual Sabbaths according to their *Torah* portion: "The Sabbath of [the name of the Pentateuchal reading]." On the other hand, some Sabbaths came to be known by their prophetic readings. An example of a Pentateuch-derived name is "Sabbath Noah," that is, the Sabbath in which the story of Noah is read. An example of a prophet-derived name is Sabbath "Comfort ye ...", the Sabbath following the 9th of Av (the anniversary of the Temple's destruction) when the *Haftarah* begins with Isaiah 40:1 ("Comfort ye ..."); or "The Sabbath of 'Return,'" the Sabbath between Rosh Hashanah and Yom Kippur, which features Hosea's call (Hos 14:2-10), "Return O Israel to The Eternal your God ..."

Sabbath names are thus derived formulaically, by citing the appropriate Pentateuchal or Prophetic reading. We can, however, distinguish names derived primarily from the readings that occur naturally as part of the continuous lectionary (Sabbath Noah, for example) and names that relate primarily to the calendar, and only secondarily to the reading (which was chosen to begin with, only because of its calendrical relevance). The Sabbath of "Return," for example, may in the narrowest sense draw its name from the first word of the Hosea lection, but that reading was selected in the first place because the calendrical occasion, the Sabbath between Rosh Hashanah and Yom Kippur, demands repentance. Calendrical determination is the norm with *Haftarah* readings, which, following no continuous cycle, were easily selected with calendrical concerns in mind. It is also true of some Pentateuch-derived names, in cases where special *Torah* readings replace or augment the continuous lectionary. The two that will concern us later (both known already before 200 C.E.) are the Sabbath of the Red Heifer (*Parah*) and the Sabbath of "This Month" (*Hachodesh*), which feature Numbers 19:1-22 and Exodus 12:1-20, respectively. These Sabbath names are not applied when the cycle arrives at Numbers 19 or Exodus 12 as part of the continuous lectionary, but only on the two occasions when they are read out of order. Here, then, we have names that are Pentateuch-derived, but calendar-determined, since the latter announces the new month of Nisan, and the former is selected the week before that (for reasons that we will see). We will return to *Shabbat Parah* and *Shabbat Hachodesh* in the next section.

Another specially named Sabbath is *Shabbat Hagadol*, "the Great Sabbath." But what kind of name is that? By the thirteenth century in Italy, at least, the term had been generalized to refer to the Sabbath preceding several holy days,[4] but its original sense, as well as its universal meaning now, is the Sabbath preceding Passover; hence, it would appear to belong to the calendar-derived category. Following the formulaic pattern of naming, which we saw above, we would expect to find the word "Great" in the Prophetic or Pentateuchal lections for the day, and in fact, we do, for the prophetic portion is Malachi 3:4-24, which promises "the great ... day of the Lord." However, the Mishnah and the Talmuds, which recognize other specially named Sabbaths, are absolutely, and mysteriously, silent about this one. Not until the Middle Ages do rabbis discuss the Great Sabbath, by which time, preferring homiletics to history, they offer a host of explanations for the name.[5] The *Tosafot*, for example—a generic term encompassing Franco-German rabbis of the twelfth-thirteenth centuries—imagine it goes back to biblical times, in that on that day, the Israelites took the lamb they were to slaughter, and forever after recalled it as the time of the "great" miracle [of Passover].[6] Easily the most amusing etiology comes from *Shibbolei Haleket*, a thirteenth-century Italian source: "On this Sabbath, people stay late at synagogue to hear the sermon of the rabbi who preaches until the middle of the day, practically into the afternoon ... so that [the day] appears to them as drawn-out and long [*gadol*, here translated as 'great' in time, not stature]."[7] Others opine that it may be a mistake, *Hagadol* being erroneously derived from the word *Haggadah* since on this Sabbath, it is customary to read the Passover *Haggadah* in anticipation of the *seder*; or it may be a transfer of terminology from *Hallel Hagadol* (the "Great Hallel"). Clearly, what we have are guesses that do not help us determine the actual origin of this important Sabbath in the Jewish year.

The problem of the Great Sabbath's origin has attracted the attention of the earliest generation of scientific scholars too,[8] who noted the oddity that even though Jews keep the Great Sabbath, early Jewish texts do not mention it; whereas, Christianity, which did not continue the Great Sabbath, bequeathed us early texts (beginning with the Gospel of John) which do contain it. Jellinek, for example, assumed that the Christian literature in question was referring to extant Jewish practice at the time; he therefore dated the Great Sabbath in Judaism not later than the first or second century.[9] In 1859, on the other hand, the great Leopold Zunz concluded that it must have originated among Christians, whence it was borrowed by the Jews.[10] Most scholars prefer Jellinek's reconstruction, but if so, how can we explain the Great Sabbath's Jewish origin?

Solomon Zeitlin turned to this task in 1948,[11] drawing on an explanation that he found in *Sefer Mateh Moshe*, an Halakhic treatise largely on the holidays, and published originally in Cracow in 1591. Noting that a "Great Sabbath" occurs in both John (19:31) and the *Apostolic Constitutions* (B. 5. 18) as the Saturday before the resurrection, Zeitlin concluded that Jews must already have celebrated the Sabbath in question by the second century, and explained its name by looking at the calendrical event and its associated *Haftarah* reading.

> It was the prevalent opinion among a group of Jews, particularly the Apocalyptists, that God would redeem the Jews on the first day of Passover, and on the eve, God would send Elijah to herald the coming of the Messiah. Thus we may understand why the chapter on Malachi dealing with Elijah was assigned ... [Since the reading in question promises, "Behold, I will send you Elijah the prophet before the coming of the *great* and glorious day of the Lord," the Sabbath when Malachi was read] was therefore called the Great Sabbath.[12]

That Elijah's coming was crucial to early Christians too, Zeitlin learns from Matthew 27:47-49 (and Mark 15:35-36) where Jesus is misunderstood by those around him as calling on Elijah to save him; and from Justin Martyr who avers, "For we all expect that Christ will be a man [born] of men, and that Elijah, when he comes, will anoint him ... Does not Scripture say that Elijah shall come before the great and terrible day of the Lord?"[13] Hence Zeitlin concludes that the church took over the idea of a Great Sabbath, but transferred it to the Saturday before the resurrection, rather than the Sabbath before Passover. The rabbis later polemicized against the church's successful transformation of the Great Sabbath, by omitting all discussion of the term from the Talmud. "However, the sages did not succeed in entirely eradicating the observance of the sabbath before the Passover as the Great Sabbath. Hence the rabbis of the Middle Ages, not finding any reference to it in the Talmud, advanced different reasons for its name."[14]

Zeitlin's reconstruction is far from foolproof, but it has its attractions, not the least of which being its solution to two grammatical problems inherent in the troublesome term *Shabbat hagadol*. (1) *Shabbat* is feminine and requires a feminine modifying adjective, and (2) *Hagadol* contains the definite article, and requires that the noun it modifies do so, too. Thus *shabbat hagadol* should read *hashabbat hagedolah*. Alternatively, we might follow the model of *Shabbat kodesh*, a normal rabbinic expression, usually rendered "the holy Sabbath," but literally being "the Sabbath of holiness"; we might then accept *shabbat gedulah* ("the Sabbath of greatness") as well. In either case, *Shabbat hagadol* will not do—unless, of course, *gadol* never did modify *Shabbat*, but was borrowed from another context where the noun it did modify was masculine—such as "the great day," *hayom hagadol*, in Malachi.[15] Moreover, Zeitlin's scheme makes this Sabbath name fit the model of the others. It is calendrically-determined, but prophet-derived, named by virtue of the *Haftarah* lection chosen to express an annual calendrical theme. Perhaps the original term was even *Shabbat hayom hagadol*, "The Sabbath of the Great Day." On the other hand, Sabbaths are elsewhere named after the first word or two of a lection, not a lectionary verse near the end, and, for that matter, we have no independent evidence that Malachi was even read on the Saturday in question as early as the first or second century.

Still, we can conclude our survey of the origin of the Great Sabbath by noting a certain plausibility in Zeitlin's scheme. The Gospel of John would appropriately have been referring to a Jewish calendrical event. The church borrowed the term, in part—I will argue, when I discuss the accounts of the martyrdom of Polycarp and Pionius—because it was found strategically in John. So here we see the first claim I am making: the validity of learning something about Jewish practice from Christian sources, not an altogether novel lesson, to be sure, especially here, where scholarly literature on the subject has been around for some time, but a lesson worth repeating endlessly anyway, if only for the benefit of parochialists who forget it.

Later, I will return to *Shabbat hagadol*, but for now, let us turn to a related problem, the special Sabbaths named *Parah* ("The heifer") and *Hachodesh* ("This month ...") which I cited earlier. They will provide a case of going in the opposite direction: from Jewish sources to Christian practice, in this case, Lent.

Shabbat Parah and Shabbat Hachodesh:
Their Impact on Lent

Talley himself has summarized a wealth of Lenten traditions known from the first several Christian centuries.[16] Egeria's fourth-century account from Jerusalem describes eight weeks of five days per week for the stipulated number of forty days. But the forty-day requirement is probably a late imposition on earlier systems that numbered something other than forty originally. Even in Jerusalem, Egeria's system could not have been universal, or else it was short-lived, since her account is not in agreement with that city's Armenian lectionaries from less than half a century later. It is therefore hard to know what Egeria's experience reflects; at the very least, it is not necessarily a measure of what people in the fourth century were doing all over Jerusalem, let alone in other centers and other times.

Earlier than Egeria, we have Hippolytus' *Apostolic Tradition* from Rome (ca. 200) where the number of days of the catechumenate was not fixed at all; one's status as a catechumen might last as long as three years. True, the last several months were kept more severely, but what months were they: any months in which the arbitrary end happened to fall, or of necessity, the months preceding Pascha? Assuming the latter—though no such fact is stipulated in the text, so that it must be assumed as the hypothesis most in keeping with other evidence—we would conclude that Hippolytus knew of a lengthy catechumenate culminating in an intensive Lent-like period for an unspecified time before Easter. Still, precisely because it is unspecified, this helps us as little as Egeria for our purposes of narrowing down specific pre-Easter time periods in which the nascent church practiced its Lent. Likewise, from that early period—in fact, about a hundred years before Hippolytus—the *Didache's* early chapters, which may be a catechesis, tell us nothing about the length of time allotted to the process.

Talley cites also Socrates' fifth-century *Ecclesiastical History*, which confirms the existence of several time periods. In Greece and Alexandria people fasted for six weeks, while unspecified "others" fasted seven. Both groups called their fast "the forty days." We are back where we started with Egeria: a time when various customs (six, seven, or—in Egeria's case—eight weeks) have been theologically harmonized to arrive at the number forty. Similarly, in 340 Athanasius writes from Rome (where he was in exile) back to his friend Serapion, saying that forty days (of some sort) are common everywhere except in Egypt. The process of theoretical standardization around the number forty seems to have been concluded, therefore, somewhere between the fourth and fifth centuries.

There is, however, one glaring exception to the rule: a Roman custom of fasting for only three successive weeks, and not calling it forty days at all. "Cet usage," says Chavasse, in his critical study, "dut naître avant la fin du III siècle [et] disparu entre 354 et 384,"[17] and a letter by Jerome written in 384 confirms the fact that the six-week fast that replaced it was then already in effect.[18] But even in the later system, we have the otherwise inexplicable application of the term *Dominica mediana* to the fifth Sunday of Lent, and *hebdomada mediana* to the week preceding it, thus signalling again an original core of three weeks to which yet other days were added later on in order to round out their number to forty. All of this merely accords with the assumption that as time went on, every effort was made by all parties to call their fasts—whatever their original length—"Forty Days," and that still in the middle of the fourth century, earlier customs prevailed to which the arbitrary designation "forty-day" had not yet been applied.

So a three-week Lent was an early custom known before the middle of the fourth century, at least in Rome, and possibly elsewhere as well. It eventually got swallowed up by other customs in an effort to arrive at the total of forty, patently impossible if there are only three weeks with which to work.

The question arises: why three weeks? The explanation favored by Chavasse, and repeated thereafter elsewhere[19] is the inherent ambiguity in the Roman calendar. On the one hand, it retained the pre-Christian empire's date of 1 March as its new year; but on the other hand, Easter Sunday could not occur until the spring, that is, 22 March at the earliest, so that the new year from a Christian perspective would not occur until then. "On a donc consacré à la préparation de la Pâques le temps minimum qui séparait le début 'chronologique' de l'année (1er Mars) et son debut chrétien 'reel' (Pâques)."[20] This certainly seems reasonable enough, but Rome may not have been alone in celebrating a three-week Lent. The *Armenian Lectionary*, composed some time between 417 and 439, indicates the possibility of a three-week fast in Jerusalem, too.[21] One can surely grant that the three-week structure posed a solution to the Roman calendrical anomaly, without assuming that the idea of three weeks was created *ex nihilo*, as it were, solely with that end in mind.

Specifically, I want to ask whether a three-week preparation for Easter may be traced to Jewish precedent. Not that it must, or even that it logically should, especially if the three-week Lent is Roman in origin, and then spread elsewhere, to Jerusalem, for example. On the other hand, a good deal of give and take characterized the late empire, so that a custom known in Rome need not have originated there; and in any case, the Jewish population of Rome, even in the first century, was considerable. Jewish influence was hardly limited to Palestine, after all. It was, for example, a regular concern of Chrysostom in Antioch as late as the fourth century, which Robert Wilken calls, "Not Yet the Christian Era."[22] At the very least, we shall see that the specially designated Sabbaths prior to Passover provide us with an interesting three week parallel for the three-week Lent.

We saw above that Sabbaths are often known by designations borrowed from the lections they carry. Even the Great Sabbath, *Shabbat Hagadol*, follows that rule, if we follow Zeitlin's theory which links it to Malachi's prophecy of the "great ... day [*hayom hagadol*] of the Lord" which is at hand. In any case, the Mishnah (ca. 200) lists other named Sabbaths which—unlike the Great Sabbath, therefore—are definitely known to us from Tannaitic tradition, and which unquestionably take their name from their Pentateuchal readings. The two which interest us have already been mentioned here: *Shabbat Parah* (The Sabbath of the [red] heifer) and *Shabbat Hachodesh* (The Sabbath of "This month ...").

The Mishnah's text is unambiguous:

> If the first day of the month Adar falls on the Sabbath, they read the Penta-
> teuchal portion "Shekels" (Ex 30:11-16); if it falls in the middle of the week,
> they read it ["Shekels"] on the prior Sabbath; and on the next Sabbath they
> take a break [reading no special portion at all then, but instead, reading the
> regularly scheduled lesson and waiting until the week after for the next
> special reading]. On the second [special Sabbath, which invariably falls
> also on the second Sabbath of the month Adar] they read the Pentateuchal
> section, "Remember what Amalek did ..." (Deut 25:17-19). On the third
> [Sabbath of the month] they read "The red heifer" (Num 19:1-22). On the
> fourth, they read, "This month shall be for you ..." (Ex 12:1-20).[23]

The Mishnah is phrased as if it counts the Sabbaths from the beginning of Adar, the last month of the year. But suppose we count backward
from the month that follows Adar, Nisan. It would then become evident
that the fourth of the special lections, "This month..." is reserved precisely for the Sabbath that introduces Nisan. Appropriately, it warns, "This
month shall mark for you the beginning of months ... the first of the
months of the year...On the tenth of this month...each shall take a lamb"
(Ex 12:2-3). Since Passover falls on the night of the 14th, there can be a
maximum of two sabbaths in Nisan before it. If, that is, Passover Day
(the 15th) fell on a Sunday, then Nisan 14 and Nisan 7 would be Sabbaths, and Nisan 1 would fall the Sunday before that. In that case, the Exodus reading "This month ..." would occur on Adar 29, the last day of
the old month, the very day before the month being heralded, and *three
Sabbaths* (!) prior to Passover.

The same scheme would hold if Passover fell on Monday through Friday. There would always be (1) two Sabbaths of Nisan before it, (2) still
counting back, Nisan 1, falling sometime during the prior week, and (3)
the announcement of the new month via the lection from Exodus on the
Saturday before that. That Saturday would also be three Saturdays—
though not exactly three weeks—before Passover itself. The only way a
difference might occur would be if Nisan 15 fell on Saturday. In such a
case, Nisan 1 would also fall on Saturday, and the reading announcing it
could occur that very day, rather than being moved up one week so as to
anticipate the new month falling some within the week following.
In such an instance, the Jewish calendar would feature *Shabbat Hachodesh*
only two, not the usual three, weeks prior to Passover, and *Shabbat Parah*
would be read three weeks before.[24]

Let us look also, then, at *Shabbat Parah*, the Sabbath of the [red] Heifer,
normally found four weeks before Passover, but sometimes (when Passover falls on Saturday) three weeks before. I said that on the face of it, the

Mishnah seems to be counting its special lections from the viewpoint of Adar. But in actuality, the text conflates two traditions, the first being the initial two readings which really are Adar-based, and the second being our two readings here, which happen to be read next, but are actually dependent not on Adar, but on Passover, just as Lent is dependent on Easter. Numbers 19:1-22 describes the biblical practice of slaughtering and burning a red heifer, the ashes of which are then reserved for the purpose of washing away the ritual impurity of those who have come in contact with a corpse. Corpse-uncleanness is directly related to Passover, since Numbers 9:9 explicitly prohibits the offering of the Passover sacrifice to "any of you who are defiled by a corpse." Continuing biblical precedent, the Mishnah aptly worries about people who "mourn their near kindred [and who would normally be presumed to have contacted impurity while guarding and preparing the corpse]…or who relocated the bones of their dead [from their temporary burial place to the permanent ossuary]"[25] The Mishnah returns to the theme of uncleanness during the Passover offering in 9:4, without, however, stipulating that corpse-uncleanness is intended; but the Tosefta glosses the Mishnah to correct the record: "when the Passover offering is eaten in a state of uncleanness: [that is] one who has contracted corpse-uncleanness."[26] To be sure, the actual practice of the red heifer as a means of alleviating corpse-uncleanness may have long fallen into desuetude,[27] but taking its place were the rabbinic enactments of ritual bathing, which appropriately are given as the proper remedy for people suspected of being impure.[28] Obviously, the purifying regulations read on *Shabbat Parah*, and *Shabbat Hachodesh*'s summons *the very next week* to prepare for the Passover, are intimately connected, as, in fact, the Palestinian Talmud itself maintains:

Rabbi Levi said in the name of Rabbi Chama bar Chanina: you may not interrupt the lectionary between *Parah* and *Hachodesh*. [If, that is, the first of the four special readings had been read early,[29]—thus necessitating an extra, fifth, Sabbath, on which one would have to return to the regular lectionary—the interruption must occur between two of the other special readings, but on no account between these two.] Rabbi Levi said: The cups of Passover wine provide an analogy to help us remember this, for the Mishnah teaches us that people may drink all they like between one cup and another, but not between the third and the fourth cup. There, no extra drinking may occur. Rabbi Levi said in the name of Rabbi Chama bar Chanina: Logic might lead you to argue that we should first read *Hachodesh* and only then [on the Sabbath thereafter, where there is no special reading] read *Parah*, since the Tabernacle was completed on the first of Nisan, and the red heifer was burned on the second. Why then is the account of the heifer read first? Because it details the cleansing of Israel.[30]

Looking back on the Mishnah's order from his vantage point at the end of the eleventh century, Rashi corroborates the connection assumed here by the Palestinian Talmud: "[We read the account of the heifer first] to admonish all of Israel to purify themselves, so that they may offer their Passover sacrifices in a state of purity."[31]

Even from the plain meaning of the biblical texts, we see that these two Pentateuchal readings, each a possible option for the Sabbath three weeks before Passover, are ideal prototypes for Lenten themes: preparation for the sacrifice (Ex 12) and cleansing from impurity (Nm 19). Let us return briefly to the calendar, to see where Easter Sunday would fall relative to the Sabbaths in question.

Martimort, Dalmais, and Jounel summarize the matter well:

> It was not until the early years of the second century that there was any thought of celebrating a specifically Christian feast of Easter, and even then, the Church of Rome waited until the second half of the century before accepting it.
>
> Until Pope Victor intervened (189-198), two ways of calculating the date for Easter were in use. The Churches of Asia Minor were bent on Christianizing the day of the Jewish Passover, the 14th of Nisan, so they stopped their fast on that day. The other Churches celebrated their paschal feast on the following Sunday, the "first day of the week." The Roman Church, in particular, followed this second way, and it became the rule for all from the beginning of the third century.[32]

In other words, the Jewish calendar was critical to the pre-Nicene Church, especially in Asia Minor, where for a while, there was no Easter Sunday at all, but instead, a Christianized Passover held on the date of the Jewish celebration itself. Alternatively, Christians outside Asia Minor, and especially at Rome, kept Easter on the Sunday after Passover. In no case, however, was there a third possibility. Easter always corresponded with Passover, or took place at the most, one week after it.

What matters even more than the actual calendrical overlap between Passover and Easter, however, is the theory behind it. For the churches in Palestine and Asia Minor, Passover *was* Easter. But even for churches outside Asia Minor, those who moved Easter to the Sunday after Passover, Easter was still seen as the Pascha, with Jesus the newly sacrificed lamb whose blood saved the new Israel, just as the blood of the lamb in Exodus saved the old. "For the Pascha was Christ afterward sacrificed," says Justin Martyr, "As the blood of the Passover saved us who were in Egypt, so also the blood of Christ will deliver those who have believed from death."[33] As the new month of Nisan dawned, then, Exodus 12's announcement to prepare for Passover was as relevant to Christians as to Jews; and so too was Numbers 20's demand for pre-paschal purity, without which participation in the sacrifice was impossible.

Of course, the best evidence for Jewish influence on the Lenten calendar would be a direct connection between the lectionaries of the rabbis and the early church, and in fact, it is there. Chavasse lists Exodus 12:1-14 as an early reading for Good Friday, albeit balanced by the prophetic text of Hosea 6:1-6, "[qui] illustre trop bien le sens du nouveau sacrifice."[34] The case with Numbers 19 is a bit more complex. I am not aware of its existence as a Lenten reading, but let us look at the prophetic accompaniment to it in the early synagogue. The Mishnah records only the Pentateuchal readings for the special Sabbaths in question, but the Tosefta supplements the Mishnah's data by giving the prophetic reading also.

> For the prophetic lection [that accompanies the Red Heifer] they read [the passage beginning,] "I will sprinkle clean water upon you, and you shall be clean from all your uncleanness, and from all your idols I will cleanse you" (Ezekiel 36:25).[35]

The early church readings from the Hebrew Bible would have preferred prophetic readings in any case, and one need not look very far before discovering this one as part of the Lenten lectionary. To begin with, in his comparison of the Georgian and the Armenian lectionaries, Lages lists Ezekiel 36:25-36 as the reading for the Wednesday of the fifth week of Lent.[36] The *Wurzburg Epistolary* too prescribes Ezekiel 36:23-28 for the Wednesday of the fourth week, which would put it roughly about two and one-half weeks prior to Easter, not very far from its placement in Jewish tradition.[37] The common usage of Ezekiel 36 dovetails with what we know of its centrality in the Jewish-Christian debate.[38] For Jews there was but one covenant, the saving blood of which was visible in two commandments: the Passover offering on one hand, and circumcision on the other. Within its homily on *Hachodesh*(!), the earliest Midrash to Exodus even polemicizes against Christian claims that a new and spiritualized covenant is intended here.[39] Apparently, the Ezekiel reading may already have been common in the second century in both Jewish and Christian preparation for their respective feasts, so that Jewish exegetes took pains to explain the Jewish understanding of its message.

Of course, there can be no certainty here. But we do have the common themes, the probability of common lections, and above all, a three-week Lent which here takes on specific meaning as a Christian application of Judaism's insistence that one count back three weeks from Passover in order to cleanse oneself and prepare for the sacrifice of the Paschal lamb.

I said above that the first case—the Great Sabbath—demonstrates how we may learn about Judaism from Christian sources. Now this second case illustrates the reverse: how knowledge of Jewish tradition sheds light on Christianity.

Great Sabbath: From Chronology to Typology

Moreover, there is still more to say about the Great Sabbath.

To begin with, the coincidence between the Christian appellation "Great Week" and the Jewish term "Great Sabbath" is, at the very least, intriguing, for the simple reason that the same Hebrew word *Shabbat* is used regularly in rabbinic literature to mean Sabbath and Week. If the church borrowed the three week counting system of preparation for Passover, it may well have borrowed other calendrical elements as well. Thus "Great Week" may be a secondary meaning of *Shabbat Hagadol*.

Of greater consequence, however, is a second point: the peculiar use of the term Great Sabbath in Christian sources. As we saw, John 19:31 understands the Sabbath prior to the resurrection to be a Great Sabbath. Translations of the Greek *mega* vary, but as Raymond Brown notes, it is "literally: 'great.'"[40] The problem is that by John's own count, the Passover sacrifice had already taken place on Friday, so that the Jewish Great Sabbath had to have been the week before.

Clearly John is using the Jewish term, but transforming it for Christians. For John, the Great Sabbath is no longer a calendrical designation; it is a concept, by which he means the Christian theological equivalent of what the Saturday prior to Passover was for Jews—namely, the Saturday preceding the day of salvation. The day of Jesus' resurrection is the equivalent of Passover in that regard. John is not telling us something about the calendrical occasion of that Saturday; he is telling us something about the nature of the resurrection, thus drawing a precise parallel between it and the Jewish Passover. The resurrection did not happen on Nisan 15; but it took the place of Nisan 15, so that the Saturday before it was, by definition, the Great Sabbath.

Seeing John's use of the term "Great Sabbath" as theological, not chronological, goes a long way toward solving the puzzle of its use in the Acts of the Martyrs. We find it twice, once in the *Martyrdom of Polycarp*, and then again in the *Martyrdom of Pionius*, both of whom are said to have been martyred in Smyrna on a Great Sabbath, the former in 155,[41] and the latter in 250. Can both men really have died in Smyrna on exactly the same day? And if so, what day was it? The martyrdoms occurred in February, while the Great Sabbath of which John speaks is tied to Passover, so cannot possibly have occurred that early in the year?

The latest attempt to solve the problem is by Robin Lane Fox, basing his reconstruction on the prior study of Willy Rordorf,[42] which, in turn, goes back all the way to Lightfoot's claim in 1889![43] Recognizing the impossibility of the Great Sabbath of Passover falling in February, Lightfoot posited the theory that the same term can be used generically for any Sabbath on which "a festival or other marked day in the Jewish calendar" falls. Thus, says Rordorf, the *Sabbaton mega* of the martyrs "bezeichne nicht den ersten Tag des Passafestes, sondern einfach einen besonderen Sabbat." But which one? Rordorf draws our attention to the account of Pionius, where we discover that the pagan population was celebrating a feast, and suggests that the author, himself a Christian, used the term *Sabbaton* not in its Jewish sense of the Sabbath, but merely as a weekday name, Saturday. Hence no particular Jewish holy day is intended. Rather we have 23 February, which is the end of the civil calendar in the Roman empire. Jews, he says, were not working, since it was a Sabbath for them, and pagans too were mischievously idle in that they were celebrating a holiday. In a festive mood anyway, the two groups conspired twice within a century to kill the two Christians. Fox accepts most of this, with embellishments and alterations. The pagan festival was the ancient Dionysia, but it must have been a Jewish holiday too, he thinks. He dismisses the special Sabbaths of Adar on the mistaken notion that they were probably not around yet in the third century.[44] Actually, as we saw, they were, but nonetheless, the term Great Sabbath is never used of any of them. Fox is right in rejecting them as a possible solution, albeit for the wrong reason. So Fox isolates Purim itself as the culprit. The pagans were celebrating Dionysia, and the Jews, Purim—the very day of bloody and vengeful deliverance from the biblical Haman. What better day than that for Christian-bashing? But Fox still has the incontrovertible problem that except for some isolated exceptions late in the Middle Ages,[45] the term Great Sabbath is never used for any Sabbath but the one known to John, the Sabbath prior to Passover.

I suggest then a different type of solution, one that does not depend on fitting a term to an actual calendar day. We have seen that John already transformed it into a theological concept, thus transferring it away from its purely calendrically fixed basis in Judaism. Now a direct line reaches from John through both Polycarp to Pionius. Eusebius quotes Irenaeus, himself a disciple of Polycarp, as testifying that the latter knew "those who had seen the Lord," but especially John, who is singled out by name. Tertullian too says he was a disciple of John, who even appointed him to his bishopric.[46] As for Pionius, it is none other than he who is credited with preparing the final copy of the account of Polycarp's martyrdom in the first place.[47] Musurillo notes that the accounts of the two martyrdoms are composed in similar style, highly dependent on gospel paradigms, full of rhetoric devices, and dedicated to the moral of "stress[ing] above all the poignant lack of sympathy which the Christians experienced as aliens in a hostile world...attributed to the malevolence of the Demon, whose aim is to conspire with Pagans and Jews to destroy the saints."[48] He doubts much of the historical veracity of the Pionius narrative, finds "undisguised anti-semitism" in both accounts, and finds an overall theme according to which the martyrs are portrayed as imitating Jesus's own death.[49]

How much of the accounts we should therefore credit as history is indeed questionable. Arguing strenuously for the historicity even of Pionius, Fox is left with the need to believe that both martyrs died on the same "Great Sabbath" ninety-five years apart. He must then explain that remarkable circumstance by locating something unique about the date; and thus, he is led to identify the "Great Sabbath" as some Jewish feast in February. Far more likely, it seems to me, is to follow Musarillo in seeing both accounts as highly skewed pictures. I cannot argue every detail here, but suffice it to say, that from the time that (1) Polycarp is arrested by the police chief conveniently named Herod (to whom "destiny had given the same name, that Polycarp might fulfill the lot that was appointed to him, becoming a sharer with Christ, and those who betrayed him might receive the punishment of Judas" [Para. 6] to (2) the "mob of pagans and Jews [who] shouted aloud in uncontrollable rage" (para. 12) until finally, (3) they "swiftly collected logs and brushwood [to burn him alive], with the Jews—as is their custom—zealously helping," we have no historical narrative, but a literary masterpiece in which theological characterizations replace historical fact.

Thus we return again to the Great Sabbath which could not possibly have occurred in February. But if the designation of the date is a typological desideratum, it need not have. It cannot be mere coincidence that (1) John is the only Gospel to make the typological breakthrough of seeing the Great Sabbath as the day preceding God's deliverance; (2) John is also mentor *par excellence* of Polycarp, who himself is the model for Pionius; and (3) the deaths of these and only these two martyrs are associated with the Great Sabbath. I suggest that the Great Sabbath for the authors of these martyrologies is no objective date in February, but simply an extension of John's typology, the Sabbath associated with the deaths of martyrs who want in every way to come as close as they can to Jesus' death, and who, therefore, are killed, by definition, on a Great Sabbath— but only retrospectively, when it was decided by the authors that any Sabbath in which they died should be so named. To be sure, the parallelism with John's Gospel is not complete: it couldn't be, since there is some historical kernel here after all; the authors could hardly make up everything. The name "Herod" may be fictitious here, but not the person of a Roman authority persecuting the Christians who refuse to recant. Similarly, the date of a Great Sabbath is fictitious, but not the idea that martyrs die as Christ did, hastening the "Great and glorious day of the Lord."

Conclusion

I began by applauding Professor Talley's call for scholarship jointly undertaken by neighboring specialists. I hope, therefore, that my own attempt to take his advice by crossing over into Christian liturgical studies will be interpreted not as an unwarranted incursion but as a mark of my respect for Dr. Talley who taught me I could do it, and for his field of expertise, where I have gingerly stepped in the course of this essay. Jewish and Christian sources really are interconnected, for the people whose liturgical lives they chronicle were themselves not so theologically disparate as we like to imagine. They shared their world as we now share the records they left of it.

Notes

1. Thomas J. Talley, "Response to the Berakah Award: Confessions of a Reluctant Generalist," *Worship* 61:4 (1987) 312.
2. See classic studies by Adolph Büchler, "The Reading of the Law and Prophets in a Triennial Cycle," *Jewish Quarterly Review*, o.s., 5 (1893) and 6 (1894), reprinted in Jakob J. Petuchowski, *Contributions to the Scientific Study of Jewish Liturgy* (New York, 1970) 181-302; and *The Bible as Read and Preached in the Old Synagogue*, vol. 1 by Jacob Mann (1940), and vol. 2, by Jacob Mann and Isaiah Sonne (1966): reprinted with superior "Prolegomenon" deserving of independent study in its own right, by Ben Zion Wacholder (New York, 1971). In addition, see modern studies by Wacholder (above mentioned "Prolegomenon"), Joseph Heinemann, "The Triennial Lectionary Cycle," *Journal of Jewish Studies* 19 (1968) 41-48, and M.D. Goulder, *The Evangelists' Calendar: A Lectionary Explanation of the Development of Scripture* (London, 1978).
3. On which, see Büchler, "Triennial Reading of Prophets," in Petuchowski, *Contributions* 240.
4. See Solomon ben Hayatom's testimony, "The Great Sabbath before Passover, Shavuot, Rosh Hashanah and Sukkot," carried in Ismar Elbogen, *Der Jüdische Gottesdienst in seiner geschichtlichen Entwicklung* (1913: reprint. ed. Hildesheim, 1962) 550-551, note d.
5. See A. Ben Ezra, *Hadoar* 25:21 (March 23, 1945) 416, and Issachar Jacobson, *Chazon Hamikra* (Tel Aviv, n.d.) 232, for synopsis.
6. See Tos. Shab. 87b, s.v. *ve'oto yom.*

7. *Shibbolei Haleket*, Section 205.

8. For early literature, see Elbogen, *Der Jüdische Gottesdienst* 550-551, note d.

9. A. Jellinek, "Literarische Analekten: Sabbat Ha-gadol," *Der Orient* 18 (1851) 287-288.

10. Leopold Zunz, *Der Ritus des synagogalen Gottesdienstes* 10.

11. Solomon Zeitlin, "The Liturgy of the First Night of Passover," *Jewish Quarterly Review*, n.s., 38 (1948) 431-460; see esp. 457-460. Reprinted in *Solomon Zeitlin's Studies in the Early History of Judaism*, vol. 1 (New York, 1973) 62-91.

12. Ibid. 458-459 (=89-90).

13. *Dialogue with Trypho*, 49; cited by Zeitlin 90, n. 320.

14. Zeitlin 459.

15. See comments by Jacobson, *Chazon Mikra* 231.

16. See Thomas J. Talley, *The Origins of the Liturgical Year* (New York, 1986).

17. Antoine Chavasse, "La structure du carême et les lectures des messes quadragésimales dans la liturgie romaine," *La Maison-Dieu* 31 (1952) 84.

18. See Chavasse, 84, and M. Ferreira Lages, "Etapes de l'évolution du carême à Jerusalem avant le V siècle," *Revue des études arméniens*, n.s., 6 (1969) 69.

19. See, e.g., Cyrille Vogel, *Medieval Liturgy: An Introduction to the Sources*, revised and translated by William G. Storey and Niels Krogh Rasmussen (Washington, 1986) 309-310.

20. Chavasse, "Structure du carême" 84.

21. Lages, "L'Evolution du carême à Jerusalem" 98.

22. Robert L. Wilken, *John Chrysostom and the Jews: Rhetoric and Reality in the Late 4th Century* (Berkeley, 1983). See esp. 29-33, and quotation from Bickerman, 33.

23. M. Meg. 3:4. Translation mine. For standard translations of Mishnah, see Jacob J. Neusner, *The Mishnah: A New Translation* (Yale University Press, 1988).

24. In the Amoraic period the possibilities were arbitrarily limited by the imposition of the rule known as BaDU, which prohibited Passover from occurring on B = the second day of the week, D = the fourth day of the week, and U = the sixth day of the week (from the Hebrew alphabet's second, fourth, and sixth letters). This rule does not concern us, however, since Passover day might still be a Sunday, and in any case, the rule stems from a period beyond that with which we are concerned, namely, the first two centuries. See Solomon Zeitlin, "The Secret of Badhu: a Specimen of 'Jewish Camouflage,'" *American Journal of Theology* 24 (1920) 502-511; reprinted in *Zeitlin's Studies*, vol. 1, 212-221.

25. Pes. 8:8. See Neusner, *Mishnah*, ad. loc.

26. T. Pes. 8:9. For standard translations of *Tosefta*, see Jacob J. Neusner, *The Tosefta: Translated from the Hebrew* (New York, 1979-1986).

27. As had the biblical practice of providing a second Passover one month later for those who were unclean on Nisan 14 (Nm 9:11).

28. M. Pes. 8:8.

29. See M. Meg. 3:4, cited above.

30. P.T. Meg. 3:5.

31. Rashi to M. Meg. 3:4.

32. A.J. Martimort, I.H. Dalmais, P. Jounel, *The Liturgy and Time* (Collegeville,

1983) 33-34.

33. *Apology* I, 66:3; for the isomorphism of symbolic systems relevant to Passover/Easter between Christianity and Judaism, see Lawrence A. Hoffman, "A Symbol of Salvation in the Passover Haggadah," *Worship* 53:6 (1979) 519-538; and extensive treatment by J. Danielou, *Sacramentum Futuri*.

34. Chavasse, "Structure du carême" 95.

35. T. Meg. 3:3.

36. Lages, "L'Evolution du carême à Jerusalem" 99.

37. See Adrian Nocent, *Lent*, vol. 2 of *The Liturgical Year* (Collegeville: Liturgical Press) 248. On the *Wurzburg Epistolary*, see Storey and Rasmussen, *Medieval Liturgy*.

38. See, for example, Bernhard Blumenkrantz, *Die Judenpredigt Augustins* (Paris: Etudes Augustiniennes, 1973), and Marcel Simon, *Verus Israel: études sur les rélations entre Chrétiens et Juifs dans l'Empire romaine, 135-425* (Paris, 1948).

39. Mekhilta *Pascha*, Chap. 5.

40. Raymond E. Brown, *The Gospel According to John: Introduction, Translation and Notes* (Garden City, NY, 1970) 934.

41. The exact date is debated. See Boudewijn Dehandschutter, *Martyrium Polycarpi: Een literair-kritische studie* (Louvain, 1979) 281; Herbert Musurillo, ed., *The Acts of the Christian Martyrs* (Oxford, 1972), Introduction, xiii; and most recently, Robin Lane Fox, *Pagans and Christians* (New York, 1987); Fox dispenses also with Eusebius' version of the year for Pionius' death; see 468.

42. See Fox, *Pagans and Christians* 468-473, 485-487; and Willy Rordorf, "Zum Problem des 'Grossen Sabbats' im Polykarp- und Pioniusmartyrium," in *Pietas: Festschrift für Bernhard Koetting* (Munich, 1980) 245-249.

43. J.B. Lightfoot, *Apostolic Fathers* 2:1, 709ff; cited in Rordorf, 246, n. 11.

44. This mistaken notion is attributed (758, n. 71) to Elbogen, *Der Jüdische Gottesdienst* 155-159. In fact, Elbogen says no such thing, but cites instead the Mishnah that we ourselves noted above. I mention it here not because I think the Great Sabbath was one of these special Sabbaths, but because I want to retain the historicity of the special Sabbaths for the Tannaitic period, for the purposes of my thesis in Part Two above.

45. See above, note 5.

46. See Eusebius, *History* 5:20; Tertullian's testimony in *De Praescr.* 32:2, and other similar accounts, all cited in E.C.E. Owen, *Some Authentic Acts of the Early Martyrs* (Oxford, 1927) 31, and in Herbert Musurillo, ed., *The Acts of the Christian Martyrs* (Oxford, 1972), "Introduction," xiii.

47. See Musurillo, *The Acts of the Christian Martyrs* 19-20.

48. Ibid. Introduction, xiv-xv, xxviii-xxix.

49. Ibid. xii, xiv, xxviii.

2

A Tale of Two Cities
The Byzantine Holy Week Triduum
as a Paradigm of Liturgical History

Robert Taft, S.J.

The Background

POPULAR MYTH WOULD HAVE EASTERN CHRISTIANITY A LIVING MUSEUM OF early Christian usages preserved intact. The fact of the matter is that during the period of Late Antiquity practically every liturgical innovation except the 25 December Nativity feast originated in the East. This creativity remained characteristic of the so-called "Byzantine Rite" into the Late Byzantine Period,[1] when changed political circumstances forced the Byzantines to give priority to the struggle for the survival of empire and church.

I call it the "so-called Byzantine Rite" advisedly, for the rites of both Romes, the Roman and the Byzantine, are hybrids. Like English, these two ritual languages showed during their formative period an astonishing capacity to absorb and synthesize new strains and outside influences, and to adapt themselves to new exigencies.[2]

This history can best be illustrated in laboratory fashion, by isolating a single specimen and placing it under the microscope as a paradigm of the broader history. In a *Festschrift* to honor Thomas Julian Talley, from whose seminal contributions to the origins of the liturgical year we have learned so much, it is fitting that our specimen be drawn from heortology. I have chosen the Byzantine Paschal Triduum.

The Jerusalem-Constantinople Axis
and the Formation of the "Byzantine Rite"

The story is basically a "Tale of Two Cities," Jerusalem and Constantinople. For it is to the hagiopolite rite of Jerusalem and to the monasteries of Palestine that we must turn for the sources of much that now characterizes the Byzantine Paschal Triduum. By the time of Egeria (384), the Jerusalem Triduum had already a developed system of stational services following the sequence of the events of Jesus' Passion.[3] Constantinople, however, remained relatively immune to these developments, retaining a very sober Holy Week liturgy throughout most of the first millennium, up until the period of monastic dominance that follows the struggle against Iconoclasm (726-775, 815-843), when it is enriched by the gradual introduction of hagiopolite elements.

That the pilgrims who flocked to the Holy Land from the fourth century on carried home with them the colorful and dramatic liturgical usages of hagiopolite Holy Week needs no demonstration. It is equally a truism of liturgical history that the Church of Constantinople became predominant throughout the Eastern Empire by the end of the fourth century, and that its rite influenced those of lesser sees, including Jerusalem.[4] The earliest extant Greek manuscript of the Jerusalem eucharistic Liturgy of Saint James, the ninth-century codex *Vatican Gr. 2282*, already shows unmistakable traces of byzantinization.[5]

This mutual exchange became especially intense towards the end of the first millennium. How this happened is known in its broad outlines, if not yet studied in all its extremely intricate details. By the ninth century the Church of Constantinople had evolved a native calendar,[6] lectionary system,[7] eucharistic liturgy,[8] and other sacramental rites,[9] as well as a cathedral liturgy of the hours, the *Asmatike Akolouthia* or "Sung Office" of the Great Church.[10] The *Akoimetoi* or "sleepless" monks of the capital had their own divine office, which need not concern us here.[11] But after the first phase of the Iconoclastic crisis (726-775), which pitted the iconodule monks against the rest of the Byzantine Church, a restoration was inaugurated under monastic auspices. Only during this struggle and its aftermath do Byzantine monks begin to play a significant role in the governance of their church[12] and, consequently, in the history of its liturgy.

This was due largely to the leadership of one of the great figures of Byzantine church history, Saint Theodore, Abbot of Stoudios (d.826).[13] Theodore summoned to the capital some Palestinian monks of the Monastery of Saint Sabas, in the Judean Desert between Jerusalem and the Dead Sea, to help in the struggle against the Iconoclasts.[14] For in the poetic chants of the Sabaitic offices Theodore discerned a sure guide of orthodoxy, he writes to Patriarch Thomas of Jerusalem.[15] The monks of Stoudios gradually synthesized this imported office of Saint Sabas with material from the *Asmatike Akoilouthia* or cathedral office of the Great Church to create a hybrid "Studite" office: a Palestinian Horologion or book of hours with its psalmody and hymns, woven into a warp of litanies and their collects from the Euchology or prayerbook of the Great Church.[16]

But the evolution of the Byzantine hours did not stop with its Studite phase. This Constantinopolitan-Sabaitic synthesis spread throughout the Byzantine monastic world, including Palestine, where it was subjected to further hagiopolite monastic developments. It is at this point, around the turn of the millennium, that our Holy Week documentation reveals a fascinating symbiosis: as the rite of Constantinople is being monasticized *via* Palestine, the rite of Palestine is being further byzantinized. This hybrid neo-Sabaitic monastic office was ultimately adopted by the hesychast communities on Mt. Athos, where it received its final codification in the fourteenth century. This synthesis, basically the Byzantine Rite we know today, spread throughout the Orthodox world (except for Southern Italy) in the wake of the reform movement propagated by the hagiorite hesychasts under the leadership of Philotheos Kokkinos, hegumen of the Great Lavra and later (1347) Bishop of Heraclea, who ascended the patriarchal throne of Constantinople in 1353.[17]

The Holy Week services of this neo-Sabaitic rite are still in use today, codified in the Byzantine liturgical book called the *Triodion*, an anthology of Lenten propers for which we have manuscripts from the tenth century. It contains a medieval mix of long and complex Triduum services, in sharp contrast to the simpler Triduum *Urqut* of old Constantinople, cradle of the Byzantine Rite.

Let us see what today's services look like, how they differ from the old rite of Constantinople, and how they got that way.

The Byzantine Triduum Today

Today's Byzantine Triodion Triduum[18] begins Holy Thursday evening with the Service of the Passion or anticipated Good Friday Orthros (matins), a three-hour marathon characterized by the chanting of twelve gospel lections, comprising the entire Passion account in all four gospels, including the Last Discourse of John. This proclamation is duplicated Good Friday during the "Great" or "Royal Hours" of prime, terce, sext, and none, celebrated usually only in monasteries, seminaries, and large churches. Each hour has a prophecy, an epistle, and a Passion gospel (in sext and none, only of the crucifixion) from Matthew (prime), Mark (terce), Luke (sext), John (none).

Early the same afternoon, Good Friday vespers are celebrated, with three Old Testament readings, an epistle, and a Passion gospel. At the end of vespers occurs the first "burial procession" of Jesus.

Holy Saturday matins, with its long and beautiful poetry, follows the same evening. It, too, has a burial cortege and readings, including a prophecy, an epistle, and the gospel of the sealing and guarding the tomb.

In these offices, three characteristics immediately stand out, especially to those with some experience of their celebration: (1) the absolutely staggering number of Passion gospel lections, seventeen in all, twelve of them at Good Friday matins. From these gospel lections alone it is obvious we face here a composite tradition that has been subjected to little attempt at homogeneity or coordination. The entire Passion gospels of Friday matins are repeated immediately thereafter, in the Great Hours. (2) The extraordinary beauty of the liturgical poetry, and its major role in communicating the sense of the liturgical anamnesis. (3) The solemn mimetic ritual of the two processions of the burial of Jesus.

Most interesting to the historian of liturgy, however, is fact 4: *none* of the above three elements is found in the rite of old Constantinople!

Triduum Services in Old Constantinople

For Constantinople, in spite of the awesome grandeur of its cathedral, Hagia Sophia, and the imperial splendor of the liturgies celebrated therein, long retained a Paschal Triduum of remarkable simplicity and primitive sobriety, redolent of an earlier age when fasting and watching and prayer were the only "ceremonial" characteristics of these days.[19] Constantinopolitan liturgical books of the entire first millennium show hardly a trace of the repetitive Passion proclamation or of the colorful, mimetic drama of today's Byzantine Paschal Triduum. According to the tenth-century Typikon of the Great Church,[20] the Constantinopolitan offices of Good Friday comprised: Pannychis[21] on the vigil Holy Thursday evening, after the Chrism Mass; Orthros and Tritoekte (terce-sext)[22] in the morning; vespers with Presanctified Eucharist in the evening.[23] The only distinctive ceremonial elements were the veneration of the Sacred Lance (Jn 19:34), the Great Church's prized Passion relic, before Orthros;[24] and the prebaptismal catechesis and renunciation of Satan, which the patriarch held in Hagia Eirene, after Tritoekte, for the *photizomenoi*.[25] The adoration of the relic, however, was but the continuation of a devotion begun at dawn on Holy Thursday, not an integral part of the Good Friday liturgy.[26] And the catechesis and renunciation were part of the paschal initiation process, not a Passion commemoration.

Basically, then, what the Church of Constantinople did on Good Friday was what it did on every other Friday of Lent.[27] Apart from the para-liturgical veneration of the lance—para-liturgical because it is not integrated into any of the normal offices of the cursus—Constantinople had no Thursday night Passion nocturns, no Good Friday day hours with Passion gospels, no reading at all of the Last Discourse of John 13-17,[28] no adoration of the cross or its relic.[29] Indeed, as Janeras has noted,[30] apart from a few chant pieces at Good Friday Orthros—and that is the sort of festive coloration found on any special liturgical day—there are few proper elements, and no scripture lections at all, in any of the Constantinopolitan Good Friday services except vespers.

The Proclamation of the Passion
in the Old Constantinopolitan Triduum Lections

So the only thing special about the Constantinopolitan Triduum are the lections of the Holy Thursday evening services, and of Good Friday vespers.

Maundy Thursday Evening

The essence of what was to be understood about Maundy Thursday was found after vespers in the *mandatum* or *pedilavium* rite with its gospel, John 13:3-17, followed by the evening eucharist with its series of five vigil lections:[31]

> Ex 19:10-19
> Job 38:1-21
> Is 50:4-11
> 1 Cor 11:23-32
>
> *Gospel Concordance*:
> Mt 26:2-20
> Jn 13:3-17
> Mt 26:21-39
> Lk 22:43-44
> Mt 26:40-27:2

The gospel cento is a chronologically arranged concordance of the Thursday night events from the Last Supper until Good Friday dawn. The epistle is the Pauline Institution Narrative. Isaiah foreshadows the Passion events recounted in the gospel cento. But the first two Old Testament lections, from Exodus and Job, have nothing to do with the particulars of the day. They are just a continuation of the Lenten *Bahnlesung* of those two books.[32]

Good Friday

Apart from the Holy Thursday *pedilavium*, old Constantinople had no triduum mimesis whatever. The Good Friday Passion anamnesis was concentrated entirely within vespers, where the lections, the same ones as in Good Friday vespers of the Triodion today, remained uncontaminated by later hagiopolite influence:[33]

> Ex 33:11-23
> Job 42:12-17
> Is 52:13-53:12
> 1 Cor 1:18-2:2
>
> *Gospel Concordance*:
>   Mt 27:1-38
>   Lk 23:39-43
>   Mt 27:39-54
>   Jn 19:31-37
>   Mt 27:55-61

The gospel resumes the events of the entire day from Jesus' condemnation through to his burial. The epistle is on "the folly of the cross"; Isaiah is the famous "Suffering Servant" pericope, an ancient Good Friday prophecy found also in such sixth-century Palestinian sources as the old Syriac and Armenian lectionaries.[34] The first two Old Testament readings are, again, from the *Bahnlesung*.[35]

Holy Saturday

Holy Saturday Orthros in the Typikon of the Great Church also has nothing special to characterize it, apart from two refrains on the themes of guarding the tomb and Jesus' accepting to be buried for our salvation, and, of course, the Word service:[36]

> *Responsory*: Ps 43:2-3 (*Rx.* verse 27)
> Ezek 37:1-14
> *Resp*: Ps 9:2-4 (*Rx.* verse 33)
> *Epistle Cento*:
>   *1 Cor 5:6-8*
>   *Gal 3:13-14*

Alleluia: Ps 67:2-4a
Mt 27:62-66

The gospel, which narrates Pilate's order to guard the tomb, "Lest his disciples steal him away, and tell the people, 'He has risen from the dead'" (Mt 27:64), is also the prelude to the resurrection, a theme clearly announced in the psalmody: "Arise, Lord, help us and redeem us for your name's sake" (Ps 43:7); "Arise, Lord God, let your hand be lifted up" (Ps 9:33); "Let God arise, and his enemies be scattered ... " (Ps 67:2)—the last being the classic resurrection psalm across the traditions.

The epistle is also paschal: "For Christ our paschal lamb has been sacrificed. Let us ... celebrate the festival ... " (1 Cor 5:7-8); "Christ redeemed us from the curse of the law ..." (Gal 3:13). And the prophecy is Ezekiel's dramatic "dry bones" resurrection scenario. But there were none of the Enkomia that characterize today's Holy Saturday Orthros in the Triodion, and nothing at all about Jesus' burial, recounted instead in the previous evening's service, in spite of the picturesque burial cortege during the Trisagion, before the lessons, of today's rite.

So in old Constantinople, originally there was nothing, absolutely nothing, of what is considered "characteristically Byzantine" in the Triduum today.

But wait—in one tenth-century codex of the Typikon of Hagia Sophia, *Stavrou 40*,[37] we find interpolated after the Holy Thursday evening Mass of the Lord's Supper a rubric not found in codex *Patmos 266*,[38] an earlier, ninth-tenth century manuscript of the same source: "This same evening at the vigil of the Passion of our Lord Jesus Christ, the Gospel according to John ... " The twelve gospel lections of today's Good Friday Orthros follow, first sign of new developments in the Paschal Triduum of the Great Church. Note, however, that in *Stavrou 40* the Passion lessons are not yet integrated into Orthros, but are read the evening before, during Pannychis.[39]

Mateos comments that these gospel readings "show a Palestinian influence on the rite of Constantinople. Their origin was the *Via Crucis* held in Jerusalem on Good Friday from midnight [Holy Thursday] until morning."[40] But as Janeras has shown,[41] the fact that there are twelve gospels, not eight as in the early Jerusalem Holy Thursday night vigil, also betrays a reworking of the lection list in Constantinople that will, in turn, affect the same vigil in later hagiopolite sources such as codex *Stavrou 43*.

The Formation of the Byzantine Paschal Triduum

This evolution can be traced through the developing books of the two source-traditions.[42] The key documents are, (1) for Jerusalem, the Armenian[43] (5th c.) and Georgian (5-8th c.)[44] hagiopolite lectionaries, and codex *Stavrou* 43, copied in 1122 A.D. but reflecting layers of liturgical material from over a century earlier, certainly before the destruction of the Holy Places by the Caliph al-Hakim in 1009;[45] (2) for Constantinople, the Typikon of the Great Church in manuscripts of the ninth-tenth centuries,[46] the Evangeliary,[47] and the Prophetologion or lectionary of Old Testament lessons.[48]

Though a veritable explosion in the composition of the new liturgical poetry in this period is perhaps the most remarkable new development,[49] I shall concentrate here on the more easily manageable shifts in structure and, especially, in the lection system, as a paradigm of this fascinating medieval symbiosis in this formative phase of liturgical history. It is one I prefer to call "the period of the unification of rites," a period of synthesis, initiated at the end of Late Antiquity, which will result in the gradual synthesis of myriad local usages into the great liturgical families, the Eastern and Western Rites we still know today.

By way of illustration, then, let us take a closer look at the structure, and especially the lections, in the services of the Byzantine Holy Week Triduum.[50]

Good Friday Matins

Good Friday Orthros—namely, matins—in today's Byzantine books has the following structure (elements not proper to Good Friday but pertaining to the ordinary structure of Orthros are italicized):

> *Hexapsalmos (Pss 3, 37, 62, 87, 102, 142)*
> *Great synapte (litany)*
> *Alleluia tone plaq. 4*
> *Troparion tone plaq. 4: "When the glorious disciples ..."*
> Gospels 1-5, each followed by: 3 antiphons
>   Small synapte
>   *Sessional Hymn*
> Gospel 6
> Beatitudes with verses intercalated
> Small synapte
> Prokeimenon (responsory)
> Gospel 7
> *Ps 50*
> Gospel 8
> *Canon, with small synapte after odes 3, 6, 9*

Exaposteilarion (refrain)
Gospel 9
Lauds with stichera (refrains)
Gospel 10
"*Glory to you who have shown us the light!*"
Gloria in excelsis
Kataxioson ("Dignare, Domine ...")
Synapte with aiteseis (biddings)
Prayer of Inclination
Gospel 11
Aposticha (refrains)
Gospel 12
Trisagion
"*Most Holy Trinity ...*"
Our Father
Troparion (refrain)
Ektene (litany)
Dismissal

This is a typical Sabaitic Orthros with gospels, antiphons, the beatitudes, and litanies intercalated. Now this rite is substantially the same as the one in *Stavrou 43*, if we prescind from some variants and, especially, from the fact that in Jerusalem the vigil was still a stational service in which the congregation went in procession, chanting antiphons, to the Mount of Olives, then back to the city, stopping at six different stations for gospels 2-7, then to Calvary for the last four gospels (8-11).[51] The lections in *Stavrou 43*,[52] *Stavrou 40*,[53] and today's *Triodion*,[54] are basically the same:

		Stavrou 43	*Stavrou 40 and Triodion*
Gospel	1	Jn 13:31-18:1	+
	2	Jn 18:1-28	+
	3	Mt 26:57-75	+
	4	Jn 18:28-19:16	+
	5	Mt 27:3-32	+
	6	Mk 14:53-15:32	+
	7	Mt 27:33-54	+
	8	Lk 23:32-49	+
	9	Jn 19:25-37	+

		Stavrou 43	*Stavrou 40 and Triodion*
Chapter	10	Mk 15:43-47	+
	11	Jn 19:38-42	+
	12	—	Mt 27:62-66

But these are *not* the same gospel lections as in the old Jerusalem stational vigil in the Armenian and Georgian lectionaries.[55] There we find only seven (eight) readings. Furthermore, they do not include the entire Passion, as in the later list of eleven (twelve), but only the events of Holy Thursday night, ending with the morning of Good Friday in the Johannine account (Jn 18:28-19:16a): the trials before Caiaphas and Pilate, the scourging and crowning with thorns, the handing over of Jesus to be crucified:

		Arm. Lect. ms J:	*Ibid. ms P:*	*Georg. Lect.:*
Gospel	1	Jn 13:16-18:1	[1] +	13:31-18:2
	2	Lk 22:1-65	[2] 22:39-46	22:39-46
	3	Mk 14:27-72	[3] 14:33-42	14:33-42
	4	Mt 26:31-56	[4] 26:36-56	26:36-56
	5	Mt 26:57-75	[5] 26:57-27:2	26:57-27:2
	6	Jn 18:2-27	-	-
	7	Jn 18:28-19:16a	[6] +	+
			[7] Lk 22:54-23:31	[7] Jn 18:3-2
			[8] +	

Where did the longer list originate? As Janeras has shown, it is a composite *Constantinopolitan* series resulting from the combination of two separate *Jerusalem* cycles, the old vigil lections of Holy Thursday night, and those of the Good Friday day hours.[56] Of the twelve gospels, 1-4 are found as gospels 1, 6, 5, 7 in the stational vigil lists of two manuscripts of the old Armenian Lectionary.[57] Of the rest, 5, 6, 8 are from prime, terce, sext of the hagiopolite Good Friday day hours in *Stavrou 43*;[58] 12 is from Holy Saturday Orthros in both earlier and later Jerusalem documents (the Armenian[59] and Georgian[60] lectionaries and *Stavrou 43*[61]); and we can recognize the source of gospel 9 (Jn 19:26-37) in none of *Stavrou 43* (Jn 18:28-19:37).[62]

Originally the Constantinopolitan series, already visible in evangeliary manuscripts from the ninth century, comprised only the first eleven gospels of the longer list.[63] Why did Constantinopolitan redactors expand the series to eleven (later twelve[64]) gospels, instead of just borrowing the Jerusalem system of eight? Probably, Janeras opines, be-

cause they wanted a series of Passion lections parallel to the eleven resurrection gospels of Sunday Orthros, and because the well-entrenched
Constantinopolitan day service of Tritoekte made them reluctant to
adopt the hagiopolite Great Hours with lections as the Good Friday day-
time services.[65]

The Great Hours

Eventually, however, in a second stage of the evolution of the Triduum, they did just that, which is why Byzantine Good Friday services today have such a burdensome and repetitious series of Passion lections.
The fact that these Great Hours are the only element of today's Triduum
services not a Constantinopolitan-hagiopolite hybrid, but were simply
borrowed as they were found in the Jerusalem books, betrays them as a
later addition, inserted alongside an already existing synthesis of the two
traditions.[66]

Good Friday Vespers

Already in *Stavrou 43*, Good Friday vespers has its present form: hagiopolite vespers with the old Constantinopolitan lections interpolated
almost intact.[67] Here, too, it is obvious what has happened: Constantinople gave to Jerusalem its lections, which inserted them into its own Sabaitic vespers—and then reciprocated the favor by donating the new synthesis to the Great Church.[68] This, of course, presents for the third time
the whole Passion story, already told at Orthros and in the Great Hours
of Good Friday, and transforms old Jerusalem Good Friday vespers, centered on the burial of Jesus in Matthew 27:57-61,[69] into a Constantinopoli-
tan-type general Passion anamnesis.[70]

A Final Problem: The Missing Burial Cortege Processions

But what of the double burial cortege procession so characteristic of
today's Triduum? I have already dealt with this question elsewhere.[71]
Suffice it to say here that we see no hint of this mimetic ritual in any of
the Holy Week Triduum services of Constantinople before the thirteenth
century. In section IV (Triduum Services in Old Constantinople) we noted the evidence for an extra-liturgical veneration of the Passion relics
during the Triduum in the capital. But the later mimetic burial processions have no connection with these older Constantinopolitan usages.
They evolved much later, beginning with the one at the end of Holy Saturday Orthros, in the following manner. In the Typikon of the Great
Church, festive Asmatikos Orthros concluded with a reading of the gos-

pel, followed by the customary concluding litanies and dismissal.[72] This reading was preceded by the solemn entrance of the patriarch and clergy, with the evangeliary, or *Gloria in excelsis* and the Trisagion that follows it.[73] By the fourteenth century, we see a new development, as this common entrance of the clergy with the gospel acquires on Holy Saturday a mimetic character. The Typikon of codex *Athos Vatopedi 954 (1199)*, dating from A.D. 1346, has the priest bear the gospel book not resting on his breast, as customarily, but on his right shoulder, wrapped in the aer like a sindon, in imitation of Joseph of Arimathea bearing Jesus' body to the tomb (Jn 19:17), while the Trisagion is sung in the funeral dirge melody.[74] The first witness to the epitaphion borne, as today, like a baldachin over the priest carrying the gospel, is in a sixteenth-century manuscript of the Slavonic Trebnik, *Moscow Synod Slav 310 (377)*.[75] But as Janeras notes,[76] early Greek printed books long ignore this procession, until it finally appears in Constantine Protopsaltes' edition of the Typikon, in Constantinople, in 1838. As late as the 1879 Roman Triodion there is no mention of either of today's two cortèges.[77]

Conclusion

The Hagiopolite Rite and the Rite of the Great Church no longer exist. In their stead the Byzantine Rite, a new synthesis of elements from the traditions of both Jerusalem and, especially, Constantinople, had come to be celebrated throughout the Orthodox East by the end of the Byzantine Era (1453). Still extant manuscripts of the ninth century show the effects of this mutual influence already, and it was undoubtedly well underway in the eighth century, if not before. It was a two-way street, and the traffic was intense. Each see borrowed from the other and joined the loaned elements to its own heritage, before sending the newly packaged synthesis home gift-wrapped for still further adaptation there. Jerusalem will ultimately prefer Constantinople's eucharist and other sacramental rites to its own. Constantinople will drop its divine office in favor of a multi-level reworking of the Palestinian monastic hours.

We have studied this process of give and take in the services of the Holy Week Triduum. By the ninth century, hagiopolite lections had infiltrated into the Triduum of Constantinople. These lections are integrated into the already existing system of the Great Church. Then the new synthesis finds its way back to Jerusalem, where it is incorporated into the corresponding hagiopolite offices by the end of the millennium. This is the situation we saw in *Stavrou 43* before 1009. It is this system that is ultimately codified in the Byzantine Triodion.

Such an historical analysis confirms one of Baumstark's "laws," formulated against the then current theory of Ferdinand Probst: that liturgical families or "rites" did not evolve *via* a process of diversification, like spokes radiating out of a single hub, but *via* a process of synthesis and unification of the variant usages within a single sphere of liturgical and ecclesiastical authority and influence—in our case, the zone dominated by the Byzantine Orthodox Church.[78]

We saw in section II above that in Constantinople alone before the city fell to the Latins in the Fourth Crusade (1204) there were three clearly identifiable liturgical uses, one cathedral—the Rite of the Great Church, i.e., Hagia Sophia—and two monastic, the older *akolouthia ton akoimeton* or "Office of the Sleepless Monks," and the more recent Studite usage. And even within the long-dominant Studite usage one sees such variety from monastery to monastery that no two Typika manuscripts are ever exactly the same unless one is copied from the other. Beyond the capital the issue is complicated still further by the usages of other traditions, especially of Jerusalem and the great monastic centers, and the local variants within each of them.

So until the period of restauration that followed the Latin occupation of 1204-1260, one cannot really speak of *the* Byzantine Rite, nor even of *the* rite of Constantinople, except as topographical designations for variant local usages that will eventually be distilled into what we know as the Byzantine Rite. Like local dialects of the same language group, such usages were at once different and alike. And the later unified rite can be compared to the standardized literary language that often evolves, political and cultural circumstances permitting, in the later history of such a language group.

Furthermore, it seems almost another "liturgical law" one could add to Baumstark's famous list[79] that whatever is considered most "characteristic," liturgically, of some service, feast, or tradition, is not one of its pristine elements! Good Friday Presanctified in Rome; the Holy Thursday "Mass of the Lord's Supper" everywhere; the enclosed, tripartite sanctuary of the Byzantine Rite; are all innovations with respect to earlier usage. Some of them, like Holy Thursday eucharist, were vigorously opposed as unthinkable novelties when first introduced.

We have seen this "law," too, exemplified here. Contrary to what is said about the historicizing and mimetic character of Byzantine Holy Week services—and, indeed, of Holy Week liturgies in general since Egeria[80]—evidence shows that the two original components of today's Byzantine Triduum offices, the lections and poetic chants, are firmly anchored in anamnesis, and indeed, one that is neither mimetic nor historicizing. For its Constantinopolitan form, unlike the Jerusalem sources, has no concern for the historical sequence of events, and even in its later Byzantine-hagiopolite synthesis, blithely ignores Passion chronology. Furthermore, today's mimetic elements are so late as to be almost modern.

But what is the point of all this, the pragmatist will ask? For the historian, of course, the point is simply knowledge itself, knowledge which leads to understanding. But understanding how our liturgies got the way they are is not just a knowledge of the past. It is an understanding of our present heritage, of who gave it to us, and of what we have done with it. If that is not worth knowing, then I do not know why we run schools.

But in addition, such knowledge is also relevant for what we do. Lenin's famous question, "*Chto delat*—What is to be done?"[81] is, after all, the fundamental question of the practical intellect, and deserves an answer. For Christian historical scholarship in the service of the church is, for me at least, a ministry with direct, practical import.[82]

Now anyone who has experienced the Byzantine Holy Week Triduum in its present form requires no great perspicacity to perceive the need for a reform of its lection system. But how? There are at least two ways of proceeding. The all-too-common way, arbitrarily, is the route taken by those unwilling to do the hard work needed to find a better basis: anyone can just cut short the existing lections or suppress a few of them. A second possibility is to proceed on the basis of an understanding of how things got the way they are. I believe such knowledge is not only useful, but essential. As Fr. Talley said so trenchantly:

> Our current discussions of pastoral praxis, of theological meaning, of spirituality, and of much more rest finally on the assumption that we know what we are talking about; and to know what we are talking about demands much more than can be generated by a mere creativity operating on data drawn only from the experience of itself.[83]

In our paradigm, the Byzantine Triduum, such an understanding will show that the problem is not simply one of too many or too lengthy pericopes. The actual Byzantine Triduum lectionary presents us with an interference of two distinct lection systems based on two opposing formative principles. The Constantinopolitan system was unitary, concentrating the entire Passion anamnesis in the lessons of a single service, Good Friday vespers. The Jerusalem system was sequential, distributing the readings throughout the Triduum according to the presumed chronological sequence of the historical Passion as narrated in the gospels.[84] Today's combination of the two systems in a single lection series that is neither sequential nor unitary creates a hodgepodge that accords with neither organizational principle.

Such understanding does not, of course, provide a solution. But it does isolate the real problem and its causes. Is not such diagnosis the usual point at which the *intelligent* solution to a problem begins?

Notes

List of Abbreviations

De ceremoniis, see Vogt.

GCS = Die griechischen christlichen Schriftsteller der ersten drei christlichen Jahrhunderte (Leipzig: J.C. Hinrichs).

Horologion = La prière des heures: *Horologion*, La prière des églises de rite byzantin 1 (Chevetogne: Ed. de Chevetogne, 1975).

Janeras, "Vangeli" = S. Janeras, "I vangeli domenicali della resurrezione nelle tradizioni liturgiche agiopolita e bizantina," in G. Farnedi, ed. *Paschale mysterium. Studi in memoria dell'Abate Prof. Salvatore Marsili (1910 - 1983)*, Analecta Liturgica 10 = Studia Anselmiana 91 (Rome: Pontificio Ateneo S. Anselmo, 1986) 55-69.

Janeras, *Vendredi-Saint* = Id., *Le Vendredi-Saint dans la tradition liturgique byzantine. Structure et histoire de ses offices*, Analecta Liturgica 13 = Studia Anselmiana 99 (Rome: Pontificio Ateneo S. Anselmo, 1988).

Janeras, "Vespres" = Id., "Les vespres del Divendres Sant en la tradició litúrgica de Jerusalem i de Constantinoble," *Revista Catalana de Teologia* 7 (1982) 187-234.

Lenten Triodion = *The Lenten Triodion*, Mother Mary and K. Ware, trans. (London & Boston: Faber & Faber, 1978).

Mateos, *Typicon* I-II = J. Mateos, ed., *Le Typicon de la Grande église. Ms. Sainte-Croix no. 40, X siècle. Introduction, texte critique, traduction et notes*, 2 vols., OCA 165-166 (Rome: PIO, 1962-1963).

OC = *Oriens Christianus*.

OCA = *Orientalia Christiana Analecta* (PIO).

OCP = *Orientalia Christiana Periodica* (PIO).

Pallas = D.I. Pallas, *Die Passion und Bestattung Christi in Byzanz. Der Ritus—das Bild*, Miscellanea Byzantina Monacensia 2 (Munich: Institut für Byzantinistik und neugriechische Philologie der Universität, 1965).

PG = J.-P. Migne, ed., *Patrologia Graeca*.

PIO = Pontificio Istituto Orientale (Rome).

PK = A. Papadopoulos-Kerameus, ed., *Analekta hierosolymitikes stachyologias* II (St. Petersburg: B. Kirschbaum, 1894).

PO = *Patrologia Orientalis*.

PO 36 = A.(C.) Renoux, ed., *Le codex arménien Jérusalem 121*, II. *Edition comparée du texte et de deux autres manuscrits*, PO 36.2 = no. 168 (Turnhout: Brepols, 1971) 139-388.

Taft, *Beyond East and West* = R. Taft, *Beyond East and West. Problems in Liturgical Understanding* (Washington, D.C.: The Pastoral Press, 1984).

Taft, "Bibliography" = id., "Select Bibliography on the Byzantine Liturgy of the Hours," OCP 48 (1982) 358-370.

Taft, *Hours* = id., *The Liturgy of the Hours in East and West. The Origins of the Divine Office and its Meaning for Today* (Collegeville: The Liturgical Press, 1986).

Taft, "Mt. Athos" = id., "Mount Athos: A Late Chapter in the History of the Byzantine Rite," *Dumbarton Oaks Papers* 42 (1988) in press.

Tarchnischvili = M. Tarchnischvili (ed.), *Le grande lectionnaire de l'église de Jérusalem (V-VIII siècle)*, Corpus Scriptorum Christianorum Orientalium 188-189, 204-205 = Scriptores Iberici 9-10, 13-14, (Louvain: Secrétariat du Corpus SCO, 1959-1960).

Triodion = *Triodion katanyktikon* (Rome, 1879).

Vogt = Constantin VII Porphyrogénète, *Le livre des cérémonies*. Texte établi et traduit par A. Vogt, I-II (Paris: Société d'Editions "Les belles lettres," 1935, 1939).

1. Roughly from the Turkish occupation of Asia Minor in the 1170s until the Fall of Constantinople in 1453.

2. For the Roman Rite, several general studies are available: E. Bishop, "The Genius of the Roman Rite," id., *Liturgica Historica* (Oxford, 1918) 1-19; Th. Klauser, *A Short History of the Western Liturgy*, 2d ed. (Oxford, 1979); S.J.P. van Dijk and D.J. Hazelden Walker, *The Origins of the Modern Roman Liturgy* (Westminster Md.-London, 1960). There is no complete overview of the Byzantine Rite, but see: M. Arranz, "Les grandes étapes de la liturgie byzantine: Palestine-Byzance-Russie," in *Liturgie de l'église particulière, liturgie de l'église universelle*, Bibliotheca Ephemerides Liturgica, Subsidia 7, (Rome, 1976) 43-72; N. Egender, "Introduction," *Horologion* 25-56; Taft, "Mt. Athos."

3. *Diary* 30-38, Egérie, *Journal de voyage* (Itinéraire), P. Maraval, ed., Sources chrétiennes 296 (Paris, 1982) 270-291.

4. Basic for the relationship between these two liturgical centers is A. Baumstark, "Denkmäler der Entstehungsgeschichte des byzantinischen Ritus," OC ser. 3, 2 (1927) 1-32; id., "Die Heiligtümer des byzantinischen Jerusalems nach einer übersehenen Urkunde," OC 5 (1905) 227-289; A.A. Dmitrievskij, *Drevnejshie patriarshie tipikony svjatogrobskij ierusalimshij i Velikoj Konstantinopol'skoj Tserkvi. Kritiko-bibliograficheskoe izsledovanie* (Kiev, 1907).

5. E.g., the presence of the *Nemo dignus* and Prothesis prayers: B.-Ch. Mercier, ed., *La liturgie de S. Jacques. Edition critique du texte grec avec traduction latine*, PO 26.2 (Paris, 1946) 178:25-180:22 (sigl. H).

6. Seen in Mateos, *Typicon* I-II. See H. Delehaye, *Synaxarium Ecclesiae Constantinopolitanae*, Propylaeum ad Acta Sanctorum Novembris, *Acta Sanctorum* XI (Brussels, 1902); A. Ehrhard, *Ueberlieferung und Bestand der hagiographischen und homiletischen Literatur im byzantinischen Reich* I-III.1, Texte und Untersuchungen 50-53, (Leipzig, 1936-1943), III.2 (Berlin, 1952) esp. I, 28-33; S.A. Morcelli, *Menologion ton Euangelion Heortastikon sive Kalendarium Ecclesiae Constantinopolitanae* (Rome, 1788).

7. Mateos, *Typicon* I-II and the references in notes 48-49 below. On the development of the Byzantine lectionary, see also, inter alia, Y. Burns, "The Greek Manuscripts Connected by their Lection System with the Palestinian Syriac Gospel Lectionaries," *Studia Biblica* 2, Journal for the Study of the New Testament,

Supplement, Series 2 (Sheffield, 1980) 13-28; id., "The Historical Events that Occasioned the Inception of the Byzantine Gospel Lectionaries," *Jahrbuch der österreichischen Byzantinistik* 32.4 (1982) 119-127; N. Dragomir, "Studiu istorico-litugic privind tentele biblice din cartile de cult ale Bisericii Ortodoxe," *Studii teologice* 23 (1981) 207-268; P.-M. Gy, "La question du système des lectures de la liturgie byzantine," *Miscellanea liturgica in onore di S.E.G. Lercaro* (Rome, 1967) II, 251-261; K. Junak, "Zu den griechischen Lektionaren und ihrer Ueberlieferung der Katholischen Briefe," in K. Aland, ed., *Die alten Uebersetzungen des Neuen Testaments, die Kirchenvaterzitate und Lektionare*, Arbeiten zur neutestimonialchen Forschung, Bd. 5 (Berlin/N.Y., 1972) 498-591; B. Metzger, "Greek Lectionaries and a Critical Edition of the Greek New Testament," ibid. 479-497; A. Rahlfs, "Die alttestamentlichen Lektionen der griechischen Kirche," *Nachrichten der kgl. Gesellschaft der Wissenschaften zu Gottingen, philologisch-historische Klasse* (1915) 28-136.

8. Overview and further bibliography in Taft, *Beyond East and West* 167-192; id., "The Liturgy of the Great Church: An Initial Synthesis of Structure and Interpretation on the Eve of Iconoclasm," *Dumbarton Oaks Papers* 34-35 (1980-1981) 45-75; H.-J. Schulz, *The Byzantine Liturgy. Symbolic Structure and Faith Expression* (New York, 1986).

9. See M. Arranz, "Les sacrements de l'ancien euchologe constantinopolitain," OCP 48 (1982) 284-335; 49 (1983) 42-90, 284-302; 50 (1984) 43-64, 372-397; 51 (1985) 60-86; 52 (1986) 145-178; 53 (1987) 59-61 (to be continued).

10. See Taft, "Bibliography," sep. nos. 48-60, 80-81, 104.

11. Ibid. nos. 3, 9, 19, 24-26, 79.

12. See H.-G. Beck, *Das byzantinische Jahrtausend* (Munich, 1978) 210-211.

13. See J. Leroy, "La réforme studite," *Il monachesimo orientale*, OCA 153 (Rome, 1958) 181-214; other studies in Taft, "Bibliography" nos. 7-8, 16-18, 20-21.

14. On Saint Sabas and monasticism in Palestine, see A. Ehrhard, "Das griechische Kloster Mar-Saba in Palästina: seine Geschichte und seine literarischen Denkmäler," *Römische Quartalschrift* 7 (1893) 32-79; D.J. Chitty, *The Desert a City. An Introduction to the Study of Egyptian and Palestinian Monasticism under the Christian Empire* (Crestwood, NY, n.d.) esp. chaps. 5-6.

15. *Ep. II, 15*, PG 99, 1160-1164; see *Ep. II, 16*, PG 99, 1164-1168. See N. Egender, "Introduction," *Horologion* 36.

16. On this office, in addition to the numerous studies listed in Taft, "Bibliography;" see id., *Hours*, ch. 17 and the bibliography, 384-387; id. "Mt. Athos."

17. On all these later developments, see Taft, "Mt. Athos."

18. Greek text in *Triodion* 665-736; English trans. in *Lenten Triodion* 565-655; French in D. Guillaume, *Triode de carême*, vol. 3 (Rome, 1978) 182-353. For those not familiar with the terminology and ordinary structure of these Byzantine hours, an outline is given in Taft, *Hours* 278-282; *Horologion* 141, 374-375, which also has a glossary of terms, 501-519.

19. The earliest evidence of a "liturgicizing" of Holy Week appears in the fourth century, when we see some churches open the Triduum with a Passion Vigil Holy Thursday night, in addition to the Easter Vigil. See Eusebius, *Church History* II, 17:21-22, E. Schwartz, ed. GCS 9.1 = *Eusebius* 2.1 (Leipzig 1903) 152; Epiphanius (ca. 377), *De Fide* 22:12-14, K. Holl, ed. GCS 37 = *Epiphanius* 3 (Leipzig

1933) 523-524.

20. Mateos, *Typicon* II, 72-91.

21. On the Pannychis of Constantinople, see ibid. 311; M. Arranz, "Les prières presbytérales de la 'Pannychis' de l'ancien euchologe byzantin et la 'Panikhida' des défunts," OCP 40 (1974) 314-343.

22. Also called Trithekte, a peculiar Constantinopolitan fast-day office said between the third and sixth hours. See Mateos, *Typicon* II, 323; M. Arranz, "Les prières presbytérales de la Tritoekt de l'ancien euchologe byzantin," OCP 43 (1977) 70-93, 335-354.

23. On Good Friday Presanctified, originally celebrated in Constantinople but later suppressed with the adoption of the hagiopolite Holy Week offices, see Janeras, "Vespres" 212-226; id., *Vendredi-Saint* 369-388.

24. Mateos, *Typicon* II, 72-73, 78-79; *De Ceremoniis* I, 43 (34), ed. Vogt I, 168. Sources from the ninth century and later speak only of this extra-liturgical veneration of the Passion relics preserved in the capital. For a time, however, in the second half of the seventh century, there was also a veneration of the relic of the true cross in Hagia Sophia. Arculf describes it ca. 670 in L. Bieler, ed., *Adamnani de Locis Sanctis Libri Tres*, II, 3:5-10, Corpus Christianorum Series Latina 175, (Turnhout, 1965) 228. According to tradition the cross relic was brought to Constantinople from Jerusalem by Heraclius, in 635, just before the fall of the Holy City to the Arabs the following year. See A. Frolow, *La relique de la vraie croix. Recherches sur le développement d'un culte*, Archives de l'Orient chrétien 7 (Paris, 1965) 73ff. Shortly before, Heraclius had recuperated the cross abducted by the Persians in 614, and returned it to Jerusalem in 631. See V.G. Grumel, "La reposition de la vraie croix à Jérusalem par Héraclius. Le jour et l'année," *Byzantinische Forschungen* 1 (1966) 139-149. But by the ninth century, when we first have substantial evidence of the Holy Week ritual of the Great Church, there is no longer any mention of the cross among the Passion relics venerated during the Triduum. Abundant later evidence of the Constantinopolitan Passion relics in G.P. Majeska, *Russian Travellers to Constantinople in the Fourteenth and Fifteenth Centuries*, Dumbarton Oaks Studies 19, (Washington, D.C., 1984) 2, 28-31, 34-37, 44-45, 132-133, 138-141, 160-161, 182-183, 186-191, 216-218, 343-344, 368-370, 378.

25. Mateos, *Typicon* II, 78-79; Arranz, "Les sacrements de l'ancien euchologe constantinopolitain (5)," OCP 50 (1984) 372-397. The text of this rite from the oldest Byzantine liturgical ms, the mid-eighth-century codex *Barberini Gr. 336*, is given in J. Goar, *Euchologion sive Rituale Graecorum* ... (2d ed. Venice, 1730; repr. Graz, 1960) 279-281; and in F. Conybeare, *Rituale Armenorum* (Oxford, 1905) 438-442.

26. Mateos, *Typicon* II, 72-73.

27. Janeras, *Vendredi-Saint* 109. I am grateful to Dr. Janeras for providing me with a copy of this excellent study even before it appeared in print. See also his "Vespres" 214, and "Vangeli" 67 note 41. I depend largely on Janeras' definitive work for what I say below about the Good Friday offices.

28. Undoubtedly because it was read as part of the Johannine *Bahnlesung* between Ascension and Pentecost: Mateos, *Typicon* II, 128-135; see Janeras, *Vendredi-Saint* 109, 151-152.

29. See note 24 above.

30. *Vendrei-Saint* 151-152.

31. Mateos, *Typicon* II, 72-77.

32. Compare the preceding and following Old Testament lections in ibid. 68ff, 80-81.

33. Compare ibid. 80-81, with *Triodion* 704-707, or *Lenten Triodion* 613-614.

34. F.C. Burkitt, "The Early Syriac Lectionary System," *Proceedings of the British Academy 1921-1923* 11 (1923) 309; PO 36, 287; see Janeras, *Vendredi-Saint* 348-349.

35. Mateos, *Typicon* II, 68ff, 80-81; see Janeras, *Vendredi-Saint* 348.

36. Mateos, *Typicon* II 82-85.

37. Ibid. 76-77.

38. Ibid. 76 apparatus 19, and 79 note 1.

39. See note 21 above.

40. *Typicon* II, 79 note 1.

41. *Vendredi-Saint* 109-111, 119-124.

42. This has been done by Janeras in *Vendredi-Saint*. See also his "Vespres" and "Vangeli."

43. Ed. Renoux, PO 26.

44. Ed. Tarchnischvili.

45. Ed. PK 1-254. On this much-studied manuscript, see Baumstark, "Die Heiligtümer" (note 4 above), and G. Bertonière, *The Historical Development of the Easter Vigil and Related Services in the Greek Church*, OCA 193, (Rome, 1972) 12-18. Corrections to the PK edition are given in Dmitievskij, *Drevnejshie patriarshie tipikony* (note 4 above) 11-60. Dmitrievskij's earlier edition of this manuscript with facing Russian translation, based on an 1804 copy (see Bertonière 12 note 25), is given in his *Bogosluzhenie strastnoj i paskhalnoj sedmits vo sv. Ierusalime IX-X v.* (Kazan, 1894). Older studies on Good Friday in this manuscript have been superceded by those of Janeras cited above.

46. Ed. Mateos, *Typicon* I-II.

47. See C.R. Gregory, *Textkritik des Neuen Testaments*, 3 vols. (Leipzig, 1900, 1902, 1909); Janeras, *Vendredi-Saint* 109-113; id., "Vangeli" 66-68, with the references given there in note 44.

48. Ed. C. Hoeg, G. Zuntz, *Prophetologium*, Monumenta Musicae Byzantinae, Lectionaria, vol. I, part 1, facs. 1-6 (Copenhagen, 1939-1970); ibid. vol.II, part 2, ed. G. Engberg (Copenhagen, 1980-1981). Vols. 1, facs. 4 (1960) and 5 (1962) contain the Triduum lections. On this lectionary, see C. Hoeg, G. Zuntz, "Remarks on the Prophetologion," in R.P. Casey, S. Lake, A.K. Lake, eds., *Quantulacumque. Studies Presented to K. Lake* (London, 1937) 189-226; G. Zuntz, "Das byzantinische Septuaginta-Lektionar ('Prophetologion')," *Classica et Mediaevalia* 17 (1956) 183-198.

49. On hymnody see the studies in Taft, "Bibliography" nos. 114-152; see C. Hannick, "Le texte de l'Oktoechos," *Dimanche. Office selon les huit tons: Oktoechos*, vol. 3 of *La prière des églises de rite byzantine* (Chevetogne, 1972) 37-60.

50. For the texts and terminology, see the references in note 18 above.

51. PK, 116-147.

52. Loc. cit.
53. Mateos, *Typicon* II, 76-79.
54. *Triodion* 665-680; *Lenten Triodion* 565-600.
55. PO 36, 269-281; Tarchnischvili nos. 642-664.
56. *Vendredi-Saint* 109-113, 120-124.
57. PO 36, 269-281; see Janeras, *Vendredi-Saint* 97-98.
58. PK 147-152.
59. PO 36, 295.
60. Tarchnischvili no. 707.
61. PK 177.
62. PK 154.
63. Janeras, *Vendredi-Saint* 112.
64. On the later addition of gospel 12, see ibid. 98-100; id., "Vangeli" 66-68.
65. Janeras, *Vendredi-Saint* 110, 120-124. On Tritoekte see note 22 above.
66. Ibid. 92.
67. Compare *Triodion* 702-709 (*Lenten Triodion* 613-614), PK 158-159, Mateos, *Typicon* II, 80-81. I say "almost intact" because in *Stavrou 43* lection 3 is abbreviated to Is 52:13-53:12 instead of extending to 54:1 as in Constantinopolitan usage. On the gospel lections in *Stavrou 43*, see Janeras, *Vendredi-Saint* 348-350; id., "Vespres" 204-205.
68. Janeras, *Vendredi-Saint* 348-350. In the pure tradition of old Constantinople, cathedral vespers has none of this Sabaitic vesperal material (Invitatory Psalm 103 [104], *Phos hilaron, Kataxioson*). There, vespers began with the Invitatory Psalm 85, followed by one evening psalm only, Psalm 140, the entrance of the patriarch, lections with Prokeimena (responsorial psalmody), the Great Ektene (litany), and, on Good Friday, the Presanctified Liturgy. See Mateos, *Typicon* II, 312-314; Hoeg, Zuntz, Engberg, *Prophetologium* (note 48 above) I, 401-409; codex *Sinai Gr. 150* (10-11th c.), A.A. Dmitrievskij, *Opisanie liturgicheskikh rukopisej khranjashchikhsja v bibliotekakh pravoslavnago vostoka*, I-II (Kiev, 1895, 1901), III (Petrograd, 1917; all 3 vols. repr. Hildesheim, 1965) I, 191-192; see Janeras, *Vendredi-Saint* 355-357; id., "Vespres" 212-218.
69. PO 36, 375; Tarchnischvili no. 702.
70. Janeras, *Vendredi-Saint* 349-350.
71. R. Taft, "'In the Bridegroom's Absence.' The Paschal Triduum in the Byzantine Church," to be published in Analecta Liturgica = Studia Anselmiana (Rome: Pontificio Ateneo S. Anselmo).
72. Mateos, *Typicon* I, xxiii.
73. Ibid. II, 82-83, see 312.
74. Pallas 40-41.
75. M. Lisitsyn, *Pervonachal'nyj slavjano-russkij tipikon* (St. Petersburg: Tipografia Smirnov, 1911) 150-151; see Pallas 42.
76. *Vendredi-Saint* 401.
77. *Triodion* 707, 709.
78. A. Baumstark, *Comparative Liturgy* (Westminster, MD, 1958) 15-19, and earlier, in id., *Vom geschichtlichen Werden der Liturgie*, Ecclesia Orans 10 (Freiburg im Br., 1923) ch. 5; against F. Probst, *Liturgie der drei ersten christlichen Jahrhunderte*

(Tübingen, 1870); id., *Liturgie des 4. Jahrhunderts und deren Reform* (Münster, 1892).

79. *Comparative Liturgy* 15-30.

80. On this question see Taft, *Beyond East and West*, ch. 2.

81. Actually, Lenin got the title of his tract (1901-1902) from the Russian socialist Nikolaj G. Chernyshevskij (1828-1889), who wrote a utopian novel by that name (1862-1863).

82. See R. Taft, "Response to the Berakah Award: Anamnesis," *Worship* 59 (1985) 311-314.

83. "Introduction," Taft, *Beyond East and West* vii.

84. Of course, modern New Testament scholars have taught us that there is no "chronological order" in the gospels: see D.M. Stanley, *"I Encountered God!" The Spiritual Exercises with the Gospel of Saint John* (St. Louis, 1986) 176. But the Byzantines entertained no such notion.

3

The Origins and Development of Candlemas: A Struggle for Identity and Coherence?

Kenneth W. Stevenson

EVERY TRADE HAS ITS PITFALLS, AND MOST HAVE TO DO WITH TERMINOLOGY. While it may be true that if ten of the world's most distinguished economists met together they could not agree on what is wrong with the western society of today, it is more likely than not that if one were to convene a meeting of liturgical scholars and ask them to identify the single most difficult problem for their trade, most would agree on terminology. Terminology, or nomenclature (perhaps more accurately) indicates the way a theory or an event is perceived and understood by people. For the study of Christian worship, it matters a great deal that the anamnesis is the anamnesis, and that the epiclesis is the epiclesis. It determines how we understand the movement of the eucharistic prayer; it also underlies different nuances to the sacrament of baptism.[1]

It is the purpose of this meager salutation to Thomas Talley to look afresh at the origins of the liturgy for 2 February. Talley has himself made significant contributions to our understanding of liturgical time, as the English are learning from Americans to call it. I well remember sitting at his feet at the 1979 meeting of the Oxford Patristic Congress under the eagle-eyes of international liturgical academe. As one formed in the Scottish Episcopalian tradition, I readily gave ear to an American of the same Anglican family, not just *historically* (how to trace the period of early origins), but *hermeneutically* (what does this mean to today's church). If you love the church of the past, you need also to love the church of your own time. Talley's own writings show a savoring of the complexity of tradition, but there is invariably a sense in which his eyes are peering through those spectacles (and the billows of pipe tobacco) with a warning glint at the mess we may—or may not—be making of our own multifariously revised rites. With a Texas lilt and a burst of laughter, the names of Dix and Botte, Macomber and Strobel flow forth as a pastiche of worship in the beauty of holiness. When you keep *that* company, you never need argue about "relevance."

Once the feast of 2 February is placed under a microscope, the question of names immediately asserts itself. But soon afterwards, two other questions rear their heads. It begins to become clear that this feast, particularly in the West, has had a varied career. For in popular piety, Candlemas[2] (*Lichtmesse* in Germany, even to this day) indicates a spectacle, rather than a theological "event."

The Three Questions

First, is the feast the Presentation of Christ in the Temple (as it is described in the 1970 *Missale Romanum*), or is it the Feast of the Purification of the Blessed Virgin Mary (as it is entitled in the 1570 *Missale Romanum*)? Each one of these ideas is to be found explicitly present in the narrative, in Luke 2:22-40. Further, is the feast one of "meeting," whether between the aged Simeon and the infant Christ, or (by extension) between ourselves and the Christ event? (Such an understanding clearly dominates the Byzantine Rite for this day.) Yet again, is it no more and no less than a feast of candles, because the procession with candles takes over as the principal feature that demarcates this feast from others (as in the medieval West)?

The second question concerns where this feast actually *belongs* in the liturgical year. Because it came to be calculated to be celebrated on the fortieth day after the birth of Christ, it is at root connected with Christmas, whether an appendage, optional in character, or a major occasion, with liturgies befitting a great Christological event. Yet the full gospel-pericope for the day does not stop short at Simeon's *Nunc Dimittis*, but goes on to prophesy that "a sword will pierce through your (i.e., Mary's) own soul also." Biblical commentators, not just modern ones, have been fascinated by the "bitter-sweet" nature of the story. On that reckoning, this feast, if it is to reflect the intentions of the gospel-writer himself, is a hinge between Christmas and Holy Week.

The third question in part extends this matter. What is the *mood* for the occasion? Evidence points to the penitential character of the procession, both at Rome and (for a time, at least) at Constantinople; a barefoot pontiff, walking as an ordinary cleric; and (as late as the 1570 *Missale Romanum*) purple vestments for the procession, changed into white for the mass. The only other occasions when such a dramatic change of vesture occurs are Palm Sunday (red into purple) and the Easter Vigil (purple into white). Interestingly, the 1970 *Missale Romanum* irons out these conflicts, in the contemporary search for slickness all round; white for the whole Candlemas liturgy and the Easter Vigil, and red for the whole Palm Sunday procession and eucharist.

Individually, these three questions do not add up to very much. When set aside from each other, they can be dismissed as reflecting another medieval muddle, or (if one is to be polite) anomaly. But together they are an eloquent expression of a deep nervousness on the meaning of this feast. Unlike the Passion narratives, which, though distinct, complement each other and tell the same basic story, this strange feast relies exclusively on a unique drama told only towards the end of Luke's infancy narrative. That is to say, so far from reflecting the central concerns of all four gospel-writers, the story of Jesus being carried into the temple as a six-week old baby boy is a peculiarity of Luke's Gospel. To that we must now turn.

The Gospel Narrative: Luke 2:22-40

The pericope is part of Luke's own sequence of ideas which began with the birth of John the Baptist, continued in the annunciation to Mary, and reached its climax in the birth of Christ. Luke's priorities dominate the drama. Matthew moves the action through dreams and Joseph, while Luke has angelic appearances direct to Mary. Matthew, the Jew, is captivated by the outsiders to Israel, hence the Wise Men from the East, and the Flight to Egypt (historically the most difficult sub-drama); whereas Luke, himself the cultured outsider, has shepherds come to adore Jesus, shepherds of simple rustic background, signs of Davidic continuity.

In the temple-drama, however, Luke himself conflates the purification of Mary after her childbirth (something necessary for every mother, hence the turtle-dove or pigeon), and the presentation (more accurately, the redemption of the first-born son); moreover, redemption of the first-born involved no sacrifice, but payment of a few shekels.[3] To compound the anomaly, Luke speaks of "their" purification, almost as if it were a family liturgy. Why?

One answer would be to say that Luke is writing for a Gentile non-

Palestinian community to whom the niceties of Jewish temple-ritual mattered little. The alternative is to suggest that Luke got it all wrong and did not know what he was writing about. Raymond Brown's classic study *The Birth of the Messiah*[4] exposes the subtleties of the infancy narratives of both Matthew and Luke, perhaps enabling us to credit Luke with more profundity than the view that he was ignorant would permit us to do.

The subtleties are everywhere present. In contrast to John the Baptist, who has only Zechariah to proclaim his birth, Jesus has angels, and then Simeon. The angels proclaim Christ as the expectation of Israel (Lk 2:10-11), whereas Simeon speaks of Christ fulfilling his destiny "in the presence of all peoples" (Lk 2:31). The balance of the devout parents with their child is matched by the two aged people, whom (Brown suggests) typify Jewish Christian *anawim*,[5] totally dependent upon God, seeing in Christ their deliverance. The *anawim*, the so-called "Poor Ones," loved the temple; the temple is also central to the dramas of Luke's infancy narrative, as witness the Zechariah scene (Luke 1:5-23), as well as the story of the twelve-year old Jesus at the Passover (Lk 2:41-52), an *innuendo*-ridden passage if ever there was one. Brown waxes eloquent:

> The Law, the prophetic Spirit, and the Temple cult have all come together to set the scene for the greatness of Jesus. The one who is called 'holy' (Luke 1:35) has come to the holy place of Israel, and he begins to embody much of what was associated with the Temple.[6]

Once again, there is contrast. Simeon is looking for the "consolation" (Lk 2:25) of Israel, whereas Anna, the prophetess, speaks of the "redemption" (Lk 2:38) Christ will bring. Both Simeon's oracles, the *Nunc Dimittis* (Lk 2:29-32) and the warning to Mary (Lk 2:34-35) rely on Isaiah's combination of consolation (Is 2:38) themes. As to the oracles themselves, the first hymns the thoughts and reflections of the aged pious one, a motif that persists in Christian spirituality, right down to tenor and bass solos in the liturgical canticle. Simeon's dual role of watchman and aged one combine with the dual emotions of joy and peace.

It could be that, like the inclusion of the canticle itself into the liturgy, the *Nunc Dimittis* does not belong to the original recension of this part of the gospel. But the second oracle poses exegetical questions wrestled with by subsequent ages. Once again, rather than try to iron out harshnesses, it is better to accept them. Mary is the first to hear of the good news of Jesus, and so is also the first to encounter its challenge and the tragedy of its rejection by many in Israel. And Luke's Christ, ambivalent about suffocating family loyalties, is perhaps saying that being related to

Jesus is not enough. The pericope ends with the statement that Jesus "grew and became strong, filled with wisdom: and the favour of God was upon him" (Lk 2:40); John the Baptist was "strong in spirit," but Jesus already has the Spirit.

So much for the gospel story. What of the three questions? It would appear that the drama (to answer the question of focus and terminology) is too complex for one theme to dominate. Luke's narrative is both purification and presentation, it is both meeting with Simeon, and Anna, and an encounter between the believer and the Christ. As to the second question of where it belongs, it would appear that Luke's Christ, always a human and trusting divine figure, ready to identify with the forgotten elements of society (here, an old man, and a woman, too), arouses conflict from the start. Whereas Matthew's sign of early tragedy is the slaying of the innocents, Luke's is the deliberate juxtaposition of the oracle of departure (*Nunc Dimittis*) and the oracle of tragic future. The narrative, then, already contains the seeds for careful and varied treatment in the liturgy. The third question, about the penitential aspect, is less easy to reconcile directly with this pericope, whether in its full form, or even in a reconstructed "early" recension. But it is not entirely concealed from view; Simeon's second oracle brings a chilling tone to a cozy atmosphere, and it could be that a spirituality that enlarges on *purification* (*our* purification, prior to making *our* offering) may supply a partial answer. It is for this reason that we must now turn briefly to look at the exegetical-homiletical tradition of antiquity.

Patristic Exegesis and Homiletics[7]

It goes without saying that the relationship between theology preached and biblical text commented upon is always an evolving one, certainly different in antiquity from what it is today in the West. Moreover, we have already seen that, although Luke is the only gospel to record this story, there is enough in the drama for considerable elaboration on various themes. None of these necessarily determines how a text is universally understood, but it is at once striking how many different ideas the story provokes from the Fathers. Origen,[8] commenting on the text, fastens his ideas on the purgation-theme, and the paradoxical character of Mary's need to purify herself, even though she has brought God into the world. A homily attributed to Timothy of Jerusalem, of uncertain date, emphasizes the second oracle of Simeon, and interprets the first "piercing of the sword" in the ensuing story, of Jesus lost in the temple at the age of twelve.[9] Ephrem, on the other hand, takes up the sacrifice motif:

> But Simeon the priest [sic!] when he had received Christ in his arms so that
> he might present him to God, understood when he beheld him that he was
> not offering Christ but was himself being offered. For the Son is not to be
> offered to his Lord by the Son.[10]

Here is a tightly-packed argument that has as much to do with evolving
Trinitarian doctrine as it has with the essentially paradoxical nature of
eucharistic sacrifice. It also gives us a foretaste of the later Byzantine spirituality of this feast—the "meeting" of Simeon with Christ, and the meeting of the believer with the savior.

Western discussion is equally Christological. Ambrose sees the story
as a demonstration of the realness of Christ's human nature. The praise
of Christ by the elderly (in the first oracle of Simeon) soon becomes the
harsh prophecy of pain (in the second), foreshadowing the pain to be experienced by Mary at the crucifixion.[11] Paulinus of Nola, poetic as ever,
doesn't like the sword theme,[12] but Augustine faces it head-on, and links
the circumcision and the presentation as yet further manifestations of the
human nature of Christ.[13] It is interesting to note that, while there is no
evidence for the feast at Hippo during the time of Augustine, it appears
that the gospel for the Christmas Day Mass was the whole of Luke 2,[14]
not just part of it, which would give credence to the view that the earliest
understanding of the celebration of the Incarnation on 25 December was
a "unitive" feast of the birth and growth of the child Jesus, and not the
somewhat sentimental preoccupation with babies as in the later West.

Evidently, the "legal requirement" of the sacrifice permeated western
comment, for we find it in Leo the Great, with a discussion of the nature
of sacrifice in the church, and it is echoed in Caesarius of Arles in a comment on the way Christ comes to fulfil the Law; Caesarius also links circumcision and presentation, a further indication that the separate feast
was some time off.[15]

Alanus of Farfa[16] spiritualizes purification and Ambrosius Autpertus[17] gives a Marian thrust, combining it with sacrifice by suggesting that
the Virgin Mary offers Christ to God in the temple. Both these writers
date from the time after the feast was established, so we may conclude
that their interpretations of the passage, interlocking as they are, reflect
an established understanding of it. Bede[18] provides us with evidence for
the ceremonies of the day, also takes in the whole sweep of the story in
its mixture of bitterness and sweetness; Mary's grief is real, as is the
praise of the elderly for the Lord, but the offering captivates him, once
again paradoxical, in that here is the poverty of humanity being the veil
under which the richness of God is prepared to dwell, a theme of humility also. It could be that Bede, who lived before both Alanus and Ambro-

sius Autpertus, has influenced them, though it is more likely that great minds do occasionally think alike.

This selection from the Fathers is clearly not a total one, but even from these sources we can make a few helpful observations.

First, the feast was established in the East before the West, which will become clearer in the ensuing discussion.

Second, whereas the East already fastens onto the notion of "meeting," western writers show an almost instinctive bias towards Mary, a factor which will, once again, become clearer in due course.

Third, both eastern and western writers are concerned to bring out the sacrificial aspects of the scene/feast—a feature which may well surprise the twentieth-century approaches. Moreover, this preoccupation is not geared exclusively to the birds killed and offered in the temple. There is a deliberate and conscious discussion of the Christological aspects of the scene: Christ is at one and the same time offered and the one being offered.

Fourth, while the writers do, naturally, bring in the poor aged one (the "*anawim*," again), the second oracle of Simeon is not ignored.

These tentative conclusions in part answer our three basic questions about the feast. First, we can already see "purification" taking over in the West, but "meeting" in the East. Second, early western reflection antedates the feast, and links with circumcision and the Lucan birth narrative, whereas the eastern calendar, more developed than the West, has the feast of "meeting" forty days after the birth. In this discrepancy is it possible to see a germ of the later problem of where the feast "belongs"? Ironically, the "bitterness" appears stronger in the West than the East. Finally, the "mood" of the occasion is hard to discern from these quotations, and in any case, homilies are notoriously selective about what they use as springboards for the instruction and devotional edification of the faithful.

We have, in any case, already arrived at the era when the separate feast has emerged. We should, therefore, look at the different types of evidence for the liturgical observance of 2 February in both East and West.

The Feast Itself

The East

There is a cluster of useful evidence from the fourth century onwards. First and foremost, Egeria gives an account of what she saw at Jerusalem, probably between 381 and 384. Because what she describes reflects the liturgical program (and possible innovations) of Cyril himself, it is worth quoting in full:

Note that the Fortieth Day after Epiphany is observed with special magnifi-
cence. On this day they assemble in the Anastasis. Everyone gathers, and
things are done with the same solemnity as the feast of Easter. All the presbyters preach first, then the bishop, and they interpret the passage from the
Gospel about Joseph and Mary taking the Lord to the Temple, and about
Simeon and the prophetess Anna, daughter of Phanuel, seeing the Lord,
and what they said to him, and about the sacrifice offered by his parents.
When all the rest has been done in the proper way, they celebrate the sacrament and have their dismissal.[19]

Tantalizing as she can on occasion be, this little account tells us a great
deal, and because she took care to note down what she saw on her liturgical journeys that differed from what she was used to back home on the
Atlantic seaboard, we can both conclude certain things and suggest others.

First, it is a major feast in its own right, no mere adjunct or afterthought. (Later Byzantine practice similarly reflects this.) Then, she goes
even further—it is so significant a feast that she compares it to Easter,
and the celebration takes place at the Anastasis, a sure sign of importance. Since she makes no mention of the *lucernare* at the Easter Vigil (but
there is no reason to believe that it did *not* take place at Easter), we can
make no firm conclusion about some *special* candle-ceremony that she
saw at this feast, though it would certainly have had the vesper candles
if it were regarded as of the same importance as Easter. What takes her
attention is that all the presbyters preach, followed by the bishop; and
she then goes on to bring out the main features of the gospel story, not
emphasizing any one in particular. We have the young parents bringing
the child to the temple; then we have the two elderly people and the
prophecies; and, finally, the sacrifice, surely an indication that something
special was said about that. This echoes completely the exegetical tradition referred to earlier, although that should hardly surprise us, in view
of the fact that there were so many homilies! Finally, it must be noted
that she gives no special title to the feast, and it takes place forty days after Epiphany, therefore on the equivalent of 14 February. She is clearly
impressed by the *whole* drama of the story, again a feature of later eastern practice. The Armenian Lectionary, of the fifth century, comes to our
help with two appropriate pericopes: Galatians 3:24-29 and Luke 2:22-40.
While the latter is obvious, it needs noting, in view of later western practice; it is the whole passage in question, not a part of it. The former, however, is a good (though, as regards later practice) unusual candidate: the
law has gone, Christ has come, we have put on Christ as baptized in his
name, and are heirs of the promise given. (The Armenian Lectionary
places the celebration at the Martyrium, not the Anastasis.)

However, the key-question, "when was the feast first introduced?" is answered in one of Severus of Antioch's homilies (513-518),[20] in which he refers to the feast as a fairly recent development at Antioch; and he goes on to say that it was introduced from Jerusalem, where some older residents can remember when it was *not* celebrated there. It is therefore tempting to suggest that it was initially a Jerusalem festival, introduced by Cyril himself. Cyril of Alexandria speaks of keeping the feast "with bright lamps" and of "fulfilling the law," which perhaps means candles.[21]

We are, however, on surer ground, when we encounter the life of Theodosius by Cyril of Scythopolis, in which it is stated that the deaconess Hikelia was the first to introduce the use of candles, around 450:

> Then the blessed Hikelia, having practised all manner of piety, was the first to introduce the celebration of the Presentation of our Lord with candles.[22]

The feast is given a title; it may well have been commemorated before, but the candles are significant. Because the venue is a church near Jerusalem, it is probable that this is no more and no less than the liturgical trade route in operation. A custom already established in Jerusalem is spreading to its environs. Sophronius (560-638) similarly mentions carrying lights.[23] Thus, from the fragmentary evidence, a clear picture is emerging of a major feast at Jerusalem, a "unitive" feast of the whole story, celebrated with great solemnity, and (either in the later fourth century or later) with special use of candles. In view of the fact that special *Easter* candle-ceremonies begin to be evidenced from the fifth century at Jerusalem, it seems likely that some special *Presentation* candle-usage dates from a similar time.[24]

First evidence of the feast's appearance at Constantinople comes from the sixth century, a development Dendy suggests results from its existence at both Jerusalem and Egypt.[25] The interplay of liturgical traditions in these three centers has been the theme of a recent study of the liturgical year by Thomas Talley, and on the basis of his conclusions, it would seem reasonable to concur that, in this instance, Jerusalem practice antedates and determines custom elsewhere. According to Theophanes' *Chronolographia*, Justinian introduced the feast, thanks to the outbreak of a plague in October 534; but it could be that the great emperor "was only extending an existing usage."[26]

Far more tantalizing is the evidence supplied by Theophylactus Simocatta, who describes a riot against Emperor Maurice in 602, "on the 40th day after the birth feast." The details of this narrative have been studied by Martin Higgins,[27] and he comes to the sobering conclusion that the

Nativity was commemorated on 6 January; that the feast of the *Hypapante*, so-called here, fell on 14 February, not 2 February, and the feast had both a vigil and a prominent procession, which was, however, penitential in character (the emperor walked barefoot in procession) but still closely associated with the feast itself.

Here are revelations indeed! The date of 14 February simply reproduces what Egeria had experienced. The title is what we have already observed in the para-liturgical evidence from the East earlier. That it should have a vigil is probably one more parallel with Egeria at Jerusalem. What *is* new is the penitential procession, which we have not encountered so far, but which we shall meet in the West.

How is this to be explained? It could be suggested that there is some pagan festival that is being christianized, but there can be no obvious candidate for this, certainly not the Roman *Lupercalia* at Constantinople![28] Another suggestion is that the supposed origin of the feast at Constantinople (plague in 534) might have brought in a penitential association; such an hypothesis needs to be considered, especially in a city where the urban character of the liturgy is (at this time at any rate) so pronounced.

Yet another, which partly links with the foregoing, is the eastern determination to keep the totality of the feast together, so that it embodies both the joy and revelation of Simeon's first oracle (the *Nunc Dimittis*) and the pain and sorrow of the second oracle. Yet another could connect the feast with the Epiphany "Lent" which Talley has suggested immediately followed Epiphany at Alexandria, but this seems unlikely.[29] What we *do* know, however, is that the penitential procession does not reappear at Constantinople.

First, what is the focus of the feast? The title *hypapante* indicates a preference we have already encountered, for whole feast; not the purification of Mary, nor the presentation of the child Jesus, but the meeting of Simeon with Christ, and ourselves also. Indeed, Egeria's full account of the possible exegesis leaves us in little doubt of how Jerusalem handles this theme.

Second, where does the feast belong? It is equally clear that it is part of the Christmas cycle, being at Jerusalem, as Talley suggests, "the closing of an Epiphany quarantine."

Third, what is the "mood"? Here the evidence is conflicting. Egeria does not tell the whole story, she is clear that the feast is comparable for its solemnity with Easter. But the early seventh-century Constantinople account under Emperor Maurice is equally clear that the procession is penitential. Whatever caused this "bitter-sweet" mixture, it brings an aura of chilling reality to the occasion, which the West takes up gradually and attempts to resolve.

The Title "Hypapante"

Much of the eastern evidence so far has included the use of the term *hypapante* for the feast. But where does the word come from? There is little doubt that by the sixth century it was well-established as the name for the day. But its first occurrence suggests that it is, in origin, a specially-constructed word with a technical liturgical meaning. Although the simpler form, *hypantao*, is found in classical and New Testament Greek, and the compound *hypapantao* is found in patristic Greek also, the noun *hypapante* is only found to describe the feast. The earliest guaranteed use appears to be in Hesychius of Jerusalem (d. after 450);[30] and it is also found in Modestus of Jerusalem (d. 634),[31] and Anastasius of Antioch (d. 599).[32] Cyrus of Scytholopis (d.c.558) even uses the peculiar-sounding *hypapantesis*.[33] However, in the sermon attributed to Cyril of Jerusalem (d. 386),[34] whose exact date is uncertain, the title of the feast is *hypapante* and Simeon is referred to as the "God-receiver." In this homily many themes recur, but two are significant. One is the idea of "meeting," for the feast clearly has an eschatological feature, in which the church meets the Lord in the celebration; in this connection, other compounds exist such as *hypantao* and *apantesis*. Second, there is the notion of light in darkness, and direct and indirect reference to the carrying of candles. It would seem plausible to assume that the deliberate adoption of a new word for the feast points to an intrinsically *eschatological* understanding of its meaning. The familiarity of the term to liturgists should not blind us from its unusual origin and meaning. Unlike anything the West dreamt up, this term is dynamic and wholesome.[35]

The Byzantine Typica

The tenth century *Typicon*[36] of the Great Church gives lavish provision for the feast and the days following. The title is significant:

> The meeting of our great God and Saviour Jesus Christ, when the righteous Simeon received him in his arms.

Solemn vespers the night before takes place at Chalkoprateia, a sign of importance itself. The three Old Testament lections are interesting:

Genesis 28:10-17	-	Jacob's ladder
Ezekiel 43:27-44:4	-	the temple shut, and then opened and filled with glory

Proverbs 9:1-11   -   the house of wisdom

The *troparion* reappears in the East and the West, and is therefore worth quoting in full:

> Rejoice, full of grace, Virgin mother of God, for from you is risen the sun of righteousness, Christ our God, lighting up those who were in darkness. Exult, also, just elder, who received in your arms the liberator of our souls, the one who has bestowed on us the resurrection.

Matins also takes place at Chalkoprateia, and meanwhile the patriarch processes solemnly from the Great Church to Blachernae, where the liturgy is celebrated. The procession halts in the forum, and the deacon sings the great *ektene*, and the feast's *troparion* is once again chanted by the singers. A fourteenth century manuscript fills out some choreographic details; the emperor arrives after the patriarch at the Great Church, receives a candle, and walks at the head of the procession. (The *Typicon's* early manuscript seems to *assume* the carrying of candles in the procession from the Great Church to Blachernae.)

At the eucharist, the lections are Hebrews 7:7-17 (Christ's priesthood compared with Melchizedek's) and Luke 2:22-40 (the whole pericope). On the following day there is commemoration of "the holy and just Simeon, who received the Lord in his arms, and Anna the prophetess." The reason appears to be to extend the festival, and because the relics of Simeon lay in the crypt at Chalkoprateia. While the two eucharistic readings are only found on this particular day, the same cannot be said of the vesper lections. Jacob's ladder (Gn 28:10-17) occurs on some significant festivals (Simeon Stylites, and the Nativity and Dormition of the Virgin Mary); Wisdom's house (Prv 9:1-11) appears on the dedication festival of Chalkoprateia (where the solemn vespers for *hypapante* is celebrated and the Annunciation of the Virgin Mary.)

This is the fullest provision we have so far seen, not least in the office of solemn vespers the night before. The urban nature of the native Constantinopolitan liturgy[37] is given fullest expression, with both patriarch and emperor taking part; and there is a procession before the eucharist. When compared, however, with the account given of the liturgy on this day under Emperor Maurice, there are obvious discrepancies. These are (1) that the feast is now on 2 February (not 14 February, as in 602, and Egeria in Jerusalem), and (2) that there is a penitential character to the procession, of which there are no indications in the *Typicon*. The similarities are: (1) the name, *hypapante*, is the same; and (2) the evening before has a solemn vespers, corresponding in part to the vigil.

The twelfth century *Typicon of St Saviour*,[38] at Messina, is a carefully worked liturgical tradition, at a special stage in creativity. Its main provisions echo that of the *Typicon of the Great Church*, as one would expect, except in two points. First, there is no procession; perhaps this was seen to be too bound up with an urban set-up like Jerusalem or Constantinople. Second, the office of solemn vespers has reached a fuller stage of development. The readings are different, though more resembling those of today's Byzantine Rite. The chants, however, are far richer, and contain two as a liturgical unit between the opening psalm and the lections which are also found in western medieval texts, and known by their *incipits* as *adorna thalamum* and *lumen ad revelationem*. The latter is taken straight from the *Nunc Dimittis*, whereas the former is a composite affair:

Adorn thy bridal chamber, O Zion,
and welcome Christ, the King;
salute Mary, the heavenly gate.
For she has been made as the throne of the cherubim,
and she carries the King of glory.
A cloud of light is the Virgin,
who has borne in the flesh the Son begotten before the morning star.
Simeon, taking Him in his arms, proclaimed to the peoples:
"This is the Lord of life and death and the Savior of the world."[39]

After the readings come chants, some of which are used today, and the office concludes, save the dismissal, with the *troparion* quoted earlier from the tenth-century *Typicon* sung as the *apolytikion*. Nothing strange characterizes the other services.

Clearly, this Italo-Greek book marks a development from Constantinople, unless this is simply explained by the fact that here is a *monastic* book whereas there it was a book made up of disparate traditions, very much for use in the imperial city, and therefore more conservative. But one feature stands out, which is that seven days after, the feast has an *apodosis* on the day commemorating also Nicephorus, when the proper for the feast is once again celebrated. Whereas the Constantinople book observed Nicephorus, it did not have this *apodosis*. Contemporary practice enlarges on this development, describing each day in the "octave" as the "Second," "Third," "Fourth" Day of Celebration. The *hypapante* has arrived.

Its arrival, moreover, solidifies its place in the liturgical cycle. To revert once more to the three questions: (1) it is still the feast of *hypapante* to the extent that, if there is a single character, it is Simeon, whose special commemoration takes place on 3 February; (2) the developing hymnody echoing the drama of Christ being received in the temple by Simeon, and, as with so much in the Byzantine tradition, chants that center on Mary only do so to meditate on the incarnation as a divine and human reality. As a postscript, from at least the eighth century, the Byzantine books contain rites for the eighth and fortieth days after birth which were celebrated as part of the life-cycle of the Christian, leading eventually to baptism.[40]

The West

From the Sacramentaries to the Early Tenth Century

The evidence we have for the West is fuller, and from it we can chart the gradual spread of the feast from Rome, with Mass-prayers, chants, and a procession; the appearance in the latter part of the ninth century, of individual candle-blessing prayers; and then, in the tenth century, the full basilican-type liturgy with a rich collection of pre-Mass prayers and chants all connected with the blessing and distribution of candles, and a procession. Thereafter, as with other pre-Mass rites such as ashing, Palm Sunday, and even the marriage liturgy itself, it is simply a question of variations on a well-established theme, throughout the local western liturgical books.

Although Gelasius frowned upon the pagan Roman *Lupercalia*[41] (held on 15 February), there is no evidence to suppose that our feast's appearance at Rome (already some way off) had anything to do with a sort of Christian one-up-man-ship, a theory that Talley has helped consign to the doldrums when matters of the liturgical year are under consideration.[42] We have already seen the different types of exegesis of the day's gospel in the classical Christian Fathers, and Bede himself bears witness to the distribution of candles by the pontiff and a procession. But we are not quite there yet.

The beginning of the liturgical story lies in the Mass for the Octave of Christmas Day in the Gelasian tradition. Chavasse and Bernard Moreton have studied the liturgical unit.[43] For our purposes, the preface is the tell-tale part, for it meditates on the whole sweep of the incarnation in gospel historical events, taking in both circumcision and presentation on the way. Chavasse (and others) are convinced that this preface is a direct quotation from a sermon by Augustine,[44] and therefore (perhaps) evidence of Roman composition; Moreton, by contrast, takes the view that this mass-set is originally Frankish. Chavasse is perhaps better followed here; but whatever the place of origin (and it must be remembered that there are no traces of a separate feast of purification-presentation in the old Gallican liturgy), this mass-set bears witness to an older "unitive" celebration, and it probably dates from an earlier time than the separate feast, and therefore could take us back to the beginning of the seventh century.

The principal evidence, however, comes from the time of Sergius I (687-701), to whom is attributed, in the *Liber Pontificalis*, the following liturgical innovation:

> that on the days of the Annunciation of the Lord, the Falling asleep and Nativity of the ever-virgin Mary, the holy Mother of God and of St Symeon, which the Greeks call *ypapante*, a procession should be made from St Hadrian's.[45]

There is much here. First, Sergius, who is known to have come from a Greek family, probably descended from immigrants from the East, had liturgical tastes that reflected his origins, notably in his introduction of the *Agnus Dei* at Mass. The author of the *Liber Pontificalis* openly uses the Greek title for the feast, as an alternative to Simeon, who figures prominently in the Greek liturgy for the day. Second, the author does, however, group this feast with Marian feasts, thus introducing a tension that will become apparent soon in the western liturgical books. Third, the procession from Saint Hadrian's is part of the gradual evolution of the stational liturgy at Rome, which began with only Ash Wednesday, Saint Lawrence and Saint Caesarius; continues with these other four; by the eleventh century includes three days per week through Lent; and eventually takes in virtually every day in Lent.[46] It need hardly be noted that Lent is a penitential season, and Rome's stational liturgy, with its complex use of special churches and solemn litanies, eventually has a strong penitential character to it.

When we look at the Gregorian Sacramentary, we discover that the mass-set begins with a "collecta," used to start the liturgy of the day before the procession to the stational church. This prayer baldly prays for inward light as the outward action of the service is performed. Fitting this together with other evidence, the sequence would have been made up of the following elements:

> "collecta"
> deaconry in the Forum
> psalms and litanies during the procession
> Mass at St Mary Major[47]

The resemblance with Constantinople is astonishing and it may even reflect what Egeria herself saw at Jerusalem.

Reverting to the sacramentaries, it is clear that the Gregorian prayers eventually take over, for in the passage between "Old Gelasian," through Gregorian "Padua," and Gregorian "Hadrianum," to (for example) Gelasian of Gellone, the Gregorian strain resists all "Old" Gelasian tendencies. In the "Old" Gelasian, the feast is called the "Purification of St. Mary" and has three mass-prayers, the first of which is about the presentation in the temple, and the second and third of which are quite neutral in tone and content: altogether, this item has all the signs of being a rush-job, ill thought-out.[48] In the Gregorian "Padua," not only is there the venerable "collecta," but the usual mass-prayers; the collect combines purification and presentation, like the Lucan narrative, and spiritualizes the theme for the worshipers; the "super oblata" is neutral; the post-communion asks for the prayers of the Virgin Mary; the "Hadrianum" adds a fourth, (a *super populum*) which meditates on Simeon. Gregorian books also start at Saint Hadrian's with the "collecta," and then move to Saint Mary Major for the Mass.[49]

For prefaces, the *Supplement* merely provides a Christmas formulation, but the ninth-century Sacramentary of Trent contains a fine composition, which sweeps through practically all the themes of exegesis we noted earlier; fulfilling the law, the poverty of the scene, the sacrifice offered; and the aged pair responding to God's Son in the temple.[50] For episcopal blessings before communion, the Gelasian of Gellone provides a prayer for angelic protection, whereas the Supplement contemplates the presentation in the temple, the fulfilling of the law's requirements, and the sacrifices.[51]

What of the titles for the feast? The Gregorian Sacramentary uses the Greek *hypapante*, and that name persists in the best manuscripts, although the *Supplement* consistently calls it "purification of St. Mary," like the "Old" Gelasian. The Gelasian of Gellone has the best of both worlds; the mass-set appears under the heading "St. Simeon," whereas the episcopal blessing comes as directed for "the purification."

The same confusion is to be found in other liturgical books, but it appears that the title which eventually wins is "Purification," perhaps the name favored north of the Alps. Frere has shown that the feast was a novelty in the seventh century, in his study of the gospel books of that time.[52] The Würzburg Evangeliary, now dated about 700, and originating in England (therefore contemporaneous with Bede) seems to regard the feast as an afterthought; it does not have a title, and it contains the standard-type gospel, Luke 2:22-32. This cutting short of the pericope may not be intentional, but it is noticeable when set alongside the eastern tradition, which includes not only Simeon's second oracle but the passage recounting Anna's presence in the temple too. Some gospel texts are even shorter, and start at the point where Simeon takes the child in his arms and recites the *Nunc Dimittis* (Lk 2:28-32).

On the other hand the "Martina" gospels prefer the Gregorian title, *hypapante* to the increasingly common "purification." For the epistle reading,[53] most books contain Malachi 3:1-4, the messenger coming before the Lord, refining the people, and then making their offering acceptable. But Ecclesiasticus 24:11-13, 15-20, the praise of wisdom, sweetness and desire from the Lord, appears in two books where it also comes as the epistle lection for the Assumption of the Virgin.

It is clear that the Latin books give the short gospel pericope, reflecting their increasing preoccupation with the first part of the temple drama, the mother being purified, and the old man taking Christ into his arms. The two epistle readings, however, reflect a comparable ambivalence. Malachi 3:1-4 is about the temple and the people being ready to worship in purity, whereas Ecclesiasticus 24:11-13, 15-20, surely, has a more Marian theme to it, lush in imagery, pointing also to the church.

As far as the Mass chants are concerned, there is nothing unusual in the prescriptions made for our feast, which consist of snippets of suitable psalmody and, for the communion, Luke 2:25.[54] But two of the Greek chants noted earlier in the Saint Saviour *Typicon* appear in the eighth/ninth century *Graduale* of Mont Blandin, and these texts appear in both Greek and Latin. Charles Atkinson has suggested that these chants may go back to the time of Sergius I himself, and therefore could have formed part of the liturgical material introduced by him with the new feast.[55] This suggestion certainly merits serious consideration, but it would be necessary to posit a date considerably earlier than the twelfth century for these chants.

The *Ordo Romanus XX*[56] is the only proper *Ordo* (apart from the Romano-Germanic Pontifical, which we shall look at shortly) to give a description of what happened on this feast. This manuscript probably dates from around 780-790 and is the work of a monk during the time of Pepin III. What he gives us more than makes up for other lack of evidence. First of all, the procession goes from Saint Hadrian-in-the-Forum to Saint Mary Major, exactly as had been instituted by Sergius on this day, as well as on the Marian feasts of the Annunciation (25 March), the Dormition (15 August) and the Nativity (8 September). Details are as follows.

Before the breaking of dawn, the procession moves towards Saint Hadrian, with the singing of the litany or antiphons, and the people carrying lighted candles. There they wait for the pontiff, who, on arrival, puts on black vestments, as do the deacons. All take from him a single candle, during the singing of an antiphon, *Exsurge, Domine*. On reaching the altar, the pontiff greets the congregation with *Dominus vobiscum, Oremus,* and before the *oratio* (the stational prayer, presumably), the deacon bids the congregation kneel, and then rise, a sure mark of the penitential character of the day's liturgy.

The procession then moves off, with seven crosses planted among the people, and presbyters and deacons bringing up the rear, with the pontiff at the end, immediately preceded by two candle-bearers, a thurifer, and two crosses. The music for the first part of the procession consists of antiphons, but when they come near Saint Mary Major, the pontiff nods to the choir to begin the litany. When the procession has entered the church, the Introit immediately begins, and the Mass follows, without the *Gloria in excelsis*.

Clearly what we have here is something akin to the penitential procession at Constantinople at the time of the Emperor Maurice. The vestments are black, there is a pause for kneeling prayer before the stational collect, and the *Gloria in excelsis* is forbidden. If these elements are subtracted, it looks like an up-market version of what Egeria recounts in Jerusalem a mere four centuries earlier. But these three elements alter the mood of the occasion. Moreover, starting before dawn means an early Mass, which would make sense of the candles, lighting up the darkness, the only such time candles are used in this way in Roman stational liturgy. It need hardly be added that the title for the feast is the Purification; there is no hint of the Greek *hypapante*.

Could it have been a Christian *Lupercalia*? Once more, this seems unlikely, even in the city where it had been celebrated during the time of Gelasius, since we would have heard about it before now. Surely this is a penitential occasion because the theme of *purification* has taken over, and the eschatological atmosphere of light in darkness requires a penitential mood. And in answering the question about where the feast belongs, I am tempted to suggest that in this particular tradition, with Lent developing its own penitential associations, our feast has already been identified as a hinge between the Christmas and Easter cycles.

Before we turn to the Romano-Germanic Pontifical, we must first look at the way the *blessing* of candles enters the Roman tradition, a feature lacking in the East. No blessings appear in the early sacramentaries, but they begin to occur in various local "supplements" in the late ninth and early tenth centuries. These compositions are varied and uneven.[57] The Collectar Pontifical of Baturich of Regensburg (817-848) contains perhaps the earliest known candle blessing, which also appears in the Reichenau Sacramentary.[58] This prayer starts twice and ends weakly, and shows signs of being an *ad hoc* composition. However, it refers to candles as *apum liquor* (a theme not unknown in antiquity); it makes a brief mention of Simeon; but two features dominate the prayer, one of which is the protection of the faithful by the blessed candles, and the other is the prayers of Mary and the saints. (There is no mention of Mary's purification, just this her feast day.) Perhaps this brings us near to the concerns that gave rise to the need to bless the candles; and it could also show us something of the mind of the prayer writer who no longer *thinks* in Latin.

By contrast, the Sacramentary of Noyon[59] (also late ninth century) is a more theological composition. It begins with a reference to the people of Israel, but moves straight into the theme of presentation of Christ in the temple, and after reflecting on the need for inner spiritual light, asks for the richness of God's blessing on those who are going to hold the candles. Mary is not mentioned; the candles are not explicitly blessed.

Shorter still is the corresponding prayer in the Sacramentary of Saint Martin's Abbey, Tours (also late ninth century).[60] Its central theme is light, and it prays that Christians may be presented in the temple of the church and may also be rich in good works and be worthy to be presented before God. There is no direct mention of the presentation of *Christ* in the temple; no explicit blessing of the candles.

These makeshift productions doubtless expressed and fulfilled a pastoral need as the feast, with its Mass prayers and its procession, embedded itself in northern Europe. Already, we can observe a subtle change in the shape of the liturgy for our feast in the West. While the theme of the purification of Mary takes over as the title, the procession spreads from Rome as a more "unitive" treatment of the feast, with a penitential tone. But, just as ashes have to be blessed at the start of Lent, and branches on Palm Sunday, so the candles have to be blessed prior to the procession. But the candles are the one feature that internalize and spiritualize the feast for the believer; candles are distributed to each person, so they must do something to each Christian; it is no longer a case of either purification or presentation. Perhaps purification explains the penitential procession that may have accompanied this liturgy; but it is presentation of the whole people of God which underlies these varied candle prayers.

From the Romano-Germanic Pontifical Onwards

The shape that has developed in the West is by now clear. The earlier Mass for the *hypapante* is now increasingly regarded as the Mass of the purification. The procession before the Mass began at Rome, in imitation of the great cities of the East. It has a penitential flavor that infects the Mass as well (no *Gloria in excelsis*). Finally, in the late ninth century, candle prayers begin to be used, probably before their distribution. All this becomes the elaborate rite of the Romano-Germanic Pontifical (*PRG*),[61] whose architecture determines the shape of later medieval rites.

PRG begins with an all-inclusive title; "the Purification of St. Mary" is the favorite, reflecting exactly the northern tendency we noted earlier, but "Ypapante of the Lord" is also listed, together with a short reference to Sergius I's innovations; "Presentation in the temple" also appears. The stational character of the liturgy is described in the move from Saint Hadrian to Saint Mary Major. There is no need to repeat what has already been described from *Ordo XX*. All the preliminaries up to and including the greeting and bidding to kneel and rise reappear. But it is in the preparation of the candles that the major difference and development is to be found.

After the "collecta," exorcised salt and water are made ready for the candles, and a long series of blessings ensues. This starts with a prayer to Mary, asking for her intercession; this (as we have noted) was an important feature of the Baturich of Regensburg prayer. The blessings are seven in number, a symbolism of some significance. The first concentrates on protection from evil; the second mentioned Raphael's protection of Tobias and Sarah and asks that the light banish evil; the third is an "ego"-type prayer, directly blessing the candles; the fourth is the Baturich of Regensburg prayer, with its balance of Simeon and Mary; the fifth dwells on Simeon in the temple and the faithful doing likewise; the sixth asks the Lord Jesus for spiritual light, and it leads into a preface which again concentrates on Simeon, and even ends with part of the *Nunc Dimittis*; the seventh recalls Moses' use of oil lamps, and asks for blessing.

The candles are now sprinkled and censed, lit and distributed, during the singing of an antiphon. A final prayer, again on the theme of Christ as the light, leads into the procession, for which there is provision of antiphons, including the Greek chant, *Adorna thalamum*, but only in Latin. (The manuscripts vary, understandably, over the antiphons at this point.) At the entry into church at the end of the procession, there are more antiphons, and a stational prayer, addressed to Christ. After the Introit, the Mass follows, but without *Gloria in excelsis*, even during Sexagesima.

PRG is a much fuller document, but it retains the penitential features of *Ordo XX*, for the vestments are still black. Three things need to be noted. First, apart from the shape developing to its medieval apogee, the interaction of word and movement has also reached its definitive stage; the candles assume an importance they never had before, hence the elaborate deep structures are:

1) the distribution of candles;
2) the "collecta" prayer;
3) the procession, with chants and litany;
4) the Mass.

Into this scheme has been introduced the surface structure of the long prayers, together with the sprinkling and incensing of the candles. Third, these prayers, taken probably from various local sources, are different in their style as well as their themes, although we can notice a progression from the early prayers (which dwell on protection), through the central prayers (which speak of the events of the day's gospel), to the final prayers (which reflect on the theology of light).

PRG's rich provisions would not have been followed by every local church, but its shape dominates all future developments.[62] When we come to the twelfth century Roman Pontifical tradition,[63] the same sequence appears, and the penitential features recur in the missal. However, the candle prayers are only five in number, and the preface-form prayer does not appear.

Interestingly, the Baturich of Regensburg prayer heads the list, and *Nunc Dimittis*[64] is sung as part of the chants, during the sprinkling and censing. But another surface structure has invaded the rite, for now there is a prayer following the sprinkling and censing of the candles, so that sprinkling and censing, together with lighting some of the candles, is a separate section of this part of the rite. The whole service takes place later in the morning, after terce, which would have an effect on the use of the candles. We observed that the candle prayers are now fewer in number; one theme does not appear so strongly, namely protection from evil. This is an important feature, because the same sequence of prayers reappears in the 1570 *Missale Romanum*;[65] the only significant difference in the rite as a whole being that the prayer between the sprinkling censing and the procession has been removed.

When it comes to local service books all over Europe in the later Middle Ages, we are faced with predictable variety of substance, but little in shape. In the collection of seven *Ordines* made by Edmond Martène, the déroulement is identical in all, consisting of (1) blessing of candles, (2) distribution, (3) procession (with or without stations), and (4) Mass. The main point of difference is usually how many candle prayers there are, and a late date does not ensure elaboration. For example, the Besançon Pontifical of Hugh of Salins (1031-1060)[66] blesses the candles with a simple prayer, followed by a preface-form prayer, which ends in *Sanctus*; and, as if this were not enough, the Lord's Prayer and *Libera nos* are borrowed from the Mass. In this rite, festal vestments are worn throughout, and terce comes between the procession and the Mass. The Narbonne Pontifical (twelfth century)[67] by contrast borrows from the Easter Vigil, and has a blessing of the New Fire, suitably rephrased, from which all the candles are lit; and the *Nunc Dimittis* is chanted during distribution. The Apamea Pontifical[68] begins also mid-morning, with terce, and has a good sequence of candle prayers, all three of which appear in the twelfth century Roman Pontifical; and it also has the separate prayer between the sprinkling/censing and the distribution. The fourteenth-century Pontifical of Arles[69] starts with terce; then processes to the Church of Saint Mary Major, whereupon the archbishop robes, and a sermon is preached; the candles are blessed (with four prayers, none of which is new); the candles are distributed; *three* prayers are said before the procession to Saint Eulalia's; the procession continues with chants, to Saint Trophome's for the Mass. Woolen vestments are worn by all the ministers, including the archbishop, probably another indication of penitence.

The remaining three French rites printed by Martène[70] are simpler, and more northerly in provenance. Rouen (fifteenth century) regards the day as *festum triplex*, and blesses a new fire and then the candles, with relative austerity; the candles are then distributed; and a prayer precedes the procession, with its chants. Argentan (fourteenth century) blesses the candles, distributes, and processes; whereas the thirteenth-century Châlons-sur-Saône blesses the candles at the Lady altar during terce. None of these latter rites has the elaborate sequence of prayers of the twelfth-century Roman Pontifical, still less that contained in the tenth-century Romano-Germanic Pontifical.

The Scandinavian[71] books show a similar shape and a comparable variety in the prayers, though none of them opts for the new fire. As with the previous rites, all of them seem to use a common core of candle prayers, never in quite the same order; the preface-form occurs in all of them. The Bystorp Manual (early sixteenth century), the Viborg Missal (fifteenth century) and the Notmark Manual (fourteenth-fifteenth century)[72] have a sequence of seven prayers, like the Roman-Germanic Pontifical, whereas the Slesvig and Lund books (both fifteenth century) are simpler by comparison.

The British books show a similar progression to France, though not quite the same divergences. The Leofric Collectar[73] in its earliest text does not contain any candle blessings, but by the time we come to the eleventh-century part of the text, there are candle blessings. The eleventh-century Missal of Robert of Jumièges[74] begins with a lacuna; but there are four blessings, followed by the elaborate procedure over the distribution of candles. At the end of the procession, there is a station at the church door, with a prayer dwelling on the theme of the church seeing the salvation brought by Christ, like Simeon. On the other hand, the late eleventh-century Missal of the New Minster[75] (Winchester), which is very similar, does not start with a lacuna, but its first prayer, (identical to Robert of Jumièges) blesses the *fire*, before proceeding to the blessing of the candles (the other three prayers). The *Nunc Dimittis* comes during the distribution of candles. It also has a "Simeon" prayer at the entry to the church; and it uses the rare lection for the epistle, Ecclesiasticus 24:23-31. The twelfth-century Pontifical of Magdalen[76] blesses the candles in four prayers (again). The twelfth-century Irish Rosslyn Missal[77] prescribes festal vestments, and blesses the candles at the Lady altar, in five prayers. The Sarum Missal[78] has silk vestments (therefore festal). One large candle is first of all blessed, and it is the same as for the blessing of the font at the Paschal and Pentecost Vigils. It would seem that only the first prayer allies to this candle, the other five, including a preface-form prayer, being for the smaller candles to be used in the procession. The stational prayer at the end of the procession, unlike Robert of Jumièges and New Minster, asks for the prayers of the Virgin Mary.

One recurring anomaly in the story has been the question of liturgical colors. We have already seen how black vestments were used in PRG, and Arles used (comparable) woolen ones. While the twelfth century Roman Pontifical does not indicate what color is used, the thirteenth-century Pontifical of Durandus has no rite for this feast, but lays down that black or violet are to be used when the pope walks barefoot in procession, a clear indication of penitence. Mabillon's Museum Italicum[79] contains two ordos which discuss colors. The first, by Benedict, a canon of Saint Peter's (twelfth century), says nothing about colors; however, the second, by Censius Camerarius (late twelfth century) directs that the pope walks barefoot in procession on this feast, but his chasuble at the eucharist is white. So here is evidence for the later Roman practice, abolished in 1970.

The Medieval West: Some Observations

What are we to make of all this variety? Clearly, the West took much longer to make up its mind on what this new feast was intended to do, in contrast with the Byzantine Rite, where its meaning and significance were worked out earlier. There are a number of anomalies which need to be highlighted.

First, there is the issue of what the feast should be called. Here, the Greek hypapante eventually gives way to Purification, as the feast takes on a Marian slant.

Secondly, the penitential tradition, which appears (briefly) at Constantinople in the seventh century, becomes a firm Roman tradition, spreading elsewhere through the Middle Ages. When western liturgical color schemes develop, a disparity surfaces between rites which use a penitential hue (whether throughout the service or just for the procession), and those which are festal for the entire liturgy. But, significantly, the choice of liturgical *texts* for the candle prayers and chants is *not* affected in any way by this factor.

Thirdly, there is the increasing preoccupation with the blessing of the candles, to the point of blessing the *source* of light, before the candles, in some places. It is interesting to note that, whereas prayers about protection from darkness and evil are strong in *PRG*, they do not occur in the twelfth-century Roman Pontifical. Perhaps the gradual shift of the service from pre-dawn to mid-morning had an influence here.

Fourth, there is the procession. Whereas in Rome, it moved from Saint Hadrian to Saint Mary Major (and this pattern was imitated in the urban churches elsewhere), in places like Arles, it could take in three churches. But it is curious to note how adhesive is the processional character of the feast, even in two tiny Danish villages, each with a small church, Bystorp and Notmark.

But underneath the local variety, the *Roman* character of the feast manifests itself all along, through Gregorian Sacramentary, *Ordo XX*, the twelfth century Pontifical, and the 1570 *Missale Romanum*, where there is a continuum not noted elsewhere in the West. The only real question mark to that continuum is the penitential mood, but that (as we suggested earlier) may have resulted from an interpretation of the events in the temple which keeps the bitter sweetness of the scene in mind throughout.

A Post-Script

At the Reformation, Lutherans and Anglicans kept the feast, although they stripped it of all the special ceremonies, ironically bringing it back to a simplicity that it once had in the "Old" Gelasian Sacramentary, namely a simple Mass with special readings, no more, no less.

In the 1549 Book of Common Prayer,[80] the feast is entitled the "Purification of St. Mary the Virgin," and the old anomaly survives the rigors of the Reformation, as the collect is a translation of the Gregorian Sacramentary prayer, which is all about being presented in the temple. But unlike any other of the calendar feasts that do not appear in 1549, there is no epistle or Old Testament; it is to be taken from the preceding Sunday. The gospel, however, is Luke 2:22-27a; this abbreviates the Roman (and Sarum) reading, which goes as far as the end of the *Nunc Dimittis*. This provision survives into 1552, but in 1662, there were significant changes, as a result of pressure from John Cosin, Matthew Wren, and others, who were well-versed in liturgical history.[81]

First of all, the title changes to "The Presentation of Christ in the Temple commonly called the Purification of St Mary, The Virgin"; then an

Old Testament reading is supplied for the epistle, but it is Malachi 4:1-5 (not 4, as Roman); and the gospel is the full pericope, not known in the West, but adhered to in the East, Luke 2:22-40, thus taking in the second oracle, and Anna. The hesitation of 1549/1552 is now more than made up for. Lutherans, on the other hand, rewrite the collect, but reproduce the Roman lections; yet they use the title "Presentation." Martin Luther himself wrote a German version of the *Nunc Dimittis* ("Mit Fried und Freud ich fahr dahin"),[82] which is also sung on this day, as witness the chorale preludes of the North German tradition, notably by the Dane, Diderik Buxtehude, as well as Johann Sebastian Bach himself. Bach's cantata for the feast, "Ich habe genug," is a bass solo throughout; it looks at the feast through the eyes of the old man who can now depart in peace.[83] Perhaps through this cantata tradition arose the custom in nineteenth-century English church music of setting the *Nunc Dimittis* to bass/tenor solo/soli voices.

The 1570 *Missale Romanum*,[84] as we have seen, represents a conservative revision of the twelfth-century Roman Pontifical; and whereas the procession is celebrated in purple vestments, white is worn for the Mass, and the title for the feast is, of course, purification, following the later medieval tradition. The two "moods" are expressed in the vestments.

In the nineteenth century, the Catholic Apostolic rite[85] adopted "the Day of the Presentation of Our Lord in the Temple" in the 1847 edition of its liturgy. The collect, Old Testament reading, and gospel all reproduce the 1662 English Prayer Book provisions, but its proper also includes *Nunc Dimittis* as the communion chant, a proper prayer of oblation which picks up the eschatalogical features of the feast, and the "Hallelujah" is to be sung after the *Gloria in excelsis*, a festal feature. The final touch comes with the 1869 edition of this liturgy, when our feast (together with the Circumcision and All Saints' Day) is given an octave, thus obtruding into the next Sunday. This particular church's interpretation of the feast is avowedly eastern in its thrust, a fact borne out by the commentary on the liturgy.

Our story is incomplete without two final remarks. First, the 1970 *Missale Romanum*[86] takes a stride out in an almost Protestant direction. For 1570's "Purification" read 1970's "Presentation of the Lord"; for 1570's purple vestments for part one, read 1970's white garb throughout; and for the elaborate sequence of blessing, distribution, and procession in 1570, there is now a more austere distribution of candles, followed by lighting (with chants), followed only now with *one* candle prayer, and the service proceeds with the procession, and continues with the Mass. The first part may take place in another church or in another part of the building. And in the era of evening Masses, perhaps this new rite has more impact than it has had since the days when it was celebrated before dawn. The Mass prayers, too, have been given a refit, to bring them into line with the new emphasis on presentation, rather than purification. Whereas the collect is the old Gregorian prayer, the *super oblata* is new, and takes up the theme of the church celebrating the one offering of Christ, the Lamb of God; the preface uses part of the Fulda Sacramentary, embroidering on the *Nunc Dimittis*; and the post-communion reproduces that contained in the 1736 Paris Missal, which asks that we may be allowed to "meet" the Lord (*in occursum Domini procedentes*), an eastern theme if ever there was one. The lections are Malachi 3:1-4 (unchanged), Hebrews 2:14-18 (required now that there is a three-reading lectionary), and Luke 2:22-40 (Anna is now at last included!).

The last thought must concern how the feast might develop further in the West. Recent revisions, from the Reformation Churches as well as the Roman Catholic, have gone out of their way to make the feast Christological, part of the Christmas cycle, with a mood that matches that scene. Perhaps in the process, they ironed out the anomalies we noticed in earlier centuries, thus removing the "bitter" character of the day, in the interests of "sweetness." Such a move has the undoubted merit of consistency but it cannot tell the whole story. The age of multiple evening eucharists could also become the era in which this feast takes on a new lease on life, in which the deep darkness of this world can be illuminated by the light of Christ in such a way that looks back to Christmas and forward to the mystery of Holy Week and Easter. The two alternative candle prayers in the 1970 *Missale Romanum* say good things, but there is a sense of loss, because all those many, rich themes that are to be found in the prolix prayers of the Middle Ages have been forgotten.

We need a feast that faithfully reflects both presentation of Christ and purification of Our Lady, since these are the two themes that are brought together by Luke as the starting off point for the gospel pericope. Yet we also need to take in the whole sweep of the drama, and include Simeon, with his twin oracles, and Anna. Here one can only lament the exclusion of the prophetess in most western lectionaries. But the most important aspect of the story, surely, is that it takes place in the *temple*, and that it is one of *encounter* between Christ and the church.

But we also need a feast that links Christmas and Easter together, and that is why the ultimate answer to the question, "where does it belong?" must really be that this feast is a hinge that holds together the two main cycles of the liturgical year. There are problems, of course, in finding a feast that seems to interrupt the ideas around it; the Annunciation falls victim to this when it comes too near Holy Week and Easter. For this reason, a renewed feast of the Presentation probably ought to remain on the fortieth day after Christmas, but there should be ways of making it point forward to Lent, Holy Week, and Easter, not least because of the crucial second oracle of Simeon.

This brings us to the third question, the "mood" of the occasion. At the end of the day, we can offer no clear-cut answer to the apparent ambivalence of the way this feast has been celebrated in Constantinople at the time of Maurice, or Rome at the end of the eighth century, or parts of northern Europe, for that matter. But my hunch is that this ambivalence results from a deep perception of the meaning of the gospel for this day. Mary is purified—we need purification. Christ is offered to the Lord—we need to be offered to the Lord. Simeon foresees pain and suffering in the life of this Christ—our witness to the faith involves many signs of contradiction.

There is an unhappy tendency to make modern liturgy slick and manageable, and that can produce a piety that does not match up to life as many people experience it. Some of these ambivalences have been explored of old, and they need to be looked at again. With the archetypal symbol of light in darkness, perhaps this feast might gain some necessary depth, and point us at one and the same time to our sins—and the infinite mercies of God.[87]

Notes

1. See, for example, N. Mitchell, "Dissolution of the Rite of Christian Initiation," in *Made Not Born: New Perspectives on Christian Initiation and the Catechumenate* (South Bend, 1972) 50-82.

2. See entry on "Candlemas" in *The Shorter English Dictionary*, 3d edition revised with addendum (Oxford, 1959) 256. The word is medieval English, as is the German "Lichtmesse."

3. See Leviticus 12:2-8 (on purification) and Exodus 13:2,12 (presentation of first-born male).

4. R.E. Brown, *The Birth of the Messiah* (New York, 1979) 435-479.

5. Ibid. 452.

6. Ibid. 453.

7. See I. Deug-Su, "La festa della purificazione in Occidentale (secoli IV-VIII)," *Studi Medievali*, 3d series, 15 (1974) 143-216.

8. PG 13, 1833-1838.

9. See B. Capelle, "Les homélies liturgiques du prétendu Timothée de Jérusalem," in *Travaux liturgiques*, vol. 3 (Louvain, 1967) 408-429.

10. CSCO., 270/271, SS 116/117 (ed. Beck); for this translation, see R. Williams, *Eucharistic Sacrifice: The Roots of a Metaphor*, Grove Liturgical Study 31 (Bramcote, 1982) 21.

11. *Corpus Christianorum* S.L. 14, 56-58, 794-796.

12. PL 61, 415.

13. PL 33, 644.

14. G.G. Willis, *St Augustine's Lectionary*, Alcuin Club Collections 44 (London, 1962) 22 (see other shorter [later] readings listed passim).

15. *Corpus Christianorum* S.L. 104, 778.

16. See E. Hosp, "Il sermonario di Alano di Farfa," *Ephemerides Liturgicae* 51 (1937) 210-240.

17. PL 89, 1291.

18. *Corpus Christianorum* S.L. 122, 73-79.

19. J. Wilkinson, *Egeria's Travels to the Holy Land*, revised edition (Warminster/Jerusalem, 1981) 128 (for Armenian Lectionary, see 262).

20. *Patrologia Orientalis* 29 (1960) 2, 47. I am indebted to Dr. Geoffrey Cuming for drawing my attention to this.

21. PG 77, 1040.

22. "Vita Theodosii," in E. Schwartz, *Text und Untersuchungen zur Geschichte der Altchristlichen Litteratur*, 49/2 (Leipzig, 1939) 236.

23. PG 87, 3749B.

24. See K.W. Stevenson, "The Ceremonies of Light—Their Shape and Function in the Paschal Vigil Liturgy," *Ephemerides Liturgicae* 99 (1985) 170-185.

25. D.R. Dendy, *The Use of Lights in Christian Worship*, Alcuin Club Collections 41 (London, 1959) 177; see also 176-181.

26. PG 108, 488b; see also Dendy, *The Use of Lights* 177.

27. See M. Higgins, "Note on the Purification (and Date of the Nativity) in Constantinople in 602," *Archiv für Liturgiewissenschaft* 2 (1952) 81-83.

28. T.J. Talley, *The Origins of the Liturgical Year* (New York, 1986) passim, for the modern rebuttal of the "history of religions" approach to this subject.

29. Talley, *Origins* 194ff.

30. PG 93, 1468B.

31. PG 86, 3276.

32. PG 89, 1286D.

33. See above, note 22.

34. PG 33, 1187-1203. For the discussion on the sacrificial language, see R.F. Taft, *The Great Entrance: A History of the Transfer of Gifts and Other Pre-anaphoral Rites of the Liturgy of St John Chrysostom*, Orientalia Christiana Analecta 200 (Rome, 1975) 132-133.

35. See above, note 30. See also E. Bickersteth, "John Chrysostom and the Early History of the *Hypapante*," *Studi bizantini e neoellenici* 8 (1953) 401-404.

36. J. Mateos, *Le typicon de la grande église*, Orientalia Christiana Analecta 165 (Rome, 1962) 220-227.

37. See J. Baldovin, "La liturgie stationnelle à Constantinople," *La Maison-Dieu* 147 (1981) 85-94.

38. M. Arranz, *Le typicon du Monastère du Saint-Sauveur à Messine*, Orientalia Christiana Analecta 185 (Rome, 1969) 117ff.

39. *The Festal Menaion* (London, 1969) 415 (whole feast, 406-434).

40. J. Goar, *Euchologion sive Rituale Graecorum* (Venice, 1730) 264ff. See also

K.W. Stevenson, "The Byzantine Liturgy of Baptism," *Studia Liturgica* 17 (1987) 176-190.
41. PL 59, 11016.
42. See above note 29.
43. A. Chavasse, *Le sacramentaire gélasien* (Paris/Tournai, 1957) 307, 376f, 285ff.; M.B. Moreton, *The Eighth Century Gelasian Sacramentary: A Study in Tradition* (Oxford, 1976) 35-37, 122ff.
44. For discussion of this text, see Chavasse, *Le sacramentaire* 212.
45. *Liber Pontificalis*, Sergius I, para. 14.
46. W.H. Frere, *Studies in Early Roman Liturgy I: The Calendar*, Alcuin Club Collections 28 (London, 1930) 24.
47. G.G. Willis, *Further Essays in Early Roman Liturgy*, Alcuin Club Collections 50 (London, 1968) 11ff.
48. L.C. Mohlberg, *Liber Sacramentorum Romanae Aecclesiae*, Rerum Ecclesiasticarum Documenta: Series Maior; Fontes 4 (Rome, 1960) nos. 829-831.
49. J. Deshusses, *Les sacramentaire grégorien: ses principales formes d'après les plus anciens manuscrits* I, Spicilegium Friburgense 16 (Fribourg, 1971) nos. 123-127 (for Padua list, see 616).
50. See ibid. nos. 1637 (preface) and 1745 (blessing).
51. A. Dumas, *Liber Sacramentorum Gellonensis*, Corpus Christianorum 159 (Turnhout, 1981) nos. 195-200 (Mass) and 2070 (blessing). This blessing recurs in later benedictionals and pontificals.
52. W.H. Frere, *Studies in Early Roman Liturgy II: The Roman Gospel Lectionary*, Alcuin Club Collections 30 (London, 1934) 5, 33, 64ff, 92, 95, and 144f.
53. W.H. Frere, *Studies in Early Roman Liturgy III: The Roman Epistle Lectionary*, Alcuin Club Collections 32 (London, 1935) 69, 80.
54. Chavasse, *Le sacramentaire* 368ff.
55. Charles Atkinson, "On the Origins of the 'Missa Graeca'," in *Nordisk Kollokvium V for Latinsk Liturgiforskning 14-17 June 1981*, (Århus, 1982) 96 and n.20 (114).
56. M. Andrieu, *Les Ordines Romani du haut moyen âge*, vol. 3, Spicilegium Lovaniense 28 (Louvain, 1933) 235-236; also discussed by John Baldovin, *The Urban Character of Christian Worship: The Origins, Development, and Meaning of Stational Liturgy*, Orientalia Christiana Analecta 228 (Rome, 1987) 137f., though the reason for the dark vestments here is not suggested.
57. J. Deshusses, *Le sacramentaire grégorien* III, Spicilegium Friburgense 28 (Fribourg, 1982) 22, 27, 32, 47, 53, 55, 56.
58. F. Unterkircher, *Das Kollektar-Pontifikale des Bischofs Baturich von Regensburg (817-848)*, Spicilegium Friburgense 8 (Fribourg, 1962) no. 402. The Reichenau text is to be found in Vienna *österreichische Nationalbibliothek*, Cod. 1815, fol. 5r.
59. E. Martène, *De Antiquis Ecclesiae Ritibus* III, (Antwerp, 1764) 45. These and the following texts should be used in conjunction with A.G. Martimort, *La documentation liturgique de Dom Edmond Martène*, Studi e Testi 279 (Vatican, 1978) 454-456.
60. Ibid. 45f.
61. C. Vogel - R. Elze, *Le pontifical romano-germanique du X siècle*, vol. 1, Studi e

Testi 226 (Vatican, 1963) 5-10.

62. See, e.g., Z. Obertynski, *The Cracow Pontifical*, Henry Bradshaw Society 100 (London, 1977) 92-95.

63. M. Andrieu, *Le pontifical romain du moyen âge 1, Le pontifical du XII siècle*, Studi e Testi 66 (Vatican, 1938) 206-209.

64. The *Nunc Dimittis* seems to the twentieth-century ear an obvious choice for this feast; however, it appears to have come into western use from the eleventh century; see the New Minster Missal (below note 75) and the Besançon rite (below note 66).

65. *Missale Romanum* (Antwerp, 1682) 542-547; see R. Lippe, *Missale Romanum 1474*, Henry Bradshaw Society 17 (London, 1899) 315-317 which has a very similar text.

66. Martène, *De Antiquis*, 46 (*Ordo* I).

67. Martène, *De Antiquis*, 46f. (*Ordo* II).

68. Martène, *De Antiquis*, 47 (*Ordo* III).

69. Martène, *De Antiquis*, 47 (*Ordo* IV).

70. Martène, *De Antiquis*, 47-48 (*Ordos* V-VII).

71. B. Stromberg, *The Manual from Bystorp*, Bibliotheca Liturgica Danica II (Edition Egtved, 1982) 46-50 (text, 120-128). There is a full discussion of the other Scandinavian texts in this useful edition.

72. K. Ottosen, *The Manual from Notmark*, Bibliotheca Liturgica Danica I (Copenhagen 1970) 19 (text, 109-112).

73. E.S. Dewick, *The Leofric Collectar*, Henry Bradshaw Society 45 (London, 1913) 203f.

74. H.A. Wilson, *The Missal of Robert of Jumièges*. Henry Bradshaw Society 11 (London, 1896) 158ff.

75. D.H. Turner, *The Missal of New Minster*, Henry Bradshaw Society 93 (Leighton Buzzard, 1962) 69-72.

76. H.A. Wilson, *The Pontifical of Magdalen College*, Henry Bradshaw Society 39 (London, 1910) 150f; see also notes on other twelfth-century books, 283f.

77. H.J. Lawler, *The Rosslyn Missal*, Henry Bradshaw Society 15 (London, 1899) 48-50. The Candlemas rite is discussed on p.xxii, and comparison is drawn between this rite and the Besançon rite, both of which bless the candles at the Lady altar (a Benedictine practice, it is suggested).

78. C. Wordsworth, *Ceremonies and Processions of the Cathedral Church of Salisbury* (Cambridge, 1901) 99-101.

79. See J. Mabillon, *Musei Italici*, vol. 2 (Paris, 1689) 130ff. (Benedict, Canon of St. Peter's, mid twelfth century), and 172ff. (Censius Camerarius, late twelfth century). See also M. Andrieu, *Le pontifical romain au moyen âge*, vol. 3, Studi e Testi 88 (Vatican, 1940) 656-659.

80. For the Prayer Book texts and their sources, see F.E. Brightman, *The English Rite*, vol. 2 (London, 1915) 564-571.

81. See the various proposals made immediately prior to 1662 in G.J. Cuming, *The Durham Book* (London, 1961) 124-125.

82. F. Schulz, "Liturgical Time in the Traditions of the Post-Reformation Churches," *Studia Liturgica* 14 (1982) 57-58.

83. See G. Stiller, *Johann Sebastian Bach and Liturgical Life in Leipzig* (St. Louis, 1984) 238.

84. See above, note 65.

85. *Liturgy and Other Divine Offices of the Church* (London, 1880) 176-178; see also K.W. Stevenson, "The Catholic Apostolic Eucharist" (Southampton University PhD Dissertation, 1975) 230-231.

86. *Missale Romanum* (Vatican, 1970) 522-526; for sources, see A. Dumas, "Les sources du nouveau missel romain," *Notitiae* 60 (1971) 41f, and 61 (1971) 76. The change of title from "purification" to "presentation" may be partially explained by the 1960 rubrics which had already laid down that it was to be a feast of Our *Lord*, following eastern tradition, instead of a feast of Our Lady. The second light-prayer is a (regrettably) abbreviated version of the Tours Sacramentary prayer (see above note 60).

87. Perhaps a new departure is needed altogether. An evening eucharist could begin with the sharing of light; the intercessions could include some references to darkness and light; and the whole liturgy *end* with a procession, from the altar to the church-door, the ministers having laid aside their outer garments; the processional chant could be the *Nunc Dimittis* (supremely appropriate after communion); the service could end with a V. and R. based on the second oracle of Simeon, and a collect like that of the Annunciation, but with a theme from the end of the canticle, *Benedictus*. The three-year cycle could also provide the opportunity of dwelling on one particular aspect of the feast in turn, whether presentation, purification, or encounter. If history teaches us anything about this feast, it tells us that there is too much in it for a mere liturgical fifty-minute "cameo."

The following deserve my thanks in the preparation of this paper: Thomas J. Talley (New York), on the eastern origins; Joanne Pierce (Notre Dame University), on the later medieval liturgical colors; and Michael Perham, on possible future paths.

The Development of the Candlemas Liturgy in the Medieval East and West

	4th Century: Jerusalem	6th Century: Constantinople	10th Century: Constantinople	Late 7th Century: Rome	9th Century: North of Alps
Date	Feb. 14	Feb. 14	Feb. 2	Feb. 2	Feb. 2
Title	"40th day after"	"40th day after"	hypapante	hypapante	Purification
Time	After vigil	After vigil	After matins	dawn	
Blessing of Candles					
Distribution of Candles				+	
Prayer				+	
Procession and Chants	+	+	+	+	
Mood of Procession		Emperor barefoot		Pontiff barefoot	
Venue: Procession	Anastasis		Great church	St. Hadrian	
Venue: Eucharist	Anastasis		Blachernae	St. Mary Major	
Eucharist: Color					
Lections	Gal 3:24-29 Lk 2:22-40		Heb 7:7-17 Lk2:22-40	Mal 3:1-4 Lk 2:22-35	Mal 3:1-4 (or Ecclus 24:11-13, 15-20)

KENNETH W. STEVENSON   75

	10th Century: Romano-Germanic Pontifical	12th Century: Rome	MR 1570	MR 1970
Date	Feb. 2	Feb. 2	Feb. 2	Feb. 2
Title	Purification (and other titles, incl. Presentation)	Purification	Purification	Presentation
Time	Dawn	After terce	After terce	(a.m. or p.m.)
Blessing of Candles	7 long	5 long and Nunc Dimittis	5 long and Nunc Dimittis	1 short
Distribution of Candles	+	+	+	+
Prayer		+	+	+
Procession and Chants	+	+	+	+ and Nunc Dimittis
Mood of Procession	Pontiff barefoot black vestments	Pontiff barefoot black/violet vestments	Violet (or no chasuble)	White throughout
Venue: Procession	St. Hadrian	Stational; but venues not	–	Stational suggested

	10th Century: Romano-Germanic Pontifical	12th Century: Rome	MR 1570	MR 1970
Venue: Eucharist	St. Mary Major	Specified	—	
Eucharist: Color		White	White	White
Lections	Mal 3:1-4 ? Lk:2-22-32 ?	Mal 3:1-4 Lk 2:22-32	Mal 3:1-4 Lk 2:22-32	Mal 3:1-4 Heb 2:14-18 Lk 2:22-40

Notes

Date: eventually settles as Quadragesima of December 25th, feast of birth.

Title: Eastern hypapante reflects interpretation, whereas West eventually concentrates on Purification, though *MR 1970* revives old alternative 'Presentation,' both in *PRG* and Anglican *Book of Common Prayer*.

Time: early tradition of pre-dawn, when candles make impact. Today's popularity of evening eucharists changes this.

Blessing of candles: not an Eastern practice, and only found in West from 9th century. Medieval clusters of prayers, including the (sporadic)N. European custom of blessing the 'fire' or the Paschal Candle, as source for subsequent lighting.

Distribution of candles: a special feature only when the candles have to be *blessing*.

Prayer: the old 'collecta,' to start the procession.

Procession and Chants: originally litany or antiphons, antiphons take over. Was the litany an indication of penitential mood?

Mood of procession: unresolved, except in *MR1970*, and, perhaps, in later East.

Venue: an old stational feature, that would not apply to a small church setting. Note *MR1970*'s desire to revive.

Eucharist: Color: color-sequences were a later Medieval feature, from 10th century (see *PRG*'s 'black').

Lections: East adheres to *whole* pericope, introduced in *MR1970* (but also in Anglican *Book of Common Prayer* in 1662). N.B. Eastern Epistle lections. *MR1970* involved three lections, hence the need to provide Epistle.

4

Why Is the Feast of the Visitation Celebrated on 2 July?

Cur 2. julii electus sit. nescitur.
—Polykarp Radó[1]

Balthasar Fischer

THE FEAST OF THE VISITATION OF THE BLESSED VIRGIN MARY, WHICH COM-memorates the meeting of Mary and Elizabeth described in Luke 1:39-56, was introduced for the Franciscan Order in 1263, when Bonaventure was Superior General. Throughout the seven centuries following its introduction in the high Middle Ages, the liturgical books of the Roman Church[2] have associated it with 2 July. This date was retained in 1441, when the Council of Basel made the feast of the *Visitatio Beatae Mariae Virginis* obligatory for the entire Western Church. The calendar of the English Book of Common Prayer adopted it with the same date.[3] The most recent postconciliar reform of the Roman calendar has given up this tradition of seven hundred years and assigned the feast a new date: 31 May, previously associated with the feast of Mary, Queen of Heaven,[4] established in 1954.[5]

Historians of the liturgical year—to one of the most prominent of whom this Festschrift is dedicated—naturally ask why the Roman tradition[6] chose this odd date from the very first. Not all of them, of course, seem as perplexed by the question as Radó, who is quoted at the beginning of this article. Most are at least aware of a lead that enables us to trace the history of this date for a considerable distance. As is almost always true in the history of the Marian feasts, this lead points to the East. There is evidence that the Eastern Church observed 2 July as a feast commemorating the "deposition" of Mary's robe in the Church of the Blachernae at Constantinople under the emperor Leo and his consort Verina (457-478).[7] We know that the gospel of the visitation was read on this feast.[8]

The advent of the robe is interpreted as representing the advent of the person, like the advent of Mary at the house of Elizabeth, described by the evangelist Luke.

The existence of a Byzantine feast of Mary on 2 July does not explain the date, but it is important. It suggests that the feast of the Visitation originated in the East. With this festival, the West borrowed from the East yet another element of the latter's much more emotional Marian devotion (while stripping it of the specific occasion that produced a Marian festival on 2 July in Byzantium).

A glance at the role played by the visitation in medieval western iconography suggests at once how deeply this motif touched the hearts of Western Christendom, which had certainly not been overly encouraged in this direction by the austere Roman liturgy.

But this observation merely shifts the problem of explaining the date of the festival. Now we must ask: Why did Constantinople celebrate the feast of the deposition of Mary's robe, with its reading of the visitation gospel, on 2 July? Lów has suggested that the date is connected with the feast of John the Baptist, observed on 24 June in both East and West since time immemorial.[9] It seems extremely contrived, however, to suggest that the date is based on Mary's return home on the day following the octave of John's birth, that is, the day after the infant's circumcision, so that the day of her return (!) came to commemorate the meeting. It is more reasonable to assume that the translation of Mary's robe took place on 2 July. If so, we would have an analogy to the feast of the Presentation of Mary on 21 November: this apparently mysterious date, common to both East and West, can be traced to an event in the history of one particular church in Jerusalem, where the observance began, namely the date of its consecration.[10]

But there is a more plausible explanation, which traces the history of our date to a substantially earlier period. The fifth-century Armenian Lectionary of the church in Jerusalem shows that in the vicinity of the Holy City an Old Testament event was commemorated on 2 July that on closer examination reveals astonishing associations with the visitation.

Here we read: "2 July: Feast of the Ark at Qiryathiarim."[11] This feast commemorates the arrival of the ark of the covenant at the house of Abinadab (1 Sm 7:1). A shrine in honor of this event was built at Kiriath-jearim in the fifth century.[12] There the annual commemoration recorded in the lectionary was observed.[13] At first glance, it appears perverse to search here for a connection with the later Marian feast on 2 July. Another entry in the Armenian Lectionary, however, furnishes incontestable evidence for the symbolic identification of the ark with Mary. On the Feast of the Theotokos—that is, the feast of Mary's Dormition on 15 August—the liturgy begins with Psalm 132, the same psalm with which the feast of the ark begins. The antiphon in both cases is: "Arise, O Lord, and come to thy resting place, thou and thy mighty ark" (v. 8).[14] In the context of the 15 August feast, the use of such a verse as a theme can be explained only on the basis of the Marian interpretation so popular later. This interpretation, therefore, must have been current in Jerusalem at an unusually early date.

How the feast of the advent of the ark of the covenant turned into the feast of the visitation (undoubtedly in the East) we do not know. Perhaps we may be allowed the conjecture that the translation of Mary's robe (a new advent of Mary) was associated with a commemoration of her visitation of her cousin Elizabeth; if so, the reading of the visitation gospel would be earlier than the commemoration of the translation.

Recent French interpreters of Luke, especially Laurentin, have suggested that Luke's account of the visitation already uses the motif of Mary as the ark of the New Testament. If this theory were correct,[15] the transition from a commemoration of the advent of the ark to a commemoration of Mary would have been natural from the very outset.

In conclusion, we note that we have been unable to answer the question of our title. Even if our whole theory is correct, it merely shifts the question we have been studying a further step into the past. It now becomes: Why was the feast of the ark celebrated on 2 July? In the absence of new evidence, we must here repeat Radó's simple answer: *Nescimus.*

Notes

1. Polycarp Radó. *Enchiridion Liturgicum*, vol. 2 (Rome, 1963) 1353. The Marian feast of 2 July is also discussed by L. Eisenhöfer, *Handbuch der katholischen Liturgik*, vol. 1 (Freiburg, 1932) 597; G. Löw, "Visitazione di Maria: Festo," *Enciclopedia Cattolica* vol 12 (1954) 1499-1501; B. Luyks, "Bezoeking (v. Maria), *Liturgisch Woordenboek* (Roermond, 1958) 260; P. Jounel in *L'Eglise en prière*, vol. 4 (Paris, 1983), 154-157; H. Merkel, "Feste IV," *Theologische Realenzyklopädie*, vol. 11 (1983) 122. See also J. Polc, *De Origine Festi Visitationis B. Mariae Virginis*, Corona Lateranesis, 9A (Romae, 1967); despite its title, this monograph does not discuss the origins of the feast but its beginnings.

2. Outside the Roman sphere the feast has other dates; see note 6.

3. The American Book of Common Prayer included the "Visitation of the

Blessed Virgin" on 2 July for the first time in its 1979 revision; see Marion J. Hatchett, *Commentary on the American Prayer Book* (Oak Grove, 1980) 62-63.

4. For a brief history of this feast (1954-1969), see Radó *Enchiridion* 1352.

5. The popularity of the feast fortunately made it possible to retain the earlier date for its observance in the regional calendar for the German-speaking church.

6. Outside Rome, we find 27 July in Paris and 28 April in Prague; see K.A.H. Kellner, *Heortologie* (Freiburg, 1911) 202.

7. See N. Nilles, *Kalendarium Manuale Utriusque Ecclesiae Orientalis et Occidentalis*, vol. 1 (Oeniponte, 1896) 200-202.

8. Jounel, *L'Eglise en prière* 154.

9. "Visitazione" 1500.

10. See Jounel *L'Eglise en prière* 156; see also my article (with F. Mussner) "Was wird bei einer Kalenderreform aus dem Fest: Praesentatio Beatae Mariae Virginis werden?" *Trierer theologische Zeitschrift* 70 (1961) 170-181. Almost thirty years later, I have to confess that the reform of the calendar has—fortunately—not accepted our recommendation to suppress the feast. Today, we see more clearly that we must not sever our many links with eastern spirituality. The problem of the legendary event that the feast commemorates has found an elegant solution in the collect assigned to the festival in the *Missale Romanum* of 1970, which substitutes the words *memoria gloriosa* for the *hodienra die* of the 1570 text.

11. See PO, Section 61: *Le codex armenien Jerusalem 121*, ed. A. Renoux, Patrologia Orientalis 35:1 (1969) 349, 351.

12. See H. Haag, ed., *Bibellexikon* (Einsiedeln, 1956) 929.

13. Observance at Kiriath-jearim rather than Jerusalem is argued by Haag, ibid.

14. Renoux (n. 11), section 64, 355, 357.

15. Schürmann and Schnackenburg have disputed it vigorously; see Heinz Schürmann, *Das Lukasevangelium I*, Herders theologischer Kommentar zum Neuen Testament, vol. 3 (Freiburg: Herder, 1969) 64-65, n.161.

LITURGICAL HISTORY

5

The Liturgy of Antioch in the Time of Severus (513-518)

G. J. Cuming*

IT HAS LONG BEEN RECOGNIZED THAT THE HOMILIES OF SAINT JOHN CHRYSOS-
tom contain numerous allusions to the text and ceremonial of the liturgy
in the years 370-398. These allusions have been collected by, among others, J. Bingham, F. Probst, F.E. Brightman, and, definitively, by F. van de
Paverd.[1] It seemed worthwhile, therefore, to search the 125 *Cathedral
Homilies* of Severus of Antioch in the hope of shedding light on the liturgy
of Antioch in the years of his patriarchate. The results of the search were
less fruitful than in the case of Chrysostom: 31 quotations against 127.
However, this rather meager harvest can be supplemented by twenty-
four quotations from his *Letters* and seventeen from his *Hymns*. Severus

---

*Geoffrey Cuming died in Houston, Texas, on 24 March 1988, while recover-
ing from major heart surgery. The doyen of English liturgiologists, he had undertaken to contribute to these essays in recognition of an American scholar whom
he greatly admired. Unfortunately, he was not able to write the piece he had intended. Instead, Kenneth Stevenson, his literary executor, has made available
here Dr. Cuming's last liturgical *opusculum* on which he was working at the time
of his death. It was typical of Dr. Cuming that he should be trying to push back
the boundaries of liturgical knowledge right to the end. Clearly, he thought
much more could be gleaned from the writings of Severus of Antioch. Perhaps
someone else will take up the challenge. Meanwhile, this modest and concisely
written contribution is offered. Barring the occasional clarification (suggested by
margin notes made by the author), this "interim report" is presented here in exactly the form he left it.

was a prolific writer: the fourteen volumes in the *Corpus Scriptorum Christianorum Orientalium* have not been included in the search: *Contra impium grammaticum* alone runs to 714 pages of closely-printed Latin. The collection below is offered as an interim report on which others may build.

Severus' main interests lay, not in liturgy, but in biblical exposition, refutation of heresies, and recounting the sufferings of the martyrs. In fact, he sometimes misses an obvious opportunity to refer to the liturgy. For example, Homily 119, on the wedding at Cana, makes no reference to the eucharist, and Homily 122 speaks about those possessed by devils, but does not mention the litany said on their behalf, though Letter 60 of Part I, Section I, Book VI shows that it was still said at Antioch.

Little has been written by scholars about Severus' allusions to the liturgy; they do not, for the most part, call for the comprehensive investigation accorded to Chrysostom by van de Paverd. Some, indeed, are self-explanatory. Some brief notes have been added below by way of commentary.

Sources

The *Cathedral Homilies*, by various editors, are in *Patrologia Orientalis*, vols. 4, 8, 12, 16, 20, 22, 23, 25, 26, 29, 35, 36, 37, 38. A table giving full details of editors, dates, fascicles, and page-numbers will be found in vol. 29, p. 250 (but vol. 26 appeared in 1948, not 1940).

The *Hymns*, edited by E.W. Brooks, are in PO, vols. 6 and 7 (1911).

Selected Letters, ed. by E.W. Brooks, are in PO, vols. 12 and 14 (1915 and 1919). (In the references below, the volume-number in PO is in Roman figures, the page-number in Arabic (e.g., xxii.221).

Letter, Book VI, ed. by E.W. Brooks, are in *Text and Translation Society*, vol. 2, Parts I and II (1903 and 1904). In this edition the letters are not numbered consecutively; the part-number is in Roman capitals and the page number in Arabic (e.g., I.187-8).

Abbreviations

AC	*Apostolic Constitutions*
CHR	Liturgy of Saint John Chrysostom
CM	*Catecheses Mystagogicae* of Cyril of Jerusalem
DBL	*Documents of the Baptismal Liturgy* (ed. E.C. Whitaker)
JAS	Liturgy of Saint James
Mer	Mercier's edition of JAS
Test Dom	*Testamentum Domini*
LEW	*Liturgies Eastern and Western* (ed. F.E. Brightman)
PO	*Patrologia Orientalis*

The Eucharist

The Peace-Greeting

1. Homily 99 (xxii.221)

> How great is the power of the first word which we address
> to the people when we say, "Peace be with you all"!

> "The reciprocal greeting with which, as is commonly
> assumed, the liturgy was begun in the fourth centu-
> ry" is established for the East only "by Chrysostom."[2]
> It is preserved in JAS (Mar, 166.7), but has disap-
> peared from CHR.

The Trisagion

2. Homily 125 (xxix.249)

> If anyone does not accept "who was crucified for us" be-
> cause it is new, let him also reject all that (act of) praise as
> not having been honored of old, but begun recently and not
> said by everyone; for the Alexandrians and the Libyans
> and the Egyptians do not sing at all in church this praise of
> the Saviour of the universe, Christ. The "Holy, holy, holy,
> Lord of hosts" said by the seraphim was reported to us by
> the prophet Isaiah ... but the "Holy God, holy, strong, holy,
> immortal" was added long afterwards. If then, we have ac-
> cepted the addition as devout, and confess as true God him
> "who was crucified," let us not call the confession of our
> faith "new," which fights against the Jewish madness of
> Nestorius and is sung thus in the holy churches of God.
> And it was begun in our city of Antioch ... and has spread
> to the churches of Asia, and is making its way beyond to-
> wards all the churches.

> The homily is a defense of the additional phrase "who
> was crucified for us," which was added by Peter the
> Fuller (Patriarch of Antioch, 468-488). It is found in
> Syriac JAS (LEW, 77.24), but not in CHR. It is not clear
> whether the phrase "this praise of the Saviour of the
> universe" above means the whole Trisagion or only
> the addition. Severus holds that the Trisagion is ad-
> dressed to Christ, not to the whole Trinity.

3. Homily 2 (xxxviii.250)

> Severus regards the omission of the addition as "an impiety."

Catechumens and the Possessed

4. Letters, Book VI (I.187-8)

> For indeed this custom has prevailed in the holy churches up to the present day. I mean that after the reading of the holy revered book of the Gospels there should be a supplication on behalf of the catechumens, one of the deacons proclaiming the names, and the presbyter thereupon offering a prayer applying to those whose names have been proclaimed, in order that they may receive the laver of regeneration and the communion of the holy mysteries; and that immediately afterwards another proclamation and prayer should follow on behalf of those who are possessed ... Further, when the holy symbols that are consecrated in the mystical sacrifice are about to be brought out into the church, and to be placed on the holy altar, the first of the deacons, looking out of the door of the deacons' chamber, utters the fearful and aweful words "No catechumen, no possessed person, no-one that is incapable"; and so, those that consecrate and those who have been consummated begin the ineffable sacred sacrifice and send upwards the mystical words.

5. Letters, Book VI (I.190)

> The intentions of the canons is to preserve the visible appearance of the church blameless. For this reason they forbade those also who are possessed by an invasion of devils to communicate in the holy mysteries.

> > *Apostolic Constitutions* (AC) has these liturgies, prayers, and dismissals, and also a set for penitents (LEW, 3.14 - 9.21), and this is confirmed by John Chrysostom's homilies.[3] No liturgy mentions a reading of the names of the catechumens.

> > The "fearful and aweful words" forbidding certain classes to stay take various forms: AC: catechumens, hearers, unbelievers, heretics; JAS Georgian: unfit, un-

worthy, unable; JAS Greek: catechumens, uninitiated, unable to pray with us. Severus is thus closest to JAS.

Earthly Thoughts

6. Hymn 233 (vii.687)

> Let no-one ... have any earthly thoughts.

> Possibly an allusion to the Cherubikon (LEW, 377.16-17); compare Cyril, CM, 5.4: "The priest bids ... all to abandon earthly thoughts".

Not to Condemnation

7. Hymn 230 (vii.686)

> Let us entreat that participation in the mystery may not be to us for judgement and condemnation, but for a participation in incorruptibility and in the kingdom of heaven.

> A liturgical cliché, which occurs in the anaphora of CHR (LEW, 330.18; see 338.22B). For "incorruptibility," see the corresponding prayer in St Mark (LEW, 134.25).

The Veil

8. Letter 105 (xiv.256)

> You should know that the priest who offers represents the great God and our Saviour Jesus Christ ... The veil therefore which, before the priest approaches, hides what is set forth, and is removed after his entry manifestly cries ... that the mystery ... by means of this spiritual and rational priestly ministration reveals Christ.

Letter 105 (xiv.257)

> In Palestine and in Jerusalem, while the priest makes the said prayer, the deacons frequently and ceaselessly lift (the veil) up and let it down again, until the end of the prayer, and so after that, the priest begins the petition over the offering of the sacrifice.

> In CHR it is the priest who both veils and unveils the gifts (LEW, 379.30, 384.1), but in the Georgian MSS of

JAS, in George of Arbela, and in the Armenian version of CHR,[4] it is the deacon or deacons who remove the veil. Again, in Syriac JAS (LEW, 85.12) it is the priest who "makes the *annaphura* to flutter." In CHR (LEW, 384.2-3) the deacon takes the fan and fans the holy things.

For "the petition over the ... sacrifice," see Cyril, CM, 5.8: "We beseech God over that sacrifice of propitiation," and *Coptic Mark* (LEW, 165.19).

The Sanctus

9. Hymn 210 (vii.673)

Myriads of myriads of angels minister to thee, and a thousand thousand angels stand before thee.

10. Hymn 208 (vii.673)

The many-eyed beasts hide their faces from thee.

Hymn 207 (vii.672)

Inclining our necks, with cherubim and seraphim let us cry and say, "Holy art thou, holy art thou, holy art thou, Lord of Sabaoth; the heaven and the earth are full of thy glory, merciful One."

11. Hymn 226 (vii.681)

Come, believers, let us approach in fear and faith. For he is the priest and the sacrifice; it is he who offers, and is offered, and receives. The multitudes of angels are standing with the cherubim and seraphim, flying while with mouths and voices that are not silent, they utter the song of victory, "Hallelujah."

"Myriads": CHR (LEW, 322.25).
"Beasts": *St Mark* (LEW, 131.25-6), *Syriac Basil*[5]
"Merciful One" appears to be Severus' own addition.
"With fear": "Let us stand with fear" is found in several liturgies just before the anaphora.
"mouths ... not silent ... the song of victory": CHR (LEW, 323.25-7).

The Benedictus

12. Homily 90 (xxiii.133)

>To the words of the Sanctus we immediately add the thanksgiving: "Blessed is he who has come and comes in the name of the Lord."

>"Has come" is in JAS (Mer, 200.5-6), Syriac JAS (LEW, 86.16), and Test Dom, I.23; not, however, in CHR.

The Institution Narrative

13. Letters, Book VI (II.238)

>The priest who stands before the altar ... says over the bread, "This is my body which is given for you: do this in remembrance of me;" while again over the cup he pronounces the words, "This cup is the new covenant in my blood, which is shed for you."

>Severus seems to be quoting Luke 22.20 rather than any anaphora. See also 18, below.

The Rational and Spiritual Sacrifice

14. Hymn 209 (vii.673)

>... in the hour of the spiritual and bloodless sacrifice.

15. Hymn 346 (vii.780)

>... the rational and bloodless sacrifice.

16. Hymn 73 (vi.117)

>(The cross) completes the rational, bloodless, spiritual sacrifice.

17. Letter 24 (xii.221)

>(The cross) is everywhere adopted ... at the celebration of the rational spiritual sacrifice.

18. Letters, Book VI (II.245)

>It is Christ himself and his mystical words which are pronounced over the bread and the cup that complete the rational and bloodless sacrifice.

>CHR (LEW, 329.13-15) has *logike kai anaimaktos latreia.*

JAS (Mer 204.9 and all versions) has *anaimaktos thusia*. *St Mark* (LEW, 126.5-6) has *logike (thusia)*[6] *kai anaimaktos latreia*. Cyril (CM, 5.8) has *pneumatike thusia anaimaktos latreia*. There appears to be little difference between *logikos* and *pneumatikos*. With nos. 16 and 18, compare Chrysostom, *De proditione Iudae*, 1.6:[7] *ten thusian apertismenen ergazetai*.

The Intercession

19. Homily 106 (xxv.665)

But now, bowing your heads towards this source full of good things, pray earnestly and actively for the establishment of the whole world, for the perfect stability of affairs, for those who fight on behalf of the orthodox faith, for the peace of men, external and internal, for that which is seen, for that which is understood.

The oldest Georgian MS (407.24) has "they bow down ... "; elsewhere it is only the priest who is mentioned in the rubric. "Stability" (*eustatheia*): see Cyril (CM, 5.8); AC (LEW, 9.30); JAS (Mer 218.23). It is strange that Severus does not mention the church here.

Communicating

20. Homily 122 (xxix.117)

You see that which is before you on the altar, as (Christ) is seated on the heavenly throne; you approach and receive him, and grasp him in your hands, and embrace him, and cover him with kisses, and bring him to your mouth, and make him enter within you, and you have him entire within you.

See Cyril (CM, 5.21-22).

Baptism

Catechesis

21. Homily 35 (xxxvi.452-3)

We speak of (the mysteries) only in a veiled way, because of the hearers who are not instructed in the mysteries.

Cyril dealt with the mysteries in his *Catecheses* only after the candidates had been baptized; Chrysostom treated of them already in Lent (DBL, 35).

Turning West and East

22. Homily 42 (xxxvi.63)

You who were catechized ... say the sacred words of David: "Let us break their bonds and cast away their yoke." Look and turn towards the sunset, and so renounce Satan and the troop of demons ... And after doing that, turn to the east and make these covenants with Christ.

23. Homily 70 (xii.47-49)

Turning yourselves first towards the sunset, you renounce the slavery of the Malicious One ... Then, turning towards the sunrise, you make afresh the health-giving profession of faith ... When you turned to the west, you stretched out your right hand and you drew back your left hand ... But at once you lowered (your left hand) and raised your right hand on high ...

When you turned towards the east and raised both your hands on high, you made a covenant with Christ.

24. Homily 90 (xxiii.159)

(After a reference to turning West and East) ... looking towards the sunrise, say the words of the profession: say clearly, "We shall pay no more tribute to the Evil One; we have become the possession of the King of heaven ... " Hasten towards the first place, I mean, towards Paradise planted in the east, for it is this which shows the external aspect of the position which we have now made you take, as is the law. Then you will go also to the spring of the Jordan, (which is) full of the Holy Spirit, of purification and the divine fire, in which you will be buried with Christ while burying the old man in the water.

25. Homily 123 (xxix.185)

Stand up and, turning yourselves to the west, renounce the darkness of the Manichees ... and turn yourselves likewise to the east; and it is by the sunlight itself that Christ will meet you ... He himself will make you descend towards the water and take a bath as a purification from all the old life, and will lead you to a new life, burying your old sins in the water ... and clothing you with infancy of spiritual status.

Cyril (CM, 1.2,4) mentions only stretching out the hand, not raising it on high, or raising both hands at the *syntaxis*. Chrysostom (DBL, 37) speaks of stretching "your hands to heaven."

"Paradise:" In CM, 1.9 Cyril writes, "There is opened to you the paradise of God which he planted in the east."

"The words of profession" in Cyril's rite were "I believe in the Father, and in the Son, and in the Holy Spirit."

The Sign of the Cross

26. Letter 24 (xii.221)

(The cross) is a thing which makes known and completes all things that are done among Christians; and it is everywhere adopted at the performance of baptism, at the consecration of the water.

27. Hymn 73 (vi.117)

(The cross) blesses and hallows the water of regeneration.

The water was consecrated by pouring chrism upon it in the form of a cross (Dionysius, DBL, 58; James of Edessa, DBL, 59).

The Triple Immersion

28. Homily 90 (xxiii.59)

By the triple immersion we make known the burial which lasted three days and the resurrection which came from it.

29. Letter 24 (xii.219)

For the same baptism is both performed in the name of the Holy Trinity, and by the triple dipping it is further signified that the man who is baptized is buried with Christ.

Cyril (CM, 2.4) also interprets the triple immersion as a symbol of Christ's three days "in the heart of the earth."

Deaconesses Immerse Women

30. Letters, Book VI (I.194)

The deaconesses in the cities are in the habit of ministering to the divine laver of regeneration in the case of women who are baptized.

Already in the *Didascalia* (ch. 16); also AC (DBL, 30); Test Dom, II.8 ("Let women be anointed by widows who sit in front").

The Seal

31. Letter 24 (xii.219)

(*Title*) Of the imprint by ointment (*muron*) with which those who have been baptized are imprinted after baptism.

32. Letter, Book VI (II.353-4)

The word of the baptizer perfects baptism also and causes the Spirit to come down upon the water ... So also the word of the anointer is mingled with the chrism ... and brings the grace of the Spirit into play.

33. Letters, Book VI (II.418)

The rite is made complete for them by the invocation, and the anointing with the holy chrism added afterwards.

For Chrysostom (DBL, 40) it is in the water that the Holy Spirit descends upon the candidate; he does not appear to have had any post-baptismal anointing. AC mentions one, but says that if there is no chrism, the water is sufficient for the seal (DBL, 32). Severus also holds that baptism is complete in the water, but by then his rite has acquired a post-baptismal anointing ("added afterwards") which "brings the grace of the Spirit into play." This is still a little short of Cyril's statement that the anointing is "the emblem of the holy Spirit." (CM, 3.3).

The Eucharist Follows

34. Letter 65 (xiv.51)

> On being admitted to the divine laver and regeneration and putting off from us the old man, we are invited by Christ to the mystic table and eat the angelic heavenly bread.

> > "Straightway after they come up from the waters, they are led to the awesome table" (Chrysostom, DBL, 41). Cyril, Dionysius, and James of Edessa concur (DBL, ad loc.).

Reception of Heretics

35. Letters, Book VI (II.348)

> These (heretics) ought to be perfected by chrism, just as the custom is for Arians and Pneumatomachi to be received.

Conditional Baptism

36. Letters, Book VI (II.422)

> (In the case of those who think they have not been baptized) it is absolutely necessary to follow the holy Cyril's expression and say, "So-and-so is baptized if he has not been baptized, in the name ... "

Emergency Baptism

37. Letters, Book VI (II.426)

> (A baby was brought for urgent baptism; no priest was available, so a deacon baptized it.) "In case of necessity, if a presbyter is not present, let a deacon baptize." The presbyter did well in paying attention to what was done by the deacon out of necessity, and performing the ceremonies that follow baptism, and applying to the boy who had been baptized the anointing with the holy chrism, and the seal of perfection that results from this.

> > The first sentence is quoted verbatim from Test Dom, 2.10.

The Daily Office

Different forms

38. Letter 54 (xii.332)

> I wish your god-loving Highness to know that the order of hymns and odes has been preserved in one form among the Egyptians, in another among the Syrians, according to the custom that has been handed down from the beginning in each of these regions.

The Evening Office

39. Homily 37 (xxxvi.478)

> Your women fast and prepare to hurry back to the church for the evening office.

40. Hymn 319 (vii.757)

> To thee, O Christ, I offer a sacrifice of praise at the hour of evening.

> Presumably vespers of the cathedral office. It was attended by lay people (Egeria, 24.4).

The Night Office

41. Homily 41 (xxxvi.26)

> If she finds (her son) on his way to church and persevering in the night office and in prayer, let her rejoice with him.

> It was held before cockcrow, with some laymen present (Egeria, 24.1).

Versicle and Response

42. Homily 87 (xxiii.86)

> Let us incline our ears to the psalmody, and in such a way that we too shall come to sing at the same time as those who sing, saying with David, "Lord, thou shalt open my lips and my mouth shall make known your praise."

> Severus thinks of the office chiefly as an occasion for singing psalms.

The Doxology

43. Homily 83 (xv.419)

> I do not know by what motive some here have been per-
> suaded to forbid women to say the doxology in the office of
> psalms: Paul says in effect, "I do not suffer a woman to
> teach," but not "to say the doxology." For if women were
> forbidden to say the doxology, by the same principle they
> would also be forbidden to sing; and if no law forbids the
> latter, have they not also freedom of the former?

>> Severus quotes the precedent of Miriam in Exodus 15
>> and deduces that the doxology is general and not pe-
>> culiar to men.

A Sunday Office

44. Homily 77 (xvi.794)

> All approve the reading of the holy gospels which we intro-
> duced on Sunday night on the subject of the Resurrection
> of our great God and Saviour Jesus Christ ... (*Title*) ... facts
> which we read every Sunday night.

>> Jean Tabet[7] has drawn attention to this office, which
>> appears to be derived from Jerusalem (Egeria, 27.2).
>> In addition to the gospel-reading, Severus wrote
>> hymns (vi.120-130) for this office. One is entitled
>> "Verses to be sung before the reading of the Gospel
>> on Sunday night; other verses to be sung on Sunday
>> night after the reading of the Gospel." It was presum-
>> ably said in connection with the ordinary night office.

The Calendar

Hypapante

45. Homily 125 (xxix.247)

> This feast and solemnity of the Meeting, which is celebrat-
> ed at Jerusalem and in the whole of Palestine ... used not to
> be celebrated in the Imperial City. Now, however, this also
> has imitated the custom which has been preserved by oth-
> ers ... And in this city of Antioch the kind of festival which
> we mentioned used not to be known. And in Jerusalem this
> festival was nothing ancient, but was invented recently, as

we have heard some old men say.

Already at the time of Egeria's visit (ch. 26) the feast
of the Fortieth Day was "observed with special mag-
nificence." Constantinople adopted it officially in 542.
Severus' "old men" must have been repeating hear-
say, and his "recently" is not to be taken too literally.

Palm Sunday

46. Homily 125 (xxix.247)
Now one could say the same about this festival called
"Palms" ... And in fact, the day of this festival, although it
had not been celebrated by many, and now, to speak generally, is celebrated by everybody, has not been rejected as a
new invention by those who have imitated those that celebrated it already.

47. Hymn 52 (vi.96)
When I see the leaves of palm-trees and hear the little children crying "Hosanna in the heights," I cry with them.

Egeria (ch.31) describes a procession down the Mount
of Olives with palm branches, but does not give the
Sunday any name. In the Armenian Lectionary it is
called "The Day of Palms."

The Easter Vigil

48. Hymn 83 (vi.124)
In the night our spirit arises early to greet thee, Christ, God.
Be among us who early honor thy Resurrection in spiritual
fashion with choirs, and send up voices of thanksgiving to
thy glory.

49. Hymn 86 (vi.126)
You who have honored the resplendent night of the Resurrection by standing all through (it).

The first quotation may refer to the Sunday Office
(see 44 above), the second more probably to Easter.

Holy Cross Day

50. Hymn 260 (vii.709)

> On the day of the commemoration of thy life-giving cross
> [thou] didst chastise us with an earthquake.

>> Egeria (48.2) describes the commemoration of the
>> finding of the cross; the Armenian Lectionary has it
>> on 14 September.

Orders

The Sign of the Cross

51. Letter 24 (xii.221)

> [The cross] is everywhere adopted ... at the symbolic and
> ineffable ordination to the priesthood.

52. Hymn 73 (vi.117)

> [The cross] completes ... the whole ministerial office and
> perfect service.

Anointing

53. Homily 80 (xx.326)

> Those who have been anointed with the oil of the pontifi-
> cate and, even more, of the patriarchate ... are the head.

The Lesser Orders

54. Homily 99 (xxii.215-6)

>> Severus describes the duties of the lesser orders as fol-
>> lows: chanters—hymns and the night office; readers—
>> the readings; subdeacons —daily distributions, light-
>> ing lamps. Of deacons he says only that they wear a
>> splendid tunic and a linen garment.

55. Letters, Book VI (I.40)

> Everywhere under the sun the order of subdeacons ranks
> before that of readers.

A Deacon May Celebrate

56. Letters, Book VI (I.194)

> The ordination of a presbyter or of a male deacon by whom
> the bloodless sacrifice is of necessity performed ...

Various

Extempore Prayer

57. Homily 16 (xxxviii.448)
>There came then the gift of prayer for him who believed in this gift and in what is fitting and useful for the whole community of the Church; he stood up, spoke, and exhorted the others ... and it is the sign of this, that it is the deacon who offers prayer for the people.

Kneeling

58. Homily 108 (xxv.147)

>Down to Pentecost we do not bend the knee to the earth when we pray ... but when the Spirit has shone to us in God-befitting fashion, we bow the knee because we cannot endure the sight.

59. Homily 25 (xxxvii.162)
>During these fifty days, we do not kneel in our prayers in any way, but stand upright and stretch out our hands, praising him who was crucified, was buried, and rose again.

60. Homily 25 (xxxvii.164)
>[After Pentecost] we bow towards the earth and kneel, glorifying the giver of these great gifts ... Further, when we have been purified by fasting ... it is the custom of those who are worthy of divine visions to kneel and proclaim by that posture the sublimity and grandeur of the vision.

>(TD 2:12): "(During) let no one fast or kneel."

Fasting

61. Homily 92 (xxv.43)
>Some women on the one hand fast every day and many on the other hand fast on Wednesdays and Fridays.

>The latter practice goes back to the *Didache* 8.1. See Egeria 41.

Frequency of Communion

62. Homily 54 (iv.63)

> Do not say to me ... "It is for this reason that once or twice a year I approach the awesome table with circumspection."

> The speaker based his practice on 1 Corinthians 11.29.

Observance of Lent

63. Two Greek fragments (Migne, *Patrologia Graeca*, 95.76)

> Severus explains that Lent is eight weeks long because there is no fasting on Saturday or Sunday (8 x 5 = 40 days). In Jerusalem it was forty-one days, as Easter Eve was a fast (Egeria, 27.1).

64. Homily 87 (xxiii.86)

> Let us pray with those who pray, let us attend the mysteries, and we shall think the day short, once we have set it apart and consecrated it to God.

65. Homily 88 (xxiii.97)

> [During Lent] beside the love of labor, put equally the wakeful office of psalmody which keeps watch during the night.

> At Jerusalem an all-night vigil was kept on Fridays (Egeria, 27.8). "The love of labour" was fasting.

The Visit to the Baptistery

66. Homily 32 (xxxvi.412)

> That is why, every Sunday, we lead you to the baptistery with a celebration, praise, prayer, and supplication, so as to recall these covenants made with God, when we renounced Satan and his wicked works, so as not to come to forget the forgiveness of our sins, the gift of the Spirit, and the grace of adoption as sons ...

> Those who like to be controversial and sharpen their envious tongues against us say in effect: this venerable baptistery ought not to be open except once a year ... In other churches you see the baptisteries open ...

67. Homily 106 (xxv.660)

> (Title:) It was delivered inside the holy baptistery, the eve-
> ning of the beginning of the holy feast of forty days, when
> we were going to forbid ourselves the entry to the baptis-
> tery which takes place every Sunday evening, until the
> holy fast of Pascha and the Resurrection. We enter every
> Sunday with psalms, petitions, and prayers.

68. Homily 40 (xxxvi.8)

> We have given you once and again the cause and reason
> why, when the beginning of the holy days of the fast
> dawns upon us, we turn aside and keep away from enter-
> ing the symbol of light.

> This ceremony, performed every Sunday except dur-
> ing Lent, seems to be peculiar to Antioch, and may
> well have been introduced by Severus. A marginal
> note gives the Greek original as *photisterion*.

Cloths for Lepers

69. Homily 122 (xxix.105)

> The chief deacon goes up to the holy pulpit and cries out in
> a public ... proclamation, and reminds the congregation to
> bring this gift and to give pieces of cloth (for lepers).

Menstruation

70. Letter 53 (xii.329)

> Menstruation and sexual intercourse bar from com-
> munion for one day. Severus quotes Test Dom, 1.42
> and the *Answers* of Timothy (V and VII).

Attendance at Heretical Services

71. Letters, Book VI (II.272)

> You ask whether some of the orthodox are doing well in
> communicating with the heretics, but listening to the read-
> ing of the holy Gospel, or even staying during the time of
> the mystical prayers, but not communicating in the rites
> that are being performed.

> Severus' answer is that they are not doing well.

Sending the Oblation

72. Letters, Book VI (II.231)

(To Count Anastasius) We have sent you the communion or oblation.

73. Letters, Book VI (II.246)

The Christ-loving brothers Ammian and Epagathus ... sent me a box and asked to have it filled full for them with the communion or holy oblation. I did not fall in with the impiety and superfluity of the request.

Architecture

74. Homily 100 (xxii.246)

No one pays attention to the venerable table of the holy priestly ministry nor to the silver columns placed near it which carry the dome situated above their heads, which is bare, ugly, and misshapen; which has been simply outlined by iron rods or bars as in a symbolic representation, but has not been covered with silver ... It represents the shape of heaven, raising itself on the arches and the corona to form the circular calotte, finding itself hung in the air, and ending in its apparent centre at the navel.

Severus is appealing for funds to pay for a ciborium. Its purpose is to show the celebrants that they are in heaven. If each member of the congregation gave only one pound of silver, the work could be finished.

Martyrs

75. Hymn 176 (vii.636)

[Martyrs,] by the limbs of your constancy you hallow prayer-house buildings in which you are laid.

Episcopal Visitations

76. Homily 56 (iv.72-82)

Several of Severus' homilies were preached during a visit to a town in the diocese. There was a regular procedure on these occasions.[8] In this homily, preached at Kinneshrin, Severus mentions that a crowd came to meet him outside the town, and he said, "Peace to this dwelling."

Notes

1. Frans van de Paverd, *Zur Geschichte der Messliturgie in Antiocheia und Konstantinopel gegen Ende des vierten Jahrhunderts*, Orientalia Christiana Analecta 187 (Rome, 1970).

2. Ibid. 83 (my translation).

3. Ibid. 140-154, 175-184.

4. J.M. Hanssens, *Institutiones Liturgicae de Ritibus Orientalibus*, vol. 3 (Rome, 1832) 336-7.

5. H. Engberding, *Das eucharistische Hochgebet der Basileiosliturgie* 9, lines 2, 36, though he is wrong about Sarapion.

6. Quoted at length in van de Paverd (note 1), 296.

7. J. Tabet, "Le témoignage de Sévère d'Antioche (+538) sur le vigile cathédrale," *Melto* 4 (1968) 6-12.

8. I.E. Rahmani, ed., "La réception d'un évêque syrien au VI siècle, *L'Orient syrien* 2 (1957) 137-48.

6

The Liturgical Setting of
The Institution Narrative in the
Early Syrian Tradition

Emmanuel J. Cutrone

SINCE THE 1966 PUBLICATION[1] OF THE MAR ESA 'YA TEXT OF THE ANAPHORA OF Addai and Mari by William Macomber, debate has continued over the presence of an institution narrative in the early Syrian eucharistic prayer.[2] Macomber, comparing Addai and Mari with Maronite Sharar concludes that the ancient eucharistic prayer did have the narrative which was removed at a much later date.[3] Others have argued that the Mar Esa 'ya text of Addai and Mari is a true representation of a tradition which did not originally have the narrative.[4] Recently E. Mazza has added his voice to those who maintain that the Syrian eucharistic tradition knew an anaphora which did not contain an institution narrative. He concludes that as late as 392 in Antioch Theodore of Mopsuestia comments on a eucharistic prayer without any mention of the words Christ spoke at the Last Supper.[5]

Since Sharar, an anaphora which shares antiquity with Addai and Mari, and *Apostolic Constitutions* VIII, which is contemporary with Cyril of Jerusalem and Theodore of Mopsuestia, are two Syrian anaphoras which certainly have the narrative, it must be demonstrated that in the same liturgical tradition some anaphoras had the narrative while others did not. If this cannot be done, then it seems that those who argue for the continual presence of the narrative must be correct, and the evidence of

Cyril of Jerusalem and Theodore of Mopsuestia must be read differently from above.

J.-P. Audet sparked a new line of inquiry with his structural analysis of Jewish prayer forms as the basis for Christian eucharist.[6] Many have amplified and redefined this line of research.[7] Thomas Talley's clarification of the distinction between *eulogein* and *eucharistein*, and his structural and thematic analysis have made major contributions to the understanding of the early evolution of Christian eucharist.[8] As profitable as this has been, there still is not agreement on the place of the institution narrative in the early development of the anaphora. The research seems to indicate that there is nothing in the structure of the prayer which either demands or eliminates the inclusion of the narrative. While strong arguments have been made in both directions,[9] it seems necessary to move the investigation elsewhere.

Beginning with the New Testament,[10] it seems clear that, from the very start, the institution narrative was part of eucharistic worship. X. Léon-Dufour is the latest voice to present a strong argument that the institution narratives come into Scripture from two different liturgical traditions: the Antiochene: I Corinthians 11:23-26/Luke 22:15-20 (Pl/Lk) and the Markan: Mark 14:22-25/Matthew 26:26-29 (Mark/Matthew).[11] This is biblical evidence that in the most influential center of the Syrian church, Antioch, the institution narrative was used in a liturgical setting prior to the composition of I Corinthians. But this does not necessarily mean that the narrative was incorporated into the eucharistic prayer. Even though Léon-Dufour does discuss various types of religious meals and gives special importance to the todah meal, he refuses to specify the liturgical manner in which the narrative was used or to suggest any particulars of the structure of the eucharistic prayer. Of course, the passages as given are not blessings or any other form of prayer; they truly are narratives.[12] But since they are descriptive of a salvific event, they could have been incorporated into a larger prayer context as an embolism, but they could not have stood alone as a prayer. As an embolism the use would have been limited to special occasions, but not the weekly eucharistic liturgy.[13] Bouley suggests that they first functioned as Christian haggadah. [14]

Whereas Ignatius of Antioch[15] makes reference to both eucharist and agape, he does not even allude to the institution narrative. *Didache* 9 and 10 give texts of prayers which most agree have the structure and content of a valid eucharistic prayer, yet the narrative is not found. Since Addai and Mari does not have the eucharistic words, this means that in the Syrian tradition the first time the institution narrative appears outside of Scripture is in the anaphora of Sharar which is a companion prayer to the anaphora of Addai and Mari dating from at least the third century.[16]

The Narrative in Sharar

If the liturgical setting of the institution narrative in the Syrian tradition is the eucharistic prayer, the earliest witness to that narrative should reflect strong influence of the Antiochene tradition (Pl/Lk). The text of the narrative as it appears in Sharar follows:

> In the night in which you were betrayed to the Jews, Lord, you took bread in your pure and holy hands, and lifted your eyes to heaven to your glorious Father; you blessed, sealed, sanctified, Lord, broke, and gave it to your disciples the blessed Apostles, and said to them, "This bread is my body, which is broken and given for the life of the world, and will be to those who take it for forgiveness of debts and pardon of sins; take and eat from it, and it will be to you for eternal life." Likewise over the cup, Lord, you praised, glorified, and said, "This cup is my blood of the new covenant, which is shed for many for forgiveness of sins; take and drink from it, all of you, and it will be to you for pardon of debts and forgiveness of sins, and for eternal life." Amen. As often as you eat from this holy body, and drink from this cup of life and salvation, you will make the memorial of the death and resurrection of your Lord, until the great day of his coming.[17]

Obviously this text does not come from Scripture, nor does it appear to be a simple expansion of the Antiochene (Pl/Lk) tradition. An analysis of the text indicates the following: (1) The bread and the cup statements are constructed so that the description of the action is parallel. Both statements have a relative clause after the identification: "... my body *which* is broken and given ... my blood of the new covenant, *which* is shed for many ..." Both statements say that the elements are for the *"forgiveness of sins "* Both statements are accompanied by a directive, *"take* and *eat* from it, and it will be to you for eternal life ... *take* and *drink* from it all of you and it will be to you for pardon of debts and forgiveness of sins, and for eternal life." Neither the Antiochene (Pl/Lk) nor the Markan (Mk/Mt) narratives parallel their statements in this fashion. (2) The account draws from all four of the biblical narratives, and not just one tradition, and at times includes things that are found in none of the four accounts. The bread statement, "took ... blessed ... broke ... and gave to your disciples ... " is closer to the Markan tradition (Mk/Mt). "This *bread* is my body" is in none of the biblical accounts. And the statement which follows, "which is broken and given ..." is from the Antiochene tradition (Pl/Lk). The cup statement definitely favors Mark/Matthew. Sharar's "This cup is my blood of the new covenant ..." is closer to Mark's, "This is ... blood ... " than to Paul/Luke which has, "This is ... covenant ... " Nowhere in Sharar is found anything close to the command, "Do this for my remembrance ..." which is unique to Paul/Luke. On the whole, then, the narrative as it appears in Sharar does not come under the heavy influence of the Antiochene biblical narratives as might be expected.

Conclusions. There is widespread agreement among biblical scholars that the institution narrative (Pl/Lk) has a liturgical setting in Antioch prior to the writing of I Corinthians. Our analysis of the anaphora of Sharar strongly indicates that the narrative was not originally in the eucharistic prayer from New Testament times because if it were we would expect to find the early textual tradition of the anaphora heavily influenced by that Antiochene tradition (Pl/Lk). But as we have seen above, that is not the case. It is possible, then, that the original setting of the institution narrative was outside the eucharistic prayer. A suggestion will be made below. At a rather early date under influences beyond the Antiochene tradition a narrative was incorporated into the anaphora of Sharar, but not into the Addai and Mari, so that at one and the same time the Syrian liturgy knew a eucharistic tradition which sometimes did and sometimes did not include the narrative in the eucharistic prayer. Indications are that this condition remained down through Cyril in Jerusalem[18] and Theodore in Antioch.[19]

Liturgical Use of the Narrative—Another Possibility

While several Church Fathers do appeal to the institution narrative as they discuss the eucharist, none of these early authors clearly place the narrative within the eucharistic prayer. When Justin Martyr quotes the words, "this is my body ... this is my blood ... "[20] he is not describing the baptismal eucharist found in *I Apology*, 65, or the Sunday celebration elaborated in *I Apology*, 67, but he is explaining the special character of the elements received at communion. If *I Apology*, 66 has any ritual context, it must be the communion rite, and not the eucharistic prayer. Similarly, the direct references to the narrative in Cyril's *Mystagogical Catecheses* IV and Theodore's *Mystagogical Catecheses* IV, 1-14 also address the nature of the elements and the food of communion. When Cyril and Theodore discuss the eucharistic prayer no reference is made to the narrative. Like Justin, their comments are independent of the anaphora. This suggests that the earliest liturgical setting of the institution narrative was in connection with the communion rite and not the eucharistic prayer. There is some further evidence that points in this direction.

Didascalia Apostolorum 12 and the parallel passage in *Apostolic Constitutions* II give witness to a blessing which should be allowed only to a visiting bishop. In *Didascalia* the blessing is over the cup, and in *Apostolic Constitutions* the blessing is over the people. What is this blessing over the cup described in *Didascalia* 12? First the text of the passage: in Funk the Latin reads, "Et in gratia agenda ipse dicat; si autem, cum sit prudens et honorem tibi reservans, non velit, super calicem dicat."[21] Brock translates the section as follows:

> And if he (the visiting minister) is a bishop, let him sit with the bishop, who should accord to him the honor of his rank, even as himself. And do you, the bishop, invite him to give a homily to your people ... And when you offer the oblation, let him speak the words; but if he is wise and gives the honor to you, and is unwilling to offer, at least let him speak the words over the cup.[22]

The passage calls for proper respect to a visiting bishop, who is to be offered a very important function within the liturgical celebration. Brock does not comment on the passage, but his translation suggests this meaning: when the eucharistic prayer is said the visiting bishop should be invited to speak that portion of the prayer which recalls the words of Jesus at the Last Supper, but if he prudently declines this honor, he should at least speak the cup statement of the eucharistic prayer. This suggests a concelebration. F.X. Funk interprets the passage differently. He thinks it means that the visiting bishop should be invited to recite the complete eucharistic prayer, but if not the whole prayer, then at least the words over the chalice.[23] Connolly thinks that this cup blessing is in a totally different liturgical celebration. He says that the tactful visiting bishop, who refuses to offer the eucharistic prayer, should at least offer the blessing over the cup at the agape.[24]

The parallel passage in *Apostolic Constitutions* II,7 can be helpful in understanding the nature of this cup blessing. Books I-IV of *Apostolic Constitutions* are, for the most part, a reproduction of *Didascalia*, with minor changes reflecting liturgical evolution.[25] As a rule, then, when *Apostolic Constitutions* agrees with *Didascalia* there has been a continuation of the liturgical tradition. They disagree when there has been a liturgical change.

The parallel passage to *Didascalia* 12 is as follows:

> ... if a bishop, let him sit with the bishop, and be allowed the same honor with himself; and thou, O bishop, shalt desire him to speak to the people words of instruction ... Thou shalt also permit him to offer the Eucharist; but if, out of reverence to thee, and as a wise man, to preserve the honor belonging to thee, he will not offer, at least thou shalt compel him to give the blessing to the people.[26]

The passages agree that it is proper to assign an important liturgical function to a visiting bishop. But the passages also differ because the blessing over the cup in *Didascalia* has become a blessing over the people in *Apostolic Constitutions*. The context indicates that this blessing takes place within the eucharistic celebration, and not at another liturgical gathering. Even though the agape is still practiced at this time[27] there is no indication in *Apostolic Constitutions* that the blessing refers to the agape. In Book VIII there is further evidence that a visiting bishop was assigned four eulogies at the eucharistic celebration.[28] Thus, it is not unusual to have the presiding bishop share different prayers of the eucharistic liturgy with a visiting bishop, a condition already practiced at the time of *Didascalia*. This blessing, originally of the cup and later of the people, must have taken place during the eucharistic celebration, and not during the agape. On the strength of the parallel passage in *Apostolic Constitutions* II, *Didascalia* 12 can be interpreted as follows: the visiting bishop is invited to pray the eucharistic prayer, but if he refuses to say the eucharistic prayer, let him then at least say the blessing over the cup, which is a blessing that takes place at another time, but still within the eucharistic celebration. Is it possible to identify this blessing further?

There is evidence in the Syrian liturgical tradition of prayers and blessings which are directly related to the distribution of the elements. First of all, the *Acts of Jude Thomas* gives a description of a blessing at the table with the newly baptized.

> And after they had been baptized and were come up, he brought bread and the mingled cup; and spake a blessing over it and said: "The holy Body, which was crucified for our sake, we eat, and Thy life-giving Blood, which was shed for our sake, we drink. Let thy Body be to us for life, and thy Blood for the remission of sins. For the gall which thou drankest for us, let the bitterness of our enemy be taken away from us. And for thy drinking vinegar for our sake, let our weakness be strengthened. And (for) the spit which thou didst receive for us, let us receive thy perfect life. And because Thou didst receive the crown of thorns for us, let us receive from thee the crown that withereth not. And because Thou wast wrapped in a linen cloth for us, let us be girt with Thy mighty strength, which cannot be overcome. And because Thou was buried in a new sepulchre for our mortality, let us too receive intercourse with thee in Heaven. And as Thou didst arise, let us be raised, and let us stand before Thee at the judgment of truth." And he brake the Eucharist, gave to Vizan and Tertia, and to Manashar and Sifur and Mygdonia and to the wife and daughter of Sifur and said: "Let this Eucharist be to you for life and rest and joy and health, and for the healing of your soul and of your bodies." and they said, "Amen;"[29]

This prayer, which is a series of petitions, does not correspond to any known structure of a eucharistic prayer. There is no blessing, thanksgiving, or memorial. This prayer, over the bread and the cup, is a communion prayer. The theme of the prayer is the Passover of Christ to which the communicant can identify by receiving the elements. As such it serves the important function of identifying the eucharistic elements in much the same way Justin did in *I Apology 66*, and Cyril and Theodore did in the *Mystagogical Catecheses*. The themes here are similar to portions of the narrative that appear in Sharar, "... my blood of the new covenant which is shed for many for forgiveness of sins; take and drink from it, all of you, and it will be to you for pardon of debts and forgiveness of sins, and for eternal life." Such a prayer would fit the category of a blessing over the cup that is described in *Didascalia* 12. Even though there is no textual evidence, a variation on this communion prayer could very well have included the institution narrative. If this is the case, the early Syrian eucharistic tradition knew a communion blessing which at least contained themes from the Passover of Christ and possible the institution narrative.

As indicated above, by the time of *Apostolic Constitutions* this blessing of the cup became a blessing of the people. In the *Mystagogical Catecheses* of Theodore there is specific mention of a blessing of the people after the eucharistic prayer and before communion. The explanation of that blessing by Theodore contains themes similar to those found in the prayer of Jude Thomas.

> When the bishop has concluded the Eucharistic Prayer in this way, *he blesses the people and wishes them peace; all present make the usual response with heads bowed in due reverence.* When the prayer is completed and all are intent on receiving Holy Communion, *the Church herald proclaims: 'Let us attend'* ... *The bishop announces: 'What is holy for the holy.'* For our Lord's body and blood, which are our food, are indeed holy and immortal and full of holiness, since the Holy Spirit has come down upon them ... This is why the bishop says: *'What is holy for the holy,'* and urges everyone to recall the dignity of what is laid on the altar ...[30]

What was previously a blessing over the cup for communion has now become a blessing of the people which Theodore describes as for peace. If I am correct that the original blessing over the cup served the purpose of identifying the nature of the elements, a change in that practice would be possible if the elements were sufficiently identified at another place in the eucharistic liturgy. As we know from *Apostolic Constitutions* VIII, the eucharistic prayer now has an institution narrative which offers very specific identification of the elements as the body and blood of Christ for forgiveness of sins and for covenant. The conclusion of B. Spinks on sacrifice in the East Syrian anaphora is also very suggestive. He sees a connection between offering and the recital of the words of institution in both the anaphora of Nestorius and that of Theodore of Mopsuestia.[31] It could be that the motivation for the introduction of the narrative into the eucharistic prayer is related to greater attention to the themes of offering and sacrifice. A cup statement similar to that found in Jude Thomas or one that contained an institution narrative would be redundant. Rather than eliminate the blessing altogether, since it is not normal liturgical evolution to simplify, the blessing takes on a new function which still stands in relation to communion—the people, not the elements are blessed.

Summary

From the sources it is possible to establish the following. (1) The institution narrative has a liturgical setting in the Syrian tradition from the very earliest times. (2) The first instance of the institution narrative in a Syrian anaphora (Sharar) does not demonstrate heavy influence from the Paul/Luke narrative. (3) At an early time there was an important blessing over the cup which took place during the eucharistic liturgy. (4) The Syrian tradition also knew a communion blessing over the elements which has strong themes of the passion of Christ. (5) By the end of the fourth century the communion blessing changed to a blessing over the people. (6) The *Mystagogical Catecheses* of Cyril of Jerusalem and Theodore of Mopsuestia make direct reference to the institution narrative only when they discuss the elements and/or communion.

In light of the above, and because of the strong evidence that the Syrian tradition did know a eucharistic prayer without an institution narrative (Addai and Mari, and the witness of Cyril of Jerusalem and Theodore of Mopsuestia), I suggest the possibility of the following: the blessing over the elements before communion originally contained the institution narrative. This prayer served the function of specifying the nature of the elements and of communion. Toward the end of the fourth century the narrative migrates from the communion blessing into the eucharistic prayer, possibly to further highlight the sacrificial character of eucharistic worship. The blessing before communion is redefined as a blessing of the people.

While the evidence to support the above suggestion is rather tenuous, it does help clarify several nagging problems in the Syrian eucharistic tradition. First, it explains how the narrative could have been in the Syrian liturgical tradition from the very beginning and not part of the eucharistic prayer. Second, it offers a further explanation of the absence of the narrative from the anaphora of Addai and Mari. Third, Sharar can now be understood as the first anaphora in the Syrian tradition to incorporate the institution narrative into the eucharistic prayer. But for a long time the Syrian tradition was satisfied to leave the narrative as a communion statement. This explains a tradition known by Cyril of Jerusalem and Theodore of Mopsuestia who seem to be the last witnesses of an earlier form of the eucharistic prayer. By the fifth century the narrative migrates from the communion statement into the eucharistic prayer. Only the Anaphora of Addai and Mari remains as a vestige of an ancient tradition.

Notes

1. William F. Macomber, "The Oldest Known Text of the Anaphora of the Apostles Addai and Mari," *Orientalia Christiana Periodica* 32 (1966) 335-371.

2. For the bibliography on Addai and Mari prior to 1966, confer my article, "The Anaphora of the Apostles: Implications of the Mar Esa 'ya Text," *Theological Studies* 34 (1973) 624-642; and for a good presentation of the present issues see, Brian D. Spinks, *Addai and Mari—the Anaphora of the Apostles: A Text for Students*, Grove Liturgical Study 24 (Bramcote Notts, 1980).

3. William Macomber, "The Maronite and Chaldean Versions of the Anaphora of the Apostles," *Orientalia Christiana Periodica* 37 (1971) 55-84; "The Ancient Form of the Anaphora of the Apostles," *East of Byzantium: Syria and Armenia in the Formative Period* (Dumbarton Oaks Symposium, 1980) (Washington D.C., 1982) 73-88.

4. Herman Wegman, "Généalogie hypothétiques de la prière eucharistiques," *Questions liturgiques* 61 (1980) 263-278.

5. Mazza concludes, "Non abbiamo elementi per dire che la liturgia commentata da Teodoro avesse il racconto dell'istituzione, inteso come racconto dell'ultima cena che comporta le parole stesse del Signore." Enrico Mazza, "La Struttura dell'anafora nelle Catechesi di Teodoro di Mopsuestia," *Presiedere alla Carità: Studi in onore di S.E. Mons. Giberto Baroni*, E. Mazza e D. Gianotti, eds. (Genova, 1988) 66-93. I have argued that Cyril's *Mystagogical Catecheses* demonstrate the same condition existed in Jerusalem toward the end of the fourth century. E.J. Cutrone, "Cyril's Mystagogical Catecheses and the Evolution of the Jerusalem Anaphora," *Orientalia Christiana Periodica* 44 (1978) 52-64.

6. J.-P. Audet, "Literary Forms and Contents of the Normal *eucharistia* in the First Century," *Studia Evangelica* (1957) 643-662.

7. The list of scholars is very long. It includes: Botte, Bouyer, Ledogar, Ligier, Talley, Cuming, Wegman, Spinks, Giraudo, Mazza, just to mention a few.

8. Two of the more significant articles of Talley on this subject are: "From Berakah to Eucharistia: A Reopening Question," *Worship* 50 (1976) 115-137; "The Literary Structure of the Eucharistic Prayer," *Worship* 58 (1984) 404-420.

9. Enrico Mazza, *The Eucharistic Prayers of the Roman Rite*, trans., Matthew J. O'Connell (New York, 1986) 22-29.

10. In 1973 L. Ligier suggested that it might be possible to begin with the

narrative as it appears in the anaphora and attempt to trace its function back to the New Testament. But Ligier admitted that such an approach has serious limitations. Louis Ligier, "The Origins of the Eucharistic Prayer: From the Last Supper to the Eucharist," *Studia Liturgica* 9 (1973) 161-185.

11. Xavier Léon-Dufour *Sharing the Eucharistic Bread: The Witness of the New Testament* (New York, 1986) 82-101.

12. Bouley, *From Freedom to Formula* 73.

13. Roger Beckwith, *Daily and Weekly Worship: Jewish to Christian*, Alcuin/Grow Liturgical Study 1 (Bramcote Notts, 1987) 32.

14. Bouley, *From Freedom to Formula* 74.

15. *Smy.* 7.

16. Bryan D. Spinks, "The Original Form of the Anaphora of the Apostles: A Suggestion in Light of Maronite Sharar," *Ephemerides Liturgicae* 91 (1977) 146-161.

17. R.C.D. Jasper and G.J. Cuming, *Prayers of the Eucharist: Early and Reformed*, third edition, revised and enlarged (New York, 1987) 48.

18. Cutrone, "Cyril's Mystagogical Catecheses and the Evolution of the Jerusalem Anaphora," *Orientalia Christiana Periodica* 44 (1978) 52-64.

19. Mazza, "La Struttura ... di Mopsuestia."

20. *I Apology* 66.

21. F.X. Funk, *Didascalia et Constitutiones Apostolorum* (Paderborn, 1905) 168.

22. Sebastian Brock and Michael Vasey, *The Liturgical Portions of the Didascalia*, Grove Liturgical Study 29 (Bramcote Notts, 1982) 16.

23. "Episcopus peregrinus ergo, si non eucharistiam totam celebrabat, saltem calicem consecrare debeat." F.X. Funk, *Didascalia et Constitutiones Apostolorum* (Paderborn, 1905) 168-169, nt.

24. R. Hugh Connolly, *Didascalia Apostolorum: The Syriac Version Translated and Accompanied by the Verona Latin Fragments* (Oxford) liii.

25. See David A. Fiensy, *Prayers Alleged to be Jewish: An Examination of the Constitutiones Apostolorum*, Brown Judaic Studies 65 (Chico, CA, 1985) 20-21.

26. AC II,7,58. *Ante-Nicene Fathers*, vol. 7, 422. Also found in Funk, *Didascalia et Constitutiones Apostolorum* 168.

27. Roger Beckwith, *Daily and Weekly Worship: Jewish to Christian*, Alcuin/Grow Liturgical Study 1 (Bramcote Notts, 1987) 35-36.

28. "Those eulogies which remain at the mysteries, let the deacons distribute them among the clergy, ... to a bishop, four parts; to a presbyter, three parts; to a deacon, two parts; and to the rest of the sub-deacons, or readers, or singers, or deaconesses, one part. For this is good and acceptable in the sight of God that every one be honored according to his dignity;" VIII, 31. *Ante-Nicene Fathers*, vol. 7, 494.

29. No. 158. *Acts of Jude Thomas*, A. Klijn, ed. (Leiden, 1962) 149-50.

30. V, 22. From Edward Yarnold, *The Awe-Inspiring Rites of Initiation: Baptismal Homilies of the Fourth Century* (London, 1971) 251.

31. Bryan D. Spinks, "Eucharistic Offering in the East Syrian Anaphoras," *Orientalia Christiana Periodica* 50 (1984) 362-365.

7

A Lenten Sunday Lectionary in Fourth Century Jerusalem

John F. Baldovin, S.J.

NO EARLY LITURGY IS AS WELL DOCUMENTED AS THAT OF JERUSALEM IN THE fourth and fifth centuries. Jerusalem, the city where Jesus died and was raised, the city where the primitive Christian community had its first center, was the recipient of massive imperial donations as well as the object of vastly increased pilgrimages in the wake of the favor shown to Christianity by Constantine and his successors. In the past hundred years new discoveries like the travel diary of Egeria (381-384),[1] a Spanish nun, and the publication of several manuscripts of the Old Armenian Lectionary (417-439)[2] have added to knowledge of worship at Jerusalem that had already been supplied by the catechetical instructions of Bishop Cyril of Jerusalem (ca.348)[3] and the mystagogical catecheses, given to the newly baptized, which have been attributed to both Cyril and to his successor, John.[4] In addition we possess a great deal of knowledge about the holy sites of fourth- and fifth-century Jerusalem, knowledge which helps us situate the liturgy in its original context.[5] Since we have no mass of evidence to equal that which we have for Jerusalem in this time period, this city's liturgy has understandably become the object of intense historical study.[6]

There are, however, *lacunae* in our knowledge and understanding of the hagiopolite system of worship. This study is an effort to fill one of

115

them. In his groundbreaking work, *The Origins of the Liturgical Year*,[7] Thomas Talley has challenged the common scholarly presuppositions with regard to a number of the most fundamental aspects of the formation of the Christian calendar, for example, the history of religion's hypothesis on the origins of Christmas and of Epiphany. One of the most striking suggestions that he makes is that Lazarus Saturday and the day following—Palm Sunday—had their origins not in Jerusalem itself but elsewhere.[8] I mean to inquire into whether or not Jerusalem in the fourth century had a Saturday-Sunday Lenten lectionary in order to see if Talley's hypothesis can be further substantiated.

The Armenian Lectionary contains several sets of readings for the season of Lent. The first set provides nineteen lessons for the catechetical lectures whose aim is to prepare the elect for initiation at Pascha. These lessons correspond closely with the eighteen cited by Cyril in his catechetical lectures of c.348 and thus were probably the standard readings for these lectures from the mid-fourth century until at least the middle of the fifth century. In the Armenian Lectionary the set of catechetical lectures is inserted in the manuscript immediately following the *canon* (order of service) for the commemoration of John, Bishop of Jerusalem, on 29 March.[9] Of course these readings would actually have begun much earlier in the liturgical cycle, i.e., at the beginning of Lent, for 29 March would come near the end of the season. Therefore, it seems that the set of readings for the catechetical lectures is somewhat artificially inserted into the lectionary. This lends credibility to the theory of M.F. Lages, who argues that the catechetical readings, Lenten evening readings, and order for Great (Holy) Week are three originally separate *libelli* (booklets) that may well point to distinct origins for various aspects of the Armenian Lectionary's Lent.[10] A second *libellus*, entitled "Readings performed during the holy Lent,"[11] is inserted after the catechetical readings. This set is composed of readings from the Old Testament for weekday evenings during Lent, i.e., Wednesdays and Fridays of every week and each weekday for the second week, up till the Friday of the sixth week of Lent.[12] These were non-eucharistic services, for the church at Jerusalem did not celebrate the eucharist on fast days, but only on Saturdays and Sundays. At the end of the *canon* for Friday of the sixth week we find: "the order of the sixth week of the holy Lent is completed." *Canons* for the eucharist on Lazarus Saturday and Palm Sunday follow and then the order for Great Week. Some kind of distinction is clearly being made between the first six weeks of Lent and the week which follows, a week of immediate preparation for the Pascha.

Talley has explained the introduction of the Lazarus Saturday and Palm Sunday services as a kind of festal interlude between Lent and

Great Week. Certainly some such break is envisioned by Egeria, who notes that the catechetical lectures are concluded before the beginning of Great Week, for there is no time for them once this week of arduous religious and liturgical exercises begins.[13] The vast majority of commentators on the hagiopolite liturgy[14] have presumed that the special liturgical commemorations of Lazarus Saturday and Palm Sunday were the creations of the Jerusalem church, inspired by the availability of the holy sites. Talley, however, argues that these commemorations stem not from a native liturgical tradition but rather were the result of hagiopolite liturgy meeting the expectations of pilgrims from other parts of the Empire, in this case the capital, Constantinople, itself.[15] He further suggests that Lazarus Saturday originally stemmed from an Alexandrian tradition associating the Friday of the sixth week of a forty-day fast after Epiphany, a fast that imitated that of Jesus in the desert. It is not possible here to go into all of the details of his argument, and so a brief summary must suffice.[16]

The Lenten lectionary for Saturdays and Sundays at Constantinople contains readings from Hebrews and from the Gospel according to Mark. On Saturday of the sixth week of Lent the continuous reading from Mark is interrupted by the introduction of the Johannine narrative of the raising of Lazarus. In the tenth-century lectionary (whose roots are probably much earlier) Lazarus Saturday also curiously functions as a baptismal day. Talley suggests that the origin of the shift from reading Mark to reading John lies in a pre-fourth-century Alexandrian practice of baptizing on the sixth day of the sixth week of the post-Epiphany fast mentioned above. He supports this suggestion by appealing to the initiatory "Secret Gospel of Mark" which is inserted into canonical Mark immediately following Mark 10:34. The gospel reading for the Fifth Sunday of Lent at Constantinople is Mark 10:32-45.

What relation could a secret passage from a gospel have to the lectionary cycle at Constantinople?[17] Talley argues that since the secret gospel recounting the raising and subsequent initiation of a young man was not part of the canonical Gospel of Mark, it needed a substitute from the canonical tradition. The closest parallel passage is John 11, the raising of Lazarus, which is followed chronologically in the Fourth Gospel by the entry into Jerusalem. By an ingenious exercise of comparative liturgical investigation, Talley has thus provided a reasonable explanation for the introduction of Lazarus Saturday-Palm Sunday festal interlude at Jerusalem. According to him, Constantinople adopted the Alexandrian Lenten pattern and Jerusalem derived the same pattern from Constantinople, probably as I have noted above because of the expectations of pilgrims. What remains unexplained is how the originally distinct post-Epiphany forty-day fast of Jesus was joined to the pre-paschal fast. In addition, it seems to me that an equally adequate explanation of the matter would be that Jerusalem derived Lazarus Saturday and Palm Sunday directly from Alexandria and that Constantinople either did the same or received the tradition *via* Jerusalem. This latter scenario is all the more attractive given the possibility that Jerusalem derived a number of practices, e.g., the earliest of its eucharistic prayers, from Alexandria.[18]

Knowledge of whether the fourth-century hagiopolite liturgy contained fixed readings for the celebration of the eucharist, i.e., on Saturdays and Sundays in Lent, would surely help to clarify Talley's argument for the introduction of Lazarus Saturday-Palm Sunday. In other words, if it could be shown that Jerusalem also derived its Sunday lectionary from another church, then it would be likely that it could have adopted this festal interlude as well.

It has been presumed that no such lectionary existed at Jerusalem because readings for the Lenten eucharistic liturgies are absent from the Armenian Lectionary. In fact, Lages claims that what is surprising is not the lack of such Lenten readings but the inclusion of any Saturday-Sunday readings at all in this fifth-century lectionary.[19] One explanation for the lack of these readings would be that in the fourth century and into the fifth readings were chosen *ad libitum*, at least at Jerusalem.

Is it possible to find any indications to the contrary? It seems to me that it is if one turns to the catechetical lectures of Cyril of Jerusalem, lectures most probably delivered in the middle of the fourth century, and so well before the Armenian Lectionary. There are two points in the lectures at which Cyril refers his listeners back to the subject of Sunday's sermons. In Catechesis 10:14 he reminds them of his exposition of the phrase "after the order of Melchizedek." In Catechesis 14:24 he mentions that "yesterday" (a Sunday) he had preached on the subject of the ascension of Christ, the very topic he is addressing himself to in the catechesis. Now these, especially the latter, seem to be rather odd topics for Lenten homilies. On one level they would make sense only in that they served Cyril's purposes for the weekday lectures themselves. But if one turns to the lectionary of Constantinople, as Talley has done for Lazarus Saturday-Palm Sunday,[20] the matter is clarified considerably.

I mentioned above that the eucharistic readings for Saturdays and Sundays in the tenth-century Typicon of the Great Church (Constantinople) are taken from the Letter to the Hebrews and the Gospel of Mark.[21] The first reading for the Third Sunday of Lent prescribed in the typicon is Hebrews 4:14-5:6—a reading which ends with the phrase "after the order of Melchizedek." For the Fourth Sunday the designated first reading is Hebrews 6:13-20, which also contains the same phrase. But this passage can also be read as alluding to the ascension of Christ: "... a hope that enters into the inner shrine behind the curtain where Jesus has gone on our behalf, having become a high priest ... " (Heb 6:19-20). Admittedly it is easier to see a reference to the ascension in the reading from Hebrews assigned to the Fifth Sunday of Lent, Hebrews 9:11-14, in which the author describes Jesus as having entered once and for all into "the greater and perfect tent not made by hands" (Heb 9:11-12).

This data does not provide irrefutable proof that the fourth-century Jerusalem liturgy employed a course-reading of the Letter to the Hebrews, but the data strongly suggests that conclusion. One cannot tell from the readings themselves whether Cyril's references were taken from readings on the Third and Fourth Sundays of Lent or the Fourth and Fifth Sundays. I favor the former two Sundays for reasons which I shall explain shortly. In any case it seems that Cyril's fourteenth catechetical lecture was not given on Monday of Great Week as Kretschmar has suggested,[22] since we have found other references which explain the references to Christ's ascension more directly. I have not found any references that would lead to the conclusion that Mark was read in the fourth-century hagiopolitan Lenten lectionary. Given the later association of Hebrews and Mark as Lenten readings in the Byzantine tradition, it seems to me that a case could be made for supposing that Mark was read as well.

Our comparison between several of Cyril's comments in the catechetical lectures and the lectionary of Constantinople has suggested that Jerusalem did indeed have a lectionary for the Lenten eucharist in the fourth century. Further, and most important, one can argue on this basis that the Jerusalem lectionary for the Lenten eucharist represented the same Alexandrian tradition that inspired the introduction of Lazarus Saturday—albeit as a festal day for initiation to conclude the post-Epiphany fast of Jesus. If this assumption is correct, then we have further evidence from Jerusalem itself to corroborate Talley's theory about the influence of Alexandrian practice on the Lenten liturgy at Jerusalem.

The coordination of the catechetical lectures of Cyril with the Byzantine eucharistic lectionary for Lent may also help to clarify another problem—the distribution of Cyril's lectures throughout Lent. Talley has suggested that the eighteen lectures of Cyril which we possess cannot represent a full Lenten course of instruction, given Egeria's comment that these catecheses took place every day in Lent and that the catechetical syllabus covered both the content of the Scriptures as well as an exposition of Christian doctrine.[23] Elsewhere I have suggested that Egeria's "daily" should be understood loosely and that the delivery of the catechetical lectures at Jerusalem was limited to days on which there were no assigned stational services, exclusive as well of Sundays, since the Sunday morning services took so long that there would have been no time for a catechetical lecture.[24] If the candidates (presumably) attended the afternoon stational services as well as the liturgy of the word at the Sunday eucharist, then they would in any case have covered the ground of a great deal of scripture exposition in the course of Lent, leaving the other days for specifically doctrinal instruction, i.e., in the catechetical lectures. In my reconstruction the tenth catechetical lecture took place on the Monday following the Third Sunday of Lent (= Fourth Monday of Lent, since the Byzantine liturgical week always begins on a Monday). The fourteenth catechesis would have been delivered on the following Monday, i.e., the beginning of the fifth week of Lent. These days coordinate exactly with the suggestion made above that Cyril was referring to readings on the Third and Fourth Sundays of Lent. If the fourteenth lecture followed the Fifth Sunday of Lent there would be too few days left before the beginning of Great Week. A lecture would have to be given on every day of that week to conclude before Lazarus Saturday. Moreover, as is likely, Cyril gave not eighteen but nineteen lectures, the eighteenth of our present collection being the last two combined, then there would be too few days in any case.

But why did the fifth-century Armenian Lectionary which reported Jerusalem practice not contain a set of Lenten eucharistic readings if one existed as I have just argued? After all, the Georgian Lectionary, which witnesses hagiopolite liturgical development from the late fifth through the eighth centuries not only contains the Lenten readings for Saturdays and Sundays but has readings which differ considerably from the lectionary of Constantinople from which I have inferred Cyril's allusions.[25] Of course one possible explanation is that the argument presented above represents nothing more than an extraordinary coincidence. Another plausible explanation, however, would be that if, as Lages has argued, the Lenten portions of the Armenian Lectionary were originally separate libelli, a libellus with the Saturday-Sunday readings for the Lenten eucharist was omitted. Why? Perhaps by this time the Armenians had their own tradition of readings for these days, a tradition that the Jerusalem practice would not replace and therefore the libellus that contained Lenten eucharistic lections was not included in the fifth-century composition.

I have argued that despite the lack of any evidence for a Saturday-Sunday Lenten lectionary in the fifth-century Armenian Lectionary, that such a prescribed course of readings did indeed exist in the fourth century, indeed from the time of Cyril's lectures to the candidates for paschal initiation. This conclusion not only helps to fill a gap in our knowledge of the liturgical tradition of Jerusalem, it lends further credibility to the inventive thesis of Thomas Talley that the Jerusalem liturgy owed far more to the traditions of Alexandria and Constantinople than has ever been supposed. Without Talley's extraordinary *tour de force* on the origins of Lent, the suggestions I have made would never have occurred to me, and so this study represents only a small portion of the debt of gratitude I owe to his scholarly achievement, not to mention his kindness.

Notes

1. Discovered in 1884 and first published in 1887 by J.F. Gammurini. For the text see E. Francheschini and R. Weber, eds., *Itineraria et Alia Geographica*, Corpus Christianorum Scriptorum Latinorum 175 (Turnhout, 1965). For the date, P. Devos, "La date du voyage d'Egérie," *Analecta Bollandiana* 85 (1967) 165-194. A good introduction to the nature of this text and its problems can be found in J. Wilkinson, *Egeria's Travels*, 2d ed. (Warminster, 1981).

2. For the edition of ms Paris Armenian 44, see F.C. Conybeare, *Rituale Armenorum* (Oxford, 1896); for ms Jerusalem Armenian 121, see A. Renoux, *Le codex Jérusalem arménien 121: introduction, texte*, Patrologia Orientalis 35 (1969) 5-197; PO 36 (1971) 211-373.

3. PG 33:1-1064. English translation in *Nicene and Post-Nicene Fathers*, 2d series (repr. Grand Rapids, 1979) 1-143.

4. Thus the mystagogical catecheses can probably be dated around the last quarter of the fourth century. For the text of these instructions and an English translation, see F.L. Cross, *St. Cyril of Jerusalem: Lectures on the Christian Sacraments* (repr. Crestwood, NY, 1977). On the question of authorship, see A. Piédagnel, *Cyrille de Jérusalem: catéchèses mystagogiques*, Sources chrétiennes 126 (Paris, 1966) 18-40.

5. For an excellent survey of current archeological knowledge of Byzantine Jerusalem, see Y. Tasfrir, "Jerusalem," *Reallexikon für byzantinische Kunst*, vol. 3, 575-588.

6. See, for example, the complete bibliography for the years 1960-1980 in C. (A.) Renoux, "Hierosolymitana," *Archiv für Liturgiewissenschaft* 23 (1981) 1-29, 149-175.

7. New York, 1986.

8. Ibid. 37-42, 176-183.

9. Armenian Lectionary 16 (hereafter AL). The citations and numbering are from Renoux's edition of ms Jerusalem Armenian 121, see above, note 2.

10. M.F. Lages, "Etapes de l'évolution du carême à Jérusalem avant le V siècle," *Revue des études arméniennes*, n.s., 6 (1969) 70-76.

11. AL 18-32.

12. Note that in the Armenian Lectionary, as in the Byzantine tradition, a week of Lent begins on Monday and not Sunday. This has often led to some confusion among western liturgical scholars who presumed that Lent begins on a Sunday as in the original Roman scheme.

13. Egeria 46:4. She had earlier noted that the Friday night vigil before Lazarus Saturday was held not in the usual place, the Anastasis, but rather at Sion. This too may have some significance for suspecting that there was originally a break between Lent proper and Great Week.

14. Myself included, see my *Urban Character of Christian Worship: The Origins, Development and Meaning of Stational Liturgy*, Orientalia Christiana Analecta 228, 1987, 95.

15. Talley, *Origins* 181-182.

16. For the details, see ibid. 183-214.

17. The question of whether or not the "secret gospel" was actually a part of Mark is not relevant here. It has been fairly well established that Clement of Alexandria did write the work in which M. Smith found the secret gospel. The crux of the matter is whether this gospel passage was used in the Alexandrian tradition. See Talley, *Origins* 205-207.

18. See G.J. Cuming, "Egyptian Elements in the Jerusalem Liturgy," *Journal of Theological Studies*, n.s., 23 (1971) 117-124.

19. See Lages, "Etapes" 77. Readings are provided for only the following Saturdays or Sundays: Lazarus Saturday, Palm Sunday, Holy Saturday, Easter Sunday, Saturday and Sunday in the octave of Easter, and Pentecost Sunday.

20. Here I show my indebtedness to Talley's method for the idea of turning to this lectionary in the first place.

21. See J. Mateos, ed., *Le typicon de la grande église* II Orientalia Christiana Analecta 165, 17-59.

22. See G. Kretschmar, "Die frühe Geschichte der jerusalemer Liturgie," *Jahrbuch für Liturgik und Hymnologie* 2 (1956) 37-38. Kretschmar's argument is based on the fact that the Jerusalem church had spent a good part of the afternoon of Palm Sunday at the Imbomon, the place of Christ's ascension. But *Egeria* 46:4 states quite explicitly that the catechetical lectures are concluded before the beginning of Great Week.

23. Talley, *Origins* 175-176; see also *Egeria* 46:1-4.

24. Baldovin, *Urban Character* 90-93.

25. See M. Tarchnisvili, *Le grande lectionnaire de l'église de Jérusalem*, Corpus Scriptorum Christianorum Orientalium 123 (Louvain, 1959) 54ff.

8

Cathedral vs. Monastery: The Only Alternatives for the Liturgy of the Hours?

Paul F. Bradshaw

IT HAS BECOME CUSTOMARY IN THE LITURGICAL SCHOLARSHIP OF RECENT decades to draw a sharp distinction between "cathedral" and "monastic" patterns of daily worship in fourth-century Christianity,[1] a distinction which is based not simply on variations in the external forms of the worship but also on significant differences in the inner spirit expressed by those divergent forms. Furthermore, the advocates of this particular classification have often tended to go on to suggest that what is needed in today's situation is a restoration of a cathedral pattern of the liturgy of the hours (as it is now fashionable to call the daily office), in place of the essentially monastic model which the churches have inherited from their medieval past. The implication of this is that the cathedral tradition of the fourth century was the authentic expression of Christian daily prayer and stood in direct succession to the practice of Christians in the first three centuries, whereas the monastic tradition was a deviation from this straight line.

All of this, however, is open to question. Although the emphasis on the twofold nature of the divine office was a perfectly understandable corrective to earlier scholarship, which had only been conscious of the existence of a single type—the monastic, yet in the end this simple dual classification fails to do full justice to the historical evidence, which reveals not just two but at least four different patterns of daily prayer in the early church. Moreover, the daily devotions of the Egyptian desert monks and also the cathedral office itself are both alike modifications of the pattern of prayer practiced by Christians in the third century. It is not therefore self-evident that a recreation of the cathedral model in the late twentieth century would be the restoration of the truly authentic form of Christian worship and the panacea for all the contemporary difficulties which surround the celebration of the liturgy of the hours.

Let us then review the historical evidence for early Christian practice:

Pattern One. Christian Daily Prayer in the Third Century

The principal sources of information concerning this pattern in its most fully developed form are the writings of Tertullian and Cyprian, supported to some extent by the *Apostolic Tradition* of Hippolytus, though the precise interpretation of this document is problematic, and its testimony will therefore not be cited here.[2] Our two North African authors are aware that the only absolute apostolic injunction binding upon a Christian is to "pray without ceasing" (1 Thes 5:17), but they both recommend that, in order to fulfill this, one should pray no less than five times each day—in the morning, at the third, sixth, and ninth hours, and in the evening—and should also rise from sleep in the middle of the night to pray again. Meals too were to be accompanied by prayer.[3] The writings of Clement of Alexandria and Origen, on the other hand, attest to what may well be a more primitive version of this horarium in Egypt, with prayers being offered just three times a day (morning, noon, and evening) and again in the night, though Clement also indicates his awareness that some do practice prayer at the third, sixth, and ninth hours.[4]

Most scholars have sought to distinguish the status of the morning and evening hours from the other times of prayer, and seen the former as obligatory for all Christians at this time and the latter as merely "recommended." However, an unbiased reading of the evidence suggests rather that all the occasions for prayer mentioned by writers of the period are considered as having equal importance to one another, as means towards the fulfillment of the end, a life of ceaseless prayer. There is, of course, no way of knowing how many ordinary Christians actually did manage to maintain this extensive daily schedule, but it should be remembered that the initiatory practices of the church at this period demanded a high level of commitment from those seeking admission to the faith, so that it was more akin to what we would think of as entering a religious order. Moreover, this pattern of prayer was probably not felt to be quite as demanding as it appears to twentieth-century eyes. Rising in the middle of the night for prayer, for example, is not as difficult in a culture where there is little to do except sleep between sunset and sunrise.

It is difficult to describe in detail the content of the daily prayers from this period, since there are very few extant early prayer-texts at all and none of them belong to these occasions. But from the allusions made by ancient writers it would seem that third-century Christians maintained the character, if not the form, of prayer reflected in New Testament documents, and especially the Pauline Epistles, and derived ultimately from Judaism, of praise and thanksgiving leading to petition and intercession for others.[5] Such prayer seems generally to have been offered either by individuals on their own or by small groups of family and friends and not in formal liturgical assemblies, which appear to have been limited chiefly to the celebration of the eucharist on Sundays, to services of the word at the ninth hour on Wednesdays and Fridays, and to the agape, the occasional communal supper of a local congregation.

Nevertheless, this does not mean that the daily prayers were thought of as being merely private prayer. As Cyprian makes clear, each person's prayer was seen as being a participation in the prayer of the whole church: "Before all things the Teacher of peace and Master of unity would not have prayer to be made singly and individually, so that when one prays, he does not pray for himself alone ... Our prayer is public and common; and when we pray, we pray not for one, but for the whole people, because we the whole people are one."[6] Such intercession was not only for other Christians, but for the whole world: according to his compatriot Tertullian, it included prayer "for the emperors, for their ministers and for all in authority, for the welfare of the world, for the prevalence of peace, for the delay of the final consummation."[7] Moreover, Christians also viewed their acts of prayer as a sacrifice offered to God, and its ceaseless nature as the true fulfillment of the "perpetual" sacrifices of the Old Testament.[8] Here then, indeed, was the royal priesthood of the church, though dispersed, engaged in its priestly task—continually offering the sacrifice of praise and thanksgiving to God on behalf of all creation and interceding for the salvation of the world.

Finally, we should note two things that were not characteristics of the hours of prayer at this time. They did not usually involve the recitation of psalms, for Tertullian tells us that the more assiduous included in their prayers those psalms which featured the Alleluia response,[9] thereby clearly implying that the rest did not. Instead the psalms were generally used in connection with meals, and especially the agape, where various individuals sang either one of the canonical psalms or a hymn of their own composition to the others, who responded to each verse with the Alleluia refrain.[10] Nor again did the hours of prayer generally include a ministry of the word, not because the reading of the Scriptures was not valued by the early Christians, but because this was normally done in other contexts, in the corporate assemblies for worship on Sundays, Wednesdays, and Fridays, briefly alluded to above, and in the catechetical classes intended for both new converts and established members of the church. This restriction was inevitable for purely practical reasons: when one considers the difficulty—and doubtless high cost—of providing additional copies of the Scriptures, to say nothing of the low level of literacy among many converts to the faith, it will be apparent that the exhortations to study the Bible at home found in a number of ancient Christian writings can only have been possible for a relatively few educated and wealthier members of the church.

Pattern Two. The Fourth-Century Cathedral Office

After the Peace of Constantine in the fourth century, when daily communal assemblies for prayer became a more realistic possibility, evidence from a variety of sources points to the conclusion that they were generally held only twice each day, in the morning and in the evening, this choice seemingly being governed primarily by the practical problems associated with meeting together during the working day or in the middle of the night. It was of course hoped that individuals and families might still continue to pray at other hours,[11] but only the exceptionally pious appear to have done so in the less disciplined environment of fourth-century Christianity. Thus daily prayer for ordinary Christians now differed in two important respects from the practice of earlier times: it had gained more of a corporate expression but its frequency was effectively reduced.

Although the shift from individual to corporate praying was in one way only making explicit what had been implicit in the previous century—that Christian prayer was always the prayer of the whole church— yet an important difference of ecclesiology underlies it and was to have significant consequences for the future history of daily prayer in the church. The vision of "church" reflected in the practice of the third century was one in which each individual was equally responsible for playing his or her part in maintaining the priestly activity of the body. This was replaced in the fourth century by a more centralized, hierarchically ordered, institutional model of the church, still involving the whole body in prayer but with much more stress on the community than on the individual. Worship was led by a number of different ministers, each charged with a specific task—the bishop or presbyter to preside and pronounce the orations, the deacon to proclaim the biddings, the cantor to chant the verses of the psalms—and the ordinary individual was now merely one member of the congregation with no specific responsibility of his or her own. What mattered was that the church should pray as an assembly, and the presence or absence of one person from the gathering did not significantly affect that activity. Except when it was their turn to perform one of the liturgical functions, even ordained ministers seemingly had no special obligation to be there above that of anyone else.

The corporate nature of daily prayer also gave rise to other differences in its form and character. Psalms and hymns, which earlier had been a characteristic of the more infrequent communal gatherings, now assume a central place in the daily services. Moreover, because of the increased size of the assembly and consequently the need for a more regular and formal structure, these are no longer freely chosen and sung by individual members of the community, but are now fixed and performed by an officially appointed cantor. Even the concluding ritual seems to have undergone a transformation: whereas formerly the participants at a Christian prayer-gathering apparently exchanged a kiss with one another as "the seal of prayer,"[12] the cathedral office ends instead with an imposition of hands by the presiding minister on each of the worshipers—a further illustration of ecclesiological shift which had taken place.

Some things, however, remain constant from the prayer patterns of earlier centuries. Prayer is still considered as a sacrifice offered to God, though the twice-daily "perpetual" sacrifices of the Old Testament are now seen as finding their fulfillment not in the ceaseless prayer of Christians but more literally in the morning and evening assemblies themselves.[13] The cathedral office still centers around the praise of God—expressed in the psalms and hymns which were appointed for use each day[14]—and intercession for others, though as time went by this activity tended to focus more on the needs of the church than those of the world, perhaps because the boundaries between the two were much less obviously marked than they had been before the Peace of Constantine. And finally, the ministry of the word still does not feature in the normal daily worship but continues to be mainly restricted to the Sunday, Wednesday, and Friday assemblies, and to catechetical instructions held during Lent and Easter week.

Pattern Three. The Worship of the Desert Monks

There had always been some whose spirituality was not satisfied merely with frequent times of prayer during the day but who wished to fulfill more literally the injunction to "pray without ceasing." Such was, for example, the attitude of Clement of Alexandria,[15] and it was inherited by the Egyptian desert fathers of the fourth century, whose aim was to maintain as near as possible a ceaseless vigil of prayer, punctuated only by the minimal interruption for food and sleep. With the emergence of the cenobitic life, however, more formal rules of prayer were established, apparently principally to school the novices of the community in this spirituality.[16] While expecting the monk to persevere in praying throughout his waking hours, these prescribed two formal occasions of prayer each day, on rising in the morning and before retiring to bed at night.[17] The evidence from the Pachomian communities of Upper Egypt indicates that these were done in common, and consisted of the alternation of biblical passages read aloud by one of the brothers with the recitation of the Lord's Prayer and silent meditation by the rest of the community.[18] In the monasticism of Lower Egypt, on the other hand, the daily prayers were said by the monks individually in their cells, except on Saturdays and Sundays, with the morning prayer seemingly being earlier, at cockcrow. The content of these prayers was very likely the alternation of psalms and silent meditation so characteristic of the spirituality of the desert fathers.[19]

Though there may be some similarity with regard to the number and times of formal daily prayer between these monastic traditions and the cathedral office, what we have here is radically different in character from that worship, and equally a deviation from the prayer-life of Christians of earlier centuries. What is retained from the spirituality of former times is the ideal of prayer without ceasing, and the emphasis on the responsibility of each individual to engage in prayer. What is new, at least compared with the mainstream of earlier Christian prayer, is the attempt to give ceaseless prayer a more literal interpretation: whereas from New Testament times onwards Christians had viewed the whole of their life as constituting an unceasing prayer offered to God,[20] these desert ascetics, on the other hand, were determined that prayer itself should constitute the sole content of their life. As Alexander Schmemann has said, "This is not the illumination of life and work by prayer, not a joining of these things in prayer, not even a turning of life into prayer, but prayer as life or, more properly, the replacement of life by prayer."[21]

What is also new is the nature of the prayer in which they engaged— meditation on the mighty works of God and supplication for spiritual growth and personal salvation. Now of course remembrance, "anamnesis," of what God has done in Christ had always been central to Christian prayer, but here it took on a somewhat different character. Mainstream Christianity had recalled God's works in order to offer praise and thanks for them, whereas the primary purpose of the extended meditation here was formation: the monk meditated on Christ in order to grow into his likeness, and prayed for the requisite grace for that. Like the movement toward more truly ceaseless praying, this again is something with its roots in the early Alexandrian tradition, which, while not denying the legitimacy or efficacy of intercession, regarded petition for spiritual rather than material gifts as the higher way. The monk's obligation to engage in prayer at certain prescribed hours or to say a particular number of psalms and prayers, therefore, sprang from what might be called a pedagogical rather than a liturgical motive: it was designed to further his ascetical growth toward what was thought of as "spiritual freedom."

Although it has to be admitted that formation is necessarily involved in all liturgy and regular participation in any rite has a significant effect upon individual spiritual development, yet by making it the principal aim of the daily office rather than a secondary by-product, the Egyptian monastic tradition seriously distorted the nature of the activity and led to an impoverishment and narrowing of its focus. Since such prayer was essentially individualistic, it obscured and lost sight of the ecclesial dimension which had implicitly undergirded the prayer-life of early Christians. Whereas prayer on one's own had been the result of necessity in earlier times, this was not so for those who had voluntarily withdrawn to the desert. It was the same prayer which was performed in the cell as in the community gathering, and neither setting was seen as superior to the other. There was nothing inherently corporate in the worship, nothing which might not be done equally as well alone as together. Although a communal assembly offered an element of mutual encouragement in the work of prayer, and afforded opportunity for supervision and discipline over the possible weakness and indolence of the more junior brethren, nevertheless the presence or absence of other people was ultimately a matter of indifference.[22]

Not only did the ecclesial dimension disappear from prayer, so too did what might be called the cosmic dimension. Whereas earlier Christians had been very conscious of their mission toward the whole world and so concerned to pray for all God's creation, prayer now became orientated inward instead of outward. The monk's primary responsibility was toward his own soul and not the salvation of others. In other words, the sense of a vocation to royal priesthood of the church had been eroded. For, as J.G. Davies has observed, a priesthood is

> never established for itself, so that for the royal priesthood to celebrate its *own* cultus for its *own* needs is to deny its very *raison d'etre*; it would cease in fact to function as a priesthood. An introverted cultus performed by the

covenant people is therefore a contradiction of their office, a rejection of their commission and a failure to participate in the *missio Dei*. It makes nonsense of the whole idea of covenant and priesthood. This means that only a cultus which is outward-looking and related to the world can be regarded as an authentic act of Christian worship. If it is not worldly, in this sense, then Christians are not exercising their baptismal priesthood.[23]

From all this it can easily be seen why it was thought vitally important that each individual fulfilled personally whatever was prescribed in the community's rule. It was not enough, for example, that the rest of the community maintained a regular time of prayer on rising each morning: if the individual did not participate in it, then he would derive no spiritual benefit from it. Nor did it particularly matter if he said this prayer earlier or later than the rest of the community: as long as he did it at some point, he would still have fulfilled his duty. Here, then, lie the roots of the idea that missed prayer can somehow be "made up" at a later time; what matters is that the work should eventually be done by each individual, rather than that the body of the church should remain in constant communion with God through a regular cycle of prayer-times.

Finally, one other important new development in this tradition needs to be noted, and this is the use of the Psalter, the whole Psalter, and nothing but the Psalter in their daily devotions. Christians of New Testament times had obviously valued the canonical psalms very highly, since they are cited more often than any other Old Testament book, and regarded them as a prophetic work—or rather as *the* prophetic work *par excellence*—which had been written by David under the inspiration of the Holy Spirit and was speaking of the Christ who was to come.[24] There is no evidence to suggest, however, that any more than certain selected psalms, mainly those in which Christological prophecy could easily be seen, were ever used in early Christian worship, and certainly nothing to support the notion that the whole Psalter was read through in its entirety.

Indeed, there is no evidence at all that the whole Psalter was used in Jewish worship at that period, or even that any of the canonical psalms had yet attained a permanent place in the synagogue liturgy,[25] and in later Jewish worship only about half of them were ever used. The claim frequently made, therefore, that in saying the psalms we are praying the prayers that Jesus himself used, lacks any sure foundation. If we did want to imitate the words of Jesus in daily prayer, we would be on much safer ground if we recited the *Shema*, ("Hear, O Israel, the Lord our God is one Lord ...."),[26] which pious Jews of his time would have said twice daily but which the early church apparently abandoned quite quickly, probably because its strong monotheistic tone did not have the right feel for a community moving toward a Trinitarian faith.

Moreover, in spite of their obvious affection for the canonical psalms, early Christians seemingly had no hesitation in composing their own psalms and hymns for use in their communal worship, and no special preference seems to have been accorded to those of the Old Testament:[27] both new and old compositions were thought of as able to communicate the word of God to the community, who listened to the verses chanted by one of their number and responded to each with a refrain of praise.

The use of the psalms in the prayer-life of the desert ascetics on the other hand, stands in sharp contrast to this. Here the Psalter was elevated to the place of honor in religious formation: the novice was expected to learn the whole Psalter by heart, and it came to be regarded as a great and worthy accomplishment to recite all 150 psalms in the space of twenty-four hours. There seem to be several reasons to account for this striking development. First, because of their supposed Davidic authorship the psalms were regarded as specially inspired: they were "the songs of the Spirit," in contrast to ecclesiastical compositions, which were dismissed as "the words of mere mortals." This attitude was greatly encouraged by the fact that at the time hymns were often used as a means of spreading and popularizing heretical beliefs. Second, the tradition of Christological interpretation made them especially attractive to those who were attempting to form their lives into the pattern of Christ: what better way was there to become more Christlike than to meditate on the words of the psalms, and allow their sentiments to shape one's spirituality? Third, since the whole of life needed to be filled with such meditation, then more than just a small selection of psalms was required. Finally, since time and seasons were of no consequence, but only eternity mattered, there was no reason to try to arrange the psalms according to their appropriateness to specific hours and occasions, and they were thus recited in their biblical order.

Pattern Four. The Prayer of Urban Monastic Communities

The daily prayer patterns of those early religious communities which did not retreat to the desert but organized themselves in more urban settings in Cappadocia and Syria are often treated merely as a variant of Egyptian monasticism. This, however, is misleading, for the foundation of their prayer-life is quite different. These groups usually prayed early in the morning; at the third, sixth, and ninth hours; in the evening; and again at some point in the night. Their prayers were generally offered in common, but might be made individually if circumstances prevented a

corporate assembly.[28] Moreover, unlike Egyptian monasticism, they did
not dispense with all outward ceremonial: as Gregory of Nyssa reveals in
his moving account of the death of his sister Macrina, the lighting of the
evening lamp with its prayer still formed a part of the daily ritual of her
religious community.[29] They are thus the direct descendants of the Christians of the third century. While the cathedral office had moved away
from this pattern in one direction and the desert monks in another, these
communities had persevered in the old family prayers of former times:
they were not innovators, but conservatives in a world which had
changed.

On the other hand, it has to be admitted that the spirituality of the
desert fathers had considerable influence on them as they developed,
and in most of the sources available to us a substantial vigil for a part of
the night is included in their daily horarium, either appended to midnight prayer or beginning at cockcrow and lasting until the morning office.[30] This, however, seems to be a secondary addition to the cycle, and
is not part of the Cappadocian pattern outlined by Basil: the vigil he describes appears to be an occasional ecclesial gathering rather than a regular monastic night office.[31] Chrysostom implies that the element of intercession for others in the daily services also gave way to prayer for
personal spiritual progress, no doubt again under the influence of the
same source.

> They ask nothing of things present, for they have no regard for these, but
> that they may stand boldly before the fearful judgment seat ... and that no
> one may hear that fearful voice which says, "I do not know you", and that
> with a pure conscience and many good deeds they may pass through this
> troublesome life and sail over the angry sea with a favorable wind.[32]

The evidence suggests, however, that, with the exception of the nightly
vigil, such communities were conservative in their use of psalmody, and
at first continued to employ a selective rather than a consecutive approach in their services. The remains of this can still be detected even in
later western monastic rules, where the Egyptian way of prayer was
more extensively imitated than in the East, strongly encouraged by Cassian's idealization of it. Indeed, while the cathedral tradition had developed communal refrains appropriate to each psalm, the monastic tradition originally tended to adhere to the more primitive custom of the
Alleluia response alone, and did not restrict this to the Easter season as
ecclesiastical usage came to do.

Conclusion

As I indicated at the beginning, it has become fashionable to regard the cathedral office as the normative expression of early Christian prayer, and as the model for today's church to follow. Our review of the evidence, however, has attempted to show that the former is not the case. The cathedral office was but one development among others in the fourth century, continuing the traditions of earlier times in some respects but modifying them significantly in others. It is not self-evident, therefore, that it constitutes the ideal model which should necessarily be imitated today; and indeed there are grounds for questioning its appropriateness to our own situation. It is formal in style and for its celebration requires a community which is able to assemble together regularly every single day, with a number of ministries represented in each assembly—bishop or presbyter, deacon, cantor. However fine this might be as a liturgical expression of the nature of the church, relatively few Christians today find themselves in a situation where such is a real possibility. For the great majority, the cathedral office is something which can only be celebrated occasionally, usually just on Sundays. It does nothing to meet the need for a pattern of *daily* praying.

For that, I would submit, we would do better to look to the pattern evidenced in the third century and continued to a large extent in the urban monastic communities of the fourth century onwards. Here we have a much more informal style of prayer, which is best done communally, but can also be performed individually if necessity dictates. It does not single out morning and evening as *the* occasions when one ought to pray, but simply emphasizes the desirability of frequent prayer at whatever times that is possible. Nor does it require the presence of ordained ministers for its celebration: in the monastic gatherings the leader of the community (who was not ordained) generally presided and said the orations,[33] as the head of the household had done in Jewish and early Christian domestic prayer, and each member of the community took an equal turn in chanting the verses of the various psalms to the others.

On the other hand, it is not without its dangers, as the history of monastic prayer shows. The Egyptian model exercised an increasingly powerful influence upon it, and still continues to shape much of the spirituality of the daily office today. Monastic communities rapidly came to adopt a cursus of psalmody which, one way or another, sought to incorporate the whole Psalter in worship, and meditation on the psalms with petition for spiritual growth replaced the praise of God and intercession for the world which were characteristic of the older concept of prayer. The absence of any liturgical expression of the ecclesial nature of the act of praying also encouraged individualism and an excessive stress on the obligation and need of each person to perform the full pensum of prayer.

This style of prayer, therefore, needs to be counter-balanced by the cathedral office, for both have something significant to contribute to Christian prayer-life. The cathedral office stands as a reminder of the kind of praying which we are called to do: it is the prayer of the church, the royal priesthood, participating in the prayer of Christ, the great high-priest, offering the sacrifice of praise and interceding for the salvation of all. However valuable meditation on the psalms and other portions of Scripture might be as a means of stimulating and feeding our prayer, it should never displace that primary focus. It also reminds us that, since we are sharing in the church's prayer, we are never really on our own when we pray, and even on occasions when we may be unable to participate in prayer ourselves, the church's work of prayer still goes on, and does not remain for us to have to "make up" at some later time.

The prayer of the small group, on the other hand, is not merely a more practical alternative to the cathedral office, but also witnesses itself to some important truths about the nature of Christian prayer. It testifies that the prayer of the church is not restricted to certain fixed hours and forms, however valuable they may be, but that the only absolute rule is to live a life of communion with God, punctuated by specific moments of prayer, whenever and wherever possible. It also testifies that prayer in the name of the church is not confined to certain deputed individuals, but that on the contrary every member has both the privilege and the duty of acting as prayer-leader on behalf of others, a tradition which goes all the way back to the Jewish synagogue.[34] In short, therefore, we have not restored the liturgy of the hours when all we have done is to popularize the communal celebration of evening prayer on Sundays, since no one individual liturgical form can ever fully express the multi-facetted nature of the Christian mystery.

Notes

1. See, for example, William Storey, "The Liturgy of the Hours: Cathedral versus Monastery" in John Gallen, ed. *Christians at Prayer* (Notre Dame, 1977) 61-82.

2. See the analysis of it made by one of my doctoral students, Edward Phillips, "Daily prayer in the *Apostolic Tradition of Hippolytus,*" *Journal of Theological Studies* 40 (1989) 389-400.

3. Tertullian, *De Or.* 24-25; *Ad Uxorem* 2.5; *Apol.* 39; Cyprian, *De Dom. Orat.* 34-36. See Paul F. Bradshaw, *Daily Prayer in the Early Church* (London, 1981; New York, 1982) 50-53; Robert Taft, *The Liturgy of the Hours in East and West* (Collegeville, 1986) 17-21.

4. Clement, *Pedagog.* 2.4,9; *Strom.* 2.23; 7.7,12; Origen, *De Or.* 12.2; *Contra Cel-*

sum 6.41. See Bradshaw, *Daily Prayer* 47-50; Taft, *Liturgy of the Hours* 14-17.

5. For further details of this see Bradshaw, *Daily Prayer*, chapters 1-3.

6. *De Dom. Orat.* 8.

7. *Apol.* 39.

8. See, for example, Tertullian, *De Or.* 27-28; Origen, *Hom. in Num.* 23.3.

9. *De Or.* 27.

10. See Clement, *Strom.* 7.7; Tertullian, *Apol.* 39; Cyprian, *Ep.* 1.16.

11. See John Chrysostom, *Expos. in Ps.* 133; *Hom in Act.* 26; *De Anna Sermo* 4.5.

12. So it is described by Tertullian, *De Or.* 18.

13. See John Chrysostom, *Expos. in Ps.* 140.3.

14. I was mistaken in my earlier claim (*Daily Prayer* 109-110) that Psalms 148-150 originated as the conclusion of the monastic night office: as Robert Taft has convincingly demonstrated (*Liturgy of the Hours* 191-209), they seem to have constituted the primitive nucleus of the morning service apparently everywhere, with Psalms 50 (51), 62 (63), and *Gloria in excelsis* forming a second stratum in many places. The canticle *Benedicite* with its strong emphasis on creation was also commonly used on Sunday mornings. With regard to the evening, the hymn *Phos hilaron*, "Hail, gladdening light," was widely used at the lighting of the evening lamp, and Psalm 140 (141) is found in virtually all later Eastern Rites, but is not so clearly evidenced in the West, where at least in some areas Psalm 103 (104) seems to have been used instead: see Caesarius of Arles, *Serm.* 136.1.

15. See Clement, *Strom.* 7.7.

16. One of the main sources which has generally been used to reconstruct the nature of this pattern of daily prayer has been the account given by John Cassian in his *Institutes*, but as Robert Taft has indicated (*Liturgy of the Hours* 58ff), Cassian was here not simply writing as a disinterested observer: he was using the example of the Egyptian monks as an ideal to promote a reform of monasticism in his native Gaul. Hence, discrepancies between his description and evidence obtained from other sources may be signs of a desire, whether conscious or unconscious, to furnish Egyptian precedents for the Gallican practices which he favored, and so his testimony needs to be treated with great caution.

17. What follows is a summary correction to my *Daily Prayer in the Early Church* (95-98) where I relied too much on the evidence of Cassian and on the reconstruction attempted by A. van der Mensbrugghe, "Prayer-time in Egyptian Monasticism (320-450)," *Studia Patristica* 2 (1957) 435-452.

18. See Armand Veilleux, *La liturgie dans le cénobitisme pâchomien au IV siècle* (Rome 1968) 307ff; Taft, *Liturgy of the Hours* 62-65.

19. Cassian's claim that twelve psalms were recited on each occasion cannot be accepted uncritically as the original practice. As Veilleux and Taft have shown, this has its roots in the tradition that twelve prayers be offered each day and twelve each night, in other words that one should pray every hour or constantly. The grouping of these prayers into two daily synaxes of twelve psalms each thus appears to be a later development. See Veilleux, *La liturgie* 324ff; Taft, *Liturgy of the Hours* 72.

20. See, for example, Romans 12.1; 1 Corinthians 10.31; Origen, *De Oratione* 12.2.

21. Alexander Schmemann, *Introduction to Liturgical Theology* (New York, 1966) 107.

22. See Taft, *Liturgy of the Hours* 66-73.

23. J.G. Davies, *Worship and Mission* (London, 1966) 95.

24. See Balthasar Fischer, "Le Christ dans les psaumes: la devotion aux psaumes dans l'église des martyrs," *La Maison-Dieu* 27 (1951) 86-109 = "Christ in the Psalms," *Theology Digest* 1 (1951) 53-57.

25. See James W. McKinnon, "On the Question of Psalmody in the Ancient Synagogue," *Early Music History* 6 (1986) 159-191.

26. Deuteronomy 6:4-9; 11:13-21; Numbers 15:37-41.

27. See Tertullian *Apol.* 39: "each is invited to stand in the middle and sing a hymn to God, from the Scriptures or of his own composition as he is able."

28. For details, see Bradshaw, *Daily Prayer* 99-106.

29. *Vita Macrinae* 22, 25; quoted in Bradshaw, *Daily Prayer* 75-76.

30. Pseudo-Athanasius, *De Virginitate* 20; Chrysostom, *Hom. in I Ep. ad Tim.* 14.4; Cassian, *De Inst. Coen.* 3.4-6.

31. Basil, *Serm. Ascet.* 4; *Reg. Fus. Tract.* 37.3-5; *Epp.* 2; 207.2-4. See Bradshaw, *Daily Prayer* 99-102; Taft, *Liturgy of the Hours* 39-41, 84-87.

32. *Hom. in Matt.* 68.3.

33. The only documented exception to this is in fourth-century Jerusalem, where, according to the pilgrim Egeria, presbyters and deacons were required to attend the monastic night office in order to pronounce the orations after the psalms, although some unease about usurping what had come to be seen as the episcopal and presbyteral prerogative of extemporizing prayer in a communal setting also seems to have been felt in other places, and hence the recitation of the Lord's Prayer was used there instead of a collect at the end of the services: see Bradshaw, *Daily Prayer* 77-78, 136.

34. See further Paul F. Bradshaw, *Liturgical Presidency in the Early Church* (Nottingham, 1983) 5.

9

The Office of Jan Hus:
An Unrecorded Antiphonary
in the Metropolitical Library
of Estergom

David R. Holeton

THOMAS TALLEY'S DESCRIPTION OF THE HUSSITE GRADUAL IN THE COLLECTION of Saint Mark's Library at the General Theological Seminary[1] was for most liturgists an introduction to a little known area of western liturgical history. Other than the restoration of the chalice, little is said in most surveys of western liturgical history about the Bohemian reformation, though it involved perhaps the most important liturgical movement in the latter half of the Middle Ages. Few specialists in the *sanctorale*, for instance, are even aware of the existence of a feast of SS. Jan Hus and Jerome of Prague. While a monograph on the liturgical history of the Bohemian reformation has yet to be written,[2] it seemed that Vaclav Novotny had collected all the extant sources for the celebration of the Bohemian Martyrs.[3] It is of no small interest, then, that a major new Hussite liturgical text should come to light providing new insights into utraquist liturgical life.

The Historical Setting

In the genesis of the Bohemian reformation sacramental and liturgical renewal antedated the appearance of Jan Hus by almost half a century.

The renewal was to remain a point of tension throughout the life of the Bohemian utraquist church. The conservative utraquists remained Catholic in both doctrine and liturgy, adhering to the rites as they inherited them with the exception of their commitment to communion under both kinds (*sub utraque specie*) for *all* the baptized[4] and the reading of the liturgical epistles and gospels and the recitation of the creed in Czech.[5] This group, often known as the "Pragers" because their center was the ecclesiastical Consistory in Prague, drew its theological resources from the faculty of the Charles University. Its principal appeal was to the nobility (most of whom had joined the utraquist cause during the fifteenth century), to the burgers of Prague and many of the other cities of Bohemia and Moravia, and to the university master.

After the death of Conrad of Vechta, the archbishop of Prague who had joined the utraquist cause, conservative utraquism did its best to maintain Catholic order. Although the Compactata, to which the Council of Basel had given its assent in 1436, confirmed the election of Jan Rokycana as archbishop of Prague, Rome refused to allow his consecration. Rokycana and his (unconsecrated) suffragans had to rely on accommodating Italian *episcopi vagantes* for the ordination of utraquist priests and deacons, a system which continued until 1620, long after the Consistory had lost any hope of obtaining the historic episcopate[6] and the utraquist Administrators ceased being bishops.

Within conservative utraquist circles liturgical life was never monochrome. Shortly after the death of Hus many churches moved quickly towards a vernacularization of the liturgy.[7] Other parishes appear to have clung tenaciously to Latin as the language of the liturgy except for the lections and creed.[8] Still others seem to have enjoyed a mixture of Latin and Czech.[9] As the sixteenth century progressed, the church experienced a period of re-Latinization when liturgical texts which had previously existed only in Czech were translated into Latin.[10]

Even by the time of Hus' death there were signs that many were not going to be content with the relatively conservative reformation lead by the university masters. Pushed perhaps in part by Waldensian influences as well as by the momentum of the Bohemian reform movement itself, these radical reformers came to be known as Taborites, after their revolutionary capital of Tabor in southern Bohemia. Here liturgical reforms were much more radical than in Prague. The liturgy passed almost immediately into Czech and most Catholic ceremonial and much Catholic doctrine was abandoned. The liturgy was simplified on what were thought to be biblical models so that its style quickly became very "free church," with hymnody assuming a major role in a liturgy that was otherwise a relatively unadorned rite focusing on word and table.

There was a tension between the conservative and radical factions from their inception. In a church and society unfamiliar with any sort of religious pluralism, the situation was exacerbated by the need to create a national front which could withstand the crusades being waged against the Bohemian nation. The alliance was always fragile, and much of what we know about the liturgical life of the Taborites comes from the acts of national synods where the Pragers were usually numerically dominant. There, under the leadership of the university masters, legislation was repeatedly enacted which was intended to eradicate the perceived liturgical abuses of the Taborites in an attempt to forge some sort of liturgical uniformity from what was obviously becoming a pluralistic national church.

The entire reform movement came to an abrupt end when the Hapsburgs defeated the Bohemian forces at the battle of the White Mountain (Bila Hora) in 1620. All public religious practice other than Roman Catholicism and Judaism was severely suppressed. The forces of the counter-reformation worked with particular vigor to Romanize utraquist hymnody,[11] to supplant devotion to Jan Hus and the Bohemian Martyrs with the cult of Jan Nepomuk, and to introduce new objects of devotion such as the Loreto and the Infant of Prague.

Liturgical Texts

Liturgical documents fared badly at the hands of the counter reformers. Most were destroyed: some, either because they were basically faithful to the Catholic rites or because of their intrinsic artistic value, were preserved. A few of these latter escaped undamaged[12] but most had the offending utraquist material—notably the feast of the Bohemian Martyrs on 6 July—removed or badly mutilated.[13] But the number of liturgical texts remaining from the Prager utraquist use are few indeed. While there is yet no catalogue of Hussite liturgical texts, there is no known utraquist Latin missal. What we know of their eucharistic practice must be pieced together from the handful of extant *Graduale* and the more numerous *Kancional*. There is one Hussite antiphonary in the Prague University library[14] but the pages which would have contained the office of the Bohemian Martyrs have been removed. The manuscript supplement to the printed Prague breviary of 1492 in the same University Library's collection,[15] provides only the office hymn *Pange lingua*[16] and three collects from the feast of the Bohemian Martyrs.[17] No utraquist *rituale* is known.

From the remaining *graduale* and *kancional* it had been possible to trace the development of the liturgical commemoration of the Bohemian Martyrs. The death of Jan Hus at the stake in Constance on 6 July 1415 was a turning point in the Bohemian reform movement which was already, by then, half a century old. His safe conduct having been guaranteed by the Holy Roman Emperor, all classes of the Bohemian realm were appalled at the betrayal and death of their popular preacher whose apparent goodness and steadfastness in the cause of ecclesiastical reform had won him a widespread following long before his death. Four hundred and fifty-two Bohemian nobles put their seals to a document protesting his death which had been immediately hailed as a martyrdom.

From the first anniversary of Hus' death there are records of his *passio* having been read[18] and sermons preached in which Hus is referred to as a saint.[19] The fathers of Constance naturally protested the practice,[20] but without effect. Jerome of Prague, who was not sent to the stake until 30 May 1416, was immediately associated with Hus in a common commemoration. The radical preacher Jan Zelivsky repeatedly invoked the sufferings of Hus and Jerome from his pulpit at Our Lady of the Snows in Prague.[21] In the atmosphere of heightened eschatological expectation which pervaded the Bohemian reformation, the sufferings of Hus and Jerome were seen as a sign of the sufferings which were to accompany the inbreaking of the eschatological age and the second advent of Christ.[22]

During the crusades against Bohemia, which began after the first defenestration of Prague on 30 July 1419, the supporters of the chalice and infant communion suffered cruelly at the hands of the invading armies.[23] These martyrs, too, were included in the commemoration on 6 July. Their death by fire, in irons, down the mine shafts of Kutna Hora, or by drowning are commemorated in the liturgical texts for the feast.

While there is clear evidence that Hus was commemorated in the liturgy from 6 July 1416, the history of the liturgical texts used for the commemoration is less clear. The use of devotional and polemical hymnody was widespread in Bohemia by the time of Hus.[24] It would appear that hymnody was the first means of commemorating Hus and Jerome at a liturgy which drew its liturgical proper from the common of martyrs or from the proper for other saints. In time, proper liturgical texts were composed for 6 July which, at first, were used in combination with other texts until a full set of propers had been composed.[25] These, then, began to be used for other feasts.[26] All this can be traced in the extant texts giving us a fairly complete picture of the eucharistic commemoration of the Bohemian Martyrs.

There was, however, a major lacuna in our knowledge of the commemoration in that office material appeared to be all but nonexistent. The office from the one known antiphonary had the propers removed while the user of the printed breviary was limited to a proper office hymn and collects along with the common of martyrs.

The Estergom Antiphonary

Sitting across the Danube, just a few hundred feet from modern Czechoslovakia in the Metropolitical Library of Estergom, is a utraquist antiphonary containing the feast of Jan Hus and the Bohemian Martyrs.[27] While the manuscript itself has been known for almost a century, the importance of its contents has not been recognized. The manuscript was first mentioned by the nineteenth-century Hungarian liturgist and canon of Estergom, Joseph Dankó, to whom the codex belonged before it passed into the archbishop's library.[28] Polycarp Radó, Dankó's celebrated successor, notes the Bohemian particularities of the manuscript in his catalogue of the liturgical manuscripts in the Estergom collection.[29] Citing some of the texts, Radó comments that he does not know if the texts for the office of Jan Hus and his companions have been edited or not.[30] Later, in his catalogue of all the liturgical manuscripts in Hungarian libraries, Radó simply refers the reader to his earlier, and effectively unavailable, work.[31]

The antiphonary is a relatively small volume (32 x 20.5 c.) containing 536 pages. It is written in a Gothic cursive which can be attributed to the second half of the fifteenth century. The notation is of the slanted lozenge type found in many of the Bohemian liturgical texts of this period and typical of the work of utraquist scriptoria.[32] The antiphonary contains the propers for the *temporale* (1-220) beginning with matins for Christmas Day but then, curiously, returning to Advent. The *sanctorale* begins with the propers for the feast of Saint Barbara (4 December) and ends with those for Saint Katherine (25 November). Additional material written in the same hand is appended to the text. Included among this material are the propers for the feast of Jan Hus and the Bohemian Martyrs (501-511) and the Transfiguration (515-524).[33]

While it is too early to say definitively, the antiphonary appears to follow the use of Prague rather than that of Olomouc, the other liturgical use within the Bohemian realm.[34] The use of Prague for the offices was of long duration and stable, antedating the establishment of the archbishopric in 1344. The variants between the earliest witnesses, which date from the thirteenth-fourteenth century, and the printed breviary of 1492 are few, the only difference being in the selection of some of the verses of the responsories.[35] Its use was enjoined on the secular clergy by the Synod of Prague in 1412[36] and confirmed for the utraquist clergy at synods in July 1421[37] and 1434.[38]

While a comparative study of the office proper is impossible, an examination of the Estergom antiphonary would lead to the conclusion that the commemoration of Hus, Jerome and the other Bohemian Martyrs followed, at the office, the same process as did the eucharistic propers. First the common of martyrs was used, later a hymn was added, and then other liturgical texts were gradually composed. The users of the Estergom antiphonary would have had proper liturgical material for first vespers, matins and first nocturns as well as some texts for second vespers, but would have had to use texts from the common of martyrs for second and third nocturns (if they were observed) and lauds. Thus, unlike the eucharist, the proper for the office remained incomplete.

A comparison of the content of the texts themselves would confirm the gradual composition of the proper rather than composition as a unified work. Some texts, such as the responsory and verse at first vespers, were composed with only Hus in mind; others, such as the antiphons for the same office or the responsory at first nocturns were written to commemorate both Hus and Jerome; still others, like the antiphon for the *Magnificat* at first vespers, included the hundreds of other martyrs who died for the chalice, though this commemoration does not seem to have been introduced until the 1430s. Two of the texts, the hymn *Pange lingua* and a variant of the antiphon *Christum regem martyrum*, were already known from other sources.[39] All the other texts are unrecorded.

Just as the compiler of the Estergom antiphonary drew on a variety of sources when assembling the office of the Bohemian martyrs, so, too, did the authors of the liturgical texts themselves. The most obvious is the office hymn *Pange lingua* which draws on Fortunatus' great hymn for the holy cross. Here, the author follows a common precedent, the hymn already having served as a source for a variety of other hymns.[40] The invitatory for the Venite, *Regem regum*, is simply a poetic expansion of the invitatory for the common of martyrs outside Paschaltide. Here, like the entire office, the prose common has been transformed into a rhythmic one, a style much in fashion in the fourteenth and fifteenth centuries. The additional antiphon, *O lumen boemie*, closely parallels the antiphon *O norma iusticie* found in Hungarian antiphonaries for the feast of Saint Emerich.[41]

In the office there is a strong and immediate sense of solidarity between the Bohemian nation and its martyrs. There is a tangible sense of Hus' goodness and of his continuing love and pastoral care for his national church. Jerome, though venerated for his martyrdom and honored for his learning ("... *arcium magister doctissimus* ...") is much more of a one-dimensional figure, having never caught the popular imagination as did Hus. Particularly vivid is the memory of the hundreds of others who went to their deaths for "the truth of the Law of God." Through fire, torture, the shafts, or drowning, they triumphed over death and live to intercede for their brothers and sisters in the faith who were, as the office itself was being sung, facing the same trials as they endeavored to be faithful to the truth as they had received it.

These new liturgical texts bring us closer to understanding the liturgical life of the utraquist church and give us a strong sense of its understanding of the communion of saints. When it seemed that all available texts had been recorded, it gives us some hope that there are yet more pieces in the Bohemian liturgical puzzle which remain to be found.

Ioannis Hus ceterorumque martirorum

In I. vesperis antiphonae super psalmos sequuntur

> Iubilans olim honorare
> adest namque nobilitas
> exhilarans sarco more
> pragensis fulget civitas.
>
> *Ps.* Laudate *per omnia*
>
> Nam duo luminaria
> ex te emerserunt
> ac per acta martiria
> ad celum migrarent.
>
> Quos dira Constancia
> flamma incendi in coro navit
> hos celi milicia
> empireo polo sociavit.
>
> Fide firma spe benigna
> Ioannes Hus Christi verna
> una cum Ieronimo
> adheserunt domino.
>
> Laus uni deo qui ethereo
> hos martires locans celo
> nobis eorum meritis
> dat uti ymnis celicis.

Responsorium: Gaude felix Bohemia
> hora nempe novissima
> te respixit dominus
> solito clemencius
> dum doctorem veritatis
> coruscantem honestatis

verbis et operibus
tibi dedit eximium
Ioannem presbiterum
predicatorem egregium
prebentum iter regium.

Versiculus: Pastor pie et benigne
lux boemice gentis
consolator desperatorum
et reprehensor vitiorum
duc nos ad regum celorum. Alleluia.

Qui propter testimonium
veri tulit martirium
et per incendium
migravit ad refrigerium
civium celestium.

Pastor pie et benigne...

Gloria patri...

Pastor pie...

Hymnus: Pange lingwa, gloriosi
prelium certaminis.
Quo bellantur studiosi
servi divi numinis
contra dolos criminosi
et perversi agimus.

Virum gignit virtuosum
Bohemorum regio,
castum, pium, fructuosum
suo fovet gremio,
viva fide animosum
transmittit concilio.

Ibi legis veritatem
forti mente profittens,
tectum cleri vanitatem
clara voce detegens
ac vivendi puritatem
per scripturas astruens,

tanquam pravus condempnatur,

verus a fallacibus
vinclis duris mancipatur
iutus a scelestibus,
sanctus igne concrematur
sevis a tortoribus.

Hic fidelis coronatur
servus vite laurea
et honore sublimatur
in celorum patria,
qui triumphat, dum luctatur
mundi cum malicia.

Patri summo atque nato
laus sit et imperium
spiritui ac beato
ultra evi terminum,
qui fideli tribulato
suum dedit gaudium. Amen.

Versiculus: Letamini in domino et exultate, iusti.
R: Et gloriamini omnes recti corde.

Antiphona ad Magnificat:

Christum regem martirum
regnantem dei patris
in gloria laudamus
hodie omnium bohemorum
spe Christi martirum
in memoria qui pro eius
legis dilecione
sacrique corporis
ac sanguinis sumcione.

Igne usti, ense cesi,
fossis iacti, undis mersi,
mire sunt opressi viventis,
eciam pueri innocentes.

O fidei auctor,
sis nostri roborator,
ob eorum merita
in tui lege agnita

da digne tuum calicem bibere,
ut possimus eciam fundere
nostrum pro te sanguinem,
timentes neminem.

O veritatis tutor,
esto nunc protector
boemice gregis
ab emulis tue legis
ut cognoscant,
quia veritas tua vincit
liberat suos et manet
in eternum. Amen.

Ad Matutinum, invitatorium

Regem regum
adoremus dominum
qui in celo
clarigero
Ioannem Hus
suis iunxit civibus
ac aurea
exornavit corona.

Venite

Hymnus: Pange lingua

In I. Nocturno

Antiphona: Quam preciosus
               martir Christi Ioannes Hus
               moribus et vita placidus
               ac exemplar omnibus
               rectam fidem sectantibus.

Antiphona: Qui se vero passus
               a clero verum non negavit
               sed necis usque terminum
               falsis obviavit.

Antiphona: Nunc Christus pro martirio
                digno dotavit premio
                dans locum celi solio
                una divo cum Ieronimo.

Versiculus: Laetamini in domino...
       R: Et gloriamini

Responsorium: Laetare gens boemie
                quod rex celestis curie
                sanctos recepit hodie
                Ioannem Hus ac Ieronimum
                sodales sanctorum civium.
          V: Promat leta
                hac dieta
                per pulcra
                quisue carmina.
                Nam athleta
                Christi celi
                conscendit culmina. Alleluia.

Responsorium: Preces Christe ascultare
                iuvans eadem intrare
                martirum consorcia
                sua divina gracia.
          V: Promat...

Responsorium: Preciosa mors martirum
                celi cum erga dominum
                qui spretis mundi ludibriis
                pro Christo dati supliciis
                meruerunt angelorum
                secum in regno celorum
                eternis fungi gaudiis.
          V: Meritas Christe
                martirum tuorum
                iungedo letari
                da loco eorum.
                Qui spretis...

Alia de martiribus.

In II. vesperis laudes antiphonae

> Verus Christe cultor fidei
> Ioanne Hus nomen ei
> martir sanctus spe in dei
> non huius luce diei
> memoratur populo.

Psalmos de martiribus.

> Est et alter Ieronimus
> arcium magister doctissimus
> quem martirio dominus
> coronavit altissimus
> in celi solio.

> Innumeriis
> gaudent Praga patronis
> quos misit deo in ore mucronis
> quorum reliquie cleicis
> sunt recondita donis.

> Dum felix boemorum regio
> de quam sanctorum legio
> lumine claret vario
> celo cum dei filio.

> Vos milites omnes Christi
> nos valle clamantes Christi
> precamus regem glorie
> prevenite oramine
> ut nos absolvat crimine.

Unus versus ut heri

> V. Letamini...
> R. Et gloriamini...

Ad magnificat:

[Antiphona:]   Iocundare germania tanto fulta
> decore animare boemia roborata
> vigore nesciens labem malicie
> sis fortis in agone
> fragrans flore pudicie.

fervens in dileccione
ob merita patronorum
sanguinem fundencium
ad pudorum al[e] mannorum
tibi resistencium quorum
collegio seve trucidanti
miro eulogio sunt excomunicati
fovearum iactu gravissimo mortificati
necnon ignis exustione examinati.

O quam preciosa mors sanctorum
quam vitam meruit angelorum
horum cetus omnium
exoret Christum dominum
pro salute fidelium. Alleluia.

Alia si libet antiphona

O lumen boemie
doctor veritatis
tu norma iusticie
lima primitatis
rosa pudicicie
gemma castitatis
codex sapiencie
cella claritatis
instita leticie
dulcor caritatis.
Ora regem glorie
nostris pro peccatis
ut det donum gracie
nobis cum beatis.

Notes

1. Thomas Talley, "A Hussite Latin Gradual of the XV Century," *Bulletin of the General Theological Seminary* 48:5 (1962) 8-13.
2. I attempted to give a short account of the background to the Bohemian liturgical movement in "Sacramental and Liturgical Reform in Late Medieval Bohemia," *Studia Liturgica* 17 (1987) 87-96. Enrico C.S. Molnár gives a somewhat over-generous account of Hus' role in the movement in "The Liturgical Reforms of John Hus," *Speculum* 41 (1966) 297-303. Beyond that the reader must turn to Czech literature notably August Neumann, *Z dejin bohosluzeb v dobe husitské* (Hra-

dec Králové, 1922); F.M. Bartos "Hus a ceska bohosluzba" in *Jihocesky sborník historicky* 21 (1952) 41-48, and the many comments of Zdenek Nejedly in his monumental collection of Czech hymnody *Dejiny husitského zpevu*, 2d ed. (Prague, 1952-1956).

3. *Fontes Rerum Bohemicarum* [FRB] VIII (1932) lxxii-lxxiii; cxx-xclviii; 243-246; 419-472.

4. For the conciliar negotiations on this question see my article "The Communion of Infants: The Basel Years," *Communio Viatorum* 29:4 (1986) 15-40.

5. This practice had been introduced by Matthias of Janov in the 1380s and seems to have enjoyed a certain popularity—despite attempts to suppress it—throughout the pre-Hussite period.

6. The last hope for acquiring the historic episcopate ended with the fall of Byzantium, with whom the Bohemians were in contact. See F.M. Bartos, "A Delegate of the Hussite Church to Constantinople," *Bysantinoslavica* 24 (1963) 287-292 and 25 (1964) 69-74 and Antonín Salac *Constantinople et Prague en 1452*, Rozpravy Ceskoslovenské akademie ved 68, 11 (1958).

7. There were early initiatives into Czech liturgy shortly after Hus' death and by 1417 Jan Capek had translated the entire liturgy into Czech. With its appearance the Taborites rejected the Latin liturgy in its entirety. See F.M. Bartos, "Hus a ceská bohosluzba" 51.

8. Synods repeatedly had to pass legislation assuring that at least these texts would remain in the vernacular. See Blanka Zilynská, *Husitske Synody v Cecách 1418-1440* (Prague, 1985) 117.

9. The Rackovsky Kancionál (MS Prague Univ. Bib. VI. C. 20a) provides an extensive collection of hymns and liturgical texts in Latin and Czech verses often alternating between the two languages.

10. The Kancionál of St. Michel's in the Old Town (MS Prague Univ. Bibl. XI. B. 1) contains a number of texts, including the eucharistic propers for the feast of the Bohemian Martyrs, newly composed in Latin during the last third of the fourteenth century.

11. The most important study of this is the unpublished doctoral dissertation of Marie-Elizabeth Ducreux, *Hymnologia Bohemica 1588-1764: Cantionnaires tchèques de la contre-réforme* (Université de Paris III, 1982).

12. For example the Gradual at General and Smiskovsky Kancionál in Vienna (MS öNB Musiksammlung 15492).

13. Among these are a number of important graduale from the late fifteenth and early sixteenth centuries: the Kutna Horsky Kancionál (1491), the Museum Kancionál (1512), the Klatovsky Kancionál (1537) and the Mladoboleslavsky Kancionál (c.1500).

14. MS Prague Univ. Bib. IV.H.12.

15. Prague Univ. Bib. *adlig* 42.G.28 *Brevarius Horarum Canonicarum secundum Veram Rubricam Archiepiscopatus Ecclesie Pragensis* (Nuremburg, 1492).

16. Ibid. Supplement ff. 2a'-2v'.

17. Ibid. f. 3b.

18. FRB VIII, cxxviii.

19. FRB VIII, 373-376.

20. F. Palachy, ed., *Documenta Mag. Ioannis Hus Vitam, Doctrinam, Causam in Constantiensi Concilio Actam et Controversias in Religione in Bohemia Annis 1413-1418 Notas Illustrantia* (Prague, 1869) 647-651.

21. Amedeo Molnár, ed., *Jan Zelivsky: Dochovaná kázání z roku 1419* Dil. I (Prague, 1953) 56, 96, 129, 240.

22. Amedeo Molnár, "Zelivsky, prédicateur de la révolution," *Communio Viatorum* 5:4 (1959) 333-334.

23. The contemporary chronicler Laurence of Brezová tells of utraquists being captured by crusaders and sent to Kutná Hora where they were tortured and thrown down the mine shafts, "In a short time more than 1600 utraquists were killed and thrown into the shafts, the executioners often being exhausted by the fatigue of the slaughter." FRB V, 351. Laurence also recounts the *passio* of Vaclav, the parish priest of Arnostovice who, with his curate and four children aged 7, 8, 10 and 11, was arrested by Albert of Austria on 6 July 1420. After being interrogated, tortured, and exhorted to renounce the chalice the six were sent to the stake where they are said to have died in Vaclav's embrace while singing utraquist hymns. FRB V, 385f.

24. See Zdenek Nejedly, *Dejiny husitského zpevu.* Dil. I: *Doba predhusitská* and Dil. II *Predchudci Husovi* (Prague, 1954).

25. FRB VIII, cxxviii-cxxxi.

26. The 1491 Graduale of Kutná Hora (MS öNB 15 501) had a full set of propers for Hus the incipits of which we know from the other feasts (S. Ursula, All Saints) which used the texts written for the Bohemian Martyrs.

27. MS Bibl. Metropolitana Strigoniensis I.313.

28. Joseph Dankó, *Vetus Hymnarium Ecclesiasticarum Hungariae* (Budapest, 1893) 80-81.

29. Polycarp Radó, "Esztergomi könyvtarak liturgikus kéziratai," *Pannonhalmi Föiskola Evkonyve* (1941/42) 111-116.

30. Ibid. 114-115.

31. Polycarp Radó, *Libri Liturgici Manuscripti Bibliothecarum Hungariae et Limitropharum Regionum* (Budapest, 1973) 541-542.

32. All noted utraquist manuscripts I have examined use this type of notation but some contemporary manuscripts from other scriptoria (e.g., the well known Dominican Graduale of Magister Wenceslas in the Prague University Library) retain the more familiar square notation.

33. It is also these two feasts which are appended to the printed breviary of 1492.

34. This will only be able to be verified when the massive comparative study of Central European antiphonaries is complete; see Laszlo Dobszay and Gabor Prószéky, *Corpus Antiphonalium Officii Ecclesiarum Centralis Europae: A Preliminary Report* (Budapest, 1988). From the beginning of the Bohemian reform movement the bishops of Olomouc were openly hostile and refused to make even the concessions legally imposed on them by the Compactata. Under such an atmosphere utraquist clergy would be more likely to follow the Prague use where their cause was better received.

35. Dobszay and Prószéky, 209.

36. Constantine Hofler, ed., *Concilia Pragensia 1353-1413* (Prague, 1872) 71.

37. F.M. Prochazka, *Miscellaneen der Bohmischen und Märischen Litteratur* (Prague, 1784) 303.

38. Blanka Zilynská, *Hustisky Synody v Cechách 1418-1440* (Prague, 1985) 114.

39. *Pange lingua* is recorded in the Malostransky Kancionál and *Christum regem martyrum* in the Rackovsky and Museum Kancionáls.

40. The best example is Saint Thomas' hymn for the feast of Corpus Christi but Guido Maria Dreves and Clemens Blume (*Analecta Hymnica Medii Aevi*) list over seventy hymns which use Fortunatus' hymn as a model.

41. Joseph Dankó, *Vetus Hymnarium Ecclesiasticum Hungariae* (Budapest, 1893) 235.

10

The Eucharistic Rite of the Stowe Missal

Marion J. Hatchett

IN 1964 A MID-SEVENTH CENTURY IRISH PALIMPSEST SACRAMENTARY, RECENT-ly deciphered by Dom Alban Dold, was published.[1] It confirmed the usual assumptions that the Celtic Rite, prior to Romanization, was closely related to the Gallican Rite as exemplified in the sacramentary known as the *Missale Gothicum*[2] and in the exposition of the Gallican liturgy of "Germanus,"[3] and that there was substantial Spanish influence on the rite.

For various days and occasions (including a feast of the Maccabees) this Irish sacramentary provides variable forms for an initial prayer, for a *collectio*, for a *Post nomina recitata*, for an *Ad pacem*, for a preface, and for a post-*Sanctus* which leads into a fixed institution narrative. The institution narrative concludes in a manner similar to the conclusions in Mozarabic, Ambrosian, and Eastern Rites, and to the memorial acclamation of various Eastern Rites[4]: "As often as you eat of this bread and drink of this cup, you make a memorial of my passion, proclaiming it to all, and you hope for my coming until I come again." This fixed portion is followed by a variable *Collectio sequitur* equivalent to the *Post mysterium* or *Post secreta* or *Post pridie* of Gallican and Mozarabic books. A variable form introduces the Lord's Prayer. Two (apparently fixed) prayers follow the communion of the people.

Dold deciphered enough of a number of the texts to determine that thirty are also found in *Missale Gothicum* and seventeen in the *Liber Moz-*

arabicus Sacramentorum Von Toledo. Three are found in an Ambrosian palimpsest, and two in the Gallican Masses of Mone. One is common to the
Celtic Stowe, Dimma, and Mulling rites for the sick. One each is found in
the Leonine and Gelasian sacramentaries and the Mozarabic *Liber Ordinum*, and one in an Irish palimpsest fragment at the Würzburg University Library. One *Post mysterium* (Item 38) is based on a prayer in the third-
century apocryphal Acts of Thomas 49-50.[5]

Even before the transcription of this sacramentary, however, Augustine had established a Roman mission in Kent, and within the century
the Synod of Whitby (663 A.D.) would decide for the Roman Rite rather
than the Celtic, and the Romanization of the Celtic Rite and the suppression of it would begin. From the beginning of the Romanization of the
rite until its final suppression our principal source of knowledge of its
eucharistic rite is the Stowe Missal.[6] Various fragments[7] add little to our
knowledge of the rite but sometimes clarify or give weight to a particular
interpretation of Stowe.

The Stowe Missal is the earliest book that can properly be called a missal rather than a sacramentary, for it apparently contains in one volume
all of the texts necessary for a celebration of the eucharist. It is the small-
est extant missal. The eucharistic rite occupies thirty-three of its sixty-
seven leaves which are approximately four-and-a-half by five-and-a-half
inches.

The Stowe Missal has generally been thought of as an *itinerarium*, a
book for a travelling monk. Hennig, however, dissents, arguing that it is
a complete Celtic missal, that the Celts had no *Sanctorale*, that their Masses were not commemorative but votive in nature.[8] That was certainly not
true of the earlier palimpsest.

Complicating any effort to reconstruct the rite of the Stowe Missal is
the fact that the book contains very few rubrics; in fact, the first edition
apparently had no rubrics at all. Surely some of the texts were for occasional rather than general use, and other texts adjacent to each other may
have been alternatives. Judging from parallels, some prayers may have
been said or sung by the celebrant during the singing of the litany or
chants. No directions are given as to how or when certain things were to
be done. For example, there is no direction for the preparation of the elements, nor for the exchange of the peace (though texts at three different
points in the rite would lead logically into an exchange of the peace).
There are no directions for the administration of communion and no
words of administration.

The original version of the Stowe Missal may date from 792 to 812 A.D.,
may be based on a prototype from the later half of the seventh century,
and may be associated with the monastery of Tallaght. These assumptions

are based on the fact that the commemoration of the departed contains the name of no saint later than the mid-seventh century with the exception of Maelruain, the founder of the Tallaght monastery, who died in 792 A.D., and whose name is given a distinctive initial capital letter.[9] By the middle of the century the eucharistic rite was re-edited by a scribe who signed himself Moélcaích.[10] This re-editing involved erasures, deletions, rearrangements of original material, and substantial additions. At a still later point additional texts were added and some rubrics and titles inserted.

The First Edition

The oldest strata of material begins with a litany (also in the Fulda fragment, the St. Gall fragment 1395, and BM Reg 2 A xx ["The Book of Cerne"]) which was probably a part of the celebrant's preparation rather than of the public rite. Initial petitions addressed to Christ are followed by a three-fold "Christ, hear us" and a one-fold *Kyrie eleison*. This is followed by a petition addressed to thirteen individual saints and then to "All saints" to pray for us and to be propitious and spare us. The thirteen are all from the New Testament: Mary, Peter, Paul, followed by seven others from among the twelve (Andrew, James, Bartholomew, Thomas, Matthew, James, and Thaddeus), Matthias, Mark, and Luke.[11] Three petitions for deliverance, addressed to our Lord, follow. A space erased by a later editor probably contained the last lines common to the various versions: three petitions to be heard, the one sentence *Agnus Dei*, and a three-fold "Christ, hear us."

The litany is followed by a prayer in the first-person singular, the contents of which would imply that it was associated with the vesting of the priest. It is associated with vesting in *Missam a Matthia Flacco Illyrico* and various French rites.[12]

The public rite probably began with a fixed collect[13] asking that our prayer ascend to the throne of God's glory and that our supplication not return to us void. This text is printed after the Creed and Lord's Prayer in the Irish *Liber Hymnorum*.[14] It is also found in an Ambrosian ordo printed in the collection of Martène.[15] Another prayer, probably for occasional use,[16] which entreats the intercessions of Peter, follows immediately in the text. This is the first prayer (Item 4) of the *Missa Romensis cotidiana* of the Bobbio Missal,[17] the first of several forms from that Mass included in the rite of the Stowe Missal.[18]

An Irish form of the *Gloria in excelsis*, found also in the seventh century Bangor Antiphonary (for use in the daily offices) and in the *Liber Hymnorum*, follows.[19] There is no indication as to whether it was a fixed part of the rite or alternated with other canticles, as in Gallican and Mozarabic

Rites,[20] or was reserved for special days or occasions, as in the Roman Rite at this period.[21]

The prayer which follows is the *collectio* of the Bobbio *Missa Romensis cotidiana* (Item 5). It is also found in the Reichenau fragment A, and as the last item in *Gothicum* (543), the only item remaining of a *Missa cotidiana Romin(sis)*.[22]

Next is the text of 1 Corinthians 11:26-32. There is no indication as to whether this was a fixed epistle or simply a provision for occasions when no lectionary or Bible might be available. The Reichenau fragment A, the St. Gall fragment 1395, and the Dimma rite for the sick all provide proper lections for particular occasions.

The prayer which follows is the initial prayer, *Oratio super populum*, in an Ambrosian Mass *pro baptizatis* for Tuesday after Easter[23] and the first prayer of the third Paschal Mass in Bobbio (Item 282). Was this a normal part of the Stowe rite, or only said on certain occasions? Was it said aloud, or secretly by the priest?

The next item is Psalm 105:4, 1-4. This is evidently a gradual, with verse four as the refrain.

The collect which follows is a prayer that the gifts may be acceptable. This is the *Ad Pacem* (Item 33) for the first Advent Mass in *Missale Gallicanum Vetus*, but a *secreta* or *super oblata* in other books.[24] This prayer may have been said secretly by the priest during the singing of the gradual.

The text of Psalm 118:14 is written out. This was probably a verse associated with Alleluia, for a later editor gave it the title "Alleluia."

The prayer which follows, asking that God behold the offerings, may have been said secretly by the priest during the singing of the Alleluia. It shows up with great frequency in other books as a *secreta* or *super oblata*.[25]

The litany which follows, which is also in the Fulda fragment, is related in placement and content to some eastern litanies.[26] It is also related to the Gallican litany following the homily,[27] to the Roman litany of Pope Gelasius,[28] and to the Ambrosian litanies which took the place of the *Gloria in excelsis* on the first four Sundays in Lent.[29] The Stowe litany seems to be early, for it includes petitions for the emperor and the Roman army and for catechumens and penitents and makes no mention of the pope. Is this placement of the litany and its mention of catechumens and penitents an indication of a dismissal prior to the reading of the gospel?[30]

The collect which follows corresponds in placement to the *Collectio post precum* of the Gallican Rite, but the petition is that God behold the sacrifice offered. This text is associated with the peace in the *Missale Gallicanum Vetus* (Item 42) and the Bobbio Missal (Item 61), but it is a *secreta* or *super oblata* in other books.[31]

At this point apparently four pages of the first edition have been removed. The gospel began on one of these pages, for when the first scribe's hand shows back up it is in the middle of a hyphenated word. Did the first edition contain, among other things, a *collectio post precum*? (The content of the prayer following the litany might suggest that it was said secretly.) Did the first edition contain a dismissal of catechumens and penitents? Did it contain the *Benedicite*, as in Gallican and Mozarabic Rites?[32] Did it contain additional prayers associated with the offering of the gifts? Or did it contain a longer version of the gospel (John 6:51-57 in the final edition) or provide alternative gospels?

The Nicene Creed follows the gospel immediately in the text. It had been inserted in the Mozarabic Rite in 589 A.D., but did not enter the Roman Rite until the pontificate of Benedict VIII (1012-1024). Though the form in the first edition of Stowe differs from that of the Gelasian Sacramentary (Items 312 and 314) in various details, it resembles those versions in its use of the first-person singular, *Credo* rather than *Credimus*, in its omission of two phrases, *Deum de Deo* and *Filioque*, and in its use of *Spero resurrectionem* ("I hope for the resurrection") rather than *Exspecto resurrectionem* ("I look for the resurrection"). This placement of the Nicene Creed is analogous to that of later western books, in contrast to its place in Eastern and Mozarabic Rites.

The Creed is followed immediately by Psalm 85:7. This corresponds to the chant following the gospel in Ambrosian, Gallican, and Mozarabic Rites. Alleluias may have been sung with this verse, for the *Treatise on the Mass* bound with the Stowe Missal refers to an Alleluia after the gospel.

The prayer which follows is the *Post nomina* of the Bobbio *Missa Romensis cotidiana* (Item 6). Does this indicate that the names of the living were read at this point? In other books this text is used as a *super oblata*.[33]

A prayer at this point, erased by a later editor, evidently began with G. It was probably the *Ad pacem* (Item 7) of the Bobbio *Missa Romensis cotidiana*.[34] Probably at one time the peace came at this point in the Celtic Rite as in the Gallican and Mozarabic Rites.

The space available under the erasures of a later editor would hardly allow for a fuller form of the *Sursum corda*, preface, *Sanctus*, and initial portion of the Roman Canon than that of the Bobbio *Missa Romensis cotidiana* (Items 8-11). On the basis of what can be made out from the erasure of the first part of the Canon, it probably contained a rubric directing the recital of the names of the living and one or two variable communicantes, as did Bobbio.[35] The work of the first editor reappears immediately after the *communicantes*. Inserted in the Roman commemoration of the living is a commemoration of departed martyrs and a petition that the builder of the church and all people may be delivered from the worship of idols. Only one sign of the cross is prescribed in the body of the prayer, at the petition to bless this oblation that it may become for us the body and blood of Christ. The commemoration of the departed may be a normal part of the Stowe prayer, though at this time it was used only on certain occasions in the Roman rite.[36] The Roman text is amplified, partly with the text of a *Post nomina* found in *Missale Gallicanum Vetus* (Item 32).[37] Within this paragraph, in parallel columns, is a list of more than one hundred names, including Old Testament patriarchs and prophets and Irish saints, all of whom had died by the mid-seventh century with the exception of Maelruain, founder of the Tallaght monastery, who died in 792 A.D.[38] Space is left in the last column for additional names. The second, third, and fourth archbishops of Canterbury are included, but not Augustine. The list has parallels in the Fulda fragment and in Reichenau B. The commemoration of Old Testament worthies has precedents in eastern liturgies and in other Gallican books. The four signs of the cross prescribed in the last paragraph may have been for the blessing of other gifts.[39]

The Canon is followed by Psalm 33:22, and that is followed by a separate paragraph consisting of Luke 24:35 and 1 Corinthians 10:16, interspersed with Alleluias. Probably Psalm 33:22 was to be used as a refrain before and after the subsequent paragraph. In its placement, between the Canon and the Lord's Prayer, and in its content, this form corresponds to the fraction anthems of the Ambrosian, Gallican, and Mozarabic Rites.

The erasures of a later scribe leave indications that the Lord's Prayer with protocol and embolism, and possibly the peace, were said at this point. The erased page which follows was almost certainly filled with communion chants.

The rite concludes with the same two prayers as the St. Gall fragment 1394 and with a dismissal. The first of these prayers is the *Post communione* of the Bobbio *Missa Romensis cotidiana* (Item 23), which also shows up in a number of other books.[40] The second prayer is the *Consummacio* of the Bobbio *Missa Romensis cotidiana* (Item 24), which is also in an Ambrosian *Cottidianis diebus* in *Triplex* (Item 72). The dismissal brings in the note of peace, as does the Mozarabic dismissal and that of many Eastern Rites.

The ordinary is followed by three sets of propers in the hand of the original scribe: (1) for apostles, martyrs, saints, and holy virgins; (2) for penitents; and (3) for the departed. The Reichenau fragments A and B apparently provided for the same three Masses. The provisions are analogous to those of the seventh-century Irish palimpsest sacramentary, the *Missale Gallicanum Vetus*, the Masses of Mone, the *Missale Gothicum*, and the Bobbio Missal. The second Mass incorporates the three texts of the first votive Mass of the Bobbio Missal (Items 421-423). Each of the three Masses provides two prayers (the first Mass also includes what is probably an alternative initial prayer for use on feasts of apostles), followed by a *Post nomina*-type prayer, a proper preface, and a post-communion prayer. The first Mass also includes a post-*Sanctus* which leads into the institution narrative. With only four exceptions the prayers are of the lengthy Gallican type rather than the concise Roman collect form. No directions for their use are provided.

This first edition of the Stowe rite is a heavily Romanized Rite: most of the prayers are in the concise Roman collect form, the Old Testament lesson has been dropped, the eucharistic prayer is the Roman Canon, and the peace has probably been moved to the Roman position after the breaking of the bread. This rite is very close kin to the *Missa Romensis cotidiana* of the Bobbio Missal. Yet a number of Gallican features have been retained: the apparently normative use of a canticle in the entrance rite, the Creed, the chant after the gospel (and Creed), the *Post nomina* and *Ad pacem* prayers, the place of the Lord's Prayer, and the *Consummacio*. Other features normal in a Roman Rite at this point in time are missing: introit, *Kyrie*, psalm at the offertory, and *Agnus Dei*. The rite also has several unusual, if not unique, features: the inclusion of prayers for use after (or possibly during) epistle, gradual, and Alleluia; the place of the litany between epistle and gospel; texts related to the offering between epistle and gospel; use of *N.* to indicate a place to insert names; and commemoration of Old Testament worthies within the eucharistic prayer. It contains relatively early forms of the *Gloria in excelsis*, the Nicene Creed, and the Roman Canon.

The Revision of Moélcaích

At an early date in its history this book was reworked by a scribe whose name was Moélcaích. Possibly the volume was carried from one monastery to another and revised to bring it into conformity to the usage or customary of its new home. This edition incorporates a number of Gallican texts not included in the first edition of the Stowe Missal and includes some titles and rubrics.

The intercession of saints in the initial litany of the original edition was limited to New Testament figures. Moélcaích inserted the names of Stephen, Martin, Jerome, Augustine, Gregory, Hilary, and twenty-six Irish saints, from Patrick who died in 493 A.D. through Samdine (Samthann, Samdann) who died in 739 A.D.[41] This possibly indicates that Moélcaích's edition was based on a mid-eighth century prototype.

After recopying the ending of the litany this editor inserted a "Prayer of Ambrose," an apologia or prayer for pardon, the first portion of which is in the first-person singular.[42]

After the *Gloria in excelsis*, Moélcaích inserted another prayer commonly found in books of the period.[43] (For an English translation, see The Book of Common Prayer, Collect of the Sixth Sunday of Easter.)

Before the epistle the editor inserted a rubric, "Here the augment." This may indicate that a prayer from among the propers after the end of the rite was to be inserted or substituted, or it may simply mean that the traditional ending is to be added to the preceding collect.

Between the prayer which follows the Alleluia and the litany Moélcaích inserted a rubric, "The Prayer of St. Martin begins, Amen, thanks be to God."

Another apologia or prayer for pardon, partly in the first- person singular, was inserted after the prayer at the end of the litany. This prayer is found in several other books.[44] According to the directions in some of those books it was to be said secretly. In this rite, would it have been said during the singing of the litany?

Moélcaích then inserted a rubric, "Half-uncovering here." This is followed by the text of Psalm 141:2, "Let my prayer be set forth in your sight as incense, the lifting up of my hands as the evening sacrifice," with directions that it be sung three times and that the linen cloth be lifted from the chalice. This is followed by a brief prayer, "Come, Lord, Almighty Sanctifier, and bless this sacrifice prepared for you. Amen.,"[45] with the direction that it also be sung three times. Do these texts and these ceremonial directions indicate a censing of the oblations? If so, this is probably our earliest indication of a censing of the oblations, for the practice did not come into common use until the eleventh century.[46]

After the gospel and Creed, but before the chant and prayer which follow, Moélcaích inserted a rubric, "Full uncovering here." Everything on that leaf after the chant and prayer (probably the *Ad pacem* [Item 7] of the Bobbio *Missa Romensis cotidiana* along with the initial portion of the eucharistic prayer) was erased and written over, and three new leaves were inserted. Three prayers were inserted at this point. The first was the third prayer of a Mass in the Leonine Sacramentary (Item 427) and the *secret* of an Ambrosian Mass in *Triplex* (Item 574). This prayer, like that immediately above it, is a petition for the acceptance of the offerings and purification of those who offer. Was it intended as an alternative? The second prayer includes a commemoration by name of the departed on whose behalf the oblations are offered.[47] The content of the prayer, which includes a reference to the book of life, is comparable to that of many Gallican and Mozarabic *Post nomina*.[48] This prayer is addressed to the second person of the Trinity, another Gallican or Mozarabic note. The prayer is fol-

lowed by a rubric, "The second part of the augment here over the oblation." This may refer to the prayer which precedes the preface in the propers at the end of the rite, indicating that on occasion it was to take the
place of the prayer which precedes or that which follows in the text or to
be inserted between them. The third prayer is the *Ad pacem* of the Bobbio
Missa Romensis cotidiana (Item 7), amplified with material which also
shows up in Reichenau fragment B, apparently for use within the Canon.
The oblation is offered not just in honor of our Lord but also "in commemoration of your blessed apostles and your martyrs and confessors
whose relics are here." The petition, "May it be profitable for salvation to
all," is extended to read "... to all our bishops and our priests and our
deacons and our beloved brothers and our beloved sisters and our boys
and our girls and our penitents." Such tender expressions are peculiarly
characteristic of Gallican liturgies.[49]

The opening dialogue of the eucharistic prayer begins with the words
Sursum corda. The salutation does not precede it, nor does it show up
anywhere else in this rite. The preface is greatly amplified with material
also found in the Fulda fragment and other manuscripts.[50] Inserted just
prior to "Per quem ..." is a rubric, "Here the *Dignum* gets the addition if
per quem follows in the text." This must refer to the use of a proper preface ending with *per quem*. Just before the *Sanctus* is a rubric, "Here the
Dignum gets the addition if *Sanctus* follows in the text." This must refer
to the use of a proper preface ending with *Sanctus*. Proper prefaces are
provided in the three Masses following the ordinary in the Stowe Missal,
in the St. Gall fragment 1394, the Piacenza fragment, and the Reichenau
fragments A and B, some of which lead into *per quem* and others into
Sanctus. As in some Eastern and other Gallican Rites the *Benedictus qui
venit* follows immediately after the *Sanctus*.

The *Sanctus* and *Benedictus qui venit* are followed by a post-*Sanctus*:

> Blessed is he who came from heaven that he might dwell on the
> earth, was made man that he might destroy the sins of the flesh,
> was made a victim that through his passion he might give eternal
> life to believers: through Lord.

This text, found also in the Fulda fragment, is a fuller version of a
Missale Gothicum post-*Sanctus* (Item 537).[51] The first set of propers at the
end of the Stowe Rite includes a post-*Sanctus* which ends in the normal
Gallican manner with the words *Qui pridie*, introducing the institution
narrative. Forms ending *Qui pridie*, normative in the seventh-century
Irish palimpsest, are also included in the Piacenza fragment and in the
Reichenau fragments A and B.[52]

The Roman Canon which follows has been given a title, *Dominical Canon of Pope Gelasius*. Moélcaích inserted a phrase, "Bishop of the Apostle's seat," after the petition for the pope, and added an intercession by name for the abbot, "our bishop." The commemoration of the living is preceded by a rubric, "Here are recited the names of the living." This intercession is greatly amplified with material evidently a part of the post-*Sanctus* in the Fulda fragment and of a post-*secreta* in Reichenau fragment B. It includes commemoration of and prayer for the departed as well as the living. Proper commemorations are provided for the Natal Day of our Lord, the feast of the Circumcision, the Day of the Star (Epiphany), Maundy Thursday,[53] the Pascha, the conclusion of the Pascha, Ascension, and Pentecost. At this point there is a return to the original edition. The only other change in the Canon made by Moélcaích is the revision of the conclusion of the institution narrative so that it reads, "As often as you do these things, doing them in my memory, you shall preach my passion, proclaim my resurrection, hope for my coming, until I come again to you from heaven." This is comparable to the conclusion of the institution narrative of the seventh-century Irish palimpsest sacramentary, of Ambrosian and Mozarabic Rites, and of many Eastern Rites, and to the memorial acclamation of many Eastern Rites.[54]

Moélcaích inserted after the doxology of the Canon and immediately before what was apparently the refrain for the fraction anthem a rubric, "It is sung three times; here the oblation is lifted over the chalice and half of the Bread is dipped into the chalice," and after the refrain another rubric, "It is here that the Bread is broken." After the fraction anthem he repeated the refrain and the first phrase of the anthem, with Alleluias interspersed.

The fraction anthem is followed by a Gallican post-*secreta*[55] which is also found in the Fulda fragment:

We believe, Lord, we believe ourselves to be redeemed in this breaking of the body and pouring out of the blood, and we trust, receiving this sacrament, to be built up so that we may enjoy the true fruits in heaven of what we have here for the time being through hope; through Lord.

In Moélcaích's edition of the Stowe Missal we have all the elements of a complete Gallican eucharistic prayer surrounding or included as an insertion in the now obligatory Roman Canon, a fact that previous commentators have not noted. A Gallican preface introduces the *Sanctus* which leads immediately into the *Benedictus qui venit*, which is then followed by a Gallican post-*Sanctus*. A typical Gallican addition to the institution narrative is inserted in the Roman Canon, and a Gallican post-*secreta* is retained at this point. The use of the Roman Canon might now be required, but this reactionary editor made sure that all of the elements of a proper Gallican eucharistic prayer were retained. This is analogous to the later Gallicanized Roman rites for ordinations and for the consecration of a church which retain the essential elements of both the earlier Roman and earlier Gallican books.[56]

The protocol which introduces the Lord's Prayer is the same as that of the Dimma fragment, the St. Gall fragment 1394, and *Missale Gothicum* Item 155.[57] The indications seem to be that the Lord's Prayer was said by all, as in Gallican rites, rather than by the priest alone, as in the Roman Rite. The embolism which follows the Lord's Prayer is also found in the St. Gall fragment 1394. It is related to but not identical with that of the Gelasian Sacramentary (Item 1258). There is no mention of the Virgin, and Patrick is substituted for Andrew. (The embolism of the rites for the sick of the Stowe Missal and of the Deer, Dimma, and Mulling fragments does not include any mention of the intercession of saints.)

The embolism is followed by this text: "The peace and love of our Lord Jesus Christ and the communion of all the saints be with us always," with a response, "And with your spirit." The St. Gall fragment 1394 has the same text and response, and it is explicitly stated there that the peace is exchanged at this point.[58] "Germanus" gives a blessing similar to this text, that is distinct from the peace, which is to be used by presbyters as a substitute for the bishop's triple blessing.[59] Possibly this form was first used in Celtic rites as a blessing, and the peace exchanged in conjunction with the *Ad pacem* collect prior to the *Sursum corda*, but in the process of the Romanization of the rite the peace was moved to this point. This dialogue is followed by a prayer comparable to various Gallican and Mozarabic *Ad pacem* forms.[60]

The text which follows, "May the commixture of the body and blood of our Lord Jesus Christ be unto us salvation unto everlasting life. Amen." certainly implies a commixture at this point. This commixture was probably for the purpose of administration in both kinds together by use of a spoon or a straw. The simultaneous reception of both kinds is certainly implied by the words of administration in both the rite for the sick and the baptismal rite of the Stowe Missal, those of the Deer, Dimma, and Mulling fragments and the Bangor Antiphonary, and by one of the communion chants of the Stowe Missal.[61] The *Treatise on the Mass* bound with the Stowe Missal, however, gives directions that would make it necessary for the bread and wine to be administered separately.

Between the commixture and the first of the communion chants is this text: "Behold the Lamb of God; behold who takes away the sins of the world." Jungmann says, "The earliest witness to the use of these words before communion seems to be the Synod of Aix (1585),"[62] but here we have witness to their use in a western rite at least seven hundred years earlier, and there are precedents in eastern rites.[63]

The remaining texts in Moélcaích's handwriting are obviously communion chants, many of which are found in other Celtic sources.[64] Eighteen of the twenty-two texts include an Alleluia in the middle and at the end.[65] The four texts without Alleluias are the *incipits* of Psalms 23, 24, 25, and 43.[66] Was one or another of these psalms to be sung with one of the other texts as a refrain, possibly varying with the season or occasion?[67] Sixteen of the eighteen that are possibly refrains are from the Scriptures.[68] One of these, "Suffer little children to come to me and forbid them not, for of such is the kingdom of heaven" (Mt 19:14), surely implies the continued communing of small children.[69] One of the two non-scriptural refrains is reminiscent of the Celtic words of administration, "This sacred body of the Lord, and the blood of salvation, receive unto yourselves unto life eternal."[70]

The last refrain is followed by the *incipit* of the first half of the *Gloria Patri*, the *incipit* of the refrain, the *incipit* of the last half of the *Gloria Patri*, and the *incipit* of the refrain. Does this indicate a pattern that is to be followed after each psalm, or at least after the last of the communion psalms? This is parallel to the Mozarabic pattern,[71] and possibly to the *Trecanum* of the Gallican Rite mentioned by "Germanus," which had some reference to the Trinity.[72]

The communion chants are followed by a note, "Moélcaích wrote," indicating the end of the work on this rite of this reviser. Moélcaích was a restorer or conserver of Celtic usages and texts. He provides some rubrics, possibly as a defense against further Romanization. The rite he knew was fuller than that of the first edition of the Stowe Missal, yet the structure was apparently basically the same. The rite as edited by Moélcaích was not unique. We have Witzel's extracts from the rite of the now lost sacramentary which he found at Fulda, which includes quotations from the initial litany, the *Gloria in excelsis*, the litany, the preface, the post-*Sanctus*, the commemoration of the living, the commemoration of the departed, and the post-*secreta*. This rite was close kin but not identical to Moélcaích's revision of Stowe.

Further Editing

Other additions were made by a later editor or by later editors. Two prayer texts were inserted. The first, immediately after the epistle, may be an addition to the rite or an alternative to the prayer which follows.

The text is found in some Gelasian books.[73] The second, "The prayer of Gregory over the Gospel," which is a Gregorian collect,[74] is inserted on a slip bound between the two pages that contain the gospel.[75] Is this an attempt to provide a parallel to the prayers after the epistle, the gradual, and the Alleluia of the first edition? An editor or editors inserted the *Filioque* in the Nicene Creed, added some rubrics,[76] and provided titles for several forms.[77]

The Treatise on the Mass

Bound with the Stowe Missal is a *Treatise on the Mass*, which may be as early as the ninth century.[78] It is a description of the ceremonies of the Mass with allegorical interpretation. It includes a description of the preparation of the elements at the altar before the *Introit* and of the complicated Celtic fraction, for which the closest parallel is that of the Mozarabic Rite.[79] It is clear that the chalice is elevated when the *oblata* is sung. It is also clear that the institution narrative, known as the *periculosa oratio*, is sung, and that in close connection with this "lesson," the priest bows in repentance, chanting "Have mercy on me, God," and the people kneel. Also in close connection with the institution narrative the priest takes three steps back, signifying sinfulness in thought, word, and deed, and three steps forward signifying "the triad of things by which he is renovated *iterum* and by which he is moved to Christ's Body."

The rite of the Stowe Missal is significant for several reasons. Although it has been highly Romanized, it is still our principal source of knowledge for the ancient Celtic eucharistic rite, and it sheds light on the sketchy sources that we have for reconstruction of other rites of the Gallican family and on the influence that they had on each other. It also sheds light on eastern influences on the Celtic Rite and on other Gallican rites. The two principal editions of the rite of the Stowe Missal raise questions and throw light on the ways in which the process of Romanization of Gallican rites and suppression of Gallican rites was dealt with by different editors or in different places. The first edition of the eucharistic rite of the Stowe Missal was closely related to the Bobbio *Missa Romensis cotidiana* and may provide answers to questions about that rite and how it was celebrated. The Stowe Missal also throws light on the process of Gallicanization of the Roman Rite. It is possibly the first witness to several features which eventually worked their way into the Roman Rite: the use of *N.* to indicate a place to insert names; the prayer invoking the Holy Spirit over the oblations, *Veni, Sanctificator*; an amplification in the commemoration of the departed and the normative use of the commemoration of the departed as a part of the Canon; and the use of the text *Ecce Agnus Dei* (Behold the Lamb of God) prior to the communion of the people. A somewhat higher percentage of texts from the Stowe Missal, and of customs such as the early preparation and presentation of the elements, show up in the British books than in the continental books of the period.[80] It raises the question of whether other peculiarly British customs or texts have roots in the Celtic Rite. The Stowe Missal also provides very early versions of several texts, including the *Gloria in excelsis*, the Nicene Creed, and the Roman Canon.

Notes

1. *Das Irische Palimpsestsakramentar Im CLM 14429*, H.C.A. Dold and L. Eizenhöfer, eds. (Beuron, 1964).

2. *Missale Gothicum*, L.C. Mohlberg, ed. (Rome, 1961).

3. *Expositio Antiquae Liturgiae Gallicanae*, E.C. Ratcliff, ed., Henry Bradshaw Society 98 (London 1971).

4. See *The Liturgies of SS. Mark, James, Clement, Chrysostom, and Basil, and the Church of Malabar: Translated, with Introduction and Appendices*, by J.M. Neale and R.F. Littledale, 3d ed. (London, n.d.) 193-247.

5. Dold, *Das Irische* 82*, 43-46.

6. *The Stowe Missal*, G.F. Warner, ed., Henry Bradshaw Society 31 (Facsimile), 32 (Text and Notes) (London, 1906, 1915).

7. For bibliographies, see K. Gamber, *Codices Liturgici Latini Antiquiores* (Freiburg: 1968), Pars. I, 130-152; J.F. Kenney, *The Sources for the Early History of Ireland* (New York, 1929), vol. 1, 683-706; E. Bourque, *Etude sur les sacramentaires romains* (Rome, 1958), Part II, Tome II, 405-416; A.A. King, *Liturgies of the Past* (Milwaukee, 1959) 186-275. The Armagh, Deer, Dimma, Mulling, St. Gall 1394, and St. Gall 1395 fragments are all available in F.E. Warren, *The Liturgy and Ritual of the Celtic Church* (Oxford, 1881) 163-186; the Piacenza and Reichenau B fragments in *The Journal of Theological Studies* 5 (1904) 49-75; and the summary of the contents of the now lost Fulda sacramentary in G. Witzel, *Exercitamen Syncerae Pietatis* (Mainz, 1555), Signature P.

8. J. Hennig, " A Feast of All Saints in Europe," *Speculum* 21 (1946) 49-66.

9. Warner, *The Stowe Missal*, vol. 32, xxxii-xxxvi.

10. Ibid. xxxvi-xxxviii.

11. On the origin of the litany of the saints, see E. Bishop, *Liturgica Historica* (Oxford, 1918) 137-164.

12. See E. Martène, *De Antiquis Ecclesiae Ritibus* (Antwerp, 1763), Lib. I, Cap IV. Art. XII. Ordines III, IV, VI, VII, et al. On the Mass of Illyricus, see Bourque, *Etude*, Part II, Tome II, 333-335 (#418).

13. A later editor inserted a rubric, "This prayer is sung in every mass."

14. *The Irish Liber Hymnorum*, J.H. Bernard and R. Atkinson, eds., Henry Bradshaw Society 13 (Introduction and Texts), 14 (Translations and Notes) (London, 1897, 1898), 13, 156.

MARION J. HATCHETT   167

15. Martène, *De Antiquis*, Lib. I, Cap. IV., Art. XII., Ordo III.

16. A later editor inserted a rubric, "In the solemnities of Peter and Christ." This collect is associated with feasts related to Peter in *Missale Gallicanum Vetus*, L.C. Mohlberg, ed. (Rome, 1958), Item 256; *Le sacramentaire grégorien* (hereafter designated as *Greg.* [the original portion] or *Greg. Suppl.* [the addition attributed by Deschusses to Benedict of Aniane], J. Deschusses, ed. (Fribourg, 1971), Item 64*; *Das frankische Sacramentarium Gelasianum* (Codex Sangall, No. 348) ("*St. Gall*") (Münster, 1918), Item 27; and later books.

17. *The Bobbio Missal*, E.A. Lowe, et al., eds., Henry Bradshaw Society 53 (Facsimile), 58 (Text), and 61 (Notes and Studies) (London 1917, 1920, 1924).

18. For comments on this Mass, see *The Bobbio Missal*, 61, 22-26.

19. *The Antiphonary of Bangor*, F.E. Warren, ed., Henry Bradshaw Society 4 (Introduction and Facsimile) and 10 (Text and Notes) (London, 1893, 1895), fol. 33r; *Liber Hymnorum*, fol. 14v. See Warren, *The Antiphonary of Bangor*, 10, 75-85, for commentary on Irish forms of the *Gloria in excelsis*. E. Bishop considered them the more ancient forms (*The Journal of Theological Studies* 12 [1911], 411 n.).

20. See *The Bobbio Missal*, Items 25-33; Ratcliff, ed., *Expositio* I 6; *Missale Mixtum*, Migne: PL 85.

21. M. Andrieu, *Les ordines romani du haut moyen âge*, vol. 2 (Louvain, 1960-1965) Ordo I, 53.

22. Phrases in this prayer are found in other books, generally in prayers associated with the first Thursday in Lent or with theRogation Days (See *Greg.* 158 and 863; *Corpus Ambrosiano Liturgicum I: Das Sacramentarium Triplex*, O. Heiming, ed. [Münster, 1968], in which various forms are designated as Gregorian, Gelasian, or Ambrosian, 616 [*Gel.*], 1762 [*Amb.*], and 1766; and other later books).

23. *Triplex* 1406.

24. *Liber Sacramentorum Romanae Aeclesiae Ordinis Anni Circuli* ("Gelasian" or "*Gel.*"), L.C. Mohlberg, ed. (Rome: Herder, 1968) 1133; *St. Gall* 476 and 1386; and *Triplex* 1139 (*Gel.*) and 1149 (*Amb.*).

25. *Sacramentum Veronense* ("Leonine" or "*Leon.*"), L.C.Mohlberg, ed. (Rome: Herder, 1956), 1326; *Gel.* 1138; *Greg.* 159,203, 257, 629, 721, *et al.*; *St. Gall* 393, 989, and 1453; and*Triplex* 617 and 917 (*Gel.*), 752, 933, and 2224 (*Greg.*), 2128 and 2513.

26. See F.E. Brightman, *Liturgies Eastern and Western* (reprint; Oxford, 1967) 216n.; see 210-211, 150-151.

27. Ratcliff, ed., *Expositio* I 14.

28. See G.G. Willis, *Essays in Early Roman Liturgy* (London, 1964) 21ff.

29. See L. Duchesne, *Christian Worship: Its Origin and Evolution*, 5th ed. (London, 1949) 198-201.

30. In Ordo Romanus XI 29 (Andrieu, *Ordines*) the deacon dismisses the catechumens before the reading of the gospel. The opening of the gospels in the Gelasian Sacramentary (Items 299-309) and in the Bobbio Missal (Items 174-182) may be remnants of this practice.

31. *Leon.* 523, *Gel.* 1129, *St. Gall* 1360, and *Triplex* 117.

32. See Ratcliff, *Expositio* I 8, and *Missale Mixtum*, and*Bobbio* (Item 33).

33. See, for example, *Greg. Suppl.* 1100 and *St. Gall* 123.

34. A variation of this prayer is found in *Greg. Suppl.* as a *super oblata* (1298).

35. The Armagh fragment substantiates the use of the RomanCanon in Ireland in the early ninth century. On the Stowe Canon, see Lowe, *Bobbio Missal*, vol. 61, 147-155; Bishop, *Liturgica* 77-155; J.H. Crehan, "Canon Dominicus Papae Gelasii," *Vigiliae Christianae* 12 (1958) 45-48; F.C. Burkitt, "St. Felicity in the Roman Mass," *The Journal of Theological Studies* 32 (1931) 279-287; F.E. Warren, *The Manuscript Irish Missal Belonging to the President and Fellows of Corpus Christi College* ("Corpus Missal") (London, 1879) 1-13.

36. J.A. Jungmann, *The Mass of the Roman Rite: Its Origins and Development*, 2 vols. (New York, 1951, 1955), vol. 2, 237-239.

37. Compare *Gothicum* 140 and 479; compare also inserts in theRoman Canons of *Bobbio* (16 and 17), *Le liber ordinum en usage dans l'église wisigothique et mozarabe d'Espagne du cinquième au onzième siècle* ("*Liber Ordinum*"), M. Ferotin, ed. (Paris, 1904), col. 228, and *Missale Francorum*, L.C. Mohlberg, ed. (Rome, 1957) 167 and 168.

38. For identification of the Irish saints, see Warner, *Irish Missal*, vol. 32, xxvi-xxxii.

39. See Jungmann, *Mass of the Roman Rite*, vol. 2, 260-264.

40. See, for example, *Gel.* 1181, *Greg. Suppl.* 1146, *St. Gall* 980, and *Triplex* 87 (*Amb.*) and 2126 (see 683, 2752, and 3015).

41. For identification of the Irish saints, see Warner, *Irish Missal*, vol. 32, xxiv-xxvi.

42. This prayer, with variations in the text, is found in several rites in Martène, *De Antiquis* (Lib. I. Cap. IV. Art. XII. Ordines V, VI, VII, IX, XIII, XIV, XV, XVI).

43. See *Gel.* 1178; *Greg. Suppl.* 1144; *Francorum* 121; *St. Gall*976; and *Triplex* 69 (*Amb.*) and 2122. In most cases it is in a Mass which includes the first of the Stowe postcommunion prayers, but in *Triplex* 69 (*Amb.*) it is in a Mass which includes the second of the Stowe postcommunion forms.

44. This prayer, with variations, is found in the Book of Cerne (see Kenney, *Sources*, vol. 1, 221), and in Illyricus and several other orders printed in Martène, *De Antiquis* (Lib. I Cap. IV. Art. XII. Ordines V, VI, XIII, XVI).

45. Jungmann, *Mass of the Roman Rite*, vol. 2, 68, says that this form was introduced into the Roman Rite from the Gallican. It is in Illyricus (Martène, *De Antiquis* (Lib. I. Cap. IV. Art. XII. Ordo IV).

46. See E.G.C.F. Atchley, *A History of the Use of Incense in Divine Worship* (London, 1909) 247-251. See J.W. Legg, *Ecclesiological Essays* (London, 1905) 91-178, on the place of the preparation of the elements in various rites.

47. On the place of the commemoration of the departed, see Bishop, *Liturgica* 96-103, 109-115.

48. See, for example, *Missale Gothicum* 1, 172, 177, 182, 188,193, 294, 365, 370, 376, 391, 437, and the Mozarabic *Missale Mixtum*, cols. 225, 286, 346, 415, 483.

49. See, for example, *Missale Gothicum* 1, 128, 230, 238, and 242.

50. *Cod. Vat. lat.* 4770 and *Cod. Ratisbonensis* (*Ephemerides Liturgicae* 74 [1960] 103-114). Some of the expressions occur in the Roman Good Friday Reproaches and others in the proper preface of the Holy Trinity in the Roman Rite.

51. Compare also *Gothicum* 4 and 482 and *Missale Mixtum*, col. 189.

52. The St. Gall fragment 1394 has several prayers between the *Sanctus* and the

Ante Orationem Dominicam which must have served as post-*Sanctus* or as post-*secreta*.

53. The scribe apparently omitted the last half of a commemoration for Epiphany and the first half of one for Maundy Thursday.

54. See Neale and Littledale, *Liturgies* 193-247.

55. *Gothicum* 516; compare *Gothicum* 19 and forms in Mozarabic books, *Liber Ordinum*, cols. 271, 321, 374, 398, 407, and 428, and *Missale Mixtum*, cols. 162, 986, 1009, and 1031.

56. See. G.G. Willis, *Further Essays in Early Roman Liturgy* (London, 1968) 167-170, and H.B. Porter, Jr., *The Ordination Prayers of the Ancient Western Churches* (London, 1967) 76-93.

57. It is also very close to that of the Bobbio *Missa Romensis cotidiana* (Item 21) and *Triplex* Item 1366b. Contrast the Gallican *Collectio ante orationem Dominicam* of the seventh-century palimpsest sacramentary and of the Deer, Dimma, and Mulling fragments. (The text used as protocol to the Lord's Prayer in the Stowe Missal introduces the Creed in the Dimma fragment.)

58. The same text is found in the rite for the sick of the Stowe Missal except that the response is "Amen." The Dimma fragment follows the embolism with a blessing, "The peace and love of our Lord Jesus Christ be always with us." The peace is then exchanged as the priest says, "The peace and communion of your saints, O Jesus Christ, be always with us" to which the communicant responds "Amen."

59. Ratcliff, *Expositio* I 26.

60. See, for example, *Missale Mixtum*, cols. 115 and 546.

61. See, for example, the Deer fragment, "May the Body with (*cum*) the Blood of our Lord Jesus Christ be health and salvation to you unto life everlasting," or the Mulling fragment, "May the Body with (*cum*) the Blood of our Lord Jesus Christ be to you health unto eternal life."

62. op. cit., vol. 2, 372.

63. Neale and Littledale, *Liturgies* 59. Though the *Agnus Dei* had been appointed to be sung here in the Roman Rite by Sergius (687-701), it is not found in the Stowe Rite except inthe initial litany. Several commentators on the rite have mistaken this *Ecce Agnus* for the other *Agnus Dei*.

64. Sixteen of the twenty-two texts are included among the communion chants of the St. Gall fragment 1394. One is included as an antiphon at the Peace in the *Antiphonary of Bangor*, and four others as communion chants. The *Antiphonary of Bangor* also includes a metrical hymn for use at the time of communion (for an English translation, see *The Hymnal* 1982, 327 or 328).

65. One text includes three Alleluias.

66. The St. Gall fragment 1394 also includes, without Alleluias, the *incipits* of Psalms 23, 24, and 43.

67. In the St. Gall fragment 1394 one refrain is designated for each of the four principal feasts, Christmas, Epiphany, Easter, and Pentecost. None of these texts is, however, among those of the Stowe Missal.

68. John 14:27; Psalm 119:165; Psalm 96:1(?); Proverbs 9:5; John 6:56; John 6:58; Psalm 78:24-25; Song of Solomon 5:1; Psalm 119:171; Psalm 34:1; Psalm 34:8; John

12:26; Matthew 19:14; Matthew 3:2; Matthew 11:12; and Matthew 25:34.

69. *The Treatise on the Mass* bound with the Stowe Missal refers explicitly to the communing of infants, and the twelfth-century *Corpus Missal* indicates the continuation of the practice (fol. 203a).

70. The other refrain for which this author cannot find a scriptural reference is: "King of heaven with peace, Alleluia, full of the odor of life, Alleluia."

71. Compare *Missale Mixtum*, cols. 316, 343, 377, 564-565, et al.

72. Ratcliff, *Expositio* I 28.

73. *St. Gall* 1302 and *Triplex* 2646 (*Gel.*).

74. Compare *Greg.* 197 and 229 and *Triplex* 735 and 840 (*Greg.*) and 834.

75. Some commentators have likened this to the "Collect over the Gospel" of the Turin fragment (See Kenney, *Sources*, vol. 1, 712-713) and of the *Antiphonary of Bangor*, items 65, 74, 79, 84, and 85. In the antiphonaries, however, this title apparently refers to the gospel canticle, the *Benedictus Dominus Deus*.

76. The prayer which follows the vesting prayer is to be sung in every Mass, the prayer which follows that is to be sung "in the solemnities of Peter and Christ," and the prayer which precedes the epistle "is said daily for those who sin."

77. The initial litany ("The Litany of Holy Apostles and Martyrs and Confessors and Virgins"), the vesting prayer ("Prayer of Augustine"), the *Gloria in excelsis* ("Hymn of the Angels"),the prayer which follows the *Gloria in excelsis* ("Prayers and supplications for mercy of the Roman Church"), the gradual, and the Alleluia.

78. Warner, *The Stowe Missal*, vol. 32, xxxix.

79. See *Missale Mixtum*.

80. Compare, for example, the number of forms from the Stowe Missal found in *The Leofric Missal As Used in the Cathedral of Exeter During the Episcopate of Its First Bishop A.D. 1050-1072*, F.E. Warren, ed. (Oxford, 1883) and *The Sarum Missal Edited from Three Early Manuscripts*, J.W. Legg, ed. (Oxford, 1916) with the number found in the first printed Roman Missal, *Missale Romanum, Milan, 1494*, R. Lippe, ed. (London, 1899). See also Legg, *Ecclesiological Essays* 91-178.

11

Hispanic Influences on Worship in the English Tongue

H. Boone Porter

TO CONSIDER THE WORSHIP OF ENGLISH-SPEAKING PEOPLES FROM A HISPANIC perspective may be surprising. Yet Spain, the historic rival of Great Britain, has contributed much to both public liturgy and private devotion in the English tongue. The present essay will not concern itself with the "Spanish symptoms" felt in the medieval Latin liturgy of the British Isles,[1] but rather with how Hispanic influence was felt in the sixteenth century in the Book of Common Prayer, how it was felt in certain later compilations, and then how in modern times a new wave of influence has been felt. This latter stage has been of a highly ecumenical nature, and those features which have affected Anglican worship have also affected versions of Roman Catholic, Lutheran, Reformed, and other rites published in the English language in recent years and in many other languages.

The Breviary of Quignon

Although some liturgical material appeared in English at earlier dates, vernacular public worship in this language on a comprehensive basis begins in 1549 with the First Book of Common Prayer of which Archbishop Thomas Cranmer is considered to have been the editor and principal compiler. This book begins with a famous preface, "There was never any thing by the wit of man so well devised, or so sure established, which in continuance of time hath not been corrupted ... " This preface reappears in many subsequent revisions of the Book of Common Prayer, or Prayer Book, as it is generally known.[2] Although this preface is primarily an introduction to the English translation and revision of the "divine service" or daily office, it sets the tone for the whole book.

This preface itself is largely a translation or paraphrase of the Latin preface which was used to introduce a drastic revision of the Roman breviary by Cranmer's older contemporary, Cardinal Francisco Quignonez—generally known in English as Quignon. The importance of this preface for the Prayer Book is not in the number of sentences Cranmer took from Quignon but rather in what it says, the outlook it expresses, and the goals which it sets up.

Knowledge of Quignon and his liturgical work is, for English-speaking readers at least, inextricably bound to the name of John Wickham Legg (1843-1922), the distinguished British physician and liturgiologist[3] who devoted many years to the pursuit of every detail of the Quignonian breviary.[4] Although Quignon was one of the most eminent and famous men of his time, many details of his life remain unknown. He was born in Spain about 1485. As a youth, he is said to have been a page to Cardinal Ximenez of Toledo (see below). As a young man he joined the Franciscan Order and was noted for his piety and devotion. By 1523 he was elected general of the order and in the subsequent years was involved in many important affairs of church and state, as with the negotiations between the pope and the emperor and the controversy over the marriage of Henry VIII in England. He is believed to have been made a cardinal in 1527 and was probably consecrated a bishop two or three years after that. He died at Veroli in Italy in 1540.

Meanwhile he was appointed by Pope Clement VII to revise the breviary and did so, it appears, primarily with the assistance of three Spanish colleagues whose names were known, in the Latin style of the time, as Didacus Neyla, Joannes Genesius Sepulveda, and Gaspar a Castro. Quignon had no personal background or experience in liturgical scholarship but, as Wickham Legg wryly observed, Clement VII, like many modern church leaders, "appears to have considered that great piety and considerable experience in affairs are the only qualifications needful for the successful undertaking of liturgical reform."[5]

Of what did the Quignonian revision consist? The breviary contained, as is well known, the "hours" or services of prayer which clergy and members of religious orders were bound to recite, in public or private, at intervals during the day. The medieval breviaries provided beautiful but very complicated services. Quignon and his co-workers undertook to rationalize the whole scheme. Three psalms (or three sections of psalms) were assigned to each hour of prayer each day, with the whole psalter being covered in a week. Nothing interrupted this cycle, not even Christmas or All Saints' Day. Sequential biblical passages were assigned for reading day by day, so that much of the Bible was read every year. Antiphons, responsories, and other items that had given charm and quaintness to the office were abandoned. All this is explained briefly in the preface.

As is seen in the sentence quoted above, "There was never any thing," Quignon and Cranmer accepted a new view of history. In the Middle Ages much of life was seen as fixed: change came mainly in the sense of accumulation. The churchmen of the Renaissance, however, saw that things change. What is good at one time may not be good at some other time. We have power to alter things, and we are periodically obliged to do so. Quignon and Cranmer, and many other learned men of their time also agreed on the importance of Scripture for divine service. Instruction, as well as prayer and praise, was seen as a major factor in daily worship.

Quignon's breviary was first published in 1535 and quickly went through several editions. It was followed by a storm of protest from professors at the Sorbonne in Paris and others. A slightly moderated second edition appeared the next year, in which the preface also had some revision. This edition showed its popularity in over a hundred editions until its use was suppressed in the 1560s by Pope Pius V. It was clearly demonstrated that given the option of using such a breviary thousands of clergy chose to do so. They carried it to Central and South America, Asia, and Africa.

Meanwhile, in England Archbishop Cranmer was experimenting with the revision of the daily office. His use of Quignon's preface was perceived by few in the sixteenth century.[6] He carried Quignon's principles to the radical extreme of consolidating the daily offices into two services, morning prayer or matins, and evening prayer or evensong, with bible readings in course as a major element in both. Early drafts of his work were discovered by Edmond Bishop. These included an adaptation of Quignon's preface, still in Latin, which was analyzed by Bishop,[7] and later by Wickham Legg.[8]

It is to be noted that Cranmer did not base either his drafts or his final rendition of matins and evensong on the exact contents of the Quignonian breviary. He used his own creativity and other sources, such as the primers, or lay peoples' books of hours, then widely current in England, and the compilations of Continental reformers. Yet it was the Spanish prelate's principles which were followed in a rationalized order, an abandonment of many aesthetic details, and a systematic reading of Scripture. Unlike the Reformers who generally expected some flexibility in worship and variation from place to place, Cranmer followed the Catholic concept of a consistent disciplined uniformity.

In the divine service or office of the Prayer Book, Cranmer achieved results which must exceed what were his wildest expectations. Unlike any of the other Catholic or Protestant reformers of the sixteenth century, Thomas Cranmer created a round of daily services which, after four hundred years, are still popular in public worship, which have been translated into many languages, and which are widely if not universally recited each day by the clergy as well as being used by devout lay people. Modern revisions have in fact restored some of the variety and seasonality which Cranmer had suppressed, but his basic pattern remains in Anglican Prayer Books the world over.

The Mozarabic Rite

The other line of Hispanic influence on the Book of Common Prayer, and more recently on many Protestant and Catholic liturgies, is the ancient indigenous Latin liturgy of Spain known as the Mozarabic or Visigothic Rite. Developing in Spain from early times, it was commented upon by the great Saints Isidore and Ildefonsus and used throughout the colorful and adventurous years of Moorish occupation. It continued in use until Spain became more closely linked with the rest of Western Europe in the eleventh century. Thereafter it continued in partial use in Toledo and no doubt a few other places. In the early sixteenth century, the distinguished cardinal, Francisco Jimenez de Cisneros (generally known in English as Ximenez), Archbishop of Toledo, undertook to have surviving manuscripts collected, consolidated and printed. Edited, perhaps not always correctly, by Canon Alfonso Ortiz, the material appeared in print as the *Missale Mixtum* (Toledo, 1500) and the *Breviarium Secundum Regulam Beati Isidori* (Toledo, 1502). The missal was subsequently reedited by the learned Scottish Jesuit, Alexander Lesley, in 1755. His edition was reprinted later as Volume 85 of Migne's *Patrologia Latina*.

A revision of the printed books of Toledo was again undertaken in the late eighteenth century by Francisco Antonio de Lorenzana. Born in Leon in 1722, he became a canon in Toledo. In 1766 Charles III appointed him archbishop of Mexico, where he quickly distinguished himself by his zeal and his support of learning and of charity. In 1772 he was recalled to be archbishop of Toledo and became a cardinal in 1789. Bringing out a selection of Mozarabic services in Mexico, *Missa Gothica* (Los Angeles, 1770), he went on to revise the breviary in Toledo, adding manuscript material. This book, entitled *Breviarium Gothicum* (Madrid, 1775) was later reprinted as Volume 86 of Migne's *Patrologia Latina*. His revision of the Missal of Toledo appeared later. It was conjectured by Bishop Coxe (see below) that Lorenzana hoped to introduce the Mozarabic Rite into Mexico. After a generous and commendable career, he died in Rome in 1804.

During the past hundred years other texts have been discovered and edited by Marius Férotin, O.S.B., and others.[9]

The Gallican Rite originally used north of the Pyrennees was closely related to that of Spain, but was not so well organized and it generally was superseded by the Roman Rite in the eighth century. Surviving documents are mostly incomplete. The Ambrosian Rite of Milan, and related usages formerly followed in some other North Italian centers, also exhibit many links with Spain.

The peculiarity of the Mozarabic Rite, and of the no longer extant rite of Gaul, is that almost every prayer changes on every liturgical occasion. Hence, in the printed and manuscript sources of Spain, there is a corpus of thousands of prayers, exceeding anything else in western liturgy. Some are very beautiful and theologically rich compositions. This ancient rite, with its romantic associations, has bequeathed several prayers here and there to editions of the Book of Common Prayer and to various devotional publications. More importantly, in recent years this ancient rite has provided important structural principles. There has also been some revival of its use at conferences and meetings.

In older editions of the Book of Common Prayer, there is but one item taken from Mozarabic sources: the series of four short "supplications," each followed by Amen, which make the transition in the baptismal liturgy from the vows of the candidate (or sponsors) to the blessing of the font. The basis of these, as has often been noted, was in the series of eight such supplications which occurred at the blessing of the font in the First Book of Common Prayer (1549).[10] Commentators on the Prayer Book in the seventeenth and eighteenth centuries do not seem to know their ultimate origin, but by the mid-nineteenth century they were widely recognized as coming from a Gallican or Mozarabic source.[11]

We possess two earlier Latin versions of the supplications. One is in the *Missale Gallicanum Vetus*, an incomplete Gallican sacramentary dating from the seventh or eighth century.[12] In accordance with Gallican custom, the blessing of the font is called a *contestatio* and is preceded by *sursum corda*. After some introductory clauses, we find a long series of supplications, all as a single prayer, unbroken by Amens. This stately composition, assimilating so well the imagery of the New Testament, must be far older than the final stage of the Gallican Rite, and would appear to date from the sixth or even late fifth century.

The second Latin source is a thousand years later, namely the printed

Missale Mixtum of Toledo, where this material appears at the blessing of the font in the Great Vigil of Easter.[13]

Following Mozarabic custom, the blessing of the font has no *Sursum corda*. After the introductory clauses comes the series of supplications, each with Amen. Such interjected Amens are characteristic of the later stages of the Mozarabic Rite, but it cannot be denied that they are extremely appropriate with this powerful procession of petitions. The text of the supplications and the ending are slightly different from that of the earlier Gallican version. It may also be noted that neither of these represents the only form of *benedictio fontis* in their respective territories.

The use of the repeated Amens makes it undeniable that the English compiler drew from a Spanish source or sources. This is confirmed by similarity to the conclusion of the Spanish form. On the other hand, at points the English text resembles the older Gallican version. We are driven to conclude that the English reformers had a Mozarabic manuscript unknown to later scholarship which had preserved a text earlier than that used in the *Missale Mixtum*.[14]

The four supplications of the English baptismal liturgy, with their repeated Amens, provide a short but striking liturgical form, unlike anything else in the English Prayer Book. It may be an occasion for regret that recent revisions in different parts of the Anglican Communion have abandoned this formulary. In the Episcopal Church in the United States, a fuller translation of the version in the *Missale Mixtum* (with thirteen Amens) in modern English is provided as a prayer for persons to be baptized in *The Book of Occasional Services*.[15] It is also interesting that prayers in the form of the supplications have now been introduced in the American Book of Common Prayer (1979) in the wedding service[16] with nine Amens and in a form of the burial service[17] with ten Amens.

Other Collections of Prayers

When Queen Elizabeth I of England came to the throne, the English Book of Common Prayer reached a stable form. Apart from internal editorial emendations, and a few additions from other Anglican sources, it remained virtually the same until the modern era. Hence there was no further Hispanic influence during this period of four centuries. The same may be said of the somewhat different Scottish and American Prayer Books. Yet, while the Book of Common Prayer remained fixed, Anglican interest in liturgical development did not cease. The official book was supplemented, as the medieval missal and breviary had been, by various books for private use and also by unofficial proposals for liturgical reform.[18] Such books are commonly eclectic and may draw on Hispanic as well as other sources.

Apparently the first Anglican writer explicitly to commend translations of Mozarabic prayers was Jeremy Taylor (1613-1667). One of the school of theological writers known as the Caroline Divines, he is usually considered the greatest English author of devotional books. In the middle period of his life, the Puritan government of Oliver Cromwell had unseated the Anglican hierarchy and banned the use of the Book of Common Prayer. Taylor's response was to compile and publish a liturgical book of his own, *A Collection of Offices*, in 1658.[19] This book was intended to be sufficiently different from the Prayer Book to be legal, but sufficiently similar to provide for the broad fabric of traditional Anglican daily and weekly worship. A second edition appeared in 1690.

This book was introduced by a lengthy preface, most of which was later used for the tract *An Apology for Authorized and Set Forms of Liturgy*, and it is printed with this latter in the nineteenth century editions of Taylor's works. It is only the last two paragraphs of this preface (nos. 48 and 49) which pertain exclusively to the *Collection of Offices*.[20] Here it is stated that the prayers "are (especially in the chiefest offices) collected out of the devotions of the Greek church, with some mixture of the Mozarabic and Aethiopic, and other liturgies, and perfected out of the fountains of scripture." He later speaks of the continued use of the Mozarabic Rite "in six parishes in Toledo, and in the cathedral church itself in the chapel of Friar Francis Ximenes; and at Salamanca, upon certain days."

Unfortunately, Taylor gives no hints as to which prayers come from which sources. Many are identifiable as translations from the Greek, and many come from Taylor's own previously published works.[21] So far, among the dozens of prayers in Taylor's *Collection*, none have yielded satisfactory identification with any of the thousands of prayers in the surviving Mozarabic corpus.

It is different with one of the greatest nineteenth-century English manuals of prayer, *Ancient Collects and Other Prayers*, translated by William Bright (1824-1901).[22] This went through many editions extending into the present century. It contains prayers, grouped according to topic or occasion, translated from the Greek Rite and from the Roman, Ambrosian, Gallican, and Mozarabic books. There are dozens of Hispanic selections. The provenance is noted for each prayer but usually no more specific reference.

The success of Bright's book inspired a learned American Episcopal priest, the Rev. Charles R. Hale, later bishop of Cairo, Illinois (within the Diocese of Springfield), to publish a handbook consisting entirely of translated Mozarabic prayers, *Mozarabic Collects from the Ancient Liturgy of the Spanish Church*.[23] Here we find collects for the church year and various occasions, and a morning and evening office, "for daily family prayer."[24] A commendatory preface by the scholarly Bishop of Western New York, Arthur Cleveland Coxe, American editor of the *Ante-Nicene Fathers*, indicates his own interest in the Mozarabic Liturgy as arising from his contact with the Iglesia de Jesus, the Mexican reform movement which ultimately identified itself with the Episcopal Church. He expresses his hope that the Mexican church might base its liturgy on Mozarabic sources, utilizing the work of Dr. Hale, who had also compiled orders for the holy eucharist and baptism.

The erudite prelate's hopes soon came to fruition, at least briefly. In 1895 appeared a diminutive bilingual volume, *Oficios Provisionales de la Iglesia Episcopal Mexicana ó Iglesia de Jesús.*[25] This was an official publication, commended by the Episcopal presiding bishop, John Williams, who declared the contents mostly from the Mozarabic Rite and "in harmony with the Catholic faith." We find here Hale's morning and evening services in Spanish and English,[26] collects for the church year, and orders for the eucharist, baptism, and confirmation. The eucharistic rite in this little and long forgotten book was perhaps the most liturgically advanced form to be adopted by any part of the Anglican Communion in that era. It contained an Old Testament lesson, the peace before the *Sursum corda*, and other Mozarabic features, although not using multiple eucharistic prayers.[27] It would be interesting to know the extent to which this rite was used by Spanish or English speaking congregations and whether recent revisers have had any awareness of it.

Various anthologies and collections of prayers in English have continued to include, on a modest scale, selections from the Mozarabic Rite. It is a source not likely to be exhausted.

Revision of the Daily Offices

The distinguished American Episcopal priest, William Reed Huntington (1888-1909), centonized material from the prayers in Bright's morning and evening sections and composed a beautiful morning and evening collect which were not admitted into the American Prayer Book of 1892, but in the 1928 revision they found a place in the Additional Prayers section at the end of the book.[28] In the present American Book of Common Prayer, 1979, Huntington's collects, entitled "A Collect for the Renewal of Life"[29] and "A Collect for Protection"[30] are in morning and evening prayer respectively. As an examination of Bright's prayers shows, Huntington's material came in part from Mozarabic selections.[31] Having conspicuous places in the daily office, these must be among the most frequently used prayers in the American Prayer Book.

A prayer which came quite directly from Spain to the American Prayer Book is the evening prayer, "O Lord God Almighty, as you have taught us to call the evening, the morning, and the noonday one day."[32] In the *Breviarium Gothicum* this is given for daily use at the end of vespers.[33]

Here, however, it is not a question of one prayer, but rather of the entire office entitled An Order of Worship for the Evening, beginning with its Mozarabic salutation, "Light and peace, in Jesus Christ our Lord."[34] The concept of a relatively brief evening service, beginning with the ceremonial action of bringing in or lighting candles or lamps, was directly inspired by the Mozarabic vespers. The contents of the service, however, have been left flexible, and they may be fitted into the regular Episcopal lectionary *cursus* of psalms and readings. In accordance with the recent scholarly awareness of the distinction between the ancient cathedral or secular choir office, and the monastic office, the Order of Worship for the Evening provides an intentional example of the former. It is a significant case of Hispanic influence in the American Book of Common Prayer. Similar arrangements are appearing in other liturgical books, as *The Lutheran Book of Worship*[35] and *The Book of Alternative Services* of the Anglican Church of Canada.[36] Here again, it is not so much in specific words as in broad principles that the Hispanic influence is felt.

Many advanced students of liturgy in different churches would also wish it to be gratefully recorded that their personal introduction to such an evening service was at a chapel in the University Church of Notre Dame University in Indiana where such a service of evensong, compiled by William G. Storey, has commended itself to a generation of worshipers.[37]

Revised Eucharistic Liturgies

In the first part of the eucharistic rite of virtually any Western Christian community which follows historic liturgical forms, we today frequently find that the first biblical reading is from the Old Testament. Such a change is astonishing when we reflect that a quarter of a century ago, such a situation was quite unknown. In the historic Roman lectionary, from which Lutheran and Anglican lectionaries were derived, an Old Testament reading occurred in the eucharist only on the rarest occasions, and on these occasions the epistle was omitted.

This has been a matter of fundamental importance for liturgical reform in the second half of the twentieth century. As soon as one has an Old Testament lesson, epistle, and gospel, together with interspersed psalmody, the vision arises of having the Ministry of the Word present the Bible in an wholistic and fully representative way.

The next step was the formulations of the three year lectionary by Roman Catholic scholars which was published after the Second Vatican Council and subsequently adopted, with some modifications, by many other church bodies.

It is the lectionary of the Mozarabic Rite, of the less well documented ancient Gallican Rite, and of the Ambrosian Rite of Milan, which provided the traditional foundation which inspired the adoption of three readings. The Mozarabic arrangement, as it is formulated in the printed *Missale Mixtum*, regularly provides an Old Testament lesson, some psalmody, epistle and gospel for Sundays and holydays. On Sundays in Lent the use of the Old Testament is massive, with a passage from the Wisdom literature, then a long episode from a historical book, prior to the epistle. In the paschal season, as at Milan, a lesson from Acts is read.[38] In Spain, but not in Milan, a reading from Revelation also occurs in this season when the Old Testament is dropped—a feature adopted in the third year of the new lectionary. The Spanish influence is thus obvious. As in some new compilations, the Spanish Rite numbers the Sundays of the Easter Season with Easter Day as the first, Saint Thomas Sunday as the second, and so forth. In all of the ancient Western lectionaries, the great signs from Saint John's Gospel are used on most of the Sundays of Lent, a tradition preserved mainly in the first year of the new lectionary.

A notable Mozarabic and Gallican characteristic that has provided traditional precedent for contemporary usage has been the highly changeable eucharistic prayer. The revised Roman Rite, and also the Episcopal Prayer Book, each confine themselves basically to four *Preces Eucharisticae*, and some other churches in America have similar arrangements. The United Methodist Church, however, now has a distinct prayer for every season and major occasion.[39]

In closing we will call attention to two specific eucharistic items in the present American Prayer Book. Form V of the Prayers of the People[40] was translated and adapted, mainly by Howard Galley, from a contemporary form used by Hispanic worshipers in the United States.[41] It is based on early eastern models. This beautiful litany is further adapted in the rites for ordination.[42]

Finally there is the famous prayer *Adesto, adesto*—"Be present, O Jesus, our great High Priest, as you were present with your disciples, and be known to us in the breaking of bread; who live and reign with the Father and the Holy Spirit, now and for ever. Amen."[43]

Given in this Episcopal source as a prayer of preparation for holy communion, it indisputably comes from the Liturgy of South India, where it is a congregational offertory prayer.[44] It was taken for the latter purpose also in the liturgy of the Consultation on Church Union, but altered so as to be addressed to the Father: "Heavenly Father, may the Lord Jesus Christ ... be present."[45] But what is its earlier source?

Adesto, adesto first appears as a silent sacerdotal devotion immediately preceding the narrative of the Last Supper in the *Missale Mixtum*.[46] The Latin form concludes, however, not with a reference to the breaking of bread but rather a petition for the consecration of the oblation. How did this prayer get to India and who changed the petition to the language of Luke 24:35? Those who have read this far will not be astonished to learn that Bright had translated the prayer, but abbreviated the ending of it.[47] It can hardly be doubted that the South India compilers were introduced to it by Bright, but added their own striking ending.[48]

We are still not at the ultimate origin of this unusual ecumenical prayer. It need hardly be said that such a prayer, interjected at such a solemn point, was no part of the ancient classic Mozarabic Rite. It is here proposed that it is an abbreviation of a longer prayer which followed the words of institution in an older Mozarabic Mass for Maundy Thursday which had gone out of use.[49] It entered the rite at Toledo sometime in between the eleventh and the sixteenth century, and hence appeared in the sources for the printed *Missale Mixtum*. Although this prayer was a latecomer to the Mozarabic Rite, it is a striking expression of the eucharistic presence of Christ in a manner acceptable to both Reformed and Catholic Christians. Invoking our Lord as High Priest is a felicitous enrichment of liturgical speech in English.[50]

Conclusion

Liturgy develops under the influence of many diverse factors: theological, devotional, political, sociological and linguistic—not to mention sheer fashion. Hispanic elements have entered the prayer life of English speaking Christians sometimes because of, and sometimes seemingly in spite of, these varied currents. Two factors stand out, however. First is the fact that the Mozarabic liturgy was and is the only complete ancient and western liturgy which is quite different from the Roman and which is adequately documented and still performed. It is thus a unique and vast mine from which to draw material. Secondly there is the extraordinary religious energy of Spain during the first half of the sixteenth century. From this came the modern codification and printing of the ancient Mozarabic Rite, and also the Quignonian reform of the Roman breviary. The publication of the Complutensian Polyglot version of the Bible (commissioned by Cardinal Ximenez), the founding of the Society of Jesus, and the spirituality of Saint John of the Cross and Saint Teresa of Avila all come from the same era. The people of Spain, and the peoples of the Spanish colonies, have left indelible marks on the history of Western Christianity. English speaking Christians have benefited in many ways, not least in their forms of public and private worship.[51]

Notes

1. See Edmund Bishop, *Liturgica Historica* (Oxford, 1918) 165ff.

2. In the U.S., see The Book of Common Prayer (New York, 1979) and subsequent printings (hereafter abbreviated BCP 1979) 866-867.

3. *Dictionary of National Biography*, supplement 1912-21, 330-331.

4. John Wickham Legg, *Breviarium Romanum a Francisco Cardinali Quignonio Editum* (Cambridge, 1888); *The Second Recension of the Quignon Breviary*, vol. 1, Henry Bradshaw Society 35 (1908) (Text); vol. 2, H.B.S. 42 (1912) (Liturgical Introduction, Life of Quignon, etc.).

5. *Second Recension*, vol. 2, 14.

6. Ibid. 78.

7. Abbot Gasquet and Edmund Bishop, *Edward the Sixth and the Book of Common Prayer*, 3d ed. (London, n.d.) 16ff, 356ff.

8. J. Wickham Legg, *Cranmer's Liturgical Projects*, Henry Bradshaw Society 50 (1915) 168ff.

9. The principal sources are still conveniently summarized by W.C. Bishop, *The Mozarabic and Ambrosian Rites*, Alcuin Club Tracts 15 (London, 1924).

10. This was not part of the regular public baptismal rite but was for use once a month when the water in the font was changed.

11. William Palmer, *Origines Liturgicae* (Oxford, 1832) ad loc. and John Henry Blunt, *The Annotated Book of Common Prayer*, editions since 1866, ad loc.

12. A convenient edition is *Missale Gallicanum Vetus*, Leo Eizenhofer, O.S.B. and Petrus Siffrin, O.S.B., eds. (Rome, 1958) 41.

13. Migne's *Patrologia Latina*, (hereafter abbreviated PL) 85:465-467.

14. This is also the conclusion of Bishop Frere, see Francis Procter and Walter Howard Frere, *New History of the Book of Common Prayer*, many editions, ad loc.

15. *The Book of Occasional Services* (New York, 1988) 128-129.

16. American Book of Common Prayer 429-430.

17. Ibid. 480-481.

18. It has been characteristic of Anglican history that there has not always been a clear line of demarcation between personal manuals and proposals for additions or changes in the official public rites.

19. Among the nineteenth-century editions of Taylor's *Works*, Reginald Heber's edition (London, 1822) vol. 15, 237ff.

20. Ibid. vol. 7, 313-314.

21. See H. Boone Porter, *Jeremy Taylor, Liturgist*, Alcuin Club Collections 61 (1979) passim.

22. *Ancient Collects and Other Prayers* (Oxford and London, 1862).

23. *Mozarabic Collects from the Ancient Liturgy of the Spanish Church* (New York, 1881).

24. Ibid. 52ff.

25. Place of publication not indicated.

26. Ibid. 3ff.

27. Ibid. 60ff.

28. Ibid., Marion J. Hatchett, *Commentary on the American Prayer Book* (New York, 1980) 126 and 143.

29. American Book of Common Prayer 56 and 99.

30. Ibid. 70 and 124.

31. Op. cit., eighth edition, 1908, esp. 8 and 11. The morning prayer, which was one ingredient in Huntington's great collect, will be found in Latin in PL 86:58, and elsewhere. For the Latin of the evening prayer, ibid. col. 705.

32. Op cit. 110.

33. PL 86:50 and 1012. For an English translation of a service including this prayer, W.C. Bishop, *The Mozarabic and Ambrosian Rites* 70-5.

34. BCP 1979, 109. For a skillfully edited amplification of this rite, *The Prayer Book Office*, Howard Galley, ed. (New York, 1980 and 1988) 58ff. This includes *lucernaria*, or anthems for the lamp-lighting, from *The Book of Occasional Services* 8ff.

35. *The Lutheran Book of Worship* (Minneapolis and Philadelphia, 1978) 142ff.

36. *The Book of Alternative Services* (Toronto, 1985) 60ff and 685ff. The Mozarabic evening order is not the only source of influence in such rites. In this Canadian book the forms given for public evensong (60ff) represent a modern adaption of material from the ancient church orders.

37. *Morning Prayer and Evensong*, compiled by William S. Storey and others (South Bend, Indiana, 1973).

38. *Documents on the Liturgy, 1963-1979*, Commission on English in the Liturgy (Collegeville, 1985) 569: "After Low Sunday there is a semicontinuous reading of Acts that derives from both the Western (Ambrosian, Hispanic) and the Eastern tradition."

39. For a discussion and extensive bibliographical data, see James F. White in chap. 5 of *New Eucharistic Prayers*, Frank C. Senn, ed. (New York, 1987).

40. American Prayer Book 389-391.

41. *Santa Misa: Accion de Gracias de la Comunidad Cristiana*, Arquidiocesis de Nueva York (New York, 1965) 16-19.

42. BCP 1979, 548-551.

43. Ibid. 834.

44. Marion J. Hatchett, *Commentary on the American Prayer Book* (New York, 1980) 569; *The Book of Common Worship* (London and Madras, 1963) 14.

45. *An Order of Worship* (Cincinnati, 1968) 28, 66.

46. PL 85:116, 550.

47. *Ancient Collects* 142.

48. See also T.S. Garrett, *The Liturgy of the Church of South India: An Introduction and Commentary* (Oxford and Madras, 1952) 58.

49. *Liber Mozarabicus Sacramentorum*, Marius Férotin, ed. (Paris, 1912) the great eleventh-century source, contains two Masses for Maundy Thursday. The first

(very long), col. 234-240, contains the formula to which we refer, no. 579, "Adesto quesumus, Domine Jhesu Christe, medius inter seruulos." The second shorter Mass, col. 240-245, which does not have this formula, is the one retained in *Missale Mixtum*, PL 85: 406-421.

50. In BCP 1979, this prayer seems to have influenced the diction of the latter part of Eucharistic Prayer C, 372.

51. Although the translation or adaptation of the Prayer Book in Spanish is not the topic of this essay, readers may be interested in chapter XV, "Liturgia Anglicana en Espanol," in David E. Bergesen, *Manual de Liturgia* (Quito, Ecuador, 1988) which discusses Spanish versions of the Book of Common Prayer.

12

The Ascension and the Vicarious Humanity of Christ: The Christology and Soteriology Behind the Church of Scotland's Anamnesis and Epiklesis

Bryan D. Spinks

WITH REGARD TO THE DOGMATIC IMPLICATIONS OF THE ASCENSION KARL Barth wrote:

> Christ is now, as the Bearer of humanity, as our Representative, in the place where God is and in the way in which God is. Our flesh, our human nature, is exalted in Him to God. The end of His work is that we are with Him above. We with Him beside God.[1]

But also, as he noted elsewhere:

> It is the movement initiated by the fact that there took place first the opposite movement from God to man, from heaven to earth, and therefore from above to below, and that it still takes place and is an event in the person of this One.[2]

Although as Thomas Talley has recently documented, the ascension did not emerge as a distinct festival in its own right before the penultimate decade of the fourth century,[3] the event which the feast celebrates is of paramount importance; it is the *katabasis* of God and the *anabasis* of saved and redeemed humanity, which are at the heart of the doctrine of the incarnation. It is these Christological and soteriological implications of the ascension which stand firmly behind the anamnesis and epiklesis of the main eucharistic prayer of the Church of Scotland's *Book of Common Order* (BCO) 1940 and 1979:

> Wherefore, having in remembrance the work and passion of our Saviour Christ, and pleading His eternal sacrifice, we thy servants set forth this memorial, which He hath commanded us to make; and we most humbly beseech Thee to send down Thy Holy Spirit to sanctify both us and these Thine own gifts of bread and wine which we set before Thee, that the bread which we break may be the Communion of the body of Christ, and the cup of blessing which we bless the Communion of the blood of Christ.

The concern of this essay is to map out the theological rationale of this anamnesis and epiklesis, with particular reference to "pleading His eternal sacrifice," and to demonstrate that despite criticism from certain Anglican Evangelicals, it is a theology which is Reformed, biblical, in accord with early catholic theology, and is ecumenical.

The Liturgical Origins of "Pleading His Eternal Sacrifice"

The phrase "pleading His eternal sacrifice" is found first in the Church of Scotland in the first order of communion in the 1940 BCO.[4] Prior to 1940, *Prayers for Divine Service* 1923 and 1929 had:

> And we most humbly beseech Thee, O merciful Father, to look upon us, as we do now make that Memorial of Thy Son's most blessed Sacrifice which He hath commanded us to make; and send down Thy Holy Spirit to bless and consecrate these Thine own gifts of bread and wine which we set before Thee, that the bread which we break may be unto us the Communion of the Body of Christ, and the cup which we bless the Communion of the Blood of Christ; that we, receiving them, may by faith be made partakers of His body and blood, with all His benefits, to our spiritual nourishment and growth in grace ...

This particular form, with its reference to sacrifice, can be traced back to James Cooper's 1917 eucharist for the General Assembly and his own previous developments of the forms of the *Euchologion*.[5] However, the first appearance of "pleading His eternal sacrifice" in a Reformed anamnesis was not the 1940 BCO, but in that of the United Church of Canada of 1932.[6]

The United Church of Canada was a union between Methodists, Congregationalists, and Presbyterians. Its 1932 liturgy has been the subject of a detailed study by Thomas Harding.[7] He suggests that the discussions for the Deposited Book 1927/8 of the Church of England were an important source of inspiration. Harding has found no clue to the exact origin of the phrase "pleading His eternal sacrifice." The Canadian Methodist and Congregational liturgies are of no help—though the eucharistic hymns of Wesley speak of the eternal sacrifice, and Watt's hymns show that the idea of Christ showing his sacrifice and pleading his blood before the throne was not entirely foreign to the Congregationalist tradition.[8] The Canadian Presbyterian BCO 1922 had the following anamnesis and epiklesis:

> Wherefore, we, Thy servants, having in remembrance His most blessed sacrifice, showing His death, believing and confessing His resurrection, rejoicing in His ascension and glorious presence at Thy right hand, abiding in the communion of the Holy Ghost, and looking for the promise of His kingdom, do present unto Thee through Him, which He has appointed, giving thanks unto Thee through Him.
>
> And we most humbly beseech Thee, O Merciful Father, to vouchsafe unto us Thy gracious presence, and so to sanctify with Thy Word and Spirit these Thine own gifts of bread and wine which we set before Thee, that the bread which we break may be to us the communion of the body of Christ, and the cup of blessing which we bless, the communion of the blood of Christ.

The leading figure behind the 1932 BCO seems to have been the Presbyterian Richard Davidson, an Old Testament scholar who also had a keen interest in worship.[9] It is perhaps not insignificant that between 1926 and 1928, Davidson's pupil, W.D. Maxwell, was a member of the drafting committee. Maxwell later removed to Scotland, where he was a member of the Aids to Devotion sub-committee preparing the 1940 BCO. Unfortunately the working papers were not retained, but the minutes of the meetings of 30 October and 27 November 1935 indicate clearly that Maxwell had a considerable hand in the eucharistic rites.[10] Commenting on the phrase later Maxwell was to write:

> What now, we may ask, is the doctrine of sacrifice in the Eucharist? This is not mentioned in our standards, but is implicit in the words of the consecration prayer contained in the *Book of Common Order*. The determinative words are "pleading His eternal sacrifice, we thy servants do set forth this memorial". The Scottish rite lays emphasis not upon "the oblation once offered", though this, of course, is there in recollection and theology, but spe-

cifically upon the eternal quality of our Lord's sacrifice: it happened once for all time, but it belongs to eternity where He continually presents Himself before the Father. Similarly, the Eucharist is of eternity, and when we plead "His eternal sacrifice", we desire Him to unite our offering and prayers with His, which is part of that eternal memorial. His sacrifice is not repeatable, but it is continually renewed; the "remembering" is not mere recollection in the psychological sense (which, in fact, is never the biblical sense), but a real uniting, possible by grace and through faith, faith which is not mere intellectual assent, but a committal of the whole person to Him. It is, thus, as Calvin declares, a *vera communicatio* with Him.[11]

It is quite conceivable that Maxwell was responsible for the phrase of the Canadian BCO being utilized in the Scottish Rite, though the phrase itself as a *liturgical* expression may have been the work of Principal Richard Davidson.

Theological Precursors:
William and George Milligan

Although the phrase "pleading His eternal sacrifice" seems to have had its liturgical origins with the 1932 Canadian BCO, the theology which underlies it was set out forcefully in the nineteenth century by two of Scotland's leading Presbyterian scholars, William and George Milligan. It is a theology which combines a strong doctrine of the hypostatic union with implications of the language of the Epistle to the Hebrews.

In his *The Ascension and the Heavenly Priesthood of Our Lord*, 1892, William Milligan insisted that the ascension is not an isolated event, but the completion of all that was involved in the incarnation.[12] The goal of the incarnation was to bring us into a state of perfect union with the Father of our spirits, and so to introduce into our weak human nature the strength of the divine nature.[13] This complete movement of incarnation and ascension is all to be understood as part of Christ's self-offering to the Father, which includes in it "a present and eternal offering to God of His life in heaven."[14] Milligan drew on recent studies on the meaning of sacrifice in the Old Testament which pointed to the importance of offering of life rather than the event of death.[15] Turning to Hebrews 8:3, he asked whether the words "that He also have somewhat to offer" take us back to the cross, and to the cross alone?[16] Milligan argued that although the verb is ambiguous in its tense, the overall context points to something not confined to what our Lord did on earth. When he died on Calvary, he presents to us the idea of offering. When he entered heaven the same idea penetrates and pervades His first presentation of himself to the Father there.[17] Since as our High

Priest he is "heavenly," the idea of his offering is also heavenly, and as heavenly, is eternal.[18]

George Milligan's *The Theology of the Epistle to the Hebrews*, 1899, makes a similar exegetical point. Discussing Hebrews 8:3, *prosenegke*, Milligan felt that the older Protestant theology which refers this back solely to the cross does not do justice to the aorist which suggests timelessness:

> The solution is to be found in connecting with the thought of offering another line of thought than that generally resorted to. So long as we think of death as offering, we can speak only of the efficacy of the death stretching forward in the future. As soon as we substitute life, the true Biblical idea of offering, for death, the thought of the life offered (the life of one who dieth no more) involves in its own nature the element of *continuousness*.[19]

Thus both Milligans established the idea of the "eternal sacrifice." William Milligan also stated that this sacrifice is remembered and pleaded.[20] However, the *purpose* of the incarnation, so he had noted, was to bring *us* into union with God. He thus expounded the unity between Christ and the church through the Spirit.

> But if the idea of priesthood was thus fulfilled in Christ it must be fulfilled also in His Church. We cannot separate the Head from the members. The Christian Church does not simply live by Christ: she lives in Him, and He lives in her. By the constant communication of His Spirit she is what she is; and, as we have seen, the Spirit is not an outward gift which may be bestowed by the Giver while different in its nature from what the Giver is. The Spirit poured out upon the Church is that which so penetrates our Lord's own being that He cannot give the Spirit without at the same time giving Himself, or give Himself without giving the Spirit. As, then, in the power of that Spirit He is a Priest in heaven, the life lived on earth by His Body, in the power of the same Spirit, must be priestly.[21]

It is in the eucharist that this offering of the church through Christ and in the Spirit finds special focus:

> As our Lord's offering of Himself to His Heavenly Father never ends, or can end; so in that offering His people, organically united to Him, one with Him, must be offered, and must offer themselves; and this they do in the expressive and touching symbols of the Eucharist.[22]

Elsewhere he was to say that Christ in his combined divine and human natures offers himself as a continual oblation to the Father; but his people are in him, and he is in them.[23]

Thus, already in this High Calvinist theology, with its emphasis on the humanity of Christ in heaven, the eternal significance of the self-offering of his obedient life, and communion between the church and Christ through the Spirit, we find the dogmatic basis of the 1940 anamnesis and epiklesis.

Subsequent Theological Elucidation:
T.F. Torrance

A number of more recent Scottish Reformed theologians have expounded a similar theology as that found in the Milligans, but now with particular reference to the BCO anamnesis and epiklesis.[24] The most extended commentary and elucidation of this theology has been by T.F. Torrance. Already in "Eschatology and the Eucharist" in 1951 he could write:

> There in heaven is the ascended Lamb Himself ever before the Face of the Father; here on earth is the waiting Church of sinners, with all saints, showing forth His death and pleading His sacrifice—"Lamb of God that takest away the sins of the world, have mercy on us"—but both are united in the *koinonia* of the eternal Spirit, through whom Christ offered Himself to the Father, and through whom we are given to participate in that oblation made on our behalf.[25]

Further theological explanation is given in Torrance's paper "The Paschal Mystery of Christ and the Eucharist" and in his book *Space, Time and Resurrection*.[26] Like William Milligan, Torrance emphasizes that the atonement is not concerned solely with the death of Christ, but the offering of his life *and* death, which was the offering of sanctified human nature:

> Although he assumed our fallen and corrupt humanity when he became flesh, in assuming it he sanctified it in himself, and all through his earthly life he overcame our sin through his righteousness, our impurity through his purity, condemning sin in our flesh by the sheer holiness of his life within it.[27]

Secondly, his role in heaven is to present our true humanity to the Father in an offering which because it is heavenly, is outside the space-time continuum, and must therefore be called "eternal."[28]

> As Mediator, Advocate, and High Priest, Christ is described as he who takes our place, represents us before the Father, moulds us, including our

prayers, in his own self-consecration for our sakes, and so offers us to the Father in the identity of himself as offerer and offering.[29]

Torrance continues:

> The resurrection and ascension, however, do not mean that Christ's priestly sacrifice and oblation of himself are over and done with, but rather that in their once and for all completion they are taken up eternally into the life of God, and remain prevalent, efficacious, valid, or abidingly real ... In the humanity of the ascended Christ there remains for ever before the Face of God the Father, the one, perfect, sufficient offering for mankind.[30]

Through the Holy Spirit we are united to Christ, and so are taken up through the eternal Spirit into his sacrifice and his eternal intercession before the Father.[31] Through his Spirit Christ dwells in the church which is his body and which constitutes the tabernacle or temple in and through which he acts as our mediator, advocate and priest, representing us before God, into whose presence he gives us entrance through himself, who is the one way to the Father.[32] Thus the eucharist focuses on the sacrifice of Christ into which we are incorporated:

> To that objective movement of redemptive descent and ascent, *katabasis* and *anabasis*, in Jesus Christ himself the Lord's Supper corresponds as through the Spirit mediated to us by the glorified Christ we participate in the self-giving of God in the incarnate Son which is consummated in his passion and resurrection, and participate in the self-offering of the ascended Son which is grounded in his passion and resurrection. That is what we do in *anamnesis* of him at the celebration of the Supper where Christ through the Spirit is really present in body, mind and will, taking up the eucharistic memorial we make of him as the concrete form and expression of his own self-giving and self-offering, assimilating us in mind and will to himself and lifting us up in the closest union with himself in the identity of himself as Offerer and Offering to the presence of the Father.[33]

Reformed, Biblical, Catholic, and Ecumenical?

Eucharistic sacrifice has been a subject of controversy ever since the Reformation. The differences which were once so apparent have been narrowed considerably, but not yet totally resolved. These differences tend to manifest themselves in the way offering is articulated or omitted in the anamnesis of the eucharistic prayers of the different churches. Careful historical investigation indicates that even in the classical rites, offering has been expressed in many different ways.[34] However, the thought behind many of the classical anaphoras which include reference to the offering of the bread and wine seems to be that the Son maintains a communion identity with the church secured by the Spirit, so that "we offer" is nothing less than the church united through the Spirit to the offerer, Christ. A High Calvinist Christology and soteriology is sympathetic to this, but the way it is actually expressed in the anamnesis suggests a dangerous identification in the self-offering of the Head; Head and Body seem identical, and the Body offers the Head. This is avoided in the Scottish anamnesis and epiklesis, where the whole eucharistic act—as all our prayer to God—is grounded in, with and through the risen and ascended Christ.

A similar (but not identical) theology to that expounded by the Milligans and Torrance was outlined by the 1958 Lambeth Conference subcommittee on Prayer Book revision, in the hope that Anglo-Catholics and Evangelicals could find rapprochement.[35] In fact, criticism was forthcoming from members of both wings of the Church of England, and although this was not totally unexpected from the Catholic wing, the Evangelical dissent was both surprising and disconcerting.

A summary of the Evangelical criticism was conveniently given by Roger Beckwith and Colin Buchanan in an article entitled "This Bread and This Cup: An Evangelical Rejoinder."[36]

(a) In the New Testament Jesus' death and his obedience to death are his sacrifice, not his obedience as such. (b) In the New Testament this sacrifice occurs on earth, once in time. The sacrifice has a definite time and place, and is complete. It is on this basis of his death that Christ enters the Holy of Holies at his ascension, and this again he does once for all. There is no biblical encouragement for viewing his sacrifice as eternally existing, though there is plenty for viewing it as eternally efficacious. (c) In the New Testament the Church does not participate in Christ's sacrifice, except in the role of beneficiary. His sacrifice was untainted by sin and atoned for sin. The Church's sacrifice of itself is different in both respects. It does not therefore offer itself as a sacrifice which is one with Christ, but owing its origin to his sacrifice, it offers itself in response, and through his sacrifice finds acceptance. (d) In the New Testament the offering of the sacrifice is one thing, the feast on it another. To assert an ontological identity of these two events is to create a theological muddle.[37]

These views have been expounded at greater length elsewhere by other Anglican Evangelical writers. Leon Morris, for example, although acknowledging that scholarship is divided on the question of whether sacrifice is concerned with the offering of a life, or the death with the shedding of blood, sides firmly with the latter view, as did A.M. Stibbs.[38] Stibbs, who regarded the type of theology outlined in the Lambeth Conference 1958 document as "modern", rejected the "eternal sacrifice" since it was not a concept taught in Scripture.[39] Once sacrifice has been defined as the moment of death and the shedding of blood, then "eternal" implies a continual sacrifice and shedding of blood, which A.J. Tait, R.V.G. Tasker, and Stibbs quite logically reject.[40]

The constant mention of "The New Testament" or "Scripture" in the Anglican Evangelical argument tends to suggest that any contrary view—such as that of the Milligans and Torrance—is unbiblical and, by inference, a departure from Reformation principles. However, as another Evangelical has recently noted:

> The Evangelical strength is its faithfulness to the data of Scripture. Its weakness is that it is prone to miss the inner connections and thus the valid doctrinal developments of Scripture.[41]

That such an approach can be a weakness is illustrated in historical theology by Arius, who had all the New Testament quotations on his side, but failed to see their logical extension. Is, therefore, the theology behind the Scottish anamnesis and epiklesis, and particularly the phrase "pleading His eternal sacrifice" unbiblical and a departure from Reformation principles?

The theology expounded by the Milligans and Torrance centers on four particular points:

(a) The hypostatic union.

(b) The eternal sacrifice in the sense that through the ascension the obedient humanity is taken up into heaven.

(c) The Koinonia between Christ and the church through the Spirit.

(d) That all worship is not simply our response to God, but that it can only be offered in, with and through the risen and ascended Christ.

Whereas Continental Reformed theology became a synthesis of the Zurich/Basel theology with that of Geneva, Scotland through Knox tended to follow Genevan theology. No infallibility can or ought to be claimed for John Calvin, but he was hardly a theologian who can be regarded as unbiblical or disloyal to Reformation principles. Although all four points outlined by Beckwith and Buchanan can be supported from the writings of Calvin, the views of the Milligans and Torrance also find full support in his writings.

(a) The hypostatic union

The two great Swiss theologians Calvin and Zwingli both protested their loyalty to the Chalcedonian definition of the hypostatic union. As they each unfolded their Christology however, it became clear that they differed on their understanding of the importance of the manhood of Christ. Zwingli inherited from Erasmus the neoplatonist separation of flesh and spirit, and this was to have an unfortunate knock-on effect on his Christology.[42] He stressed Christ as God rather than man.[43] In his Berne sermon on the Creed, he urged that the godhead cannot suffer, and therefore the manhood was necessary for the suffering. At the same time no man could satisfy God's righteousness, but only God—hence the important role of the divine nature.[44] However, he had great difficulty with John 1:14, and his statements elsewhere about the sharp contrast between flesh and spirit contradict his profession of an orthodox christology. As Stephens remarks:

> The dominant place afforded to the divinity and the sharp distinction made by Zwingli between the divine and human seem at points to call in question the genuine humanity of Christ.[45]

Calvin takes much more seriously the manhood of Christ. In the *Catechism of the Church of Geneva* (Catechism) he wrote:

> M. Was it of consequence then that he should assume our nature?
> S. Very much so; because it was necessary that the disobedience committed by man against God should be expiated in human nature.[46]

Calvin certainly stressed the importance of the death and the obedience to death;[47] but he also asserts that Christ purchased righteousness through obedience of his manhood, "from the moment when he assumed the form of a servant."[48] "In the Confession of Faith, called the Apostles' Creed, the transition is admirably made from the birth of Christ to his death and resurrection, in which the completion of a perfect salvation consists."[49] The voluntary nature of this servanthood is stressed in his commentary on Philippians, together with his humility.[50] In his commentary on Hebrews he notes that his birth included his priesthood (5:5) and his obedient life and his teaching are stressed.[51] In a searching study of Calvin's Christology, Willis correctly states:

> What is saving in Christ's teaching, miracles, and death is not simply that they occurred voluntarily. The heart of the reconstituting act is the free obedience of the Second Adam which displaces the willful disobedience of the first Adam, and frees the members of the Second Adam for new obedience in place of their inherited disobedience. That the whole course of

Christ's obedience, the act of the Incarnation being but the first and continuing stage, was a voluntary submission, is an affirmation guarded by the
"extra Calvinisticum".[52]

The obedient life, therefore, is quite in line with Calvin.

(b) The eternal sacrifice

Concerning the Ascension of Christ Calvin wrote:

Having entered the temple not made with hands, he constantly appears as
our advocate and intercessor in the presence of the Father; directs attention
to his own righteousness, so as to turn it away from our sins; so reconciles
him to us, as by his intercession to pave for us a way of access to his
throne, presenting it to miserable sinners, to whom it would otherwise be
an object of dread, as replete with grace and mercy.[53]

He also stressed that the power of his death has the effect of a perpetual
intercession for us.[54] Whereas Lutherans, followed apparently by some
Anglican Reformers, tended to regard the intercession as vocal, Calvin
regarded it as including the presentation of redeemed humanity through
the cross to God.[55] Commenting on Hebrews 10:19, he could thus write:

The blood of beasts did not long retain its power because it immediately
began to decay, whereas, since the blood of Christ is not corrupted by any
decay but flows continually in unadulterated purity, it will suffice for us to
the end of the world. It is no wonder that beasts slain in sacrifice had no
power to give life because they were dead, but Christ who rose from the
dead to give us life pours His own life into us. This is the continual consecration of His life that the blood of Christ is continually being shed before
the face of the Father to spread over heaven and earth.[56]

In the Catechism he can speak of the one perpetual sacrifice (le sacrifice
unique et perpetuel; *unicum perpetuumque sacrificium*).[57] A.J. Tait tried to
excuse such statements on the grounds that Calvin was misled by the
Vulgate version of Hebrews, particularly Hebrews 8:3, *unde necesse est et
hunc habere aliquid quod offerat*, the *"est"* suggesting a continual offering.[58]
In fact Calvin gives his own text, had a good knowledge of the Greek
text, and we may assume that like many commentators before and after,
felt that the Latin did justice to the Greek aorist in Hebrews 8:3.[59]

Calvin emphasized time and again that the sacrifice on the cross was
once and for all, and he denies that it is a continual sacrifice. However,
since for Calvin intercession was inseparable from Christ presenting his
High Priesthood in heaven, which was now, with his obedient manhood,

eternally before God, he could quite legitimately speak of a perpetual or eternal sacrifice.

(i) As Beckwith and Buchanan argued, so too did Calvin, that the sacrifice was eternal in the sense that its efficacy is eternal. "Since that one sacrifice which Christ offered once for all has eternal power, and is therefore perpetual in its efficacy, it is no wonder that the eternal priesthood of Christ is supported by its power which never fails".[60] "The power of the one sacrifice is eternal and extends to all ages".[61]

(ii) It is also eternal in the sense that Christ is no longer on earth but is in heaven. Against the Lutheran concept of heaven, Calvin insisted that although he ascended to heaven, it was beyond the heaven of heavens, at the right hand of God, which means the power of God.[62] His body "carried above the heavens is exempt from the common order of nature".[63] "He does not mean here the heaven which we see with our eyes and where the stars shine, but the glory of the Kingdom of God which is higher than all the heavens".[64] He has been received into eternal bliss.[65] In other words, the humanity of Christ which lived an obedient life, and was obedient to death, is now in eternity and no longer in space and time. Thus Calvin can speak of "the sacrifice of eternal atonement."[66]

(iii) The sacrifice can also be called eternal because this once for all act was something foreseen by God from the creation of the world. Before the first man was created, God in his eternal counsel had determined what he willed to be done with the whole human race.[67] He had ordained Christ by his eternal counsel.[68] God sent Christ in the fullness of time; "it was the fulness of that time which God had determined by his eternal decrees."[69] Thus the term "eternal sacrifice" is not modern, but can be traced back to Calvin, who felt that the term did justice to the biblical data.

(c) Koinonia through the Spirit

Calvin expounded a strong Trinitarian doctrine, and developed the *filioque* to underscore that the Son is never effectively active in creation or redemption without the Spirit.[70] In the *Institutes* he carefully describes how the benefits of Christ are communicated to us by the Spirit, so that "he is called our Head, and the first-born among many brethren, while, on the other hand, we are said to be ingrafted into him and clothed with him, all which he possesses being, as I have said, nothing to us until we become one with him."[71] "The whole comes to this, that the Holy Spirit is the bond by which Christ effectively binds us to himself.[72] "It is by the Spirit alone that he unites himself to us."[73] Communion in the Lord's Supper is also due to the Spirit; we are by the Holy Spirit made partakers of him, and the Spirit effects this since he is the virtue of the living God proceeding from the Father and the Son.[74] Appealing to Cyril of Alexandria, Calvin insists that the faithful communicate in the flesh and blood of Christ and at the same time enjoy participation of life; this comes about by the Spirit which "truly unites things separated by space."[75] "The Lord by his Spirit bestows upon us the blessing of being one with him in soul, body and spirit. The bond of that connection ... is the Spirit of Christ, who unites us to him, and is a kind of channel by which everything that Christ has and is, is derived to us."[76] Indeed, Calvin's teaching on the place of the Holy Spirit in uniting us to Christ in the eucharist is the basis of the epiklesis of the Church of Scotland.

(d) Worship through Christ

On the subject of the priestly office of Christ, Calvin stressed that Christ is a perpetual intercessor, and that through him we have access to God:

> Christ now bears the office of priest, not only that by the eternal law of reconciliation he may render the Father favourable and propitious to us, but also admit us into this most honourable alliance. For we, though in ourselves polluted, in him being priests (Rev.1:6), offer ourselves and our all to God, and freely enter the heavenly sanctuary, so that the sacrifices of prayer and praise which we present are grateful and of sweet odour before him. [77]

In the *Institutes* he wrote:

> We do not appear with our gifts in the presence of God without an intercessor. Christ is our Mediator, by whose intervention we offer ourselves and our all to the Father; he is our High Priest, who, having entered into the upper sanctuary, opens up an access for us; he is the altar on which we lay our gifts, that whatever we do attempt, we may attempt in him; he it is, I say, who "hath made us kings and priests unto God and his Father" (Rev.1:6).[78]

And in a fine passage commenting on Hebrews he wrote:

> It is He alone who hallows our lips which are otherwise defiled to sing the praises of God, who opens the way for our prayers, who in short performs the office of Priest standing before God in our name.[79]

Thus ultimately the theological rationale of the anamnesis and epiklesis of the BCO may be traced to Calvin, who believed that he was not only establishing Reformed theology, but that it was also fully in accord with the Bible.

However, Calvin also believed that Reformed theology was a return to a purified patristic theology. We cannot enter here into an investigation of patristic sources, but others have shown how Calvin's Christology and soteriology has its roots in, and is in harmony with the writings of Cyril of Alexandria, the Cappadocians, and Athanasius.[80] It can legitimately be called a catholic Christology.[81]

Of equal importance in an ever increasing ecumenical context, is the fact that this emphasis in Calvin is also in harmony with *Baptism, Eucharist and Ministry* (BEM). Para. 4 of the latter notes:

> Christ unites the faithful with himself and includes their prayers within his own intercession so that the faithful are transfigured and their prayers accepted. This sacrifice of praise is possible only through Christ, with him and in him.

BEM argues that Christ with all he has accomplished in his incarnation, servanthood, ministry, teaching, suffering, sacrifice, resurrection, ascension and sending of the Spirit is present in the anamnesis (para. 6). In thanksgiving and intercession the church is united with the Son its great High Priest and Intercessor (Rom 8:34; Heb 7:25).

BEM urges that churches should test their liturgies in the light of the eucharistic agreement. The Church of Scotland's anamnesis and epiklesis are, as Max Thurian observed, excellent examples of one expression of BEM.[82] Our contention is that these forms should commend themselves to all those who genuinely seek an anamnesis and epiklesis which are not only patient of an ecumenical understanding, but also are forms which are biblical, and have their roots in patristic Christology and soteriology.[83]

Notes

1. Karl Barth, *Dogmatics in Outline* (London, 1966) 125.

2. Karl Barth, *Church Dogmatics* 4/2 (Edinburgh) 29.

3. T.J. Talley, *The Origins of the Liturgical Year* (New York, 1986) 63ff.

4. From this source it passed into other English Reformed rites, such as *The Presbyterian Service Book* (England) 1948 and 1968, and the Congregational Union's *A Book of Services and Prayers* 1959. For the latter, see Bryan D. Spinks, *Freedom or Order? The Eucharistic Liturgy in English Congregationalism 1645-1980*, Pittsburgh Theological Monographs, n.s., 8 (Allison Park, 1984). For a wider background to the phrase, see J.M. Barkley, "'Pleading His Eternal Sacrifice' in the Reformed Liturgy," in Bryan D. Spinks, ed. *The Sacrifice of Praise: Studies on the Themes of Thanksgiving and Redemption in the Central Prayers of the Eucharistic*

and Baptismal Liturgies in Honour of Arthur Hubert Couratin, Ephemerides Liturgicae Subsidia 18, C.L.V. (Rome, 1981) 123-140.

5. My thanks to Rev. C. Williamson who kindly drew my attention to this. See also H.J. Wotherspoon, *James Cooper. A Memoir,* (London, 1926).

6. It was direct from this Canadian source that the phrase was used in the English Congregationalist compilation *A Book of Public Worship* (1948).

7. Thomas R. Harding, "The Major Orders of the Book of Common Order of the United Church of Canada (1932). Sources and Development." Thesis submitted in partial fulfillment of the requirements of the degree of Master of Theology, Vancouver School of Theology, 1986. I am grateful to the Rev. Thomas Harding for so readily answering my questions on the Canadian BCO.

8. See J. Ernest Rattenbury, *The Eucharistic Hymns of John and Charles Wesley* (London, 1948) Hymns 99 and 124; Selma L. Bishop, ed. *I. Watts. Hymns and Spiritual Songs* (London, 1962) Hymns CXLV; CXLIX; CXVIII.

9. John Dow, "Richard Davidson: Churchman" in Harold W. Vaughn, ed. *The Living Church* (Toronto, 1949) 1-26. I am indebted to the Rev. Thomas Harding for a copy of this memoir.

10. Minutes of Meetings of the Aids to Devotion Sub-Committee 176-177. I am grateful to Colin Williamson for kindly furnishing me with copies of the Minutes.

11. "The Elements of Liturgy: Reformed," in P. Edwall, E. Hayman and W.D. Maxwell, eds. *Ways of Worship* (London, 1951) 115-116.

12. W. Milligan, *The Ascension and Heavenly Priesthood of Our Lord* (London, 1892) 27.

13. Ibid. 30.

14. Ibid. 116.

15. Ibid. 119.

16. Ibid. 120.

17. Ibid. 125.

18. Ibid. 126-127.

19. George Milligan, *The Theology of the Epistle to the Hebrews* (Edinburgh, 1899) 144.

20. W. Milligan, *The Ascension* 142-143.

21. Ibid. 243-244.

22. Ibid. 266.

23. Ibid. 307.

24. For example, Donald Baillie, *The Theology of the Sacraments* (London, 1957) 116-122; T.F. Torrance and R. Selby Wright, revised edition, H.J. Wotherspoon and J.M. Kilpatrick, *A Manual of Church Doctrine* (London, 1960). James B. Torrance, "The Vicarious Humanity of Christ" in T.F. Torrance, ed. *The Incarnation. Ecumenical Studies in the Nicene-Constantinopolitan Creed A.D. 381* (Edinburgh, 1981) 127-147. See Alasdair Heron, *Table and Tradition* (Edinburgh, 1983) 167ff.

25. D. Baillie and J. Marsh, eds., *Intercommunion* (London, 1952) 303-350, 326.

26. T.F. Torrance, *Theology in Reconciliation* (London, 1975) 106-138; *Space, Time and Resurrection* (Edinburgh, 1976).

27. Torrance, *Space, Time and Resurrection* 53.

28. T.F. Torrance, *Space, Time and Incarnation* (London, 1969).

29. Torrance, *Theology* 113.

30. Torrance, *Space, Time and Resurrection* 114-115.

31. See ibid. 64.

32. Torrance, *Theology* 113.

33. Ibid. 118-119.

34. See the recent study by Kenneth W. Stevenson, *Eucharist and Offering* (New York, 1987).

35. *The Lambeth Conference 1958* (London, 1958). The Eucharistic Sacrifice 2:83-85.

36. In *Theology* 70 (1967) 265-271. Not all Evangelicals shared or now share the views expressed in this article.

37. Ibid. 267.

38. Leon Morris, *The Apostolic Preaching of the Cross* (London, 1955) 122-124; A.M. Stibbs, *The Meaning of the Word 'Blood' in Scripture* (London, 1947).

39. A.M. Stibbs, *Sacrament, Sacrifice and Eucharist* (London, 1961) 41; 27ff.

40. A.J. Tait, *The Heavenly Session of Our Lord* (London, 1912); R.V.G. Tasker, "The Priestly Work of Christ," in J.I. Packer, ed., *Eucharistic Sacrifice* (London, 1962) 47-57, esp. 54-55; A.M. Stibbs, *Sacrament*.

41. C.J. Cocksworth in a typescript communication to the Church of England Liturgical Commission 11.2.1988.

42. Roland H. Bainton, *Erasmus of Christendom* (New York, 1969); John B. Payne, *Erasmus: His Theology of the Sacraments* (Richmond, 1970); W.P. Stephens, *The Theology of Huldrych Zwingli* (Oxford, 1986).

43. Stephens, *The Theology* 111.

44. Ibid.

45. Ibid. 116.

46. In *Calvin's Tracts and Treaties*, H. Beveridge, trans. (Edinburgh, reprint, 1958) vol. 2, 44.

47. *Institutes* II.16.3.

48. *Institutes* II.16.5.

49. Ibid.

50. T.H.L. Parker, trans., *The Epistle of Paul The Apostle to the Galatians, Ephesians, Philippians and Colossians* (Edinburgh, 1965) 246 and 249, commenting on Philippians 2:6-8.

51. William B. Johnston, *Calvin's Commentaries. The Epistle of Paul to the Hebrews and the First and Second Epistles of St. Peter* (Edinburgh, 1963) 16-17; 54 (Hebrews), commenting on 1:14, 4:14.

52. E. David Willis, *Calvin's Catholic Christology* (Leiden, 1966) 85.

53. *Institutes* II.16.16.

54. *Institutes* III.20.20.

55. Tait, *The Heavenly Session* 150.

56. Hebrews 10:19, 140.

57. Catechism, op.cit. 90.

58. Tait, *The Heavenly Session* 106, 129.

59. I am grateful for Dr. T.H.L. Parker's advice on this matter, and for mak-

ing available to me the various versions upon which Calvin drew.

60. Hebrews 9:25, ibid. 129.

61. Hebrews 9:26, ibid.

62. Catechism, op.cit., 49.

63. Second Defence of the Faith Concerning the Sacraments in Answer to Joachim Westphal, in *Calvin's Tracts and Treatises* 290.

64. Hebrews 9:24, 128.

65. Hebrews 7:25, 101.

66. Hebrews 9:14, 121.

67. Articles Concerning Predestination, in J.K.S. Reid, ed., *Calvin: Theological Treatises*, Library of Christian Classics 22 (London, 1954) 179.

68. Hebrews, commenting on 1 Peter 1:20, 249.

69. Hebrews 9:26, 130.

70. E. David Willis, *Calvin's Catholic Christology* 83.

71. *Institutes* III.1.1.

72. Ibid.

73. *Institutes* III.1.3.

74. Summary of Doctrine Concerning the Ministers of the Word and the Sacraments, *Calvin: Theological Treatises* 175.

75. *Institutes* IV.17.9-10.

76. *Institutes* IV.17.12.

77. *Institutes* II.15.6.

78. *Institutes* IV.18.17.

79. Hebrews 13:15, 211.

80. T.F. Torrance, "The Mind of Christ in Worship: The Problem of Apollinarianism in the Liturgy," in *Theology in Reconciliation* 139-214; "Athanasius: A Study in the Foundations of Classical Theology," ibid. 215-266. Alasdair Heron, "Homoousios With the Father," in T.F. Torrance, ed., *The Incarnation* 58-87; James B. Torrance, "The Vicarious Humanity."

81. Willis., *Calvin's Catholic Theology.*

82. M. Thurian, "The Eucharistic Memorial, Sacrifice of Praise and Supplication," in M. Thurian, ed., *Ecumenical Perspectives on Baptism, Eucharist and Ministry* (Geneva, 1983) 90-103, 100.

83. It is one source of inspiration for a modern eucharistic prayer being considered by the Church of England Liturgical Commission:

Father, as we plead his sacrifice made once for all on the cross, we remember his dying and rising to glory, and rejoice that he prays for us at your right hand: pour out your Holy Spirit over us and these gifts, which we bring before you from your own creation; show them to be for us the body and blood of your dear Son; unite in his eternal sacrifice all who share the food and drink of his new and unending life.

13

Sunday, Socialism and Sorcery: The Question of Historical Revisionism and the Study of Sacred Time

Paul Marshall

DURING THE LAST CENTURY IT HAS NOT BEEN AT ALL UNCOMMON FOR HISTO-rians to interpret religious movements with primary reference to their social significance. This has been, perhaps, a healthy corrective to the tacit assumption often made in older introductory texts that the person on the street in the thirteenth century had as primary topic of conversation issues of sacramental metaphysics. Similarly, the silence of seminary courses on the political and economic implications of the shift of power away from Jerusalem in the late first generation of Christianity needed to be broken. These two examples could be followed by many more illustrations of the need to distinguish an inclusive *Kirchengeschichte* from a much narrower *Dogmengeschichte*, a need which has now been largely met in general studies of Christianity, and to a growing extent in studies of the church's liturgical life.

There have however, been casualties along the way, and one of them has been our understanding of the Sabbatarianism of post-Reformation England, an important subtopic in the history of the Lord's Day if only for the numbers of people it affected and still affects. Consequently, it is the goal here to test some of the hypotheses of Christopher Hill, whose "The Uses of Sabbatarianism" is the only in-depth treatment of the controversy in our time, and one which is rigorously revisionist.[1] Hill's views have, furthermore, been carried over to some extent in Horton Davies' widely-consulted Worship and Theology in England.[2] In the first place, Hill took the position that the anti-Sabbatarian Laudians, unlike the Puritans, were not standing in the English legal tradition (both civil and ecclesiastical) in their enforcement of legislation barring work on holy days rather than laws affecting Sunday work. He further concluded that the Sabbatarians were by and large interested in providing relief for the overworked by their observance of the Sabbath, and that the prohibitions of sports that the Puritans sought reflected the fact that the traditional country sports were rites of a pre-Christian religion surviving as what Christians called "witchcraft." For him, Sabbatarianism was not a religious issue at all, but a legal and economic one, tainted by the witch-panic of the mid-seventeenth century.

It is important to make adjustments to Hill's presentation of the material because the question of Sabbatarianism is already a difficult one to assess. The primary literature is of daunting proportions. The number of books written in the sixteenth and seventeenth centuries whose primary subject was the manner in which Christians should observe Sunday is in excess of two hundred. To that number the researcher must add the many published sermons and pamphlets, as well as the legal, social, and general theological sources needed for the study of Sabbatarianism.[3] Nineteenth- century work, which cannot be reviewed here, tended to be highly detailed and frankly partisan. The exceptions are the works of Robert Cox and James Augustus Hessey, to which one still turns for much of the detail of the controversy which occupied so many writers.[4] Sunday literature abounded into this century, and apparently climaxed with W.B. Whitaker's two books on the "English Sunday,"[5] English Sabbatarianism is still to receive its definitive treatment. Christopher Hill's essay has increased interest in the question, but has only added to the number of unresolved questions by approaching the social issues underlying the Sabbatarian controversy from the point of view of a Marxist historian.

The Question of Civil and Religious Law

Hill maintains that in 1641, when the Long Parliament ordered the laws of England relating to the observance of Sunday be enforced, and that the King's Book of Sports be burned by the public hangman, the members were standing squarely on pre-Caroline English tradition, and that the Laudians had been the innovators in permitting Sunday labor in harvest time, and by doing nothing to suppress Sunday sports.[6] The issue is not as simple as that, and it *is* an issue to be considered here, as the case of the legally-trained Hamon L'Estrange demonstrates. His *God's Sabbath* (1641) was the blueprint for the Sabbatarian pronouncements of the Westminster Assembly, and thus the book's evidence for the view of Puritans is not unimportant. Although L'Estrange cites more than his fair share of legal maxims for the writer of a theological treatise, he only once alludes to the contemporary legal situation in England. Why did he omit so potent a weapon, if as Hill claims, it really was one of the most potent in his arsenal? The question becomes more pressing when one discovers that it was L'Estrange's anti-Sabbatarian opponent Peter Heylyn who devoted much more attention to the actual state of the law in his *History of the Sabbath* (1637).

A review of the development of laws governing personal conduct on the days of worship in England indicates that Hill's assertions are oversimplified. To be sure, there was a legal tradition in England from the seventh to the seventeenth centuries regarding abstinence from work and from certain recreations on days of worship, but there was no consistent understanding of which days were holy, of whom the laws were to govern, and of which activities were to be regulated. It seems rather that there were elements in the legal tradition of England on which each side of the Sabbatarian question could draw in the English Church's new situation on the eve of enlightenment and in the process of industrialization, a situation which Hill believes to have been determinative of their theological positions.

The fact seems to be that each side had *some* of the tradition behind its understanding of how the English nation had for centuries interpreted the biblical words which were now become the liturgical formula they had all used since 1552. On the Sabbatarian side, when Nicholas Bownd wrote *The True Doctrine of the Sabbath*[7] at the end of the sixteenth century, English Protestants had begun the celebration of the "second service" for some fifty years with the Decalogue. There they heard the Sabbath requirement of the Fourth Commandment.

> Minister: Remember that thou keep holy the Sabbath day. Six days shalt thou labor, and do all that thou hast do; but the seventh day is the Sabbath of the Lord thy God. In it thou shalt do no manner of work, thou, and thy son, and thy daughter, thy man-servant, and thy maid-servant, thy cattle, and the stranger that is within thy gates. For in six days the Lord made heaven and earth, the sea, and all that in them is, and rested the seventh day: wherefore the Lord blessed the seventh day, and hallowed it.

> People: Lord, have mercy upon us, and incline our hearts to keep this law.

How were they to "keep this law"? The Homily, "Of the Time and Place of Prayer" took the position more or less held by the Sabbatarians: "For we keep now the first day, which is our Sunday, and make that our day of rest, in the honor of our savior Christ ... God hath given express charge to all men, that upon the Sabbath-day, which is now our Sunday, they should cease from all weekly and work-day labour."[8] That homily, with its Puritan interpretation of the words of the Fourth Commandment, makes a case of Hill's understanding of the Sabbatarians as conservators of English religious tradition, but they are best understood as conservators of but one expression of that tradition alone, that of the Reformation.

The most scrupulous observers of that tradition found themselves separated from the legal authority of Church and Crown. Some seventeenth century Englishmen, such as the first seventh-day Baptist, John Traske, and his follower and popularizer, Theophilus Brabourne, suffered public punishment for taking the words of the Decalogue in their simple sense.[9] Many similar cases illustrate the point that in England the Sabbatarian issue did indeed involve the question of how a Christian society was to obey the biblical law, but they also demonstrate, contrary to Hill, that for most Englishmen, it was always the biblical law as applied to the new Christian institution of the Lord's Day. The difficulty they had in defining the demands of that ancient Israelite law in the new situation of Christianity can be seen in the fact that even under the Sabbatarian Commonwealth the uncertainty and intensity of the issue of the interpretation of the Fourth Commandment led to public acts of violence.[10]

That uncertainty itself may be the tradition for England. Christians had, of course, addressed themselves to the relationship of the Lord's Day to the Sabbath since Paul's objection to the Sabbath-keeping tendencies of some early believers.[11] There is no record of the early Sabbath/ Sunday controversies reaching England in their first form, however. The earliest English legislation on the subject of Sunday observance makes no use of Sabbatarian terminology, but that law, the Edict of Ina, king of Wessex, as adopted by the English synod of 691/92, orders rest from all labor:

If a yeowman works on a Sunday by his lord's command, he shall become free, and the lord is liable to a fine of thirty shillings.

1. If, however, the slave works without the cognizance of his master, he shall undergo the lash or pay the fine in lieu thereof.

2. If, however, a freeman works on that day without his lord's command, the penalty is forfeiture of freedom or a fine of 60 shillings, and twice as much in the case of a priest.[12]

The edict concerns Sunday itself, not other holy days. The same is true of the ninth-century Celtic *Cain Domnaig* (Law of the Lord's Day), which specifies more than a hundred activities which must be forgone "from vespers on Saturday till after matins on Monday," and concludes with no mean threat. *Cain Domnaig* warns that "it is on account of transgression of the Lord's day that God brings plagues upon the fields. It is this that sets back every kind of produce that sea or land brings forth ... For worse than demons are they who would destroy the Law of the Lord's day." [13]

In the tenth century, Aelred's son Edward ordered the forfeiture of goods which were displayed for sale on Sunday and holy days, and added that on feast days and Sunday trials by ordeal and oaths are forbidden, and "If it can be so contrived, no capital offender shall ever be put to death during the feast of Sunday, but he shall be arrested and kept in custody until the festival is over."[14]

The industrial activities of spinning and weaving had been forbidden on Sundays and feast days since 1354; in addition, some recreations (*jeux importunes*) had been forbidden by Henry IV in 1409. Why then, is no appeal made to these laws by the Sabbatarians?

Although the prohibition against work and some amusements had been the subject of worship-related legislation, all the English laws since the turn of the millennium clearly referred to other holy days as well as to Sunday. The Laudian divine Peter Heylyn was able to demonstrate that fact, and devoted the final chapter of the First Book of his *The History of the Sabbath* (1636) to his claim that Sunday was just another holy day, and not the chief one, as far as the broad legal tradition was concerned.

When the Puritan Sabbatarians and others seeking Sabbath observance appealed to laws, then, they were forced to appeal only to those which dated from the Reformation, but even these have a mixed character, with regard to their Sabbatarianism, to no one's satisfaction. Henry VIII's *Injunctions* of 1547 speak consistently of "every Sunday and holy day," through most of the text, but become unclear as to which day is meant when addressing cessation from work on the "holy day." Although the injunctions had followed some theological and economic trends in combining all parish feasts of dedication in a single day, they were of further dissatisfaction to the Puritans in that they expressly *permitted* Sunday work in harvest time:

> All parsons ... shall teach ... unto their parishioners, that they may with a safe and quiet conscience, in the time of harvest, labour upon the holy and festival days, and save that thing which God hath sent. And if any for scrupulosity abstain from working upon those then they should grievously offend and displease God."[15]

Although Henry's opening rebukes against drunkenness and other unseemly behavior would appeal to the Sabbatarians, the equation of Sunday with other feasts and the express permission given to labor on Sunday and holy days made the injunctions an unlikely source of authority for the Sabbatarians. Even the lawyer L'Estrange mentions the injunctions only in passing.

The 1552 *Act of Uniformity*, which brought England its most reformed prayer book, provided little support for Sabbatarianism, in that its provisions were framed in the very language of the old system, with a cycle of sacred time spanning the year rather than the week:

> II. From the feast of All Saints next coming, all and every person ... [shall] endeavor ... to resort to their Parish Church of Chapel accustomed; ... upon every Sunday and other Days ordained and used to be kept as Holidays upon pain of punishment by the censures of the Church."[16]

The Act further provided for twenty-seven holy days "commanded to be kept," to which the "and none other" added to the catalog of the days imposed came as little relief to the Puritans, who were, after all, seeking escape from what they perceived to be the superstition operative in the observance of holy days. The statute imposing the Kalendar was revived by James I, directly in the face of the Millenary Petition, which had asked that the number of the days be lessened, and that the observances of them by cessation from work be relaxed.[17]

In 1604, under James I, a statute of Edward VI was reenacted which also permitted work on Sundays in harvest time, "or any other times in the year where necessity shall require to labour, ride, fish or work any kind of work, at their free wills and pleasure."[18]

Despite Hill's claims, the legalities of Sunday rest were against the Sabbatarians: the laws, ever since the Reformation, although forbidding work on Sundays out of harvest time, did not distinguish Sunday from the other holy days. A study of court records indicates that the laws were enforced quite unevenly by the church courts: Puritans and other working on the holy days were prosecuted much more than those who profaned Sunday.[19] Furthermore, the Puritans believed that entirely too much recreation was permitted on Sunday and feasts. The *jeux importunes* of Henry IV had been defined as "drunkennes, quarrelling and brawling" by Henry VIII, but to many Puritans that prohibition of rude behavior did not seem enough to insure the dignity of the Lord's Day. For forty years attempts in Parliament to further curtail Sunday activities failed to win the royal assent. Finally, in 1625, a bill was passed forbidding some Sunday recreations, and then in 1628 came the one law to which L'Estrange could and did appeal, one which forbade various kinds of work and travel, as well as meetings of people outside their own parish for common plays.[20] To these Puritans appealed for punishment of Sabbath-breakers. It was only to these recent prohibitions that the Puritans of 1641 could refer without also encountering the embarrassment of the (to them) papist holy days.

The Church Fathers provided each side with only partial support, and each side had its own catena of patristic quotations. The homily "Of the Time and Place of Prayer" and the words of the Decalogue in the liturgy were on the side of the Puritans, but even those words of divine command were contained in a prayer book whose Kalendar was an item to which they specifically objected. This left it for the Sabbatarians, who could find no absolute support in Church or Crown, to employ the traditional protestant counter-authority to decrees of church and state, the Bible, interpreted by their own hermeneutic. Thus the Westminster Assembly looked for biblical authority alone in planning its Sabbatarian scheme, and leaned primarily on a book whose title tells the tale, L'Estrange's *God's Sabbath Before the Law, Under the Law, and Under the Gospel* (1641).

Was Sabbatarianism a Disguised English Social Movement?

Was it, in fact, English? When he retailed the work of his father-in-law Richard Greenham, Nicholas Bownd was not the first to express rigid views on the Sabbath rest. Where did he get them? One cannot accept Douglas Brackenridge's contention that such views originated in Scotland in the late sixteenth century.[21] Earlier evidence is found in Europe. At least by the time of Bullinger's death in 1575, Swiss Calivinists had heard rigidly formulated Sabbatarian views. In his *Decades* Bullinger taught that Christians were obliged to keep an internal rest of the soul on Sundays as well as observe a public Sabbath. His notion of the legal ramifications of his teachings must have inspired many an English Puritan:

> It is the duty of a good Christian magistrate or at leastwise of a good householder to compel to amendment the breakers and contemners of God's Sabbath and worship. The peers of Israel, and all the people of God, did stone to death...the man that disobediantly did gather sticks on the Sabbath-day. Why then should it not be lawful for a Christian magistrate to punish by loss of goods, or by death, the despisers of religion ... and of the Sabbath-day?[22]

Bullinger's *Works* were published in English in London in 1587, before

Greenham and Bownd wrote, and are cited by L'Estrange and other Sabbatarians. Although John Knox opposed days of worship other than Sunday, he never undertook a Sabbatarian campaign, and Sabbatarian laws
in Scotland came well after his death and after the publication of Bullinger's *Decades* and Bownd's first work. Daniel Augsburger and Gerhard
Hasel have explored other continental Sabbatarian developments of the
sixteenth century. Although these do antedate English developments,
their link to the English situation has not been demonstrated.[23] It does
seem clear that one looks for the ideological roots of Sabbatarianism in
Bullinger or the continental Reformation, not in Scotland, or in native labor movements, when one goes beyond the native English expression.

Why did Bullinger's ideas take hold in England to the extent that they
did? Why was the question so urgent in England, when it was of smaller
consequence in England? My reading of the evidence is that the Puritan
commitment was primarily and intensely theological—at the time in
question their American cousins were busy building totalitarian theocra-
cies in New England. Hill's belief is that economic pressure, the demand
of "the industrious sort" for as much time as possible in which to labor,
which the Sabbatarians opposed on humanitarian grounds, made the difference in England. The theory is certainly attractive, for England was indeed undergoing rapid economic development, in which the small proprietor needed every available hour of his and his help's time.
Nonetheless, it cannot handle a very large block of the data, namely the
Sabbatarian's insistence on prohibition of the very sports which would
have recreated these weary labor forces, if that had been the Sabbatarians' intent. Reading back from the reminiscences of a *nineteenth* century
miner's child, Hill sees Sabbatarianism as the intentional guarantee to
the proprietor of six days of regular work, but also as the guarantee of
the protection needed for his workers from his ambitions and their own;
they all, laborer and employer, needed time off.[24]

The fact is that Sabbatarians did not consider the Sabbath as an opportunity for time off, but time devoted to a different kind of work, worship,
and acts of charity.

Stated thus, this was not an entirely un-Anglican sentiment. A generation before, Hooker had written that "ordinary labour, the toils and cares
whereof are not meet to be companions of such gladdness" as the "new
revolution" begun at the resurrection of Christ offered, must be abandoned on the new Sabbath, but he also said, "let us not take rest for idle-
ness."[25] On the Sabbatarians' own part, the distinction was drawn more
sharply. Bownd had insisted that Sabbath devotion excluded "all honest
recreations and lawful delights" because they could not be enjoyed and
the whole day still spent at worship.[26] Puritan John Cotton thought that

no fewer than two sermons should be heard on a Sunday.[27] Canon 13 of those agreed upon in 1603 directed that time outside of worship be spent in visiting the poor and sick and "using all godly and sober conversation," although, since the time of James it was a settled point of law that the canons were only enforceable against the clergy in the courts; the laity must be governed by statute law. John Ley insisted that the rest taken on the Lord's Day be "a religious rest."[28] In this they all followed Bullinger, who wrote in the *Decades* that Sabbath rest was *not* for physical comfort or well-being, "but so that we should have the leisure to attend unto our spiritual business."[29] Archbishop Whitgift approved, and at the 1586 Convocation directed his clergy to study the *Decades*. Lancelot Andrewes had held a similar view of the Sabbath rest, but his lectures on the commandments were not published until 1630, and they are not cited by the Sabbatarian authors of 1630s and early 1640s.

It was to ensure freedom for religious *work* that Puritans sought to enforce a Sabbath cessation from ordinary labor. It was to the same end that they opposed Sunday recreation. Bownd made no exceptions: it is to be noted that he urged Christians to abstain from *all* "honest recreations and lawful delights" on the Lord's Day.[30] The prohibition that Puritans sought against all Sunday recreations can thus hardly be said to demonstrate the concern Hill believes them to have had for the working population. L'Estrange demands cessation from all labor in *God's Sabbath*, but never does he directly express a concern for the working classes of his own day. L'Estrange nowhere suggests that the Christian Sabbath is for any purpose other than the worship of God. Like Bownd, he wanted Christians to abstain from all recreations as well as from all work.[31] In November 1644 the Westminster Assembly voted that masters ought to have simple meals on Sundays, and this was a custom known among many Sabbatarians. But again, the emphasis was on getting the servants to church, not in giving them time off.[32] Bownd, it seems, did feel some difficulty over the fact that the servants of the very rich missed church in order to prepare and serve elaborate Sunday dinners for their master, for the Preface to the 1601 edition of *The True Doctrine of the Sabbath* contains lengthy instructions to servants to obey any Sabbath-breaking commands received from their masters. Bownd goes on to deal with the Sunday dinners of the wealthy in a classic passage:

> Concerning the feasts of noblemen and great personages, or their ordinary diet upon this day (which in comparison may be called feasts), because they represent in some measure the majesty of God on the earth, in carrying the image as it were of the magnificence and puissance of the Lord, in so much that they are called gods (Psal lxxxii.6), much is to be granted unto them ...[33]

Bownd, it should be noted, was not insensitive to the plight of working people, and also undertook to "exhort them that be in goverment to give some time to their children and servants for their honest recreation, upon others days."[34] It was not until later in 1641, after L'Estrange had published *God's Sabbath*, that George Harkwell declared that if there were a class of people who deserved leisure on Sundays, it was the working people, not the "gentlemen, who for the most part make every day holiday in following their sports."[35]

Were Sunday Recreations Witchcraft?

When he does come to deal with the problem of Puritan opposition to sports, Hill does not center his attention on the freedom to go to church which abstinence from sports provided, but upon witchcraft. "The traditional sports clearly were survivals of pre-Christian fertility rituals ... The campaign against the traditional sports linked up the campaign against the witches."[36] He bases this conclusion not on the writings of the Sabbatarians themselves, but upon his acceptance of the theories of Margaret Alice Murray. Murray was an Egyptologist who in the early 1920s took up seriously the views of the tellers of folk tales, notably Jacob Grimm, and combined them with the statements of witch-hunters and with the forced confessions of accused witches. She then postulated the existence of an organized pre-Christian religion surviving in England to her own day, which, she believed, had been unfairly termed "devil worship" by its Christian opponents. This cult of Diana she believed to be one which ultimately demanded human sacrifice, of a king to the Divine King.[37] What may have impressed Hill from her work, in addition to her belief that seventeenth-century dwellers on the English countryside were still *consciously* practicing an active pre-Christian religion, is her naive description of the "sabbaths" witches were said to celebrate with an abandon very much in contrast to the Puritan notion of behavior appropriate to worship on their Sabbath.[38] However, simply limiting ourselves to the evidence available before Hill wrote, we can arrive at another view of the matter.

By the time Hill published *Puritanism and Society*, Murray's work, although still read on the popular level, and found for a brief period in the *Britannica*, had been almost completely discredited by a long line of historical researchers into English and continental witchcraft. The first of these was Cecil L'Estrange Ewen. Ewen's *Witch Hunting and Witch Trials* (1929) and *Witchcraft and Demonianism* (1933) set new standards for the investigation of the subject by the study of trial records and other related sources. He would not base conclusions on the sensational pamphlets of the witch-hunters and the forced confessions of the accused, items upon which Murray had uncritically relied. Certainly folk-magic was and is practiced, but Ewen ended forever serious belief, for instance, in a thirteen-member "coven" as a standard organizational unit of members of the alleged religious groups, or that the "sabbaths" ever took place. Ewen's work has been followed by other investigators of the data, virtually all of whom find the evidence all contradicting the notion that local seers, hags, spell casters, and enchanters were part of any organized religion, let alone of a nation-wide fertility cult set upon resisting and outliving Christianity. The work of Ewen and his colleagues makes it clear that much of the twentieth-century practice of witchcraft is *based on*, not *evidence for* Murray's theories.[39]

Hill's contention is, again, most vulnerable to the objection that no seventeenth-century Sabbatarians mentioned that they were opposing the traditional pastimes of the people in order to defeat a dangerous opponent to Christianity. The literary monuments of Sabbatarianism evidence no concern with witches, nor is there a record of any other coincidence of Sabbatarianism and the prosection of accused witches. The silence of L'Estrange, Ley, and Harker is quite relevant here, for they wrote on the eve of the greatest English witch panic of all times, that of the mid-1640s. American perspective on the connection between Puritanism and witch-hunting has been distorted by the Massachusetts trials—the only people in authority there were Puritans. In England the case was much different, and it has been demonstrated that there was no particular connection between witch-hunting and English Puritanism.[40] I would add that there is much less connection between that persecution and Puritan opposition to the traditional country sports. The language of *The King's Book of Sports* and of Charles I's declaration reissuing that book take no notice of any association of the "customary sports" with witchcraft. The bishop of Hereford went so far in 1640 as to overlook entirely the undisputed occurrence of drunkenness, brawling, and illicit sex at church ales and organized Sunday sports, commending them instead for their civilizing influences. One of the writers whom L'Estrange opposed in *God's Sabbath*, Bishop Ironside, described the social value of the very May games and morris dances which Hill thinks were patently anti-Christian witchcraft.[41] Puritan writers never challenged Ironside on the issue of sports as relics of the old religions, although they are critical of him on many other points.

The dread of witchcraft aside, what evidence is there for the Puritan motivation in opposing sports? The unsensational answer is that they were, quite simply, what the Puritans believed to be an offense against God on the day devoted to divine service. Sabbatarians were motivated by religious rather than social concerns in the attempts to prohibit labor on the Sabbath. It was those same concerns which caused them to oppose Sunday sports in a situation in which the legal tradition was only partially on their side.

It seems, then, that while the social study of Christian institutions and doctrines is a valuable one, due regard must be paid first to the theological matrix which generates them. In the present case, the data allow no other conclusion than it was in fact the search for religious truth and the attempt to be obedient Christians that motivated the Sabbatarians. It cannot be denied that two kings misunderstood and mistreated Sabbatarian Puritans, and it certainly must be admitted that they became increasingly alienated from their government, church, and civic life in pre-1641 England, but these must be assessed to be consequences of their beliefs, not the primary reasons for holding them.

Notes

1. In Christopher Hill, *Society and Puritanism in Pre-Revolutionary England* (London, 1964) 145-218.

2. Horton Davies, *Worship and Theology in England. From Andrewes to Baxter and Fox, 1603-1690* (Princeton, 1975) 222ff.

3. A good guide through the morass of three centuries' worth of material is Max Levy, *Der Sabbath in England* (Leipzig, 1933), which has the added advantage for Anglo-American readers of indicating how an English institution (adopted to varying extent in America) appeared to members of another culture in the 1930s.

4. Robert Cox, F.S.A., was an editor of and frequent contributor to the *Edinburgh Phrenological Journal* and created the index for an edition of *The Encyclopedia Britannica*. His attention was turned to the Sabbatarian question in *The Whole Doctrine of Calvin About the Sabbath and the Lord's Day* (Edinburgh, 1860) and in the exhaustive *The Literature of the Sabbath Question* (Edinburgh, 1865). James Augustus Hessey addressed himself to the question in the Bampton Lectures for 1860, which appeared in print as *Sunday, Its Origin, History, and Present Obligation* (London, 1860).

5. W.B. Whitaker, *Sunday in Tudor and Stuart Times* (London, 1933), and *The Eighteenth Century English Sunday* (London, 1940).

6. Letter of Robert Reyce to John Winthrop in 1636, *Mass. Historical Society Collections*, 4th Series, 6, 396-409, in Hill, "Uses" 159.

7. Nicholas Bownd, *Sabbathum Veteris et Novi Testimenti: Or, the True Doctrine of the Sabbath* (London, 1601), completes the thought begun in his *The Doctrine of the Sabbath, Plainely Layde Forth and Soundly Proved* (London, 1595).

8. Church of England, *Certain Sermons or Homilies Appointed to be Read in Churches in the Time of the Late Queen Elizabeth* (Oxford, 1840) 303.

9. Church of England, *Certain Sermons or Homilies Appointed to be Read in*

Churches in the Time of the Late Queen Elizabeth (Oxford, 1840) 303.

10. Donald McAdams, "Riots as a Measure of Religious Conflict in Seventeenth and Eighteenth Century England," *Andrews University Seminary Studies* 14 (1976) 289.

11. A complete survey of the New Testament and Patristic issues is found in Willy Rordorf, *Sabbath und Sonntag* (Zurich, 1972). It is Rordorf's view that the Lord's Day and the Sabbath were observed separately in the early church.

12. Text in Levy, *Der Sabbath in England* 61f.

13. Translation in Donald Maclean, *The Law of the Lord's Day in the Celtic Church* (Edinburgh, 1926) 3f, 15.

14. Text in Levy, *Der Sabbath in England* 61f.

15. *Injunctions* of 1547, sec. 6.

16. 5 & 6 Edw. VI, cap. 1.

17. The petitioners had also asked that "the Lord's Day be not profaned; the rest upon holy days not so strictly enforced."

18. 6 Edw. VI, cap. 1.

19. The legal studies are summarized in Hill, "Uses" 155.

20. 3 Car. I., cap. 2.

21. Douglas R. Brackenridge, "The Development of Sabbatarianism in Scotland 1560-1650," *Journal of Presbyterian History* 42 (1964) 149.

22. Second Decade, Sermon Six, my emphasis.

23. Daniel Augsburger, "Sunday in Pre-Reformation Disputations in French Switzerland," *Andrews University Seminary Studies* 14 (1976) 265. Gerhard F. Hasel, "Sabbatarian Anabaptists of the Sixteenth Century," *Andrews University Seminary Studies* 5 (1967) 101; 6 (1968) 19.

24. Hill, "Uses" 166.

25. Richard Hooker, *Of the Laws of Ecclesiastical Polity*, V, 71, 70.

26. Nicholas Bownd, *Sabbathum Veteris et Novi Testamenti* (London, 1601) 271f.

27. In Hill, "Uses" 174.

28. John Ley, *Sunday a Sabbath* (London, 1641) 200.

29. First Decade, Sermon Eight.

30. Bownd, *Sabbathum* 271.

31. Hamon L'Estrange, *God's Sabbath* (Cambridge, 1641) 130.

32. Lightfoot kept a *Journal of the Assembly of Divines*, where he recorded for 31 November 1644: "[proposed] That there be no feasting on the Sabbath. This Mr. Marshal opposed, and Dr. Temple and I myself. They instanced in Christ's feasting, Luke xiv, and in his feasting, at least dining, with all his desciples in Peter's house, Matt. viii. Therefore it was proposed thus, 'That the diet on the Sabbath-day be so ordered, that no servants or other be unnecessarily kept from the public service'." (327-0) The Westminster *Directory* quotes the resolution almost verbatim.

33. Bownd, *Sabbathum* 211. The question of the conflicting duties owed God and master for those whose employers ordered them to work on Sunday rose to its highest degree of intensity in the barrage of books fired between Edward Brerwood and Nicholas and Richard Byefield, the Byefields maintaining that servants must disobey their masters when ordered to break the Sabbath rest.

34. Bownd, *Sabbathum* 271f.

35. George Harkwell, *A Short but Cleare Discourse of the Lord's Day* (London, 1641) 36.

36. Hill, "Uses" 187.

37. See particularly her *The Witch Cult in Western Europe* (repr., London, 1962) and *The God of the Witches* (repr., New York, 1952). Murray's views enjoyed something of a vogue and still continue to inspire made-for-television and other low-budget motion pictures. Anthony Schaffer's screenplay "The Wicker Man" is one rare first-rate dramatic adaptation of her views, and combines them with some of Julius Caesar's less responsible observations upon the Druids.

38. Murray, *The God of the Witches*, Chapters 3 and 4.

39. Modern works which add more depth than is required here abound. Helpful for beginning further study on this question are the following. Julio Baroja, *The World of the Witches* (Chicago, 1968); A.D.J. Macfarlane, *Witchcraft in Tudor and Stuart England* (New York, 1970); Wallace Notestein, *A History of Witchcraft in England* (New York, 1952).

40. A.D.J. Macfarlane, *Witchcraft in Tudor and Stuart England* (New York, 1970), especially Chapter 14.

41. Gilbert Ironside, *Seven Questions of the Sabbath* (Oxford, 1637) 271-275.

LITURGICAL THEOLOGY

14

"Successio Sanctorum"

Herman Wegman

BESIDES MY ESTEEM FOR THE SCHOLARLY WORK OF THOMAS TALLEY, THE OC-
casion for my contribution to this collection arose from the review which
I wrote of his book *The Origins of the Liturgical Year*.[1] Therein I said: "Talley's study seems to suggest that the memorial of the martyrs does not
have any relevance for his topic. If so, I question his thesis."[2] In a personal letter the author clarified to me that the reason he omitted memorial
days for saints and martyrs from consideration in his study had not to do
with a low estimation of this topic, but with practical decisions taken in
relationship to the publication of his book. I am pleased with that answer; for I have gradually become convinced that the so-called *sanctorale*
has exercised just as great, if not greater, an influence upon the religious
imagination and piety of the majority of the faithful as has the *temporale*,
the origin of which Talley has so creatively reinterpreted in his study of
the sources. It seems good to me as my contribution to the present collection in honor of Thomas Talley to elucidate this conviction.

Several years ago I radically altered the core question of my research
into the history of the liturgy. Until then, through the study of the sources, like those for the eucharistic prayer, I had pursued a strictly "liturgical" analysis, namely, an analysis of the textual material, without much
regard for the context, for the users and for the "makers" of the liturgy.
However, I discovered that such an analysis remained superficial because being purely "liturgical" it was not equipped to see the liturgy as a
faith confession of and in the assembly. The danger was that liturgy was

studied as an *ens in se*, with the consequence that only the worship of the literate higher clergy would be researched. Eventually this would mean that the piety of the faithful would be ignored, a piety which was and is not so affected by the churchly liturgy as the makers of that liturgy had intended. The sense of faith among church folk (to use a somewhat prejudicial term), in whom over the "long run" (*la longue durée*) the church's life is most invested, is however an extremely important element to remember in testing the churchly liturgy.

That liturgical experts often forget this piety, treat it somewhat patronizingly, or (in the worst case) reject it, is proved by the recent production of liturgical scholarship. What has now for some time belonged to the normal tool kit of the church historian is still mostly absent from that of the liturgical researcher, at least as far as I can observe. This absence is apparent in many recent studies and commentaries which deal with innovative or restorative projects found in the new liturgical books of the churches. These commentaries dwell for the most part on the narrowest terrain of liturgy. The attention devoted to the assembly is imaginary: "the faithful" are discussed as they ought to be, not as they are. The liturgical renewal of the Roman Rite effected since the Second Vatican Council is impressive, but the commentaries on that renewal circle around the liturgy as *ens in se*, without any critique arising from a history of popular mentality. The study of worship by the liturgical scholars deals with the superstructure and not the infrastructure. This is precisely my objection against this sort of research: it is too limited, too narrowly "churchly," too hierarchical both in intention and in execution.

In German Roman Catholic liturgical studies, which have been especially marked by their high-church approach, there are however other voices heard. In the collection presented in 1986 to E.J. Lengling[3] critical observations about the renewed liturgy are included. Angenendt points out a lack on the part of liturgical scholars of genuine interest in the Middle Ages;[4] and Vorgrimler has both criticism and questions for the liturgy as a *"Thema der Dogmatik."*[5] One can say that both writers object to purely "liturgical" approaches and to unambiguous explanations of (in this case) the Roman Rite, which go on as if the *lex orandi* had no importance. I have myself given voice to this concern in a short article:[6] using the expression of Hayden White—"the liberation of the present from the burden of history"[7]—I opine that the churches must be relieved of the burden of historical liturgy (*"la pesanteur de la liturgie"*).

But a great problem affects the scope of my research's results. How can you distinguish what theology and the theologians have contributed in worship from what has come from the piety of the faithful? How do you research the influence of the liturgy on the mentality of the faithful, and vice versa? These questions demand a different mode of inquiry, which is not immediately achievable but can be found only gradually. On the basis of what has already been established through study of the sources about calendars and the devotion to the saints, I intend in this article to attempt *a theological re-evaluation of the cult of the saints*, to which at the same time the piety of the faithful will be related. The thesis from which I work is this: in spite of the current desacralization of nature and cosmos surrounding humanity, the cult of the saints has been continually present in the mentality of the faithful, even when it has been forced into a somewhat cryptic form by the didactic violence of high-church liturgical instruction. Thus I present here not an historical but a theological contribution, in which theology lets itself be counseled by the piety of the people. My theological thesis is this: the devotion to the saints through the ages makes it apparent that, besides the apostolic succession, *there is surely a second and not less important pillar of the church: the "successio sanctorum," the coherent array of evangelical witnesses and prophets.* This succession, based on the *sequela Christi*, can be of decisive significance for an ecumenical ecclesiology. It can unite where the other form of succession has up to now divided the churches.

The Calendarium

Everyone at home in the theological tradition of the Roman patriarchate knows that behind the words "Roman calendar," at first sight a purely technical term, more is hidden, just as behind the title "Roman liturgy." These terms are components of the Roman ecclesiology, which proceeds from the conviction that in spite of schisms and heresies the true church of Christ in this world is to be found in the church which calls itself Roman Catholic. This church is *the* representative of what is called in the Creed "the one, holy, catholic and apostolic church." This church is universal in time and space and unites in itself all local and regional churches around the central bishop of Rome. The church of Christ spread throughout the world is one under the leadership of the Apostolic See. Thus, on this basis, there is only one liturgy and, within that liturgy, only one calendar.

In contrast to other churches, the universal liturgy and calendar of the Roman patriarchate are part of its ecclesiology, in which final responsibility for the life and teaching of the church, as it is theologically founded, rests with the Apostolic See. This means that an essentially local (namely, *"stadtrömische"*) church organization and liturgical tradition has, through the development of Roman ecclesiology, grown to be *the* universal tradition of the Roman patriarchate. In the practical elaboration of the liturgical principles of the Second Vatican Council (it is actually strange in itself that the liturgy was a subject of conciliar pronouncement, but according to this ecclesiology it is completely fitting) this unity principle has been consistently pursued and complied with. In spite of local adaptations of worship provided for here and there in the liturgical books of the Roman liturgy we must conclude that the Roman liturgy is one and the same everywhere it is celebrated. This is so precisely on the grounds of the aforementioned theological principle.

The *"stadtrömische"* liturgy has become the universal liturgy. The same holds for the calendar. In spite of proper local or regional calendars, the core of the Roman calendar has been declared as the universal calendar. One can doubt whether the attempt to achieve this universal character has succeeded; the critics of the Roman calendar suggest that it has not.[8] P. Jounel has demonstrated that finally very little of "universality" remains: the calendar is Roman in its basic text and it has remained Roman.[9] The development of the canonization process, in which the official declaration of who is a saint is reserved to the bishop of Rome,[10] has further strengthened the Romanization of the universal calendar.

As far as I have been able to ascertain, other liturgical traditions, such as the Anglican, the Evangelical-Lutheran, and the Reformed-Calvinist, have not been so strictly tied to an ecclesiological principle. In these traditions there have been historic attempts to bring about more unity in the celebration of the liturgy, principally out of practical theological and strictly liturgical motives. People have striven toward more centrally regulated forms of liturgical renewal. But such a massively applied theological principle as in the Roman patriarchate is not known in the other churches.

Even if I, as a Roman Catholic liturgical scholar, would want to choose a less fixed and a less theologically determined conception of liturgy, the fact of this theological principle is still there. An historical-theological reflection such as I propose in this article is made rather difficult since a good many theological arguments foreign to the liturgy itself are at stake and cannot be avoided. Writing about an historically rooted *successio sanctorum* can present an interesting panorama, but the view is very quickly narrowed by attendant theological principles. Although historical research into calendars can demonstrate that the cult of the saints might be just as important, if not more substantial, a foundation for the church, the universalistic ecclesiological principle, on which the Roman patriarchate rests, will nonetheless insist upon the last word of unity. I recognize this theological problem, but for the moment set it aside to give my thoughts free course. I proceed from the "calendar" as such, without these ecclesiological implications. With J. Hennig,[11] I understand by that term a list of the memorial days of the saints according to the course of the year's cycle, a list intended as a key to the other liturgical books, such as the sacramentary and the lectionary. The *calendarium* serves for the celebration of memorial days and preserves for posterity the death day of saints and martyrs.

The ancient world knew a calendar which determined religious festivals and the worship of the gods at fixed times and days. That calendar memorialized the dedication of temples and the honoring of emperors. The Jewish religion knew festivals, with a salvation-historical woof, which were fixed yearly according to definite calendrical calculations. In both cases, the word *calare*, which is heard behind "calendar," fits: on the basis of precise calculations the length of the month, the ides and the calends, or (as in the Jewish tradition) the feasts in the cycles of the year, were fixed and promulgated. In these matters, the early Christian congregations had no need to create something new, but could make use of pre-existing customs and patterns of marking time. And so the Christians did: they fixed their memorial days, taking them up into the calendar. They annually calculated on what day a martyr had died (beginning with Polycarp, the bishop of Smyrna), in order to remember this martyr, who was proposed every year on that fixed date as an example for the congregation. Already very early on, lists must have existed of this *locale* and perhaps also of an *interlocale*. Could it be that only apostolic letters and Gospels were exchanged and not the dates and the stories of the deaths of the martyrs? Lacking any data, we have only guesses, unless the "memoirs of the apostles" about which Justin writes (*apomnemoneumata*, Apology 67:3) contained more than the Gospels. Might the passion story of Jesus, told in different versions (the synoptics and John), early on have been exemplary for other passion stories, first of all for that of Stephen in Acts 7?

This much we know: we are on sure footing only in the middle of the fourth century with two documents—the Roman Chronograph (354) with its list of *depositiones* (death days) of the Roman bishops and martyrs,[12] and the Syriac Martyrologium (second half of the fourth century).[13] From that time on, the calendar tradition is a firm datum in the local or regional churches.[14] If we add to this the *martyrologia* which, although not the same as the calendars, cannot be conceived of without local calendars, the *Martyrologium Hieronymianum* in the first place,[15] then the image is complete. What image? Quite simply this: from time immemorial in an unbroken continuity (the "long run") Christian congregations have remembered the grace-filled men and women who in their living and in their dying after the model of Jesus bore witness to the Good News, as martyrs, as "confessors," and, if we may use this word here, as prophets.

How interested the *historici* are in the "holy man!"[16] There is, howeverer, silence about the "holy woman." One fears that this topic cannot be unearthed from the sources. Or is this lack the consequence of a blind spot in the researchers?[17] The time has passed in which Christian hagiography can be held in low esteem; the "too tired model" of the separation between the religion of the people and that of the elite has been taken under fire by Peter Brown.[18] The interest in the saints and in their *vitae* is apparent in many recent publications,[19] and all of them, in one way or another, are looking for the mentality or the pious impulses at the roots of the writing of the lives of the saints. There is a "new blossoming of 'hagiology'."[20] Each of the researchers has a different approach, but they are united by their interest in the lives of the saints and in the veneration which these lives are given by believers. If we add here the studies of popular religion, in which the cult of the saints and the phenomena of exorcism play a large role, then the "output" of the scholarship which concerns us would be immense.[21] One can speak of an historical "hagiographic discourse,"[22] to the discovery of which many researchers have contributed.

Of course, the opinions differ about the construction of this hagiographic discourse; it would have to be called a miracle if the interpretive patterns of all these scholars had been the same. J. Fontaine[23] and C. Pietri[24] regard as a reduction P. Brown's sociological explanation of the origin and growth of the cult of the saints. They plead for the religious or theological dimension of the *vitae* and of the cult which came to be based on them. From the life of the saint, so they posit, the *sequi Christum* cannot be discarded. In the foreword of his book *Unquiet Souls*, Richard Kieckhefer notes the difference between his theological reading of the sources and that of Vauchez and of Weinstein and Bell,[25] and there is indeed a differing result in the three research projects. Kieckhefer echoes the essence of the holiness ideal of the fourteenth century in his title: unquiet souls experience the way in which human existence in this earthly life remains unfulfilled, and they share the certainty that life elsewhere will find fulfillment and plenitude. Both death and the ascetic life are directed toward that fulfillment.[26] On the other hand, Andre Vauchez is able to dig out of the canonization documents of the fourteenth century (more precisely, 1330-1370) a conception of holiness which is based not so much upon evangelical poverty as in the preceding period, but upon a new respect for culture. Holiness is brought into relationship with study and with cultural interest and development.[27] Furthermore, similarities seem to exist between the typology of the miracles in the Christian tradition of late antiquity as van Uytfanghe gives it—he interprets the miracles as *caritatieve mirakelen* intended in imitation of the *pertransiit benefa-*

ciendo ("he went about doing good," Acts 10:38)[28]—and the results of the study of P.-A. Sigal in regard to the eleventh and twelfth centuries.[29] Differences in nuance can thus certainly be noted in these successive studies, but it is also striking how a basic typology can be made out of the many facets of the cult of the saints through the ages. It is this basic typology which concerns me.

When I consider the prayers, the Mass texts, the songs, and the *vitae* which I have had in my hands and read, a mere fraction of the total hagiographic output, what especially strikes me is a clearly recognizable undercurrent in piety which draws people to the saints. The honoring of the saints on their memorial days, the veneration of the relics, the processions and the translations, are supported by real human experiences of need: powerlessness to change one's own social world, inability to break away from the tyranny of others, incapacity to raise oneself either to resistance or to full life. This powerlessness is not removed by the surrounding society. On the contrary, society is often intent upon maintaining this very weakness. Who were the saints? Women and men of God, belonging to the good world of God, who in their earthly lives did what they could to alleviate this great need and who in their heavenly existence continue the task in God's name, but now more powerfully and more surely, led by the finger of God. The invocation of the saints has been encouraged both by lament over suffering, pain, loneliness, and injustice, and by certainty that the heavenly patrons were able and prepared to lighten this yoke. Relics, images, graces, and churches with the names of patron saints were beacons of hope and of transcendent certainty. Precisely for this reason "local" saints became known and revered also outside their own city, being taken up in an "inter-local" pattern of remembrance and veneration. Seen in this way, it is not strange that there exists a global calendar with commemorations of holy people.

According to the reception of the faithful, the saints are prophets, even if many Christians would not use this word to describe them. A prophet proclaims the good news of God, in images and in unambiguously clear language, with examples borrowed from daily life, in parables, and with miraculous signs of healing and liberation. When this proclamation of God collides with the social arrangements which human beings make with and at the expense of each other, and with the idols which are set up here and there, then the prophet speaks directly of what is going on and does so for the sake of those who have suffered. The prophetic witness of the saints creates possibilities of resurrection and resistance: this in the end constitutes the power of attraction the faithful feel in the saints. Added to this is the powerful witness of their giving of their lives. *There is not just one passion and resurrection account, that of Jesus; there are* many. There is not one *vita* of Christ, set down in the Gospels, *but "une biographie continuée du Christ" in the vitae of the saints."*[30]

Here we meet the specific character of Christian hagiographic discourse, of which van Uytfanghe gives a typology. I entirely subscribe to this typology, in spite of the objections which cleave to such a generalizing approach. Van Uytfanghe describes the following elements:

1. *The saint is a person of God*, who lives out of the grace of God, knows himself/herself to be dependent on that grace, and senses that he/she is free to live in the dominion of God. This makes the soul of the saint restless (the title of Richard Kieckhefer's book is to the point: *Unquiet Souls*), because he or she experiences that the divine dominion is veiled in this earthly life. The saint knows that if one wants to live from and with God, it is necessary to invert ordinary values, so that the longing for God can continue to shape human existence. The saint receives grace to continue seeking for the fullness of existence with God. The only value and truth for the saint is this: God's grace can seize us, and so seized we seek for heavenly fullness in earthly emptiness. As is apparent from many *vitae*, this is a painful and joyful process. Saints are believers who, in the estimation of their fellow believers, have gone through this process and have admitted the dynamic of God's Spirit to their lives. They are on journey, even though they may live in a cell. They are not divine (*theioi anthropoi*), but are being "divinized." They feel the beckoning *eschaton*.

2. The *sequela Christi*[31] determines the life of the saint, whether it is as a martyr or as a confessor (a tautology!). The life-story of Christ is continued in that of the saint, and one can speak of the saint sharing the lot of Jesus, both his passion and his resurrection. This means that in hagiography after the death of the saint his or her life is regarded as a pure image of the Lord. The *virtus* of the saint is situated not primarily in wonder-working and miracles (even though the participants in the cult of the saints may most often have their hearts set there), but in the virtue of *imitatio*. The love of Christ, his *amor Dei* and his *caritas*, imbue the saint, so that the history of salvation and of healing is carried on. The life of the saint actualizes in the saint's own time the lives of many prophets who serve as examples, and it culminates in the *sequela Christi*. The model for this following of Christ is inimitably expressed by the evangelist Matthew (25:31-46): "Truly, I say to you, as you did it to one of the least of these my brethren, you did it to me" (25:40). This existence for the sake of the other, motivated by the perception of the marks of the Lord in the other, is also the actual impulse for the asceticism and penance which play so large a role in the lives of the saints. It may be true that in the successive periods and differing cultural settings of Christianity asceticism has marked an attitude toward life which is individualistic, directed to-

ward one's own salvation and motivated by a certain contempt for the earthly (the somewhat dualistically colored *terrena despicere*). Nonetheless, it is apparent in the hagiographic material that the actual impulse for penance and asceticism is the imitation of Jesus: the saint wants to be like Jesus and to live for the other. The ego was to be set aside. Asceticism envisions a radical end of egoism, even though some radical forms of penance from the past suggest a masochistic egoism. The same impulse comes to expression in the miraculous powers of the saints: they do not do the miracles, but they hand on the miracles of God and make current the healing power of the Lord. Of the five thousand miracle stories which have been studied by P.-A. Sigal,[32] the great majority are concerned with the continuation of the *caritas Christi*. The miracles are *"caritative,"* as van Uytfanghe remarks.[33]

In connection with sanctity as *sequela Christi*, yet another fact should be recorded: the *vitae* of the saints are not informative or historical in the meaning which we give to these words; they are performative. The stories intend to stir up and to stimulate the hearer to imitation, in order to perpetuate the *"biographie continuée du Christ."* Is there a life-description of a saint in which doctrine and dogma, orthodoxy and truth, the "theological competence" of the saint, play a role? Even in the canonization processes of the counter-Reformation or later, which processes dealt with holy proclaimers of the faith, the interest was not so much in their risk for the sake of true doctrine as in their efforts for the preaching of the true faith, the faith which brings felicity and blessing. The lives of the saints which are available to us in an unbroken line from the early church into our own time are intended not to offer proof for the *ecclesia apostolica*, founded upon apostolic succession, but to stir up believers to imitate the imitators and so keep the life of Jesus graphic and visible. The stories continue the line. I detect here no separation of doctrine and life, truth and holiness, but it can be asserted that the vast majority of hagiography demonstrates no doctrinal ambitions. Hagiographic discourse intends to urge believers to become like those whose story is being read. It is therefore important to understand that in the liturgy of East and West it is not only the Bible which is publicly read, but the lives of the saints. However much the principle of *sola scriptura*, passed on to us in the Reformation of the church, is to be understood and honored, most liturgical traditions have neither known nor applied this principle. The stories of Jesus and of his holy ones are read and held in balance, even though, as I understand it, in the piety of the faithful often a superstitious imbalance is imputed to the saints in the question of the mediation of grace. In the forward of the *Passio* of Perpetua and Felicity stands the following:

If examples of faith from the ancient past, bearing witness to the glory of God and working human edification, were written down with the express intention that by their being read aloud, as if that were the vivid presentation of the events themselves, God might be honored and humanity comforted, why should not new examples which are just as much in accord with both purposes be set down? The more so because these later texts will also at some time in the future be ancient and necessary for posterity, even if they are given less authority now in their own time because of the presumed venerability of what is old ... We acknowledge and honor the new visions then, according to the promise, equally with the old prophecies ... And so we proclaim to you, brothers and children, what we have heard and touched, so that you who were there may continue to remember the glory of the Lord and you who now learn of it through hearing may have communion with the holy martyrs, and through them with our Lord Jesus Christ, to whom belong splendor and honor in the ages of ages. Amen.[34]

The *nova fidei documenta* are set next to the *vetera documenta*! According to Augustine, for example in Sermon 280, the account of Perpetua and Felicity was still being read in the liturgy on their feast day. This tradition was long preserved and deserves to be restored again.

3. In the lives of the saints much attention is given to the fascination with and the *aversion of evil*. The many apotropaic rites and prayers which the tradition has passed on are a link for us to the spirit of the *vitae*. The devil and his *pompa* have gotten plenty of attention in the popular expressions of faith. There certainly has been a clear development in the understanding of the *abrenuntiatio* (the renunciation of evil) and of exorcism, moving from a more personally active role for the one who makes the renunciation (as, for example, in the baptismal rite of the *Tradition Apostolica*) to the more passively experienced casting out of demons. But there has always been the conviction that we have to do with an evil Power which opposes the coming of the dominion of God.[35] The prototype of the power and the impotence of evil is the narrative of the temptation of Jesus (Mt 4:11). It may indeed be true that, in the monastic tradition, this narrative was the model and the first example of a great deal of ascetic literature, in which the battle with wicked desires tempting the monk stood as a central concern (the *Vita Antonii*, to begin with!). In any case, it is clear that popular piety has known about possession by the devil, about the malicious power of the devil in humanity and in the world of humanity, but also about the possibility of resistance to and rejection of evil. It is no wonder, then, that in the lives of the saints the saint's imitation of Christ is primarily concentrated in an undaunted conflict with and power over wrong. Thus the saints became in the piety of the faithful the warriors, assigned to the heavenly *militia*, against all the

forms of evil with which humankind must deal: sickness and sin, suffering and death. From the hagiographic point of view, the saints gave convincing proof, during their lives and after their deaths, that evil can be conquered. Thus have the faithful, in their painful earthly existence, turned to them for help and deliverance, since such help was frequently not available in human concourse, with the world and society presenting a mostly satanic face. Virtue is the earnest of holiness, which is itself pure grace; and holiness is the final surprise attack on evil. Such language makes up a significant part of hagiographic discourse, which discourse intends to be performative, that is, it intends to lead to the conviction that evil has neither the first word nor the last.

To summarize: in the continuous succession of biographies of the saints, toward which we in our time ought to be more receptive,[36] the *foi veçue* comes to expression: saints are grace-filled God-seekers with a mystical receptivity for the dominion of heaven; they are followers and imitators of the prophet "who went about doing good" (Acts 10:38); they are living witnesses of the power over evil in and between people and over evil itself, witnesses of the resurrection from sin and from death. Moreover, this continuous succession of narratives demonstrates an unbroken *successio sanctorum*, a chain of holy lives, who show forth the strength of the Gospel of Jesus.

Ought not this *successio sanctorum* receive more attention in the churches? Could it not be of pre-eminent importance for the doctrine of the church, for ecclesiology? That is the intention of the title of this article and, at the same time, the content of its thesis. I am aware that hereby I walk an untrodden path, having found nothing anywhere which appeared to be an ecclesiological valuing of the *successio sanctorum*, not even in the otherwise splendid "Lima document" of the World Council of Churches,[37] in which, in the chapter on ministry, the saints have apparently nothing to contribute to a conception of "ordination." Ordained ministry is regarded, apparently, as belonging to another and a higher order.

Interpretation

By "interpretation" I mean here my interpretation of the above described typology of the saints, with an eye to the grounding of an ecumenical ecclesiology. The list of books I read which contribute to such reflections is not only theological in character, but it is also limited. I am aware that hagiographic data can also admit of other interpretations and can lead to a socio-cultural paradigm. I consider that for this latter I am not prepared, demanding as it does a more detailed study.

Concerning the line in the Creed, "We believe in one holy ... church," Hans Küng writes as follows:

> The history of the Church is not only a very human history, but a deeply sinful history ... No excuses can avail us here; we must accept the realities of the case ... Because it is not an idealized and hypostatized pure element, distinct from human beings, but it is a fellowship of believing men, the Church is a sinful Church.[38]

The concept "holy church," found in the Creed, is not found as such in the New Testament. The Christian communities of the New Testament were too deeply rooted in the faith of Israel for them to have forgotten that there is only one who is holy—God. "Holy" is, as it were, a synonym for divine. God is the Other, the Holy. Although it is true that the song "Holy, holy, holy" (see Is 6:1-7; Rv 4:2-11) only later came to be part of the eucharistic prayer, that song is now, together with the Lord's Prayer, part of the memorable traditional core of the liturgy which continuously forms and transforms our image of God. The old visions of the prophet and of the seer give an unearthly glow to our worship in the present day. This means that the word "holy" must be used critically and cannot easily be applied to people. Only one is holy, and God's creatures are sanctified through God's own holiness. The New Testament is no place to find a magical form and experience of holiness. *Lumen gentium,* the Constitution on the Church from the Second Vatican Council, expressed the faith that the church is indestructibly holy in lapidary words,[39] but it combined that pronouncement with the confession, "You alone are the Holy One."

It therefore follows ineluctably that *the expression "holy church" is a derivative confession.* The church, and the people in and of the church, can be called holy because they are sanctified, graced by God the Holy One, touched by God, immersed in God's Spirit. And even this expression, "sanctified by God," is sanctified in the believing people who are being sanctified. All must turn from sinful existence in the grace-enabled turn toward the Holy. The confession, "we believe in one holy ... church," is then an expression of unwavering hope: the church shall be sanctified. Its future and that of its members shall be hidden in God the Holy One. Sin and death are not the final categories of the Creed, but holiness and life.

One can easily look all this up in learned commentaries on the Creed and theological studies of the church.[40] But what strikes me is that in such ecclesiological studies the saints remain continuously out of purview, even though the writing concerns the holy church. The saints have their place in ascetical or mystical tractates, but they are absent in the theology of the church. "Ecclesiologists" know how to make clear to us that the church is both sinful and holy—sinful as an institution carried on by human beings, and holy in the sense of being graced by God—but none of these scholars points out the phenomenon of holiness as it is experienced by the faithful, by the "common sense" in the church. The theological tractate on the holiness of the church undervalues and forgets the *successio sanctorum*, which is in fact the only phenomenon capable of giving concrete form to the confession of faith in the holiness of the church. Where is the holiness of the church shown? Not in the writings of the theologians but in the *vitae* of the saints. I intend not to sound polemical, but to register a genuine lack, a missed chance for giving flesh and blood to the confession of a holy church. When I reflect upon the holy church, the vision of the prophet comes to mind:

> And he said to me, "Son of man, can these bones live?" And I answered, "O Lord GOD, thou knowest" ... Then he said to me, "Prophesy to the breath, prophesy, son of man" ... and the breath came into them, and they lived, and stood upon their feet, an exceedingly great host. (Ez 37:1-14)

The dry bones, of which the church seems to consist, come to life through the Spirit of God, and it appears that the Spirit has transformed the church into a church of saints, re-created with the breath of life.

Thus I come to the core of my own interpretation of what has been distilled above from hagiographic discourse: the saints, whom the church through the ages has always had in its midst, are the living and positive proof of the credal assertion *credo sanctum ecclesiam*. That the church is a community of sinners is verifiable, but that it nonetheless can be characterized as holy is not only a hopeful prospect, directed toward the *eschaton*, but also a confession based upon the actual and realized experience of holiness by so many men and women in all the periods of church history. *The credal confession of the holy church is no free-floating pronouncement, but is filled with the life stories of people who have been sanctified and graced by God though the ages.*

Yet another element significant for our subject can be unearthed out of hagiographic discourse. Many *vitae* indicate that the life of the saint is regarded as proof of the ongoing flow of salvation history. No separation is made between the first and the second Testaments, between then and now (the lectionary of the renewed Roman liturgy might well learn something here). Rather, the history of God with humanity is seen and experienced as ongoing and as one, and therein lies the basis of the hope "that is in us" that the times shall be fulfilled. In the early church there was a much stronger presence of typology—in which past, present and future were united in an all-embracing confession of Christ, the same yesterday, today and forever (Heb 13:8)—than in the following periods. Even so, the church has always confessed that the history of God with humanity was not only to be projected into the past, but also could be experienced as present, could be relied upon now, could form current prayer. There have been chiliastic movements in the church. There have been doctrinal propositions which separated the God of the Old Testament from the God of the New. But the Creed, the liturgy, and hagiography have all confessed the unity of salvation history. It is entirely possible (though it would require further research to clearly affirm) that the *vitae* have been influenced by the liturgy, for in the liturgy the typology of saving events and persons (Moses and the exodus, Elijah, Samuel, King David, Solomon) plays an enormous role. What is certain is that a network of biblical allusions and *exempla* are found in hagiography, and that the imitation of biblical figures is of great importance. Does this explain the fact that in not a few Christian calendars persons from the Hebrew Scriptures are presented for veneration? In any case, the Moses/ Peter typology, which C. Pietri has extensively described,[41] is no exception. *L'amour des lettres et le désir de Dieu*[42] of the medieval monk bears the same pattern of thought.

If then we describe the saint, in the manner of hagiographic discourse itself, as a person touched by the Holy (a "holy man") who follows Christ, the prophet who "went about doing good," and who combats and overcomes evil, and if we add to this that the *vitae* see the saints as imitators of exemplary figures from the Hebrew Scriptures (Moses the precursor, Elijah the wonder-worker, etc.), then we may summarize this entire image with the word "prophet." The *nabi* or *prophetes* is a person graced and gifted by God and inspired by the Spirit who conveys the message of God in words and in symbolic actions. This message has to do with the holiness of God and the conversion of human beings who live in covenant with the Holy One. The conversion which is preached has individual and social implications, being required of the king as well as of the people. In the Gospels, Jesus too is characterized as a prophet (for example, Lk 4:24; 13:33; 24:19,21; Mt 16:14). The *sequela Christi* thus implies the prophetic character of the saint, who receives the message of God, lives and experiences that message, and hands it on to the church and the believers. The prophetic saint offers to his or her congregation a "program of behavior"[43] that the saint has interiorly realized and experienced. *Thus, the saint is not only the representative of the Prophet, but also serves the continuation of the prophecy.*

This leads me to the *conclusion* of my interpretation: the churches must relate the concretely experienced forms of holiness, perceived by the "common sense" of the faithful or by one or another form of churchly approval or canonization, to the pronouncement *credo sanctam ecclesiam*. This is not merely to fill out this confession or to enable one "to believe in" holiness, but also to see the communion of saints (*communio sanctorum*, confessed in the baptismal Creed) as embracing heaven and earth and yet anchored here and now—in our world. It is not only the heavenly spirits who stand before God's throne. Also our saints participate in that liturgy and bring about the inclusion of the churches in the *communio* of the saints and even the unfolding of the churches themselves toward *communio*. Indeed, the credal confession is, at the same time, the assertion of the trust that the sin of church divisions and disunity shall be forgiven by the cloud of holiness out of which the Holy One speaks. I am of the opinion—and this is my interpretation of the *vitae* of the saints— that the succession of prophetic saints or of holy prophets is of fundamental importance for the theology of the church of Jesus, namely, it lays down a second and distinct basis upon which the church is founded. We have become accustomed to the image of the Rock, coming out of the churchly tradition of that image. The Rock is hard and often unapproachable; such a metaphoric basis can contribute to fundamentalism. I wish that another and equal metaphor might be introduced as basis for the church: the flowing river, the unceasing stream of *vitae*, which is described by the phrase *successio sanctorum*. In this stream the ship can sail toward the horizon; the compass has been experimentally set and verified—so we learn from hagiographic discourse. The text of Tertullian occurs to me:

> Moreover, the boat is an image of the church, which is tossed to and fro at sea, that is this world, by the waves of persecutions and temptations, while the Lord appears to sleep peacefully until the last moment, when he, *awakened by the prayers of the saints*, subdues the world and gives rest to his own.[44]

Possibilities

In the ecclesiological traditions of several churches the so-called apostolic succession is a central concern, one that serves to determine the apostolicity of the church and, as a consequence, to give a satisfactory answer to the truth-question.

The question is: are we, who are separated in time and space from the source of our faith, that is, the life of Jesus as proclaimed by the apostles and passed on to the following generations, still in contact with that source? How can we be certain that we are promoting the message of Jesus faithfully and in the spirit of the apostles? Is our interpretation of the Gospel the right one? Are our theological formulations in accord with the spirit or the letter of the apostolic teaching? What criteria can apply sufficient demarcation between reliable and unreliable members of the congregation? How should judgments and choices be made between the factions which lead to disunity (see 1 Cor 11:18-19)?

Very early on answers were sought to all of these questions, enabling a reaction to new developments and new doctrines. In synods and councils people of differing persuasions were excluded. The quartodeciman conception of the paschal feast led to disunity. So did the reaction to the followers of Marcion and of the gnostic movements; it is clear that the determination of the canon of the New Testament took place at least partly out of this reaction. Gatherings of several bishops, who together spoke in the spirit of the tradition of the apostles, developed into councils which defined the common confession of faith. It was assumed that the assembled bishops, gathered in council, offered the best guarantee of orthodoxy, because they were called the successors of the apostles and of the Twelve. Moreover, by means of the laying on of hands and prayer, celebrated in a liturgy in which three bishops consecrated the new bishop, this bishop was connected to the apostolic community, for in that community the apostles themselves had provided for their successors in the same manner. In short, apostolic succession became and remained *the* remedy of the true church against heresies and divisions, even though this concept was differently filled out in the different churches. The caution with which the aforementioned Lima document of the World Council of Churches deals with the porcelain image of *successio apostolica* (under the title, "Succession in the Apostolic Tradition," see nos. 34-38) is a lively demonstration of the importance of this concept and of its diverse application.

It would show little regard for tradition for us to minimalize or to discard this idea of the apostolicity of the church. It should be possible, however, on the basis of the historical facts, to expose the misformed developments of this idea in theological thinking and speaking, although that is not the direct concern of my argument. This alone: a concept of conforming truth based on the apostolic succession leads easily to intolerance, smugness, and rigidity. This tendency can be found in history before and after the Reformation and into our own time. I meant to indicate that by mentioning the Rock-metaphor: how many arrogant pronouncements have been made in the spirit and on the basis of this metaphor, and how reactionary have been the counter-pronouncements! The one and true church, with right on its side, encountered churches which had the rightness of the *sola scriptura*, and not much that was constructive came out of the engagement. Churches which exclusively appeal to the principle of apostolic succession and churches which more or less exclusively present the proclamation of the Word of God as their foundation all suffer from a modern sort of fundamentalism, one which makes an ideology out of the basis of one's own estimation of correctness. In the long run, such an ideology means the enfeebling of the apostolic succession. If one can still feel something of an incubating warmth in the churches, that warmth can hardly be attributed to the chilly truth claims of the churches, claims which, moreover, do not correspond to the conception of truth as it occurs in the Gospels. In the Gospel, truth is not an administrative, juridical, or intellectual idea, but relates to the true nature of God and of God's Son, of humanity and of things. The one-sided concept of apostolic succession needs a corrective, and I propose to have found this in the notion of the *successio sanctorum*. What possibilities are contained in such a notion?

The *successio sanctorum* is, given its development in the history of the church, *all-embracing*. It is widely known that the faithful, from high to low, have held the saints in great affection (albeit with a corresponding difference in reverence from tolerance to adoration). The festivals and memorial days of the saints have received at least as much interest from the faithful as have those of the so-called *temporale*. Academic and other dating, weather forecasting, and proverbs all use language that often can be traced to a saint's feast. The saints and the stories of their lives have influenced the imagination and the emotions of the faithful more than the teaching of the church and of its theologians. This means that in the *successio sanctorum* the whole church, the *ecclesia* in all of its branches, is affected. The saints have smitten the faithful, and around the images of the saints and their memorial places forms of liturgy have developed, forms which the churchly functionaries have entitled "pious exercises" (*pium exercitium*). But this liturgy is precisely what is meant by the word; it is the prayer of the people. More than the *successio apostolica*, the *successio sanctorum* is anchored in the reverence and the piety of the people, perhaps because the saints, more than the apostolically based clergy, are near to the people, coming to them in their needs and fears. The veneration of the saints by believing people has an ecclesial dimension frequently ignored: it is they, the faithful, who have declared the saints to be saints and have taken their prophetic witness seriously. In the saints the faithful have encountered God's Spirit and God's Son, for the grace of God and God's generosity, the source of salvation for all people, have appeared upon earth (Ti 2:11). The *successio sanctorum* offers the church the vital and emotional strength of faith; that can be concluded from the honor accorded the saints by the faithful. These saints knew little of dogmatic positions; all the more did they know the real values of faith. They respected these values above the truth, in the spirit of Jesus who in the parable of the Samaritan sketched out an image of the neighbor—*the* imago of the saint. The succession of saints in all the periods of church history, with the constantly changing socio-cultural prospect of these periods, grounds the church as *communio sanctorum* and makes it one. Dogmatic pronouncements remain of relative importance, but they need to be filled out with piety and prayer. The veneration of the saints offers this amplification and provides for the warmth of faith in the church. *Credo sanctam ecclesiam* because there are holy women and men who have lived out the holiness and the *virtus* of the church before us.

The veneration of the saints, which has continually graced the church by its presence, is *structural and global*. These words seem to me to be best for translating the concept "catholic" (*ecclesia catholica*). The veneration of the saints is not tied to a certain period or a certain class of the population (the "people" as over against the "elite"), but is part of the psycho-religious structure of the human search for contact with the holy. In all religious cultures of the past and present, veneration of the ancestors and heros plays a large role because of the living conviction that by means of such veneration one is in contact with the sacral world, albeit after the necessary apotropaic rites and customs. Christian hagiographic discourse, then, although it may give evidence of a very particular context and content, clearly demonstrates the same structure as that of the pagan veneration or the Jewish commemoration. In other words, the veneration of the saints is rooted in the religious behavior of humanity and is no exception. One may speak then of the anthropological substratum of what we have called an ecclesiological foundation. This is the more true because here the global aspect of the cult of the saints also comes into view. Since this cult is part of the socio-religious character of humanity, it also bears global character traits, corresponding to the nature and essence of the *ecclesia* which is intended for all peoples (Mt 28:19; Acts 1:8). The veneration of the saints is in essence proper to the religious human being, and therefore it is, by definition, universal, catholic, capable of affecting also the believing human being. In this regard, the cult of the saints enlists and corresponds to the religious needs of the human being, also the Christian human being. Seen in such a way, a global calendar of memorial days (formed in some other way than that of the Roman patriarchate) can support the catholicity of the church and participate in setting out its basis. The veneration of the saints is thus, in yet another way, a proof of the confession *credo ecclesiam sanctam et catholicam*. This part of the Apostles' Creed is strengthened by the cult of the saints, as that comes to expression in hagiographic discourse, and the church is thereby more firmly based, namely in the religious vitality of its faithful.

Still one consideration ought to be added: the matter of critical judgement. There continues to be a need for a critical consideration of the cult of the saints through the course of the centuries, of its accommodations to the socio-cultural context, and of its magical implications. Just as one can critique the implementation of the principle of *successio apostolica* in ecclesiology without affecting the principle itself, so also one may critically evaluate the religious impulses in hagiography and in the cult of the saints. It could appear that in their adoration of holy men and women the faithful have gone too far, as did the inhabitants of Lystra (Acts 14:11), seeing the saints as gods in human form. They may have seen the saints as direct miracle workers and not as distributors of the miracles of God. In their great admiration for these supernatural creatures, they may have forgotten to follow their way of life. In short, it is not impossible that in the *vitae* themselves, but especially in their reception by the faithful, magical elements have crept in which are more connected with a cyclical conception of fate than with the continuing history of God's covenant with humanity. A critical evaluation of the defense against evil remains especially necessary, since it often seems that the power of evil is sought outside of the human, and not in the human and in interhuman structures. Moreover, the conflict over images, iconoclasm, did not simply yield an unambiguous victory for the "iconodules," but at the same time showed that the objections of the iconoclasts were not without ground. The image theology of John of Damascus,[45] filled with high honor to the icons, begins with the proposition that the veneration of the image returns to and depends upon the Primal Model; therefore one ought not speak of the worship of an idol. In the defense of the images one can hear that there were indeed also negative influences at play in the general esteem for images. The veneration of the holy people, who have given form to the *sequela Christi* in a continuous line and who contribute to the grounds of the confession of faith in the holy church, has developed in the church through the centuries. But here and there, now and then, it can show evidence of malformation, affecting its foundational function and requiring continuous and careful critique. In this regard, there is no difference between the *successio sanctorum* and the *successio apostolica*. The foundations of the holy church need to be given as much care as does the superstructure. Both require *une restauration permanente* in order to serve their purpose: to support and to lead the pilgrimage of the people of God.

Conclusion

After the foregoing I can be brief. I hope that my thesis has been made sufficiently clear and, at least to some extent, plausible: the *successio sanctorum* is an important concept for an ecumenical ecclesiology. *Credo sanctam ecclesiam* is a jewel-like expression; more, it is a text which, like the entire Creed, ought to be sung. This song of praise is possible not only on the grounds of the hope which lives in us but also because of the succession of saints, the immense multitude from every nation and tribe and people and tongue (Rv 7:9).

Augustine was mistaken when he wrote:

> For even now miracles are wrought in the name of Christ, whether by his sacraments or by the prayers or relics of his saints; but they are not so brilliant and conspicuous as to cause them to be published with such glory as accompanied the former miracles.

By "the former miracles" he meant those which were recounted in the Gospels and constantly read aloud in the churches. He could not foresee that in a later time many celebrated miracle stories would be eagerly heard in order "to confirm that one grand and health-giving miracle of Christ's ascension to heaven with the flesh in which he rose."[46]

The same Augustine brings me to recognize the relativity of any *successio*:

> We, therefore, who are called and *are* Christians, do not believe in Peter, but in him whom Peter believed—being edified by Peter's sermons about Christ, not poisoned by his incantations; and not deceived by his enchantments, but aided by his good deeds. Christ himself, who was Peter's master in the doctrine which leads to eternal life, is our master too.[47]

Notes

1. Thomas J. Talley, *The Origins of the Liturgical Year* (New York, 1986).
2. *Worship* 60 (1986) 461.
3. K. Richter, ed., *Liturgie: ein vergessenes Thema der Theologie? E.J. Lengeling zum 70 Geburtstag, Quaestiones Disputatae* 107 (Freiburg, 1986).
4. Ibid. 99-112.
5. Ibid. 113-127.
6. H. Wegman, "De la pesanteur de la liturgie catholique romaine," *Praxis juridique et religion* 4 (1987) 168-175.
7. "And it follows that the burden of the historian in our time is to reestablish

the dignity of historical studies on a basis that will make them consonant with the aims and purposes of the intellectual community at large, that is, transform historical studies in such a way as to allow the historian to participate in the liberation of the present from the burden of history." *Tropics of Discourse: Essays in Cultural Criticism* (Baltimore, 1978) 40.

8. P. Harnoncourt, *Gesamtkirchliche und teilkirchliche Liturgie: Studien zum liturgischen Heiligenkalender und zum Gesang im Gottesdienst unter besondere Berücksichtigung des deutschen Sprachgebietes* (Freiburg, 1974); J. Torsy, *Die Eigenkalender des deutschen und neiderländischen Sprachgebietes* (Sieburg, 1977).

9. P. Jounel, *Le culte des saints dans les basiliques du Latran et du Vatican au douzième siècle* (Rome, 1977).

10. A history and an analysis of the legal procedure is offered by the splendid book of A. Vauchez, *La sainteté en occident aux derniers siècles du Moyen Age d'après les procès de canonisation et les documents hagiographiques* (Rome, 1981), with a very extensive inventory of sources, 654-683.

11. J. Hennig has published a summary of his earlier studies in "Kalendar und Martyrologium als Literaturformen," *Archiv für Liturgiewissenschaft* 7:1 (1961) 1-44.

12. The text can be found in H.A.P. Schmidt, *Introductio in Liturgiam Occidentalem* (Rome, 1960) 540-542. See also C. Kirch, *Enchiridion Fontium Historiae Ecclesiasticae Antiquae* (Freiburg, 1923) nos. 543-544.

13. B. Mariani, *Breviarium Syriacum seu Martyologium Saeculi IV*, Rerum Eccl. Documenta, Series Minor, Subsidia 3 (Rome, 1956).

14. See the overview in Schmidt, *Introductio* 532-539, supplemented by such works as the Martyrologium of the Sacramentary of Gellone, A. Dumas, ed. Corpus Christianorum 159, 498-513). The schema of the evolution of the Roman calendar with historical notes from the Bollandist work *Propylaeum Ad Acta Sanctorum*, in Schmidt, *Introductio* 545-685, is very handy.

15. H. Delahaye, "Commentarius Perpetuus," in H. Quentin, *Martyrologium Hieronymianum ad Recensionem*, Acta Sanctorum, Nov. II,2 (1931).

16. P. Brown, *Society and the Holy in Late Antiquity* (London, 1982) 103-152; H.J.W. Drijvers, "De heilige man in het vroege syrische christendom," in A. Hilhorst, ed., *De heiligenverering in de eerste eeuwen van het christendom* (Nijmegen: 1988) 11-24; G. Fowden, "The Pagan Holy Man in Late Antique Society," *Journal of Hellenic Studies* 102 (1982) 33-59; R. Kirschner, "The Vocation of Holiness in Late Antiquity," *Vigiliae Christianae* 38 (1984) 105-124.

17. See, however, H.J.W. Drijvers, "Clarissimae Feminae en de christelijke ascese," *Jaarbeok voor Vrouwengeschiednis* 4 (1983) 13-40.

18. P. Brown, *The Cult of the Saints: Its Rise and Function in Latin Christianity* (Chicago, 1981) 12-22.

19. M.J.M. van Uytfanghe, "Het 'genre' hagiographie," in Hilhorst 63-98, with an impressive bibliography; A. Vauchez (note 10, above); D. Weinstein and R.M. Bell, *Saints and Society: The Two Worlds of Western Christendom, 100-1700* (Chicago, 1982); R. Kieckhefer, *Unquiet Souls: Fourteenth Century Saints and Their Religious Milieu* (Chicago, 1984); R.E.V. Stuip and C. Vellekoop, eds., *Andere Structuren, andere middeleeuwen* (Utrecht, 1983); and the congresses, such as "As-

pekt frühchristlicher Heiligenverehrung" (Erlangen, 1977) and "Hagiographie, cultures, et sociétés, IV-XII siècles" (Paris, 1981).

20. Uytfanghe, "Het 'genre' hagiofraphie" 64.

21. I list here only: A. Gurjewitsch, *Das Weltbild des mittelalterlichen Menschen* (translation into German from the Russian; Dresden-Munich: 1982) 352-400; P.H. Vrijhof and J. Waardenburg, eds., *Official and Popular Religion: Analysis of a Theme for Religious Studies* (The Hague, 1979); J. Delumeau, ed., *Histoire vécue du peuple chrétien*, 2 vols. (Toulouse, 1979).

22. M. de Cherteau, "Hagiographie," in *Encyclopaedia Universalis* 8 (Paris: 1968) 207-209; G.L. Muller, *Gemeinschaft und Verehrung der Heiligen: Geschichtliche-systematische Grundlegung der Hagiologie* (Freiburg, 1986).

23. "Le culte des saints et ses implications sociologiques; réflexions sur un récent essai de Peter Brown," *Analecta Bollandiana* 100 (1982) 17-41.

24. C. Pietri, "Les origines du culte des martyrs (d'après un ouvrage récent)," *Riv. Archeol. Christ.* 60 (1984) 293-319.

25. Kieckhefer, *Unquiet Souls* 20; see 15-20.

26. Ibid. 180-201.

27. Vauchez, *La sainteté* 455-474 (on the "sainteté officielle" and the "valorisation de la culture").

28. Van Uytfanghe, "Het 'genre' hagiographie" 80.

29. P.-A. Sigal, *L'Homme et le miracle dans la France médiévale (XI-XII siècle)* (Paris, 1985). See also G. de Nie, *Views from a Many-Windowed Tower: Studies of Imagination in the Works of Gregory of Tours* (Amsterdam, 1987).

30. J. Fontaine, ed., *Sulpice Sévère: vie de Saint Martin*, Sources chrétiennes 133 (Paris, 1967) 68. For the following typology see van Uytfanghe, "Het 'genre' hagiographie" 77-81.

31. This term can be found in the *Missale Romanum* 1970. It is also already present as a variant in a prayer of the *Sacramentarium Veronense* (no. 556): with this variant, the *postcommunio* of *fer.* 1, *hebd.* 5, of the *Quadragesima* reads as follows: "Sacramentorum tuorum benedictione roborati, quaesumus Domine, ut per haec semper emundemur a vitiis, et per sequelam Christi ad te festinanter gradiamur. Per Christum."

32. See note 29.

33. See note 28.

34. *Passio Sanctarum Perpetuae et Felicitatis* 1: "Si vetera fidei exempla et Dei gratiam testificantia et aedificationem hominis operantia propterea in letteris sunt digesta ut lectione eorum quasi repraesentatione rerum et Deus honoretur et homo confortetur, cur non et nova documenta aeque utrique causae convenientia et digerantur? vel quia proinde et haec vetera futura quandoque sunt et necessaria posteris, si in praesenti suo tempore minori deputantur auctoritati propter praesumptam venerationem antiquitatis ... Itaque et nos qui sicut prophetias ita et visiones novas pariter repromissas et agnoscimus et honoramus ... Et nos itaque quod audivimus et contrectavimus, annuntiamus et vobis, fratres et filioli, uti et vos qui interfuistis rememoremini gloriae domini et qui nunc cognoscitis per auditum communionem habeatis cum sanctis martyribus, et per illos cum domino nostro Iesu Christo, cui est claritas et honor in saecula saeculorum. Amen."

35. A. Angenendt, "Religiositat und Theologie; ein spannungreiches Verhältnis im Mittelalter," *Archiv für Liturgiewissenschaft* 20/21 (1978/79) 28-55; G. de Nie, *Views* 133-161, 230-251; J. Delumeau, *Le péché et la peur* (Paris: 1986).

36. Ours is, after all, a time in which "science fiction" has developed into a genuine form of discourse. I do not mean to compare the *vitae* to science fiction, but to indicate the points of contact, such as the new approaches to myth (as opposed to "mythoclasm") and the multi-facetted perception of the religious world. See H. Timm, "Remythologisierung? Der akkumulative Symbolismus im Christentum," in K.-H. Bohrer, ed., *Mythos und Moderne* (Frankfurt, 1983) 432-456.

37. *Baptism. Eucharist and Ministry*, Faith and Order Paper No. 111 (Geneva: World Council of Churches, 1982) 22-32.

38. Hans Küng, *The Church* (New York, 1976) 414, 416-417.

39. *Lumen Gentium* no. 39.

40. I have already referred to the work of Küng. As examples, I think here also of these studies: J. Moltmann, *Kirche in der Kraft des Geistes* (Munich, 1975); and L. Bouyer, *L'Eglise de Dieu: corps du Christ et temple de l'Esprit* (Paris, 1970).

41. C. Pietri, *Roma Christiana: recherches sur l'église de Rome, son organisation, sa politique, son idéologie de Miltiade à Sixte (311-440)*, vol. 1 (Rome, 1976) 314-401.

42. Title of a book by J. Leclercq (1957).

43. Drijvers (see note 16), 24; see also J. Fontaine, "Une clé litéraire de la Vita Martini de Sulpice Sévère: la typologie prophétique," *Mélanges Chr. Mohrmann* (Utrecht, 1963) 84-95.

44. *De Baptismo*, 12:7 (Sources chrétiennes 35:84): "Ceterum navicula illa figuram ecclesiae praeferebat quod in mari, id est in saeculo, fluctibus id est persecutionibus et temptationibus inquietetur domino per patientiam velut dormiente, donec orationibus sanctorum in ultimis suscitatus compescat saeculum et tranquillitatem suis reddat."

45. PG 94:1249-1252. See H.-G. Beck, *Kirche und theologische Literatur im Byzantinischen Reich* (Munich, 1959) 300.

46. *De Civitate Dei* 22:8; M. Dods, ed., *The City of God* (New York, 1950) 820.

47. *De Civitate Dei* 18:54; Dods, *The City* 668.

15

The Liturgical Roots of Theology

Leonel L. Mitchell

WHEN I FIRST MET THOMAS JULIAN TALLEY HE WAS A STUDENT AT THE GENER-
al Theological Seminary doing his field education at the parish of which
my father was rector. Ten years later we were both Th.D. students in liturgics, working with H. Boone Porter and Alexander Schmemann. I am
sure his laugh is resounding still through Sherrill Hall. Although we
have usually contrived to place half a continent between us, except for a
few summers when we taught together at Notre Dame, I count Tom a
good friend and colleague and am happy to contribute this essay on a
topic I know to have been one of his early interests.

Defining Liturgical Theology

For several years past I have been concerned with the question of
"What is liturgical theology?" Like most Episcopalians I was accustomed
to "proof text" theological statements out of the Prayer Book, to quote
the Prayer of Humble Access to "prove" that the church taught the real
presence, or the preface to the Ordinal to defend the validity of Anglican
orders. I was aware that there was such a thing as a theology of worship,
by which I really meant both a theological reason for worshiping and a
rationale for worshiping the way we did. I had also studied, and even
taught, sacramental theology, in which I began with theological defini-
tions of the sacraments, such as those in the catechism,[1] and then looked
at the liturgical practice of the church to see how it embodied these principles. This, however, is not what I mean by liturgical theology, nor what

243

the term means to those liturgists today who describe themselves as liturgical theologians.

Two quotations from Aidan Kavanagh's *On Liturgical Theology*, the 1981 Hale Lectures at Seabury-Western Theological Seminary, will provide a starting place:

> The "thing" about which systematic theology forms propositions is the encounter between God and the world which liturgical rite enacts among those of faith.[2]

and:

> As we approach the core of liturgical structures and endeavor, what we encounter there is not data or issues but the Presence of a Holy One who must mask itself in Word and flesh and sacrament and sense out of respect for our weakness if we are to be able to sit at table with it as "friends."[3]

At the heart of Christian life and thought is the encounter with God, an encounter for which the primary locus is the Christian assembly. When the persecutors wished to destroy the early church it was its weekly assembly for worship which they attempted to prevent, and they were right. Massey Shepherd in *The Worship of the Church* quoted the acts of the fourth-century martyrs as they testified to the Roman authorities: "Don't you know that a Christian is constituted by the Eucharist and the Eucharist by a Christian?"[4] This single statement epitomizes the core of an understanding of liturgical theology.

In various ways contemporary liturgical theologians have been attempting to show that the liturgy is not simply the constitutive force in Christian life and faith; it is constitutive for Christian theology as well. What we generally call theology is primarily reflection on that divine encounter. Aidan Kavanagh, in his book already mentioned, has reminded us that this theology is properly called secondary theology, and that primary theology arises directly out of the assembly's encounter with God.[5]

My own, somewhat modest contribution to the contemporary discussion has been a book entitled *Praying Shapes Believing*,[6] which attempts to do theology on the basis of the liturgy of The Book of Common Prayer 1979. Without entering into the finer points of the contemporary discussion, in which Kavanagh and Geoffrey Wainwright are probably the best known protagonists,[7] I would begin by affirming that what we say and do in our worship simply *is* the primary factor in what we believe. The *lex orandi*, which is more than the text of the Prayer Book, establishes the *lex credendi*. The tap roots of theology are liturgical.

While we can, of course, begin with what we believe and devise a ritual to embody and proclaim that belief, this will more likely result in ideological indoctrination than liturgy. In my youth I remember the terrifying newsreel pictures of Hitler haranguing throngs of uniformed Nazis who thundered back in unison, "Sieg, Heil!" It was frightening, and very real. Ideology called the tune, and the world marched to it, willy-nilly. At the other end of the spectrum are the heavily didactic Reformation liturgies which begin with a eucharistic theology and construct a liturgy to drive home the doctrine, so that the worshiper cannot miss the point. Zwingli, for example, wrote in a prayer to be recited in place of the Canon:

> Our souls are spiritual, made in your image; therefore they can only by refreshed with spiritual food, and that food can only be given by your word ... Never deprive us of the food of your word, but ever feed us in your goodness. That is the true bread which gives life to the world ... He himself said that the flesh profits nothing, but it is the Spirit which gives life.[8]

And Calvin, in his Geneva liturgy, prayed:

> And although we see only bread and wine, yet let us not doubt that he accomplishes spiritually in our souls all that he shows us outwardly by these visible signs; in other words, that he is heavenly bread to feed and nourish us unto eternal life.
>
> ... Let us not be bemused by these earthly and corruptible elements which we see with the eye, and touch with the hand, in order to seek him there, as if he were enclosed in the bread and wine. Our souls will only be disposed to be nourished and vivified by his substance, when they are raised above all earthly things, and carried as high as heaven, to enter the kingdom of God where he dwells. Let us be content therefore to have the bread and wine as signs and evidences, spiritually seeking the reality where the word of God promises that we shall find it.[9]

Whether or not one agrees with the particular eucharistic theologies expressed in these prayers, they are classic examples of the subordination of worship to particular expressions of systematic theology and the use of the liturgy to propagate those expressions. Usually, as in the case of the Reformers, this is done in the cause of truth for the highest possible motives, evangelistic and educational. Once the liturgy itself has been crafted in this manner, of course, the liturgy itself takes over and begins to shape the beliefs of those who use it, so that the theology so carefully written into the liturgy either becomes the theology of the community which prays it or a public embarrassment causing them to amend or replace it.

The Liturgical Act

Let us then return to the question of what the *lex orandi* is. We have said that it was more than the text of the Prayer Book. It is the liturgical act itself, not the book, and the act is more than text; it is rite, and ceremony, and context. Morning prayer will be experienced quite differently by those who attend it every day before their work, and by those who participate alternate Sundays at eleven o'clock. The text may be identical, but the context will say different things. In the same way the eucharist seen as a quarterly event for the pious will be different from the same service, with the same ceremonial, celebrated week by week as parish and family worship. The context will, in fact, begin to shape the text itself, as the worshiping community demands that it express more accurately what they actually do. It is not the text but the liturgical act which is formative of the Christian life.

Liturgical theology is often compared to biblical theology, and the comparison is valid, as long as we remember that the Bible is primarily the book of the church and its proper context is the liturgical assembly. It is the Bible as Word, not as written text, which is the core of biblical theology, and it is the celebration not the text that is the root of liturgical theology.

It is in the celebration of the eucharist, the office, baptism, and the other sacraments and rites of the church that we not only encounter God but form the firmest basis for our reflection on that encounter which we are accustomed to call theology.

Professor Michael Aune of Pacific Lutheran Theological Seminary asked in a review of *Praying Shapes Believing* whether what contemporary liturgical theologies are attempting to do is, in fact, possible. Can the liturgy really speak for itself? Does not the very act of extracting "meaning" from it require one to place it within a theological framework? He asks:

> How can I as a member of a community of faith talk *with* God or with anyone else for that matter unless we have some kind of framework within which such "liturgical conversation" can occur and within which such talk can be interpreted? Do we not need an idiom of interpretive scheme in order to make sense of what we say, hear, and do in the church's worship just as we do when we communicate with one another?[10]

While Aune is certainly right that no communication can take place without a common medium of communication, I would suggest that the liturgical act is itself the framework in which the conversation takes place. The ordering and structuring of the liturgy is the context for the conversation. Any attempt to "extract meaning" from an act necessarily involves going outside of the act itself and placing it within a framework of intelligibility. Systematic theologians will attempt to examine the liturgy according to the categories which they have devised. The liturgy is mined for data to support the doctrinal framework which the author brings to it from outside. This is what Wainwright does in his monumental work *Doxology*.[11] He does it very well and shows that the conceptual framework which he uses is congruent with the liturgical tradition of the church. In a similar way a philosophical theologian like David Power[12] begins from certain contemporary theological assumptions and then discusses the liturgy in terms of those assumptions. To the extent that we share the author's philosophical presuppositions, we shall find such works valuable in fitting worship into our world view.

What I am suggesting is that the less we import into our liturgical theology, the better. The closer the meanings we extract hew to the theology proclaimed by the rite itself, the more faithful we shall be in proclaiming "the church's teaching" as opposed to contemporary, or outdated secondary theological systems. As soon as we begin to reflect on the act and "extract meaning" from it, we are, of course engaged in secondary theology, and we are involved in reducing the multivalent polysemantic language of prayer to a series of univocal propositions. The famous response of the ballet dancer to one who asked her the meaning of the dance, "if I could have told you I wouldn't have gone to all the work of dancing," needs to be engraved on the minds of those who seek to explain liturgy. We never get it all. As in all theology, the object of our investigation is literally beyond our grasp.

If we, nevertheless, wish to undertake this investigation, we need to examine what happens when Christians come together to worship God, and instead of attempting to deal with this abstractly I propose to deal with a specific act of worship.

Eucharist as Theology

Since the Prayer Book describes the eucharist as "the principal act of Christian worship," the eucharist will be not only a convenient but a significant place to start, bearing in mind that, however central, it is not the totality of worship, and therefore this example needs the complement of similar discussion of all of liturgical worship—a reasonably monumental task—if it is to give a true picture. I feel I have just begun to do that in *Praying Shapes Believing*.

The eucharist takes place within the context of the life of the church. It is the major liturgical occasion of the parish community on Sundays and major feasts.[13] The assembly is presided over by the bishop or a priest. The ideal picture which the Prayer Book paints of the assembly shows us the bishop presiding, flanked at the altar by presbyters, and assisted by a deacon, and by lay persons who both form the body of the assembly and fulfill particular roles, such as reader and offerer.

The presider, especially a bishop, usually presides from a chair in the sanctuary, or standing toward the center of the altar table, facing the people. Other than that chair, the significant furniture is a stand from which the Bible can be read, placed where the reader can be seen and heard, and the altar, a table on which are placed the bread and wine and around which the celebrant community gathers.

Without even considering the text of a single prayer, we are already prepared to say something about the centrality of this gathering to the church, the significance of the Bible and its public reading, and the nature of the eucharist as a meal. We are also prepared to make statements about the structure of the assembly itself. The special position of bishops and presbyters, the ministries of deacons and lay people, and the corporate nature of their common activities.

The assembly is the *synaxis*, the gathering of Christ's people in his name with the assurance that he will be present in their midst.[14] They engage in two overlapping activities. They gather to listen to the proclamation and exposition of the Word of God from the Bible and to engage in common prayer, hence the reading desk/pulpit, and to participate in a meal, hence the table, the plate, the cup. The place in which they gather is both a lecture hall in which the sacred text is read and expounded and a banquet hall in which the feast is served. The bishop or priest presides over the community in both of these activities, but the actual reading of the Scripture is assigned to lay members of the congregation, presumably to those who will do it well.

The presider or another authorized teacher expounds, or breaks open, the Word in a sermon. The common prayers, or prayers of the people, are led by a deacon, or a lay person, the presider joining with the people in prayer and response and summing all up in a final collect. The prayers rise from the whole people expressing their common and individual concerns. They are the prayers not of the presider, but of the whole praying church.

After the prayers the members of the assembly exchange the greeting of the peace with each other, thus defining themselves as the eucharistic community, a community both reconciled and reconciling in the peace of Christ.[15]

For the eucharistic banquet the gifts of bread and wine are brought to the altar by representatives of the people. The deacon, the chief "servant" of the congregation sets the table in preparation for the feast, and the presiding bishop or priest stands at the altar to offer thanks.

It is, of course, possible to turn all of this around and to say that we arrange our churches in this manner and assign the roles to these people because we hold certain theological positions about the nature of the church, the Bible, and the ministry. I am suggesting rather that we hold these beliefs because this is the way our worship is structured, and we have supported that structure both by doctrinal statements and by canonical enactments and rubrics which define the parameters of our practice. Anthropologists say that "Creed follows cult." Our explanations are secondary to our practice and depend directly upon it.

The classic example of this in Christian worship is the doctrine of the Trinity. It was the practice of Christian prayer "to Christ as God" which compelled theologians to reflect upon the relationship of Christ to the One God. There is, of course, secondary influence in the other direction, and, once the Arian controversy was upon the church, the desire to affirm the divinity of Christ resulted in an increase in liturgical prayer addressed to him.

We do not have the space to go through the text of the entire eucharist even to suggest the possibilities of detailed reflection on all of its prayers and actions, but we can at least look at the Great Thanksgiving and some of the possibilities of starting from the liturgy to do theology. I am not so foolish to think that either I or anyone else can comment either definitively or exhaustively on the eucharistic prayer, no matter how extensively we write, but we can lay out some broad outlines.

The Great Thanksgiving

Historically the Great Thanksgiving is the central prayer of the service and a proclamation of the core of its theology. Again, we need to consider not simply the text of the prayer, but the context of its proclamation.

The Word of God has been read from the Bible and broken open in the sermon. The congregation has joined in petition and intercession in the prayers of the people. The bread and wine have been brought to the altar by members of the congregation and prepared by the deacon. The bishop, flanked by presbyters, stands at the table, the deacon standing by to assist, and the congregation are at once greeted and invited to participate in the act of Thanksgiving: "Let us give thanks to the Lord our God."

The action is that of the entire assembled church. The presiding bishop or priest gives voice to the words. The people assent both at the beginning by joining in the dialogue and at the end by saying "Amen" to the prayer. It is then the prayer of the church, not simply of the chief celebrant.

The invitation "Lift up your hearts" invites the congregation to leave the "lower" things behind and turn heart and mind to the "higher." The metaphor is clear and commonplace, but nonetheless significant. This is not a magic rite to bring Christ down from heaven, but a prayer of praise and thanksgiving to raise our affection to "things" that are above, where Christ is "seated at the right hand of God."[16]

The prayer itself begins with thanksgiving. In most of western eucharistic prayers, including those of the Book of Common Prayer, the thanksgiving begins with a proper preface which states the particular ground for our thanksgiving on this occasion, while affirming that it is both proper and joyful to do this "at all times and in all places." Reflection on this preface can lead into the theology of prayer and begin to open the question of the relationship of human beings to God, of which thanksgiving for what God has done for us is a prime ingredient. The proper prefaces provide a means of examining the mighty acts which comprise the redemption of the world. Over the course of the liturgical year they raise up different aspects of the mystery of salvation, looking at that same mystery as it were from different viewpoints.

The Easter preface, for example, rejoices in the paschal mystery of Christ's dying and rising again for the salvation of the world, and our participation in the eternal life which he has won. The Ascension preface affirms not only Christ's resurrection but that we shall be with him and share in his glorious reign. So too, the Incarnation preface proclaims not only the birth of Christ, but that through his becoming flesh we have been freed from sin and given power to become the children of God. In a similar way the prefaces of Advent, Epiphany, Lent, the Lord's Day, and those for holy days and special occasions highlight some aspect of our celebration in the light of which we see into the central mystery of our redemption in the death and resurrection of Jesus Christ.

The words in which these mysteries are proclaimed are not dogmatic propositions, but poetic, metaphorical proclamations. They are, however, certainly theological. They are expressions of theology as we proclaim it to God's people in thanksgiving and doxology to God.

The preface goes on to proclaim that we not only give thanks, but join in a celestial choir of praise, with which the people audibly join in singing the *Sanctus*, the angelic hymn of Isaiah 6 and Revelation 4.

After the *Sanctus* the Great Thanksgiving continues with thanksgiving for creation. The texts of the various prayers differ, but the content of those which follow the traditional West Syrian-Scottish-American structure,[17] that is all but Eucharistic Prayer C and Form 1 in An Order for Celebrating the Holy Eucharist, is parallel. We shall follow Eucharistic Prayer A for an example.[18]

In a sense, the topics for which thanks are given in the Great Prayer are those which are central to the ongoing life of the church. It is these which we mention at the heart of our principal liturgy. First, we give thanks that God made us out of love and for himself. We are from God and for God, and the reason for our being is the love of God. This is a significant statement of Christian anthropology. It is followed by reference to the fall and our subjection to sin and death. The human condition is proclaimed, and we give thanks for the divine response of redemption in Jesus Christ.

God, in mercy, sent the Only-Begotten Son, to share our human nature, "to live and die as one of us," and to reconcile us to God, the Father of all. This is certainly the heart and core of Christology and soteriology. The atonement and the perfect sacrifice offered freely upon the cross for the whole world then become the object of thanksgiving. The Great Thanksgiving does not spell out the various theories. It proclaims what God has done, and gives thanks for it. It is this relationship with God here proclaimed to which we assent in the final "Amen." How it all happens is grist for the secondary theologian's mill, but that will be a theory, however plausible and widely accepted. Its roots are in the primary theology of creation and redemption. In fact, the Creed, the ancient formulation of secondary propositional theology which is most at home in the liturgy, follows this same order as the Great Thanksgiving in setting forth its dogmas.

The thanksgivings for creation and redemption culminate in the narrative of the institution of the eucharist, for this is the specific occasion of our *eucharistia*. On the night Jesus was handed over to suffering and death, he instituted in the Holy Supper, the sacrament of bread and wine, the means of our participation in his saving acts, by doing this as his *anamnesis*.

To eat the bread and drink the wine over which thanks have been given is to celebrate the "memorial of our redemption." The offering of the eucharistic gifts to God in union with Christ's own self-offering is the pivot which moves the Thanksgiving from the recounting of what God has done in history to our celebration of it. Whatever secondary theology we may choose to espouse to explain how, when we eat the bread and drink the cup, we receive the body and blood of Christ, and how this present eucharist is linked to the actions of Christ in the upper room, on the cross, and in the resurrection, we begin with the proclamation that it is for this purpose that we do these things, and that by offering thanksgiving, we do recall, commemorate, and enter into the celebration of Christ's mighty acts. Past, present, and future, what God has done in Christ, and what he is doing and will do in us are all joined together in this act. It is the church's great act of self-offering in union with the self-offering of our divine head.

It is, in fact, here, in the eucharistic *anamnesis*, rather than at the offertory, that we can most properly speak of offering either the bread and wine or "ourselves, our souls and bodies" to God. We have no gifts of our own to offer. The only offering we have is to return to God in thanksgiving what he has given to us, and we do this in union with the priestly offering of Jesus Christ, apart from whom we are unworthy to do even this.

Finally, as we do this, we ask the Holy Spirit to descend upon us and upon the gifts, sanctifying them and claiming them for God, that Christ's promises may be fulfilled: that we may receive the body and blood of Christ, the food of eternal life, be united into one holy church in God's service and have a share with the saints in the eternal kingdom. Eucharistic Prayer D, following its ancient models, includes intercessions after the *epiclesis*. Although our other eucharistic prayers do not include intercessions, their presence here reminds us that our action in the eucharist is that of the catholic church, not simply of the local congregation. The saints on earth and in heaven with whom we claim a share in the eternal kingdom are one with us in our eucharistic celebration.

None of these concepts are self-explanatory, but they are what needs to be explained. They are the liturgical roots from which our theology grows. And that theology is primarily the interaction, the encounter with God which is proclaimed, signified, and effected in this eucharistic meal, and then, it is our reflections on it. But all are offered to the Father, through Jesus Christ, in the Spirit, by us as members of the church, to God's honor and glory, and to this doxology of praise and thanksgiving the people of God respond "Amen," signifying the assent of the assembly to what is done and their participation in it.

From this Great Thanksgiving, we move to the common recitation of the Lord's Prayer, the breaking of the bread, and our eating and drinking in and with Christ at his heavenly table. The Thanksgiving is set in the context of the meal, which is an integral part of the action. It is not simply our verbal assent to the words of the Great Thanksgiving, but our common participation in the heavenly banquet which Christ sets before us which unites us with him in the mystery of his saving death and resurrection. Thus we are taken up into the saving acts of the Holy Trinity and united with God in Christ, through the power of the Holy Spirit poured out upon the gifts and upon us.

The congregation's participation in the eucharistic action is signified first by their bringing forward of the gifts, then by their response to the opening dialogue of the Great Thanksgiving and saying "Amen" at its conclusion. Finally it is climaxed by eating and drinking the communion of the body and blood of Christ.

There is enough theology here for a new *Summa Theologica*, or, if you prefer, a new *Institutes of the Christian Religion*. But there is also enough theology here for the assembly of Christian people to offer their prayers and praises to God and to be united with Christ forever, without recourse to either Aquinas or Calvin, or to their contemporary counterparts. To be a theologian is first of all to call upon the name of God and to enter into conversation with the Holy One, and that is the theology which the liturgy makes available to all who pray. But for those of us who aspire to be wise and learned, God offers unbounded and unending joy of reflecting upon this and trying to express the inexpressible, search the unsearchable, and comprehend the incomprehensible.

Aquinas, at the end of his life, is supposed to have said that he had not begun to scratch the surface of the knowledge he sought, but he died in the assurance that he, no less than the simple folk who could not read his books, had entered into the true knowledge and love of God.

My claim is simply that it is the liturgy where this primarily takes place, and that this encounter is the tap root of all of our theology.

Notes

1. Book of Common Prayer, 1979, 857-861.
2. Aidan Kavanagh, *On Liturgical Theology* (New York, 1984) 145.
3. Ibid. 169.
4. Massey H. Shepherd, *The Worship of the Church* (Greenwich CT, 1952) 4.
5. Kavanagh, *On Liturgical Theology* 74ff.
6. Leonel L. Mitchell, *Praying Shapes Believing* (Minneapolis, 1985).
7. A good point of entry into that discussion is Kavanagh's treatment of Wainwright in *On Liturgical Theology* 123ff and Wainwright's review of Kavanagh's book in *Worship* 61 (1987) 183-186.
8. *Epicheiresis Canon Missae* (1523), translation in R.C.D. Jasper and G.J. Cuming, *Prayers of the Eucharist*, 3d ed. (New York, 1987) 184ff.
9. *Form of Church Prayers*, Geneva (1542) translation in R.C.D. Jasper and G.J. Cuming, *Prayers of the Eucharist* 217ff.
10. Michael B. Aune in *Currents in Theology and Mission* 14:1 (February 1987) 58-59.
11. Geoffrey Wainwright, *Doxology* (New York, 1980).
12. David Power, *Unsearchable Riches: The Symbolic Nature of the Liturgy* (New York, 1984).
13. Book of Common Prayer 13.
14. Matthew 18:20.
15. See Mitchell, *Praying Shapes Believing* 142ff.

16. Colossians 3:1-3.

17. The West Syrian structure of the eucharistic prayer is that of the Byzantine and Antiochene anaphoras. Its classic exemplars are the eucharistic prayer of *The Apostolic Tradition* of Hippolytus, the so-called Clementine liturgy of *Apostolic Constitutions, Book 8,* and the anaphoras of the liturgies of Saint James of Jerusalem, Saint Basil, and Saint John Chrysostom. The Scottish Nonjurors conformed the Prayer of Consecration of the Scottish Prayer Book of 1637 to that pattern in their *Wee Bookies* in the belief that it represented the tradition of the apostolic church, and from that source it was adopted by the Episcopal Church in 1789 as the eucharistic prayer of the First American Prayer Book. It is Eucharistic Prayer I in the present American Book of Common Prayer, but its structure and outline are shared by Prayers II, A, B, D, and Form II.

18. Book of Common Prayer 362ff.

16

Seeing Liturgically

Aidan Kavanagh

THIS ESSAY WILL ATTEMPT TO IDENTIFY FOUR WAYS OF SEEING WHICH RESULT-
ed as the church gradually changed the root metaphor[1] of late antique
culture. Having identified these, it will then propose that all four still
have fundamental relevance to the way we see as Christians.

Pagan and Judaic root metaphors tended to come from nature and to
be expressed in images drawn from agricultural husbandry; for example,
offering "first fruits," sacrificing animals, fertility observances, and die-
tary restrictions meant to enhance the unity and distinctiveness of a People among alien neighbors. Participation in such observances put people
in touch with social and religious coherence in the strongest and most accessible way.[2] The community of believers in Jesus the Christ altered all
this, replacing it with an unprecedented root metaphor which both ab-
sorbed and transmuted what had gone before. This new root metaphor
was lodged not in the recurring cycles of nature husbandry but in the
historical incarnation of the invisible and inconceivable Judaic YHW in
the person of one Jesus, a rabbi called the Anointed One, the Messiah,
the Christ. In its most powerful expression the metaphor took the form
of the Pauline "Body of Christ"; a Body which could be dined upon at a
new Table around which sat the same Body, a new corporation of people
who conceived of themselves as reconciled to God and at peace both
with each other and a redeemed world.[3] The cultural potency of such a
metaphor produced what Peter Berger has called a new "sacred canopy"
beneath which the entire world could be viewed, and it gained force as

255

late antique civilization peaked and then slid into decline from around the middle of the second century, when its political focus shifted eastward and its economic and military fortunes declined.

Enculturating the New Root Metaphor

The new root metaphor held out to the late antique world's divisions and anxieties an offer too good to refuse, namely, a fresh coherence which the old metaphors finally could not provide. It rendered them obsolete, subsumed them into itself, transforming them and giving them an altogether new sort of life. The God incarnate in Jesus the Christ was the new and final sacrificial lamb who consummated all previous offerings in himself.

Yet it was not enough to propose the new metaphor; it had to work and to be seen to work. It had to be demonstrated culturally, to be enculturated in plausible and accessible ways. Nor could it merely be "proclaimed"; it had to be "manifested" in every cultural analogy the civilization was able to perceive.[4] These analogies clustered mainly in the lived human experience of the *civitas*, from which civilization took its name. Had Christians shrunk from the risks involved in taking the metaphor of the Body of Christ public on a civil scale, the church would have perished along with its competing "mystery religions" (which might be seen as vigorous attempts to resuscitate the old metaphors in terms of their helpfulness to individuals). The subsequent influence of the new root metaphor, reverberating down through the power centers of rural cultures such as Armenia, and of uncivilized tribes such as the Franks, Germans, Goths, and Slavs, could not have taken place. The result would no doubt have been that modern Europe might still be tribal to a degree seen today only in central Africa. Nor would Kievan Rus have been Christianized a millennium ago, an event attributed in the oldest Russian chronicle directly to events of public worship in the city of Constantinople in 988.

The question for now, however, is how the new root metaphor managed to overwhelm and finally transmute those that had been in possession of the culture. The answer is not simple and is capable of almost unlimited nuance. But for our purposes here, recent research has been helpful in clarifying some of its general lines.[5] The Body of Christ metaphor penetrated late antique civilization as Christian worship became public, urban, and mobile, thus helping to win the great cities of the Mediterranean world—Alexandria, Antioch, Rome, Jerusalem, and Constantinople—whence it spread into hinterlands east, south, north, and west. In the streets and buildings of these great cultural centers Christians proclaimed and manifested the Body of Christ metaphor as urban *cultus*, enacted as a holy company dining upon a non-carnal (*pneumatike*, as in *Didache* 10) food which filled souls, minds, spirits, imaginations.

The *cultus* in which the metaphor was manifested can already be sensed in *Didache* 9-10, which seems to have originated in Syria, perhaps in its oldest passages from ca. 40-60 A.D.[6] But it is expressed clearly by Ignatius Theophorus (+107), third ruler of the church in Antioch, in a series of letters he wrote to small urban churches of Asia Minor and to Rome while on his slow way to martyrdom in the latter city. The church, he says, comes together around its bishop, who presides at the holy meal called, as in *Didache*, the Thanksgiving (*eucharistia*).[7] To the meal's bread Ignatius compares himself: "I am God's wheat, ground fine by the lion's teeth to become purest bread for Christ."[8] What has been called this "strange cry of ecstasy, never heard before, sent a thrill of wonder through the Christian world,"[9] along with a similar statement about Ignatius' colleague and friend, Polycarp of Smyrna (+155), who was compared by those who witnessed his own martyrdom at the stake to "a loaf baking in the oven,"[10] an image with eucharistic overtones similar to that of Ignatius. The enculturation of such unconventional sentiments, explicable only by recourse to the gathering power of the Body of Christ metaphor at so early a period, can be seen in the subsequent explosion of the pious veneration of martyrs and in the erection of *martyria* to enshrine their bodily relics beginning in the early fourth century. The martyrs were, quite literally, personal and physical manifestations of the new root metaphor as it was becoming *cultus* in the most concrete, public, and accessible way. The association of the ranks of martyrs with the eucharistic Body of Christ which lay upon the table and sat around it, seen already in Ignatius, becomes overt in the Roman *Canon Missae*, with its lists of martyrs both female and male.

But there was an even larger setting within which the new metaphor expressed itself. This was the move of the Christian *cultus* into the whole complex of urban public worship in the cities of late antiquity. These cities had to be won for Christ if the church enlivened by the new metaphor were to survive, and victory was neither easy nor quick. In Rome, at least, paganism remained alive and entrenched well into the fifth century, long after the much newer cities of Constantinople and Jerusalem had become solidly Christian. The agency of winning these and other cities was, especially on the popular level, liturgical. A mobile and rapidly developing system of worship in public and on an urban scale carried the new metaphor and its cultic expression into the corners of late antique cultural centers, moving from site to site (cemeteries, shrines, and churches) through changeable processional routes to the singing of psalms, antiphons, litanies, and sometimes scriptural readings. There were already at least nine such Christian sites in Rome prior to Constantine. By the end of the fourth century these had grown into an array of some twenty neighborhood *tituli*, four or five large episcopal basilicas, and a series of martyrial shrines in cemeteries ringing the city.

In those cities from which evidence has survived, this system of urban worship had several distinctive features. First, it centered on the bishop. As ruler of the city's church, he was the living source of its unity as Christ's corporate Body and host of its holy banquet. In Ignatius' terms, where the bishop was, there was the church catholic celebrating its *eucharistia*. The imagery is Pauline: "One body and one spirit, as you were called in one hope of your calling, one Lord, one faith, one baptism, one God and Father of all, who is over all and through all and in all" (Eph 4:4-6).[11] Second, this episcopal liturgy, wherever in the city it was celebrated, was the common and singular worship of the entire urban church.[12] Third, as the cities became more thoroughly Christian by the latter half of the fourth century, public processions from one worship site to another increased in frequency. In the tenth-century *Typikon* of Hagia Sophia in Constantinople, there are still at that late date sixty-eight processions listed during the course of the year (an average of one every five days), and indications are that this number was fewer than in earlier centuries.[13] These processions, moreover, were not separate events but an integral part of the whole urban pattern of worship,[14] so much so that their execution and contents helped to structure the *eisodos* and *introit* of both Byzantine and Roman eucharists.[15]

Christians picked up these processional observances from pagan antecedents. Ignatius intimates just such a thing when he alludes to pagan practice at the great shrine of Artemis (Diana) at Ephesus. He instructs the Christians of that famous city: "You are all pilgrims in the same great procession, bearing your God and your shrine and your Christ and your sacred treasures on your shoulders, every one of you arrayed in the festal garments of the commandments of Jesus Christ."[16] Indeed, Ignatius' own description of the most intimate aspects of the new root metaphor, such as the cross and the conception of Jesus by Mary, as the "loud-shouting mysteries" would no doubt have encouraged Christians after his time to let their new metaphor shout in public through such urban processions,[17] shorn now of their pagan associations.

The liturgy by which Christians enculturated the new metaphor of Christ's Body from the second century onward was episcopal, urban in scope, and mobile. What all this gradually displaced were the pagan *pompae* such as those mentioned by Ignatius. This should make us aware that early Christians no less than their pagan predecessors, "who lived in societies before the invention of printing, experienced their cities vertically by moving about their streets and walls and public places. They did not experience the urban environment horizontally, as it is now possible to do with elaborate maps and plans, not to mention rapid transport ... It is important to note that it was the urban stational liturgy that made these movements and their topographical arrangement a dynamic aspect of the lives of the city's inhabitants."[18] More even than the fact of Christian buildings, it was the urban liturgy which threw open the new metaphor to the city's denizens by "covering the city with liturgical action that had the bishop as its main participant ... It made the *civitas* not only a civilization, but also holy civilization, a civilization defended as much by icons and relics and processions as by its walls and military and political power."[19]

In other words, Christian liturgy made the civilized urban corporation into a new Body manifested worshipfully. This result was an evangelical success of astounding proportions which affects us still, even if not as much as it could. We receive the tradition created by this success, but often without insight into what made it work. We pass the tradition on materially but without having really entered into it formally, as does one who cooks by recipe or paints by numbers without ever penetrating either art or gaining formal mastery of its techniques and possibilities. We receive the liturgical tradition without quite knowing how to respond to it on its own terms, thus tapping into its power. "When the human response factor is minimized, the forms that worship takes will be *adiaphora*, relatively unimportant. However, if the human response to divinely communicated grace is important, then the cultural forms in which worship is enacted must be taken seriously."[20]

Taking those forms seriously means in part learning *to see* as did the liturgy's progenitors. For liturgy is never merely text. It is something people do; they see themselves doing it, and doing it causes them to see differently. As we learn to see with the liturgy's progenitors (to the extent that this is possible), then texts otherwise humdrum take on depth and color and dynamism, especially if we learn to see vertically and in motion. For convenience we might break this down into four categories for treatment: seeing interior spaces, seeing surfaces, seeing liturgy, and liturgy as a way of seeing.

Seeing Interior Space

All Christian churches, as distinct from shrines and baptisteries, "are heirs of that compact and unassuming building of the fourth century, which contains them all in essence—the building called a 'basilica'."[21]

This is so because church buildings are functions of that enculturation of the root metaphor of Christ's Body manifested in the liturgy enacted as a public event on an urban scale. The very word church is derived from *ecclesia*, assembly. Christians look at their buildings and call them an event: a worshiping act by those who are assembled by that act. The basilica was built to house this act and its performers. It was entirely different in form and purpose from a pagan temple, which was built to house the image of a god whose worship was most often conducted outdoors; the worshipers were not housed.

Telos: The Longitudinal Space

The basilica was matter-of-fact and without complicated engineering problems; a roofed and paved "street of columns," its lines of perspective converging in a semicircular apse or conch which staged the chair of the bishop and his clergy. Before the apse stood a small covered table surrounded by low barricades for crowd control. In front of this rose a high ambo from which lections were read and cantors conducted the singing of psalms and antiphons. The building was either orientated or occidentated, the only feature which would have suggested to an outside viewer that it was used for some sacred purpose. It was usually surrounded by a complex of colonnaded courtyards and other buildings which were as extensive as topography and endowment allowed, apparently in order to insulate the basilica and remove it from the ordinary noise and bustle of the streets.

Inside it was a sober and silent hall, full of a certain emptiness outside the time of divine service. Interior surfaces were hard, sheathed if possible in marble beneath either an open-beamed or flat, sometimes coffered, wooden ceiling. Draperies were often hung between the columns of the nave, making the side aisles dim in contrast to the nave, lit brightly from above by clerestory windows. The building was rigorously longitudinal: a visitor would have been drawn down the nave, between lines of rhythmically marching columns, toward the apse. It was a space filled with the typical Roman public virtues of *gravitas* and *auctoritas*, somewhat stoic on the whole. In the apse stood the chair (which even today the Byzantines still bless and reverence) from which the bishop passed on to his people apostolic teaching, often illustrated in fresco or mosaic panels called *sacrae historiae* and located in series running the length of the nave on each side above columns. Examples can still be seen in Saint Mary Major in Rome and Saint Apollinare Nuovo in Ravenna. Functioning in somewhat the same manner as the stations of the cross in modern Catholic churches, these amounted to visual preaching of canonical and noncanonical Scriptures—biblical preaching for ordinary people in fresco and mosaic, the stimulus for the same effort in stained glass windows centuries later.

People experienced these interiors the same way they experienced the cities in which they were located: vertically and in motion. The walls and vertical columns carried them, instructing them along the way, toward the *telos*, or final end, of the great chair in the apse, with the small table before it, whence issued back to the people the divine Word in holy Scripture, apostolic teaching, and prayer. Here were Ignatius' loud-shouting mysteries of the Lord's Body, on the table and gathered around it, manifested in quiet gravity, authority, and a gentle but firm sense of order. The experience as a whole was what we today would call counter-cultural; secular busyness, political cunning and factionalism, and cultural anxiety were meant to be transmuted here (with what effort and partial success we can only imagine) into purpose, peace, wisdom, and unity. And wherever Christians went, they found this same sort of interior, shouting the same mysteries, manifested in the same way from Spain to Eastern Syria and beyond, as the fourth-century western pilgrim Egeria notes repeatedly in the diary of her travels in the East.[22]

Dynamis: The Centralized Space

But if the basilica's main psychic emphasis may be characterized as solemnly teleological, another type of interior complemented it in terms of *dynamis*, power. This was an architectural form not special to Christianity, as was the cultic basilica, namely, the *tholos*, a domed space not unknown in the West (for example, the Roman Pantheon) but more common in the East prior to the Christian era. The *tholos* axis is not longitudinal but vertical and concentric, producing a pavillioned space focussed on a central point, as in the Jefferson Memorial and the Capitol Rotunda in Washington today. Such a space requires a central focal point from which the walls seem to bloom upward and outward, a phenomenon which invests the center with great psychic power both civil and religious.

Not surprisingly, such spaces tended to be used as shrines and mausolea, less usually as churches, although there are exceptions such as the Great Church in Antioch, founded by Constantine, and Saint Vitale in Ravenna, built in the sixth century under Justinian and adopted as suitably "imperial" church design by Charlemagne in his chapel royal at Aachen in northern Germany. But the *tholos* form was used more regularly among Christians for their baptisteries, the architectural center of power being the pool of running water in which one died to death and rose to a new life intimated in the resurrected body of the Lord himself. Early Christian baptism had its own liturgy distinct from that which was housed by the basilica, and therefore its own building, as one can still see in the Lateran, Ravenna, Florence, Pisa, Constantinople, and elsewhere.

But there is more to it even than this. The death-life dynamism of the *tholos* was further enhanced by its use as the shrine which contained the Lord's own tomb, the Anastasis ("resurrection") of the Constantinian Great Church on Calvary in Jerusalem. This particular *tholos*, as though to demonstrate the psychic and spiritual power such a shape insinuated in the expanding Christian culture, kept being reproduced for the next thousand years in baptisteries, reliquaries, eucharistic vessels from pyxes to turrets and tabernacles,[23] as well as in artistic representations of the holy city of Jerusalem, the center of the great cosmic *tholos* itself.

Every *tholos* thus manifested the root metaphor of the Body of Christ dead and risen among his people; every *tholos*, whether large or small, was an "anastasis." To grasp this is to understand why pilgrims from all over the Christian world traveled to Jerusalem from the early fourth century onward, and why the Crusades were mounted first against the Persians and later the Muslims. This was to secure the integrity of the city made holy by the presence of the Anastasis at its heart. At almost every baptism and eucharist and Easter Vigil they attended, Christians were reminded of this specific building, for it was here that the new Eve of the church was born from the wounded side of the new Adam as he slept in the bosom of the earth, the mother of all.

So deeply etched into Christian consciousness did all this become that by the sixth century *tholos* and basilica had come to be sometimes united in the domed basilica, such as that of Hagia Irene in Constantinople. More important, however, were the more complex architectural unions of *tholos* and basilica in the building of Saints Sergios and Bacchos in the same city, built as a domed octagon within a square, and of Justinian's astonishing rebuilding of Hagia Sophia. Except for an attached apse and only two pairs of columns standing across from each other, Saints Sergios and Bacchos has all but lost the basilica's longitudinality in its floor plan; the great dome rises over the center of a nave which is defined by side columns as longer than it is wide, organizing perspective which focusses in the apse with its synthronon. The building was thus as conservative in its liturgical floor plan as it was daring in its superstructure. Even more conservative was Rome, which seems not to have erected domed basilicas until the Renaissance, almost a thousand years later. In Rome, vaulting (necessary for domed interiors) was used in public baths and mausolea, but was apparently thought unsuitable for liturgical purposes.[24] But in the East, from Armenia to Constantinople and up into the lands of Rus, the hybrid basilica and *tholos* became the standard after the seventh century and domes multiplied.

It could perhaps be argued that the deep psychic association between *tholos* and shrines such as *martyria* and the Jerusalem Anastasis containing the Holy Sepulchre encouraged those who worshiped in domed churches to see the liturgy in terms of Christ's death. Germanus, patriarch of Constantinople (+ ca. 730), when he describes the paradigmatic interior of Hagia Sophia in his commentary on the Divine Liturgy, moves in this direction. The apse is both the cave where Christ was born and the cave where he was entombed. The altar is the spot in the tomb where Christ was laid. The ciborium over the altar represents "the crucifixion, burial, and resurrection of Christ" from this tomb. Even the altar-area barricades of bronze "are like those around the Holy Sepulchre," and the ambo "manifests the shape of the stone at the Holy Sepulchre."[25] The roots of this passion and death emphasis, "even to the point of seeing in individual details of the concrete ritual a dramatic reenactment of those awesome events,"[26] are Syrian, an area in which *tholos*-martyria were numerous, and can be seen already in the fourth-century commentaries of the great Syrian mystagogues Saint John Chrysostom and Theodore of Mopsuestia.[27] Domes, with their subliminal associations with mausolea, martyria, and the Anastasis-Holy Sepulchre, may well have helped focus the eyes of eastern Christians especially on the passion-and-death aspects of Christ's own *sacra historia* in their liturgy. Thence it spread to the West through mystagogues such as Ambrose of Milan, who read Greek (unlike Augustine), admired John Chrysostom, maintained close contacts with imperial courts in both West and East, and was generally the most important figure in the West for a generation.

But no more vivid sense of seeing interiors vertically can be had than by contemplating the Orthodox baptistery of the mid-fifth century in Ravenna. The decoration descends in five programs to the floor from the cupola, to which the eye rises on entering, lifted by vertical perspectives which meet there. The cupola medallion is a mosaic of Jesus's baptism in the Jordan, and it hovers exactly over the baptismal pool in the floor below. The programmatic band below the medallion contains twelve apostles in white and gold togas against a deep blue mosaic background, each figure carrying a wreath of victory. The style is classical, the billowing vesture almost baroque, the faces individually modelled in the style of portraiture. Below this is another band of twenty-four scenes: four vested thrones, four tables supporting the four gospels lying open on them, eight chairs in conches (perhaps the bishop's apsidal chair), and eight garden scenes. The band as a whole suggests the paradise of a new Eden (the garden scenes) now restored by Christ (the thrones and gospels) in the church (the episcopal chairs). Below this is a band of eight shallow arches, each containing a window flanked by two stucco figures in low relief, sixteen in all, framed by a conch above and by trabeated columns. The figures wear togas, hold scrolls or codices, and their framed stance altogether suggests that they are authoritative teachers, perhaps catechists. The lowest band is composed of eight shallow arches resting on columns which stand on the floor. The walls are covered in swirling tendril patterns done in blue-green and gold mosaic, a motif which ascends up through all the bands to the baptismal medallion in the cupola over the pool, sustaining the paradise theme throughout.

This octagonal interior is perhaps the most splendid surviving room of late antiquity. Its composition from cupola to floor integrates sixty-one images which cascade from top to bottom. It is complete in its summing up of the root metaphor of Christ's Body only when the figure of the naked Jesus of the cupola medallion emerges in its antitype—a naked catechumen stepping into the baptismal pool in the floor beneath. The intervening program-bands disclose visually how the type above and antitype below are related. What happened to him (medallion) is known by apostolic eyewitnesses, the Gospels as passion narratives, and the authoritative teaching of bishops and catechists (bands 2, 3, and 4). This knowledge is not dated chronology; it is life (band 5). The baptized are drawn up into all this as they descend into the pool, there to die to all they were in order to rise, reborn by being conformed to him (Rom 6, Jn 3) and constituted thereby new and eschatologically egalitarian creatures (Eph 4-5, Gal 3:25-29).

This is anything but mere interior decoration. Only actual baptisms, as at the Easter Vigil, complete the circuit of meaning that descends from the cupola medallion to the pool below. When that happens, the viewer is swept into an emphatic manifestation of the root metaphor—a complete and dynamic theology both of Christian life and of the church in its people, the living members of Christ's mysterious Body corporate. The table around which the baptized will stand in the church next door has nothing on it but an open gospel in Word and food, and what they give thanks for there is Ignatius' loud-shouting mysteries which they can see cascading all around them in this splendid room. It is the story of creation and the fall played backwards until all rest, in an astonishing new way, in the simplicity which is God. Every one of the sixty-one images in the octagon itself are transparent. Surface and frames disappear; one sees only perspectives of light which converge into a single point deep in the bosom of light itself. Mosaic, it has been said, is about optics.[28]

One might say that the Orthodox baptistery is an enactment of fundamental theological sensuality, a visual analogue to Methodios of Olympos' (+ca.311) lyric statement: "The Apostle could apply directly to Christ all that was said of Adam. It is in excellent accord with this that the Church has been formed from His flesh and bone. For it was for her sake that the Logos left His heavenly Father and came down to earth in order to cling to His Spouse and slept in the ecstasy of His passion ... cleansing her with the laver for that blessed spiritual seed which sows and plants; and like a woman the Church conceives of this seed and forms it."[29] There is nothing prim in this, rather as there is nothing dull in the Orthodox baptistery. Both exhibit technique and imagination which transformed the way conventions of the time saw the world.

At least by the ninth century in the East, after the victory over iconoclasm, this way of seeing had led to a general canon for locating images in a church. Christ, Mary, and the angels occupied the dome, high vaults, and conch of the apse, the "sky" of the church, the kingdom of heaven. On the lowest half of the walls saints mingled with the *ecclesia* on earth. The intermediate sphere of the walls was the link between heaven and earth, where the *sacrae historiae* of Old and New Testaments were displayed, sometimes in great detail, as we shall see. The church itself had become a great cosmic icon centering on the incarnation of the Logos in the Body of Christ become an abiding real presence in the world.[30]

This perspective has nothing to do with pious fancy nor with a certain neoplatonic regard of images as emanations of ideal types in the mind of God. On the contrary, early sources of the tradition insist that, far from being abstract, ideal, or merely aesthetic in nature, an image was praiseworthy precisely to the extent that it was utterly lifelike, true to life rather than to some obscure type. This is why early icons are fully modelled in the manner of classical portraiture.[31] Definite canons were evolved concerning how the Lord, his Mother, the saints and certain key events were to look, so that the ordinary person could recognize them at a glance—Paul as balding, Peter the ruddy fisherman with full beard and thick white hair, the visitation of Abraham at Mamre, the birth of the Lord, the resurrection, the transfiguration. Moreover, the *sacrae historiae* programs such as can still be seen in Saint Mary Major and Saint Apollinare Nuovo in Ravenna are plainly expressions of fundamental doctrine rather than "mystical" icons. But into this we shall go presently.

Seeing Surfaces

The liturgy's progenitors saw basilical interiors as they saw their cities, vertically and in motion. One column led to another, one image to another. The verticality was experienced in motion along a longitudinal route—much as the lives of male and female martyrs on the nave walls of Saint Apollinare Nuovo in Ravenna move from one site (the palace of Theodoric or the harbor of Classe) toward either the enthroned Mother of God on one side or the enthroned Christ on the other. In the Orthodox baptistery, as we have seen, the bands of images orbit the vertical axis established between the *typos* of Christ's baptism in the cupola medallion above and its *antitypos*, the pool of Christian baptism in the floor below. In Hagia Sophia longitudinal and concentric movement blend architecturally in a domed basilica to create a complex space not unlike a great urban plaza lying open beneath the sky, down from which pours one of the most potent scriptural manifestations of God, namely, light.

There is not a static brick or random image in any of these or hundreds of other examples that could be cited for at least the first thousand years. Putting immoveable pews in such a space could never have crossed anyone's mind until after the invention of printing in the fifteenth century, an event which severely damaged the way we see liturgically. What liturgy's progenitors saw was not a text producing concepts, but people filling churches, an assembling which gave rise to the repertoire of images Germanus of Constantinople used in the mid-eighth century to begin expounding the meaning of liturgy to his people, who saw the same things he did.[32] Even the death-of-Christ imagery used to explain the liturgy is filled with motion; the entry of the gifts is the funeral cortege from the cross to the tomb of the altar.[33]

What is evident in such treatments is that the people were not expected to see the utilitarian movements of getting from one place to another merely for what they were, but to see deeper meanings in them— meanings doctrinal, moral and spiritual, and eschatological.[34] These deeper meanings are very solemn indeed, and they escape the bonds of ritual necessity. Nor are they idle allegorical fancy. Rooted firmly in what was actually happening in the liturgy, commentaries such as those of Germanus link the ritual theologically to the fundamental motives for which the Body corporate of Christ comes to stand in him before his Father in worship. Here Christians see space and motion and surfaces, out of which loom toward them the very reasons for which space and motion and surfaces are there in the first place. This *space* exists because the ineffable God became effable in space and time by the incarnation of the Logos in Christ Jesus, who died for everyone's sins and reconciled all to his Father. The swirling *motion* of clergy and people into the church, and the emergence of the bishop out of all this as he mounts the synthronon, follow the law of creation when God brought order out of chaos. Vertical *surfaces* reflect back to believers the beauty of their faith and the world and of *sacrae historiae*, all manifestations of the saving love which lies at the core of creation and redemption in Christ.

The arts practiced by Christians for the first thousand years, including the great and complex art of liturgical ceremonial, were meant not merely to communicate meanings but to transform the viewer into a witness of an event in progress[35] and to envelop them in it. Words issue from this involvement, but they do not constitute it; nor is the involvement exclusively with concepts, but of the entire person in "the typological interconnection of the whole process of salvation" related throughout the Holy Scriptures.[36] We today view or hear a work of art and ask what it means. Earlier Christians would begin more typically with the event, say, of Abel's murder by Cain and then be aware of "the blood that would cry out to heaven louder than the blood of Abel, made present again on their altars,"[37] where they were transformed into witnesses of the event in progress. Their witness projected mosaic scenes of Abel's death, of Abraham's sacrifice of Isaac, and of the sacrifice of Melchisedech, priest of Salem (Peace), in bread and wine—as around the altar of eucharistic sacrifice of the New Covenant in Saint Vitale in Ravenna. "The bishop of Ravenna, as he celebrated at this altar, would then have translated into explicit phrases the thoughts that lay behind this composition, when he recited the main eucharistic prayer,"[38] in this case the old Roman *Canon Missae* witnessed already by Ambrose in his *De Sacramentis* and still said today.

An even more massive example of this was in the great basilica of Saint Paul Outside the Walls in Rome.[39] Finished in 402, it was restored under Leo the Great by 450, when the program of *sacrae historiae* may have been installed or completed in the immense three hundred by eighty-foot nave, capped by a coffered ceiling one hundred feet above the floor. "In this grand central nave, about thirty feet of wall space below the sills of forty clerestory windows was reserved for a double band of frescoes. Their vertical frames corresponded to the axes of the twenty columns of each arcade. Allowing for the frames, each panel was about ten feet wide and twelve high. There were forty-two such panels on each wall; Old Testament on the left, New on the right, reading from the triumphal arch where the cycles began—six hundred feet of painting, twenty-four feet high. The statistics put this cycle on a par with the reliefs of the columns of Trajan and Marcus Aurelius."[40]

So much effort and planning could not have been merely random or purely decorative. The eighty-four biblical scenes were there to give present life to the texts themselves. As Leo said, so fixed in the hearers' hearts was the story of Christ's passion "that for each listener the reading itself makes a kind of vision" (Sermon 70:1); gospel readings are "so open and lucid, that for committed and devout hearts to hear what is read is to see what was done" (Sermon 52:1). "Hold the sequence of events so plainly in mind as if you had reached them all in bodily sight and touch" (Sermon 19:3). When Leo urged his hearers to visualize the gospel story, he was not calling on them to remember the texts. "He wanted the events present to their sight so they could respond directly to them and emotionally inhabit them."[41] This is the role which the *sacrae historiae* in Saint Paul's and elsewhere were designed to play. What the viewers saw is what they heard: in the liturgy people were transformed in the most actual and fundamental way into witnesses of events in progress, saving events caused still by and in the Body of Christ. This continuum is what the tradition has called the *mysterion,* the *sacramentum.* All that was actual in the life of Christ remains actual in this continuing modality. Apart from this continuum, ecclesial art forms are drained of their intent and separated from the *sacramentum* and from each other. All that is left are engineering problems, "art" works, scores, and texts. One can get with ease from the *sacramentum* to the forms, but it is almost impossible to get from the desacramentalized forms to the events which the *sacramentum* sustains. This is why a Soviet tour guide can praise Russian icons by saying that religions come and go, but the works of man survive—a supreme statement of aestheticism shorn of content and peculiar genius. What the guide said is not untrue; but it is only a small part of a greater truth.

Early Christians, liturgy's progenitors, did not look at their art and wonder what it meant. Rather, they were expected to steep themselves in the sacramental mystery of the Word made flesh and then rejoice in the beauty to which this gave rise, and which beauty was suffused by it with an inner light of hard-headed, flat-footed presence. The strong young man with a lamb on his shoulders is neither a shepherd nor Orpheus nor some ideal type. He is the same person as the beardless boy who sits on the cosmic orb in the apse of Saint Vitale in Ravenna, a sealed scroll in one hand and the crown of victory in the other. And both of these are the same One seen presiding in the twenty-four scenes of creation and fall in the right-hand dome of the entrance hall of Saint Mark's in Venice, undergoing his passion in the *historiae* on the south wall of Saint Apollinare Nuovo in Ravenna, performing his miracles in the *historiae* of the north wall, sitting as an infant in his mother's lap just beneath, and coming as food and drink to his people on the holy table in all the churches of Christendom. The Creator Logos, perfect image of the Father whom no one has seen at any time (a canon violated spectacularly by Michelangelo on the Sistine Chapel ceiling), is the One who took flesh of a Virgin in the world's greatest-ever act of philanthropy (Phil 2:5-11), and who in his resurrection bore all home to his Father, sustaining all on the food of his own Body along the way. "'We have now heard the fact,' Augustine was in the habit of saying, when he had taken his seat to preach after the reading of the Gospel, 'now let us search for the mystery that lies hidden behind it.'"[42] Artists and those who commissioned them strove to do likewise.

This is one reason why mosaic was so appropriate for manifesting the loud-shouting mysteries in artistic form. Articulating mystery and form was a high discipline, "the art of calculation, applied geometry, of optics and mechanics" applied by *noetos* (mind) to *aisthetos* (matter).[43] Mosaic technology was not concerned merely with covering surfaces with colored cubes. It was a form of optics designed to trap light *within* the surface, of geometry which showed artists how to place figures in a hemisphere without allowing the curve of the surface to distort the figure. Most especially, mosaic strove to harness light within the surface so that the mystery represented seemed not to lie hidden behind the image but, shimmering, to inhabit it—enlivening *aisthetos* with a *noetos* that went beyond ordinary artistic competency. No one can quite know what this is like who has never moved through a mosaic interior lit by artificial light. The mosaic sparkles and lives. Hence the inscription in the episcopal chapel in Ravenna: *Aut lux hic nata est aut capta hic libera regnat* ("Whether light is born or caught here, it reigns freely"). Part of the *noetos* was the awareness that in Scripture the primordial chaos was dark, so that the first act of creation was God's command, "Let there be light; and there was light. And God saw that the light was good" (Gn 1:3-4). At that moment the divine mystery was in space and time on the first day. The mosaicist's creation, an extension of God's, began with light.

Furthermore, the light in a mosaic does not remain there, but streams out to the viewer. The depth of the scene was conceived as being in front of it, not behind it; its perspective point was not off somewhere behind the scene but in the viewer. The scene is thus not an "open window" into which one gazes, immobilized. Rather, the light-filled scene creates its space out in the room or church where the viewer, the focal point, carries the scene's perspective point with him as he moves about. "The *Ekphraseis*, Byzantine descriptions and panegyrics upon buildings, emphasize repeatedly that the eyes should not rest on decorations but should wander."[44] It is not as though the viewer looks at God through the scene, but that God regards the viewer through the scene. Perspective in iconography is dynamic and always in motion, never static or immobilizing.

To think that all this can be adequately summarized by calling liturgy's perceptions of space and surface "symbolic," in the sense of one thing standing for something else, is to reduce the complex and subtle and grand to the bland and obvious and pedestrian. It is to scale the Orthodox baptistery down to a traffic sign, and to miss entirely how its progenitors perceived liturgy to work.

Seeing Liturgy

Although liturgy is not primarily done to be seen, doing it means that it will necessarily be seen. If its progenitors saw as sketched above, then it follows that when they did the liturgy they would have seen it in similar ways: vertically, in motion, sacramentally, its perspective point in themselves, and flooding their entire urban environment. Like any composed scene, it would have been utterly lifelike—not "symbolic" or abstract, not like a view through an open window at mysteries whose meaning receded into some golden haze, immobilizing the viewers in the privacy of their own subjectivity. Rather, the liturgy for them was suffused with the dynamic and active presence of the *sacramentum* just as light filled a mosaic and streamed to the viewers, filling them with the same light whose origin constituted the first day of creation itself and was the *doxa tou theou*, the glory of God.

The Creator Logos, who became incarnate in Christ Jesus, walked in the liturgy as he had walked in the cool of the Garden of Eden and asked the man and the woman who had told them they were naked (Gn 3:8-13); who stands now amidst a great multitude which no one can number "before the throne and the Lamb, clothed in white robes, with palm branches in their hands, and crying out with a loud voice, 'Salvation belongs to our God who sits upon the throne, and to the Lamb'" (Rv 7:9-10). Both scenes, one at the beginning and the other at the consummation of time, are simultaneous in God and exhaustively frame the liturgical assembly at every point in its existence: fallen yet saved by the blood of the Lamb who is Jesus the Christ of God, the fresh-faced boy sitting on the orb of the cosmos and hanging dead on a cross. In the liturgy one is dealing with a *noetos* that goes beyond what human mind might devise as light goes beyond darkness. To enter its assembly one must undergo *photismos*, enlightenment; only thus can one stand at the table of Life, where all give thanks to God for the divine glory revealed in Christ amidst a gathering from the four winds (*Didache* 9 and 10), an *ecclesia* in the midst of which gestates "the Passion at the heart of the World."[45]

Unless I am mistaken, this is not drama.[46] Although the historic liturgies of Christianity may appear "dramatic" to many moderns, and although these liturgies have often engendered paraliturgical and nonliturgical drama in something akin to the modern sense, it would be a mistake to read the modern sense of drama back into these historic liturgies and then conclude that this explained anything fundamental about them. On those liturgies' own evidence, something more was afoot in their enactment than is encompassed satisfactorily by the category of drama. For they strove no more for dramatic effect than an iconographer or mosaicist strove for striking visual effects. What all these strove for was the divinizing actions of the Body of Christ in humanity, a humanity transfigured in his incarnation, ministry, passion, death, and resurrection. This was so because the church celebrating the liturgy is "in actuality the state of kenosis in which the flesh of the Word communicates his life to the world until the day when death is destroyed forever (1 Cor 15:26). [The church's liturgy] is the transfiguration continuing today."[47]

Here once again we run into the Christian root metaphor, something so vertiginous that whatever may be done in accordance with it must necessarily be so out of the ordinary as to seem "dramatic." But although the liturgy may be dramatic in this sense, like a great mountain or the Grand Canyon, this does not make it drama, at least in Aristotle's sense of an imitation of an action, not the action itself.[48] The liturgy is not an imitation or mime of anything, even of the life of Christ. It is its own unique thing, deeply connected at every point with space and time and human cultures, but energized by that present and effective Reality which transcends and transmutes them all.

Perhaps a category more useful than drama in helping us see the liturgy as its progenitors did is that of "scene." By scene I mean the sort of meticulously crafted compositions that came to cover the walls, apses, and domes of interiors in which the liturgy was done. As we have seen, these were never random or capricious, but were often organized into programs more or less vast, with increasing sophistication from the third century onwards. As they evolve, these scenes absorb influences from all over the Christian world and lay the groundwork for all subsequent iconography, even to the point that a quick glance is usually enough to identify an image's multivalent contents and personae. These latter are what we today might characterize as plot and cast, but to our predecessors they were Augustine's "facts" or *aisthetos*; what they looked for was more the *noetos* which loomed at them out of the facts of the composition. The entire scene is matter transformed by mind, the mind knowable only by the transformation of matter it accomplishes.

This can be seen in the way even individuals were regarded as "scenes." In describing the beauty of Empress Irene Dukas, the *Alexiad* dwells on her hands and eyes: "her hand acted as a charioteer for her speech, in perfect harmony bringing forward the wrist with the arm," and "the iris of her eyes resembled a calm sea radiating forth its blue in deep waves of serenity."[49] Not too different from the description of the beloved in the Song of Songs, Irene's beauty becomes a literary scene in which the *aisthetos* of her physique is transformed into utter charm and beauty by the *noetos* of her elegant persona. The scene, furthermore, associates life and light on one hand, and light and the immaterial element in material things on the other. Color is conceived as light materialized. Changing color is conceived of in terms of rhythm. Mathew concludes: "Perhaps both painting and mosaic were in some fashion apprehended as music and the color combinations conceived in terms of harmony."[50] The iconic scene, like the liturgical scene, is fundamentally one of the perfect symmetry and pacific order originating in God, a manifestation of *noetos* writ large, a "seen music" filled with a harmony going beyond what the ear could hear. The alternative is chaos, the darkness of mere meaning.

For this reason, if for no other, the scenes of the liturgy would be composed as carefully as an iconographer would compose a painting or mosaic. The enacted scene conserved the fecund association between *noetos* and *aisthetos*, between the Light which is Life and that element in material things which is the ultimate immateriality of their divine cause. For Germanus, the matter of *aisthetos* in the entrance into the church is motion and climbing stairs. But its *noetos* consists in the souls of Christians being "called together to assemble with the prophets, apostles, and hierarchs in order to recline with Abraham, Isaac, and Jacob at the mystical banquet of the Kingdom of Christ."[51]

This is not drama. Germanus is striving to probe the *noetos* of each *aisthetos*, or practical part, of the liturgy as it occurs for the imagination and faith of his people. As he does this, liturgical events become rooted scenes accessible even to the most unlearned, and of a depth none of them will ever exhaust. From each scene Light and Life flow into the participants, who become living mosaics that trap in themselves the loud-shouting light of the "mystical banquet of the Kingdom of Christ," a flow enhanced by ceremonial rhythm and visual harmony. As such, the liturgical scene does not constrict and immobilize: it broadens and liberates. The Scriptures themselves are a tissue of such scenes, which is why they appear all over the walls of churches, until the modern period. The low level of church art in our day is both cause and effect of the non-scenic liturgy which afflicts us: we sit and we think, but there is nothing to see. It is as though seeing and thinking are mutually exclusive.

When scenes of faith are no longer enacted in the liturgy, when they cease to glow from our walls, then the mystery that manifests itself in them ceases being attended to. What takes its place is mere proclamation of a narrow band of theological and social concerns which fail to fire imaginations, to engender a warm and robust faith, a truly popular piety. The two attitudes have about as much in common as do the British crown jewels and a subway token. And lest it be thought that the latter is all we can reasonably be expected to work with, in those areas where liturgy has remained scenic, as in Russia, Poland, and Africa, paradoxes abound. The Soviet government, which for seventy years has allowed the Orthodox to do little more than worship liturgically in a hostile environment, must now reckon with the church's burgeoning hold on the working masses. In Poland the Catholic Church is the only real opponent of the socialist state due to its hold on the masses—producing Solidarity, the first non-Italian pope since 1522, and two out of three of all the new churches currently being built in Europe. In Africa Christians have increased fourfold, to one hundred million, between 1950 and 1975.[52]

The point is not to belabor but to call into serious question the attitude that modern Christians can no longer see the mystery as vigorously as they once did, that today their celebrations must be laments over their not having been socially omniscient, that the concerns expressed in an essay such as this one are obsolete or quaint. But it is not our eyes which have dimmed. Rather, the scenes we allow ourselves seem to have become pernicious by inadvertence on our part, more or less in passing. The images and scenes of a consumer culture have been allowed to become our fare, to build our churches, to compose our liturgy. The Christian root metaphor cannot be enculturated in such scenes, but only relativized or denied. Lacking better, we quickly come to see as everyone else does. The liturgy, meanwhile, slips from being a rich, new, countercultural way of seeing and becomes a tertiary ecclesiastical form of entertainment for Sunday mornings: tiresome, bland, alleviated only by the rarely apprehended sincerity of the preacher. The Body which sits at the table quietly disperses; its antithesis locks itself deep and unseen within us, taking over our lives. The problem is illustrated not by the fact that Christians do not find anything nice to say about the Trinity, but that it never occurs to them to say anything eschatalogical about the beauty of Elizabeth Taylor. Meanwhile, the liturgy slips into being little more than a prolix commercial for a dry "spiritual" product delivered by a statisticalized system of "pastoral" services.

No surviving ancient building, image, or ceremony is as flat, dull, or deadening as this. People still have their rhythms, movements, and scenes, most of which have been drained of everything but short-term or utilitarian significance at best. Rock video projects strong scenes as difficult to ignore as they are bereft of serious meaning. What looms out at one from them is what assaults one in much modern art, namely, the grotesque barrenness of life in our day. These are major visual homilies driven home without, or in spite of, words: celebrations of glandular urges, summonses to amass possessions, ideological programs where law becomes confused with justice, wisdom no longer prevails, and charity gives way to outrage or lust.

Conclusion: Liturgy as a Way of Seeing

The liturgy, being essentially something done and therefore seen, forms its participants on the deepest levels. We are what we see, taste, smell, and touch. Prayer texts heard help clarify and anchor this total perception, but they do not produce it nearly so tellingly as do the liturgy's ceremonial scenes. Hence the early liturgy's pronounced visual character in images and ceremony. These fired the imaginations of liturgy's participants and gave irresistible force and confidence to their faith which no cultural inertia or assault finally could overcome. They remain potential in today's liturgy. Three examples from eucharistic prayer texts may illustrate the point.

The eucharistic prayer, being the sacramental prayer par excellence, is replete with literary scenes which should form Christians to see all things in a unique way. One such scene is the Sanctus, the hymn of the angelic beings before God in the vision of Isaiah 6, a vision brought full term in that of the heavenly liturgy of already present messianic times in Revelation 7. More often than not, this hymn, which entered the eucharistic prayer prior to the fourth century, is sung as the first climactic part of the prayer. In some of these prayers it climaxes the thanksgiving to God for creation; in others, such as in *Apostolic Constitutions VIII*, it climaxes a long section thanking God for the work of Christ. In all cases, however, it defines the relation between God and the world as fundamentally one of worship; all things are given a voice in this worship as humanity is enabled to join the heavenly host surrounding the awe-inspiring God in singing pure praise: "Holy, Holy, Holy Lord ... " The scene is one of all things giving cosmic credit where credit is due; in the realization that everything which is comes from the Holy One who cannot but fill all things with his own holiness. Christians look around them and see, therefore, nothing but existential holiness, and they do so with wonder, awe, and thanksgiving.

Sticking close to Isaiah 6—where the prophet, on seeing the divine scene, is filled with a sense of his own unworthiness—Cranmer in 1552 had the priest kneel after Sanctus and say the so-called Prayer of Humble Access: "We do not presume to come to this thy Table, O merciful Lord, trusting in our own righteousness ...," thus creating a visual scene illustrative of devotion in receiving holy communion. Luther, on the other hand, has the Sanctus hymn sung at the elevation-showing of the sacrament, creating a different sort of visual scene altogether, one which maintains the greatest visual scene of medieval eucharistic climax in the old *Canon Missae*.

The elevation is the second example of scenic emphasis in the eucharistic prayer. Entering western ceremonial usage at this point only from the eleventh century, it glossed the literary scene of the institution of the eucharist by showing the consecrated sacrament of bread and wine in closest proximity to the statements of Christ at the Last Supper: "This is my Body ... this is the cup of my Blood." Whatever else may be said of this ceremonial introduction, which came to be expanded by lighting extra candles, ringing bells, and singing motets, the enacted scene deeply gripped the medieval imagination, even to the point of altering perceptions regarding the text, typography, and theology of the prayer itself. But the entire scene was a strong affirmation of the root metaphor of the Body of Christ on the table, if not around it. If it was emphatic sacramentally, it was ambiguous ecclesiologically. But a strong and compelling scene it was in any case, producing lasting piety, spiritual orientations, and even certain types of religious orders.

The third example is the often unremarked Old Testamental verbal scenes evoked in the Roman *Canon Missae* of eucharistic types, already mentioned: the death of Abel, the sacrifice of Isaac by Abraham, and the sacrifice of Melchisedech, priest of Salem—scenes displayed in the sanctuary of Saint Vitale, Ravenna, as we have seen, and elsewhere. Moreover, the prayer for acceptance of the church's offering by God is cast in a temple scene reminiscent simultaneously of Isaiah 6, Hebrews, and Revelation 7: "We humbly beseech you, almighty God, to command that these offerings be carried by your holy angel to your altar on high, in the sight of your divine majesty..."

These three verbal scenes, in only one liturgical text of the Roman tradition, might illustrate the inadvisability of allowing ceremonial scenes to disappear while the liturgical texts remain so rich. This may be one reason why such literary scenes eventually lose their imaginative richness; people come not to see them just as they have nothing left to see ceremonially. Worse, the blandness of ceremony in contrast to the rich imagery in the texts may suggest to people that textual images are not to be taken seriously because those who conduct the ceremony do not seem to do so. Thus a certain distrust of verbal scenes imperceptibly sets in, making the texts seem to be overblown rhetoric unsupported by the ceremony surrounding them. No longer can the texts' verbal scenes be imagined, and the texts themselves come to be discounted, distrusted, or ignored altogether. In any case, the liturgy's ability to form its participants into a richly common way of *seeing the world and the mystery at its heart* weakens, yet another motive for community coherence is lost, and the root metaphor of Christ's Body becomes a source of dispute or mere speculation. When the imagination of Christians goes flat, enculturating the metaphor becomes impossible, and the force of the mystery manifested drains away.

To move in this direction is to encounter one negative after another, as it were in a descending spiral that can only end in disaster liturgically, theologically, and pastorally. To move in the opposite direction seems the only alternative. Attending to the liturgy's strong *textual* scenes is one way to begin, going on from them to reestablish the liturgy's strong *ceremonial* scenes as complements. When both begin to support each other, the participants' way of seeing the world might begin to take on a distinctive Christian quality once again, and their evangelical and sacramental self-confidence may begin to return.

Notes

1. The phrase was coined by S. Pepper, *World Hypotheses* (Berkeley, 1942) 38-39.

2. Thus H. Eilberg-Schwartz, "Israel in the Mirror of Nature: Animal Metaphors in the Ritual and Narratives of Ancient Israel," *Journal of Ritual Studies* 2 (1988) 1-30, passim.

3. Ibid. 21-23. W. Meeks, *The First Urban Christians: The Social World of the Apostle Paul* (New Haven, 1983): "When Paul became a Christian, new rituals had already been created to commemorate the dying and rising of Jesus and to incorporate believers into his 'body.' Among the radicals at Antioch, these rituals and a new set of human relationships were replacing circumcision and other halakic observances as the distinctive boundary markers of the people of the one God." (p. 168)

4. D. Tracy, *The Analogical Imagination* (New York, 1981) 202-218. The Emmaus story illustrates the distinction between proclamation and manifestation; Luke 24:13-49.

5. J. Baldovin, *The Urban Character of Christian Worship: The Origins, Development, and Meaning of Stational Liturgy* (Rome, 1987); W. Meeks, *The First Urban Christians*, especially 140-192.

6. J. Hazelden Walker, "A Pre-Marcan Dating for the Didache: Further Thoughts of a Liturgist," published in vol. 3 of the *Proceedings of the VI International Congress on Biblical Studies* (Oxford, 3-7 April, 1978) by the *Journal for the Study of the New Testament* (Sheffield, 1980).

7. For example: Ephesians, passim; Philadelphians 4; Magnesians 6, 7.

8. Romans 4.

9. M. Staniforth, *Early Christian Writings* (New York, 1968) 70.

10. *The Martyrdom of Polycarp* 15.

11. See Smyrneans 8; Meeks, *The First Urban Christians* 166-167.

12. See Philadelphians 4.

13. Baldovin. *The Urban Character* 196-197, 212. R. Krautheimer, *Rome: Profile of a City 312-1308* (Princeton, 1980) 58, notes that there were ninety-eight stational observances, including solemn processions, in Rome by the twelfth century, one every four days.

14. Baldovin, *The Urban Character* 211.

15. Ibid. 214-226, 238-247.

16. Ephesians 9. See Staniforth, *Early Christian Writings* 83.

17. Ephesians 18-19. See Staniforth, *Early Christian Writings* 84.

18. Baldovin, *The Urban Character* 256-257. Also: L. Mumford, *The City in History* (New York, 1961) 277; and J. Dougherty, *The Five-Square City* (Notre Dame, 1980) 57-59, both quoted by Baldovin.

19. Baldovin, *The Urban Character* 257.

20. Ibid. 253.

21. F. van der Meer, *Early Christian Art* (London, 1967) 53. Krautheimer, *Rome* 21.

22. J. Wilkinson, *Egeria's Travels to the Holy Land* (London, 1981) passim.

23. See O.Nussbaum, *Die Aufbewahrung der Euchariste* (Bonn, 1979); G. Dix, *A Detection of Aumbries* (London, 1955); S.J.P. van Dijk and J. Hazelden Walker, *The Myth of the Aumbry. Notes on Medieval Reservation Practice and Eucharistic Devotion* (London, 1957); E. Maffei, *La réservation eucharistique jusqu'à la Renaissance* (Brussels, 1942).

24. Thus van der Meer, *Early Christian Art* 66.

25. P. Meyendorff, *St. Germanus of Constantinople: On the Divine Liturgy* (Crestwood, NY, 1984) 59-63.

26. R. Taft, "The Liturgy of the Great Church: An Initial Synthesis of Structure and Interpretation on the Eve of Iconoclasm," in *Dumbarton Oaks Papers* 34/35 (1980-1981) 58.

27. Ibid. 62-65.

28. G. Mathew, *Byzantine Aesthetics* (London, 1963) 41.

29. Quoted by G. Mathew, 41.

30. Ibid. 106-107. See W. Loerke, "'Real Presence' in Early Christian Art," in T. Verdon, ed., *Monasticism and the Arts* (Syracuse, 1984) passim.

31. See C. Mango, *The Art of the Byzantine Empire* (Toronto, 1986) 22-24.

32. Meyendorff, *St. Germanus* 73-77. See Taft, "The Liturgy" 50-52.

33. See Taft, "The Liturgy" 62-65.

34. Ibid. 60.

35. Loerke. "'Real Presence'" 37.

36. Van der Meer, *Early Christian Art* 96.

37. Ibid. 95.

38. Ibid.

39. See Loerke, "'Real Presence'" 39.

40. Loerke, "'Real Presence'" 39, using R. Krautheimer, *Corpus Basilicarum Christianarum Romae* 5 (Vatican City, 1977) 151-153, 155-156.

41. Loerke, "'Real Presence'" 38-39, 40-41.

42. Van der Meer, *Early Christian Art* 97, 123-126. Mathew, *Byzantine Aesthetics* 38-47.

43. Mathew, 24.

44. Ibid. 30. See his chapter "The Mathematical Setting," 23-37.

45. Ibid. 106.

46. Mathew (p.7) disagrees.

47. J. Corbon, *The Wellspring of Worship* (Mahwah, NJ, 1988) 63.

48. P. Bayes, "Drama and Worship," in J.G. Davies, ed., *The New Westminster Dictionary of Liturgy and Worship* (Philadelphia, 1986) 214-216.

49. Quoted in Mathew, *Byzantine Aesthetics* 4-5.

50. Ibid. 5.

51. Meyendorff, *St. Germanus* 101.

52. Paul Johnson, *Modern Times: The World from the Twenties to the Eighties* (New York, 1983) 701.

17

Proclamation of Faith
in the Eucharist

Louis Weil

A SIGNIFICANT EFFECT OF THE LITURGICAL RENEWAL OF THIS CENTURY HAS
been an intensified awareness of the structural aspects of liturgical rites.
This awareness is the result of the historical study of all the basic ritual
forms of Christian worship and has served to free students of liturgy
from a naive approach which tends to see a rite as a monolithic whole.
Every rite is a mosaic of numerous elements, each element having its
own particular history, its origin and evolution amid factors which often
have little direct relation to the primary intent of the rite.

The impact of such historical reflection upon one aspect of the liturgy
or another is not direct. Even where historical knowledge has changed
the way in which some ritual form is understood, this impact upon the
authorized rites of a tradition is very gradual. Whereas scholarly reflection may come upon a moment of illumination, an instant in which
something is seen in a completely new way, liturgical piety works very
differently. Where change is even allowed, its process is gradual, slowly
reshaping the liturgical mentality which has been formed through years
of experience within the context of the presuppositions of a given set of
liturgical attitudes.

Liturgical piety is thus a very conservative aspect of a person's religious views as a whole. The prayers which were meaningful in childhood
often continue to find a place in an otherwise very different life situation.

Similarly, the pattern of liturgical prayer which church goers have experienced, often for a period of many years, continues to shape the worshiper's expectation of what a liturgical celebration will involve. Radical change disrupts that expectation, even if there has been an attempt to address the reasons for such change through some form of educational program. The mind may be able to deal with information about the rite, but it is at a much deeper level that the experienced change is felt.

This distinction helps to explain why the 1979 Book of Common Prayer (BCP) is a transitional document. Whereas it reflects to an unprecedented degree the impact of deepened historical insight upon the structure of our liturgical rites, and along with that some important shifts in theological emphasis, the 1979 BCP nevertheless preserves structural elements, even vestiges, which work against the ritual clarity which liturgical renewal has generated. This simultaneous presentation of both the old and the new may well be a sign of pastoral sensitivity to the fact that a new ritual form (even if in fact a restored ancient one) cannot simply be inserted as a replacement for a familiar form. Liturgical piety requires an experience of continuity with the prayer forms which have constituted the believer's participation in liturgical prayer.

An obvious example of this simultaneity is seen in the inclusion in both Rite I and Rite II of the Holy Eucharist of the *Kyrie eleison* as an optional part of the entrance rite. This is an extremely familiar element in the liturgical experience of Episcopalians, on Sundays often sung in a hymnic setting. It would never occur to the typical worshiper to ponder its role at this point in the rite, nor to note that it somewhat duplicates the function of the opening hymn. These are structural questions which cannot compete with the cherished familiarity of the *Kyrie* within the liturgical experience.

The fact that the *Kyrie* is optional in the 1979 BCP is itself a sign of the book's transitional character. This use of the *Kyrie* must be held in balance with an important restoration in the book, namely, the prayers of the people. Here is an item of major importance which is characteristic of the new rites in various liturgical traditions, that is, the restoration to the people of their fundamental role as intercessors, a liturgical role which had come to be identified with the priest since the fifth century. The six forms of the *oratio fidelium* (Prayers of the People) attached to Rite II bring back into our common experience a primary action of God's people, and the source from which the vestigial *Kyrie* was gradually derived. The historical relation between the two is especially clear in Form V. Thus the present rite includes both the structurally significant *oratio fidelium* as an expression of the full participation of the laity, and at the same time, in continuity from earlier versions of the Prayer Book, its truncated response in the entrance rite.[1] For a transitional period, this type of duplication reflects a gentle conservatism in regard to a familiar element in the rite. The presentation of the *Kyrie* in these two contexts permits both the renewed emphasis upon the participatory role of the laity and also the continued use of beloved musical settings of the *Kyrie* (as well as new musical settings) at the beginning of the rite at a point established in centuries of Anglican liturgical experience. Preoccupation with such details from liturgical history can seem little more than a rarefied area of academic interest, a scholarly passion for the specialist but of little importance to the worshiping community as a whole. This is not the case, however, when reflection upon an established liturgical custom leads to the conclusion that a matter of fundamental importance has been thereby obscured, as when a secondary element in a rite assumes an importance which undermines the foundational role which another part of the rite is intended to bear. When such a shift of priority has taken place in the eucharist, "the principal act of Christian worship,"[2] the result can profoundly affect the way in which that act both forms and expresses the faith of the church.

The use of the *Kyrie eleison* in both its original and its derived forms does not produce a shift of priority: as structured, the eucharistic rites of the BCP 1979 clearly indicate that greater importance is given to the prayers of the people than to the *Kyrie* in the entrance rite. Whereas the *Kyrie* is optional as well as brief, the prayers of the people is a required and substantial element in the rite. The duplication is innocent even if it is something of a structural anomaly. Of far greater importance is a duplication which has been pointed out by liturgical writers for many years but has not yet affected our pastoral models in any significant way. It has to do with the way in which the eucharistic liturgy is the occasion of a profession of faith.

If one were to ask the typical churchgoer *how* the liturgy of the eucharist is a profession of faith, the question would probably confuse them. This is simply not the way that people have been taught to participate in liturgical rites. Participation is holistic rather than analytical: the rite unfolds as it has countless times before, and the worshiper engages the particular celebration in ways which are deeply rooted in one's whole religious formation and experience. The entire liturgy is a renewal of the shared faith into which all Christians have been baptized, even when that commonality is not consciously focal for an individual believer. Christian faith finds its most profound expression in such shared acts of worship, acts whose nature is to proclaim that common faith. Christian worship is an act of Trinitarian faith: the proclamation of that faith permeates the rites.

Yet is there a point, for example, in the eucharistic rite at which the people assembled are most aware that a profession of faith is taking place? The probable response which most liturgical participants would give to this question would be in the recitation of the Creed. Yet there is an anomaly here. The so-called Niceno-Creed, or more correctly the Nicene-Constantinopolitan Creed, is a summary of the faith which gradually emerged from the conciliar debates of the fourth century. Its purpose was as a test of orthodoxy among the bishops rather than for liturgical use. A liturgical Creed developed in the context of Christian initiation, and is essentially the one which we call the Apostles' Creed.

In the eucharistic rite, the primary focus for the proclamation of Trinitarian faith is found in the eucharistic prayer, the Great Thanksgiving. Within its single encompassing form, the common faith is proclaimed before the assembly of those baptized into that faith. But if this might be accepted in theory, it is evident in the attitudes of both clergy and laity that it is not confirmed in experience. The understanding of the eucharistic prayer as the proclamation of the church's faith has been obscured through attitudes and general norms of celebration in which the congregation sees itself as the silent observers of a clerical ritual. A friend of mine who is now a priest commented to me on his personal experience of this as a teen-aged acolyte. Once the *Sanctus* was over, as the priest read "the two long pages," my friend felt that he could tune out for the time being. The prayer did not pertain to him.

It is the purpose of this essay to explore the historical background of this question, to show how the introduction of the Nicene Creed into the eucharist was as a kind of unconscious surrogate for the loss of the proclamatory character of the Great Thanksgiving as the eucharistic prayer became more narrowly identified with the role of the ordained priest. On the basis of this historical and theological perspective, a concluding section will address the implications of this for the further reform of the structure of the eucharistic rite, and for the reshaping of our models for eucharistic presidency.

Inclusion of the Creed in the Eucharist

Many years ago I was struck by the late date at which the Nicene Creed was incorporated into the eucharist of the Western Church. Although, as we shall see, its use had been expanding throughout other parts of Europe, it did not gain official papal approval at Rome until 1014. I had naively assumed, taking the holistic approach discussed above, that it had always been there, or at least since Nicaea! In my own experience, the Creed was a significant moment in the eucharistic celebration, a moment in which I was substantially involved. By contrast, the eucharistic prayer belonged to the celebrant. I had no awareness that the Great Thanksgiving pertained to all of us.

The historical fact of its late introduction led me to reflect more deeply on the Creed's structural role within the eucharistic rite. As the nature of the Great Thanksgiving as proclamation of faith became more evident to me, the more I felt led to question the inclusion of the Nicene Creed within the eucharist. It amounted to a duplication, and unlike the rather innocent duplication which we have noted with regard to the *Kyrie*, in the case of the creed/anaphora issue, there was a duplication which inhibited the authentic function of the eucharistic prayer, being indicative of a narrow association of the prayer with the sacramental ministry of the ordained priest. I found this insight confirmed by a comment made by Robert Taft in his discussion of the Creed in his masterly study of the rite of Saint John Chrysostom: "Like so many other later additions to the liturgy, the creed is really superfluous. The eucharistic prayer itself, with its account of salvation history and its repetition of the banquet of the New Covenant, is an entirely sufficient profession of faith."[3] Since so much of the work of liturgical renewal is aimed at greater clarity in the church's rites and consequently the elimination of accretions which had obscured their original intent, this suggestion that the Creed is superfluous within the structure of the eucharist struck me as a serious matter indeed.

Given the form of the eucharistic prayer most familiar to us from the BCP 1928, the parallels between the content of both Creed and anaphora would not be immediately obvious to most Episcopalians. In Prayer D of the BCP 1979, the credal content is much more obvious, but we are not accustomed to looking at the content of the Great Thanksgiving from this perspective. The parallels are much more evident if we look at some of the older formulations of the eucharistic prayer which vary little in content from a credal form. This parallel is particularly clear in a comparison of the baptismal Creed found in the *Apostolic Tradition* of Hippolytus with the text of a eucharistic prayer which he gives in the context of the rite for the ordination of a bishop.

According to the evidence available to us, the two forms (Creed and anaphora) would never have been used within the same liturgical rite with the exception of the paschal liturgy, on which occasion they would have been widely separated in time as well as immediate ritual context. There is certainly no evidence that the Creed had any place in the usual celebrations of the eucharist on Sundays. The parallels between the two forms are thus significant in that at the regular Sunday eucharist it was in the eucharistic prayer that the common faith into which all had been baptized was proclaimed: the prayer reverberated with the faith which each person had professed at baptism.[4]

When we compare the texts, the most obvious parallel is found in their Trinitarian structure. In the baptismal rite, the Creed is stated in a series of questions by the deacon who is baptizing the candidate, and the one being baptized responds three times, "I believe." The text offers a brief summary of the Christian faith, appropriately structured for the initiatory context. The eucharistic prayer fills out the credal structure with a kind of theological elaboration upon the events of salvation history. Like the Creed, the eucharistic prayer is Christocentric, giving great verbal weight to the phrases on the second Person of the Trinity. In basic sequence, the two texts are closely parallel. This is all the more interesting since Hippolytus gives the eucharistic prayer as his own model, whereas the credal interrogation appears to be an aspect of his claimed witness to the "tradition which has remained up to now,"[5] and thus at least of the generation before him.

Brief as it is, the text of the eucharistic prayer of *Apostolic Tradition* is much longer than the credal summary. The eucharistic prayer seems by any critical analysis to stand out as the principal *item* of the rite. Being cautious not to assume naively what we cannot prove, it nevertheless appears reasonable that the eucharistic prayer had a dominating role, a focal significance within the celebration as the proclamation of the community's common faith.[6] But how do we move from this model to one in which the eucharistic rite incorporates a formal conciliar Creed? The shift is important because it not only suggests a loss of the experience of the eucharistic prayer as a proclamation of faith, but also that the understanding of the use of credal statements had itself changed. Gregory Dix comments that the Creed "was no longer to be only a test of belief for those entering the church from outside. Since misbelief had shown itself to be prevalent in the East not only among those who had been baptized but amongst bishops and clergy, the creed was to be made a test for those already within the church."[7] The presence of the Creed within the eucharistic rite is thus indicative of a change of purpose from that of credal origins: it is not an echo of baptismal profession but rather a demarcation of orthodoxy.

When we turn to consider the historical data around the introduction of the Creed into the eucharist, we find that its use in opposition to heresy is itself rather clouded. The Creed known as the Niceno-Constantinopolitan Creed was the text sanctioned by the bishops at Chalcedon in 451, and is the form that was eventually introduced into the eucharistic rite. But how? Ironically, the use of the Creed in this context seems to have begun among the Monophysites late in the fifth century.

But was it the form approved at Chalcedon, or the earlier version as formulated at Nicaea? The evidence suggests that it was the latter. The Monophysites rejected Chalcedon, and had instituted the custom of reciting the "pure" Nicene version in the liturgy at Antioch in 473 A.D. This custom spread among the Monophysites, being subsequently introduced by the Patriarch Timothy (511-518) at Constantinople, apparently to gain the support of the monophysite Emperor Anastasius (491-518). Once Constantinople was again in orthodox hands, the now established custom could not be abolished without giving offence. The shift to the Chalcedonian text was accomplished, however, when, as J.N.D. Kelly suggests, the orthodox "cunningly substituted" the form sanctioned at Chalcedon for the earlier version of Nicaea.[8]

It was in the same century that the Creed was introduced into the eucharist in Spain, and thus began its progressive use in the rites of the Western Church. As in the East, its use in Spain was in opposition to heresy, specifically in the rejection of Arianism by King Reccared in 589, at the Third Council of Toledo. The recitation of the Creed was inserted in a place which became characteristic of the Mozarabic Rite, after the eucharistic prayer and before the Lord's Prayer. Given our earlier discussion of the eucharistic prayer as a profession of faith, its immediate juxtaposition with the Creed suggests that the proclamatory character of the anaphora had been radically obscured through the manner of its celebration, namely, that by this time the celebrant recited the text of the eucharistic prayer with his voice inaudible to the assembly.[9]

Although it cannot be claimed that the Creed was inserted into the eucharist consciously as a surrogate for the loss of the eucharistic prayer proclaimed audibly in the liturgical assembly, there is a certain type of phenomenological replacement which occurs in this significant shift. In the century of its introduction—the sixth—there was a kind of culmination to the process of clericalization which had gradually refocused the classical rites of both East and West during the previous two hundred years. With the collapse of the catechumenate, the inferiority of lay status was inevitable as all fundamental liturgical acts fell definitively to the ministries of the ordained clergy. The loss of the prayers of the people was a powerful sign of this shift. The sixth century is a watershed for this process and set the pattern of clerical domination of the church's life for the centuries thereafter.

Two centuries later the Creed was introduced into the eucharist in France, during a period of reaction against the heresy of Adoptionism.[10] The route by which the custom of the recitation of the Creed in the eucharistic rite moved from Spain to France has been the subject of debate,[11] but when the Emperor Charlemagne introduced the custom in his palace chapel at Aachen toward the end of the eighth century, the Creed was placed after the gospel, the point at which it has remained in the western tradition.[12] In spite of this imperial use, the custom spread slowly through northern Europe, and was finally brought to Rome only in 1014, when the Emperor Henry II convinced Pope Benedict VIII that the Creed should have a place in the eucharist at Rome, as was the custom elsewhere. With usual Roman reserve, the practice was limited to Sundays and certain major feasts. The list of such feasts gradually expanded until the Creed became almost a fixed element in the Roman Rite. Jungmann makes the interesting comment on this development that the Creed "was thus conceived simply as a means of enhancing the festivity."[13]

This is the pattern for the use of the Creed in the eucharist until the Reformation, and is thus the source for the Sarum Rite from which Archbishop Thomas Cranmer developed the eucharistic rite of the 1549 Book of Common Prayer. In regard to the inclusion of the Creed, Cranmer appears to have accepted its place in the western tradition without question, although some Reformers on the Continent rejected the Nicene Creed because it included nonscriptural phrases. The 1549 BCP allowed for its omission only if a sermon was preached, "or for other great cause." The Creed became a fixed element in the 1552 BCP, and continued so in subsequent editions of the English book.[14]

In America, the Proposed BCP of 1786 ran into difficulty when it was reviewed by the English episcopate at the time after the American Revolution when the now nationally independent American Church was seeking the episcopal succession. Due to its use of unscriptural phrases, but perhaps also because of a certain Latitudinarian attitude, the Nicene Creed had been dropped from the Proposed Book. This omission was not acceptable to the English bishops, as also to Bishop Samuel Seabury and the clergy of New England, and the Nicene Creed was restored to the eucharistic rite of the first American BCP in 1789, with the Apostles' Creed as an alternative. The 1892 BCP specifically required the use of the Nicene Creed on the five major feasts for which proper prefaces were supplied. That rubric continued in effect in the 1928 BCP.

In the 1979 BCP, the Nicene Creed is more strongly favored for the eucharist and yet more restrained in frequency. In the eucharistic rite itself, there is no mention of the alternative use of the Apostles' Creed, and in the Additional Directions attached to morning and evening prayer, it is indicated that "the Apostles' Creed is omitted from the Office when the Eucharist with its own Creed is to follow."[15] Yet the rubric preceding the Nicene Creed in both eucharistic rites indicates its use only on Sundays and major feasts. The list of such feasts, however, is rather long.[16] This usage still echoes Father Jungmann's comment on the gradual expansion of the use of the Nicene Creed quoted earlier, that is, "as a means of enhancing the festivity."[17] It further reflects a hesitancy about according to the eucharistic prayer the role of proclamation of faith.

Pastoral and Practical Implications

This discussion of the historical evolution of the use of the Nicene Creed in the eucharist is not a matter of merely academic and theoretical interest. It relates directly to the establishment of pastoral and ritual norms for the public worship of the church. For many, liturgical experience has confirmed the impression that a rite is a long series of elements strung together. On the whole, liturgical renewal has fostered the idea that there is an internal logic to the way in which a rite is structured and that the meaning of a rite touches the worshiping community most effectively when that meaning is not clouded by obscurities and needless duplications.

Commenting on complex musical settings of the Creed, Jungmann indicates the basic problem linked to the inclusion of the Creed within the eucharistic rite:

> Often (the Creed) became the show-piece amongst the chants of the Ordinary. In fact, because of its broad presentation and because of the musical unfolding of its inexhaustible contents, it has attained such an importance in the full course of the Mass that it leaves the eucharistic prayer (which, in its design, is much akin to it) quite in the shadow.[18]

But this is a problem not only with elaborate musical settings. The experiential impact of the recitation of the Nicene Creed unbalances the structure and undermines the proclamatory character of the eucharistic prayer. This is a serious problem because the Great Thanksgiving is the primary prayer of the rite and, as Jungmann goes on to say, has much the same aim as the inserted Creed, "to survey ... the achievements of the divine plan of salvation which we grasp by faith."[19] On the whole, this underlying purpose in the eucharistic prayer is not claimed in the attitudes of the majority, it seems, of both clergy and laity.

Attitudes of piety generally operate at a deep level of the unconscious. Although a priest may try to justify the norms of celebration of a liturgical style by an appeal to some aspect of tradition, these norms are often based upon early religious experience and observation which have shaped the particular model. Further, these norms are seldom confronted with conscious critical evaluation. What a person does at the altar, their general liturgical attitude, the use of voice and the use of gesture, is usually what that person has done for many years, often with the gradual accretion of idiosyncracies of which the priest is seldom aware. It is very difficult to address this situation without painful confrontation because, often unconsciously, a priest's sense of identity is linked to decades of sacramental ministry. Yet the fact remains that one can find many situations in which the eucharistic prayer is distorted from its natural role through the use of altered voice patterns, artificially low levels of vocal projection, the eccentric dislocation of particular phrases (notably the Words of Institution), as well as distracting patterns of gesture which exist in a world of their own, detached from the theological sense of the text.

The problem of attitude does not rest only with the clergy. The fact is that for vast numbers of the laity, the eucharistic prayer is not seen as pertaining to them: it belongs to the priest. This non-relation is articulated through an almost inevitable inattention to the prayer simply because of a passive self-understanding in regard to it. This passivity is characterized by the kneeling posture and a piety turned in upon itself while the prayer is said. Although *no* posture assures a sense of active participation, and although one may participate fully from any posture, the witness of the first several centuries of Christianity to the self-understanding of the ecclesial assembly at worship suggests a standing posture as a normative expression of the awareness that all the baptized are celebrants in the eucharistic rite.

Such an awareness, however, must be met with a renewed sense of the role of the ordained celebrant as presiding over a common action of the whole assembly. This will manifest itself in every aspect of the presider's manner—in voice, in gesture, and in an attitude which draws forth the participation of all those who stand around the altar and share the sacred gifts.

A transformation of this kind cannot happen overnight simply because liturgical attitudes are reflective of experience deeply etched over a period of years. The transformation must be undertaken at various levels at the same time: in the way these matters are approached during the years of seminary formation; in diocesan workshops at which clergy are enabled to analyze the sources of their own liturgical style and to confront without fear the ways in which that style might appropriately be modified; and in the programs of adult Christian formation through which the baptized may come to understand themselves as active participants in the whole liturgical action. In none of these is the question merely the substitution of one liturgical model for another. The issues are much deeper than that, being rooted in a reclaiming of our sense of the church of the people of God. That is not a matter of gimmicks, but rather of deep reflection upon the Christian faith undertaken by the church as a whole. In such a context, the entire eucharistic rite would be seen as the primary articulation of that faith by the Christian assembly, and the eucharistic prayer would be, at its heart, the "credal" proclamation of that faith into which all have been baptized.

Notes

1. It is said that the use of the *Kyrie* in the penitential introduction to the present Roman Rite was a personal decision of Pope Paul VI, and may be seen as another modern example of the preservation of the vestigial *Kyrie* in a modified context. Readers interested in the historical background on the origins and evolution of the *Kyrie* should see T. Klauser, *A Short History of the Western Liturgy* (Oxford, 1979) 47-52; see J.A. Jungmann, *The Early Liturgy* (Notre Dame, 1959) 293-295. For a discussion of this issue in the wider perspective of liturgical structure, see my *Gathered to Pray* (Cambridge, MA, 1986) 59-85, esp. 71-76.

2. BCP 13.

3. Robert F. Taft, *The Great Entrance*, 2d ed. (Rome, 1978) 404-405.

4. G.J. Cuming, ed., *Hippolytus: A Text for Students* (Bramcote, Notts., 1976) 19 n.21 (baptismal Creed); 10-11 n.4, (eucharistic prayer). My comments about the use of the Hippolytan forms do not indicate a definitive stance as to whether or not any of the texts of *Apostolic Tradition* were actually used in liturgical worship by a body of Christians at Rome or elsewhere. From the evidence available, that tantalizing speculation cannot be known. The emphasis upon the parallels is rather as illustrative of credal content in an early example of the eucharistic prayer.

5. Ibid. 8 n.1.

6. Note J.A. Jungmann's comment on the intrinsic relationship between the Creed and the eucharistic prayer, that this is seen "most impressively ... in the *Eucharistia* of Hippolytus of Rome." Jungmann, *The Mass of the Roman Rite*, vol. 1 (New York, 1950) 473 n.74.

7. Gregory Dix, *The Shape of the Liturgy* (Westminster, 1945) 485.

8. J.N.D. Kelly, *Early Christian Creeds*, 3d ed. (New York, 1972) 349-350. See Taft, *The Great Entrance* 398-400; Dix, *Shape*, 486; Jungmann, *Mass*, vol. 1, 468. Edmund Bishop discusses the debate as to whether Timothy may not have introduced the Niceno-Constantinopolitan version as "a polite concession ... to the current of feeling of the people and monks of Constantinople which soon after (Timothy's) death was to carry everything before it." See E. Bishop, *Liturgical Comments and Memoranda*, IV, *Journal of Theological Studies* 12 (1911) 387 n.2. In support of this opinion, see Taft, *The Great Entrance* 400-401. Bernard Capelle argues that the custom of reciting the Creed in the eucharist, although indeed of monophysite origin, did not originate in Antioch, but rather at Constantinople under the initiative of Timothy. See B. Capelle, "L'Introduction du symbole à la

messe," in *Travaux liturgiques,* vol. 3 (Louvain, 1967) 60-63.

9. Jungmann, *Mass,* vol. 1, 82-83. (There is some debate as to whether the Creed came before or after the Lord's Prayer.)

10. Jungmann, *Mass,* vol. 1, 469.

11. B. Capelle, "Alcuin et l'histoire du symbole de la messe," in *Travaux liturgiques,* vol. 2 (Louvain, 1962) 211-221.

12. Jungmann, *Mass,* vol. 1, 469.

13. Jungmann, *Mass,* vol. 1, 470. See T. Klauser, *Short History* 76-77.

14. It has been suggested that in the 1552 BCP the replacement of the ninefold *Kyrie* with the decalogue meant that the rite offered the occasion for the public repetition of the three things which every child was to have learned prior to confirmation: the Ten Commandments, the Creed and the Lord's Prayer. See M. Hatchett, *Commentary on the American Prayer Book* (New York, 1980) 310.

15. BCP 142; see 326 and 358.

16. BCP 15-17; see Hatchett, *Commentary* 334.

17. Jungmann, *Mass,* vol. 1, 470. For a perspective on the idea that increased length is characteristic of festal celebrations, see my article, "The Liturgy on Great Occasions: Notes on Large-Scale Celebrations," *Living Worship* 14:2 (1978).

18. Jungmann, *Mass,* vol. 1, 473.

19. Ibid.

18

In Time and Community: Individualism and the Body of Christ

J. Neil Alexander

The Problem

THE FAITHFUL COMPRISING OUR PARISHES PARTAKE OF THE FULLNESS OF LIFE in the Body of Christ in only partial, fragmented ways. Life in the church is just one more activity performed alongside countless others; one more thing competing for their time, money, and devotion and generally with little sense of integration with the totality of life. And, one might ask, is it any wonder that many of our people experience this fragmentation of their life in faith given the manner in which most parishes respond? The "successful" parish is the one touted as having "something for every-one"—a "cafeteria-style" program undergirded by little more than "shopping mall" ecclesiology, that is, plenty to feast your eyes on, but very little, if anything, you actually need. The question so often asked, "what will our people take away from this liturgy, or class, or meet-ing?"—is a question for which I see little warrant, scriptural or other-wise. Only recently are we beginning to ask, "what gifts are people bringing to the upbuilding of the body of Christ?"—a question that is central to the witness of the New Testament, particularly the Pauline lit-erature. Both questions, however, are framed somewhat dangerously. In the former question, the emphasis is upon the benefit, the "goody" if you will, that will be received as a result of an individual's participation. With respect to the latter question, although its premise is certainly much stronger, it is not always helpful to assume that a gift brought to the community is a gift the community actually needs. Either way, the potential exists for participation that is individualistically conceived and experienced.

One way of understanding the tendency toward individualism is to see it as the result of persons experiencing and understanding their experience as fragmentation. It goes without saying, perhaps, that a cherished sense of individualism is endemic to the North American experiment. We should not assume, however, that all individualism is of the same nature. The survivalistic individualism of northern Canada is quite a different thing from the anonymous individualism of a major urban center, or the rugged individualism of the classical western wrangler.

Charles Gerkin has recently offered several helpful perspectives on the problem of fragmentation and individualism.[1] On the basis of the historical work of Brooks Holifield, Gerkin writes:

> ... an interpretive awareness that had been taking shape all through the twentieth century, had to do with the priority placed on self-realization. The metaphors that best caught up the primary human strivings all tended to emphasize one or another aspect of that historically shaped human purpose. Self-actualization, self-fulfillment, self-determination, self-motivation—no matter what the words might be, they all pointed to the realization of the self and the self's potentials. The second awareness was that many if not most corporate institutions and structures of society were experienced as interfering with rather than supporting the fulfillment of the self.[2]

According to Gerkin, the response of the pastoral care movement was concerned with assisting persons to face these "self-conceived" issues. The focus of the task was "helping persons to free themselves from family constraints, the moralistic constraints of social class respectability, and whatever interference with the realization of individual freedom might be coming from corporate authorities of one kind or another ..."[3]

Gerkin then defines the contextual matrix in which pastoral care must now work, the parameters of which are as useful to pastoral liturgists as they are for the theoreticians of pastoral theology. Perhaps the best way to establish these parameters is to use the illustration that Gerkin himself uses. As an example of a person caught in fragmentation, Gerkin offers the following description of a young, adult male:

> He had been brought up in a conservative southern home in a small com-

munity where the family went to church regularly, both on Sunday and during the week. He attended the "training union" of his local church faithfully through high school and then went off to the state university, where he joined a college fraternity and was introduced to a different way of life. After college he was employed in a large bank in his state's largest city and soon learned both to dress conservatively and to attend carefully to the bottom-line profit expectations of his employer. As he received sufficient promotions to afford it, he moved into a large apartment complex designed for the avantgarde single lifestyle. There he met and married an Irish Catholic girl from Boston who had come south to escape the close confines of her family. Before and after marriage, the young man continued to visit his parents biweekly, still attending church with them, now over his bride's objection.[4]

You will not be surprised to hear that Gerkin's first observation is that this young man is caught in the grips of pluralism! It is a pluralism that forces upon individuals a compartmentalization of life simply in order to survive one's daily experience. "Pluralism has now so penetrated every nook and cranny of Western social life that given individuals in the course of their normal activities on a given day may be required to move from one social context governed by one primary language of interpretation to another governed by another, and often, to yet a third or fourth. This makes not only for fragmentation of language worlds among members of a social context but also for fragmentation within the day-to-day experience of the individual."[5]

As a result of his experience of contextual pluralism, the young man in Gerkin's example is faced with what Don Browning has referred to as *the loss of moral context*.[6] Of the young man in his illustration, Gerkin writes:

> There is apt to be little consensus on moral values among his parents, his hard-nosed businessman boss, his fellow dwellers in the singles complex, and the deeper recesses of his wife's Irish Catholic upbringing. His confusion is basically moral. Not only that, but the various worlds he moves among in the course of daily life each comprise a moral universe whose values are taken for granted and unquestioned. To which of these worlds is he finally to belong? Or, what is more likely, is he simply to live chameleonlike in fragments of worlds, not fully identified with any?[7]

Persons caught by pluralism and the consequent loss of moral context often attempt to validate their experience by living out a particular "solution" or "reaction." Of the several potential solutions Gerkin articulates, two are of particular interest to pastoral liturgists: tribalism and privatism.

Tribalism results from bonding together with other persons of shared viewpoint in a social, political, or religious sphere, or in some workable hybrid thereof. The shared unity of mind and purpose, often expressed in very black and white terms, shields the adherents, or at least pretends to do so, from the experienced fragmentation of life. Tribalism, one might observe, is precisely the operative reality in such enclaves as the Ku Klux Klan, the John Birch Society, or any number of religious cults whose existence theoretically protects the adherents thereof from a particular manifestation of reality. One might also observe that something of the tribalist mentality is operative is many of the mainline churches in North America. What is important for our reflection is that tribalism is the result of a "refuge mentality" that serves common purpose only insofar as it serves an individual's need to overcome fragmentation.

The other potential "solution" is privatism. Simply put, privatism is a clear distinction between the life that an individual lives publicly, that is, a person's work, and one's private life. The response to one's public life, potentially another root cause of fragmentation, is to tolerate the incongruities and accept a tolerable level of fragmentation as inevitable, while at the same time expanding the private sphere to accommodate as much of one's life experience as possible. This solution is played out in the life of the church among those for whom the weekly assembly is experienced as a "filling station," or among those whose participation in the body is the fulfillment of a sense of obligation. In either event, a highly individualistic life-concept is operative.

In 1985 Robert Bellah and his colleagues produced a major study of individualism and commitment in American life and published their results in the delightfully readable book *Habits of the Heart*.[8] Every section of the book broadens one's understanding of the culture in which we live, and one is tempted to draw a parallel between each cultural observation and the implications of it for the life of the church. Such an exercise would prove highly instructive, but in this brief essay it is possible to highlight only two observations that complement the thoughts of Gerkin and that will, perhaps, give us still more precision on the problem before us.

Bellah and colleagues make a very useful distinction between "lifestyle enclaves" and "communities."[9] Characteristic of a "lifestyle enclave" is the fragmentation of the individuals who participate in the group, that is, they invest only partially in the group, keeping entire areas of life divorced from the group's interactions. A secondary characteristic is that the group generally shares a fragmented agenda as the result of a very clear, and usually narrow, understanding of itself and its reason for existence. Negative or antagonistic relationships with those outside the enclave are a possibility, but the more likely scenario is that outsiders will be invisible if not entirely non-existent. A community, on the other hand, "attempts to be an inclusive whole, celebrating the interdependence of public and private life and of the different callings of all," whereas a lifestyle enclave "is fundamentally segmental and celebrates the narcissism of similarity."[10] In the enclave, the unity of purpose is the result of the collection of persons of the same position. In the community, certain values, viewpoints, or positions belong first to the group and are then shared by those who are members of it.

The usefulness of this distinction is the realization based upon it: that life in the modern church and in most of its parishes, while aspiring, perhaps, to be communities in Christ, are in fact lifestyle enclaves gathered around something less than the fullness of Christ. The church, and specifically congregations, often function less as communities and more as lifestyle enclaves—collectives of individuals with similar values, viewpoints, ethnic roots, or some other identifiable uniting characteristic. If, in fact, our congregations are lifestyle enclaves, then individualism will always be rampant among us because we are powerless to do anything more than institutionalize it. Our institutionalization of individualism is not, however, merely an external reality that our cultural context has callously thrust upon us. It is deeply rooted in our theology and practice.

The Problem Deepens in History and Tradition

Most of what you are about to read is confessional, not in the sense of theological documents, but with respect to the recent struggles of the writer with the ever widening gap within the church between faith and practice. These struggles arise less from being a member of the clergy or a professor of liturgics than they do from the discomforts of living a graceful life in the interface between what the church is and a vision of what the church could be. As a result, four issues are offered that clearly have impact upon the life of the church and that are worthy of the reflection of pastoral liturgists.

The first issue is doctrinal. For the major traditions that had their birth in the sixteenth century re-formation of the church, the doctrine of justification by grace alone through faith alone has been essential to the formation of all other doctrine and has had profound impact upon the myriad details of ecclesial life. The central thrust of the doctrine, while couched in different terminology, is surely no less significant in the Roman Church and in other ecclesiastical communities. It is precisely the fundamental nature of the doctrine of justification that makes it so troublesome.

With its roots in Paul, refracted through the writings of Augustine, and re-formed by Luther and the other reformers, the doctrine has become centered on the salvation of individuals. It has become a means by which to speak of the relationship between God and the individual believer. The church has popularized a picture of an unaccompanied "free agent," standing terrified before the throne of judgment, and just before the divine boom is lowered the acquittal takes place and the prisoner, whose chains had been eternally locked, is miraculously set free.

The problem is clearly not the *gospel* at the core of justification theology, but the manner of the church's appropriation of it. The primacy of justification theology gives us no choice but to focus our mission and ministry on individuals and individual salvation, and forces a notion of the church as a collective of the justified as over against a community in the Risen Christ.

One obvious retort to this suggestion is to note that justification by grace alone through faith alone has its roots deeply imbedded in scripture, particularly in the Pauline corpus. If by such a response we mean to say that Paul believed that we are inserted into a saving relationship with God as an act of divine grace based upon the merits of Jesus Christ alone, then there is little difficulty so long as we understand "inserted into a saving relationship with God" as meaning incorporation into the body of Christ. Paul was concerned with living a graceful life as a result of the community's present encounter with its risen Lord, whereas the question for Augustine, and Luther, and for many in the church has been "how do I find a gracious God?" Paul assumed a corporate dimension of life in relationship to God that our interpretation of his thinking has largely subverted.

The second issue that may be identified is our historical approach to doing theology. Theology, by its very nature, is time and situation bound. That is to say that western theology, at least as it has been formulated since Augustine, has been restricted to the delineation of and reflection upon *past* events, understood to be *for our salvation*. Most attempts at articulating an alternative to a time and situation bound theology fall short because the assumption remains that God's activity "for our salvation" was in the past and past alone, and that it is present to us anamnetically, by the power of faith or Spirit, or as the result of some sort of cooperation thereof. Whether the gap between past event and present reality is understood to be closed by some sort of spiritual leap, or by some notion of the prolongation of the past, the past is still the operative time-frame reference. The past can only be experienced as past because when communities gather to tell their stories and celebrate their past they do so only through the historical imaginations of the individuals gathered together. Consequently, our theology and doxology will continue to be individually conceived and collectively celebrated recapitulations of the history of salvation as long as our primary time-frame reference is past tense.

A third issue to be identified is that of church structure and leadership. Our co-opted democratic forms of church government are simply another level of the institutionalization of individualism. There is no such thing as radical equality either inside or outside the church. To understand baptism and eucharist as "the great equalizers" in the life of the body, or to hold tenaciously to the "democracy of death," clearly have their spiritual value for our life together. But such concepts are quite a different thing from espousing a position that asserts that we are all equal, or of equal value, in the church's organization of itself for mission and ministry. While it is true that the New Testament does not lift up any particular political system as normative for the body of Christ, and while furthermore the New Testament affirms the importance of all members of the body and their full participation, it does not suggest at any point that we are all equal in strength or influence. The biblical affirmation that every member of the body is gifted, and that every gift is important, does not mean that every gift is equally honored in every situation in which the church finds itself. Democratically organized churches will always be fighting individualism. Congregational autonomy, in addition to being an insult to the body of Christ, represents nothing more than a collective institutionalization of individualism.

The fourth issue that may be identified might be referred to as "pastoral." In conversations with parish clergy one hears a great deal about the time spent in one-on-one ministry with persons. Hospital calls, crisis ministry, marriage counseling, grief therapy, and a host of other singular encounters demand an extraordinary percentage of the clergy's time. That individuals in our parishes need pastoral care and that some portion of the clergy's time will be devoted to such ministry is a given. The question, however, is how much of the pastor's time should be spent in direct one-on-one ministry, and in what context, and toward what end, is such ministry to be accomplished? Much of what passes for pastoral ministry is not "pastoral" in any honest sense of the word, and while important, would best be left to others within the faith community, including many laypersons.

Toward the Restoration
of the Community of Christ

Having now raised four issues that to one degree or another face us as we move toward the future, it is important to point toward some possible solutions, or perhaps more accurately, possible alternatives.

One must confess no small degree of uneasiness at the assertion that "the church stands or falls on the doctrine of justification." One's more pietistic side may well react to such a statement because of the certainty, at that point where faith dwells, that the church never has, nor ever will, stand or fall on a doctrine. To whatever degree that it does, to at least that same degree, we must work towards its falling so that it might be rebuilt upon some other, more secure, foundation. In moments of theological lucidity, one may well argue that the church does not stand or fall on anyone's conception or embodiment of individual salvation, but that the church stands, and never falls, because of the utter faithfulness of her Lord. If the church is to be found faithful, it must be a faithfulness defined not in terms of our personal salvation, but in terms of our corporate identity in the Risen Christ. In the New Testament, God does not single us out for salvation so much as he calls us into a saving relationship with Christ and with each other.

It is interesting to note that in the *Smalcald Articles*,[11] Luther writes, "We shall now return to the Gospel, which offers counsel and help against sin in more than one way." Luther then proceeds to set forth the classic list of the means of grace. What is profoundly striking is that Luther's description of the means of grace is "corporate" in its best sense. Through preaching, baptism, eucharist, confession and absolution, and mutual conversation and consolation—all means of grace that are either corporate or deeply rooted in the corporate experience of the body—by these means we have the gospel of the forgiveness of sin. This is representative of one of the dimensions of Luther's thought that is potentially very exciting. While it may be impossible to argue away that Luther's primary emphasis remained on the justification of the individual sinner before a gracious God, he developed a concept of the community in Christ broader than he could have inherited and more eschatologically centered than other major reformers save, perhaps, the Anabaptists.

Potentially then, there exists the possibility of understanding the church, not as a lifestyle enclave of sinners with similar batteries of sins, but as inclusive communities of grace. We become, at once, a preaching community, a baptizing community, a eucharistic community, a confessing and forgiving community, and community of consolation and mutual support. At yet a higher level, it means that when we preach we do not preach the Bible, nor do we preach toward the goal of individual conversion or personal salvation, but we preach Jesus Christ—risen, ascended, and coming again—present in our very midst! It means that in baptism we can be less concerned with ritualizing all of the Augustinian baggage concerning original sin and personal salvation, and focus more fully on incorporation of persons willing to lose their individual identity and who are willing to be shaped by the corporate identity of those "in Christ." It means that in the eucharist we can be less concerned about what it means, and more fully focused on the fact that obedience calls us to "do this" without ceasing "until he comes." It means that the specific content of an individual's confession pales in significance over against the restorative power of absolution. It means that friendship will be the fundamental icon of life lived in Christ.

The most exciting dimension of all, however, is that we are no longer merely recipients of the means of grace, but we are transformed into being means of grace to the world—the precise vision of the church for which Christ gave his life. This dimension was so powerfully captured by Robert Taft when he wrote:

> We do all this together because we *are* a "together," and not just individuals. Christian salvation is by its very nature "Church," a "gathering," a one Body of Christ, and if we do not express this, then we are not what we proclaim to be. Redemption in the New Testament is a coming together, a solidarity in the face of the evil of this world. It necessarily leads to community because only in common can new human values be effectively released and implemented. Christ came not just to save individuals, but to change the course of history by creating the leaven of a new group, a new People of God, paradigm of what all peoples must one day be.[12]

The constantly longed for renewal of the church and the vitality of her witness to the world are to be found in our corporate expression of the movement between being recipients of the means of grace, to becoming, in Christ, means of grace for the world.

There is a marvelous little story about an exchange between a priest and a parishioner following the Ascension Day eucharist. The parishioner was heard to ask, "Now that Christ has gone away from us into heaven, how long will it be before he comes again in glory?" To which the priest replies, "Well, I'm not really sure, but it is sooner than it has ever been before!" The value of that quip is that it forces us to keep things in proper perspective. When I harp on keeping our historicized theology in proper perspective, I do not intend to suggest anything but the deepest reverence for our past as the people of God. At the same time, as long as our primary time-frame reference is past tense, then our experience of God and the interactions of the people of God will largely be individualistically conceived and played out. Why, for example, do many of our people have difficulty understanding and accepting the church's restoration of at least weekly eucharist? At least one reason is that our eucharistic catechesis has largely been cast in past tense. The eucharist in the minds of many of the faithful is less an eschatological banquet of the resurrection as it is a pious repristinization of the historical Last Supper of Jesus with his disciples. As long as the eucharist appears to be little more than a rerun of the Upper Room, and as long as whatever gets attached to it celebrates what happened way back when, then its reception will be individualistically conceived and experienced, and our people are correct when they say, "We don't need it that often," because as individuals, they don't. Those who would confess to a more frequent need for the eucharist have come to that position because they hold a less historicized, more profoundly eschatological eucharistic doxology learned by having been immersed in eucharistic communities that gave them no choice.

The past events of God in history are just exactly that—past. There is a limit to how much of them one can understand as is the degree to which those events may be appropriated for the living of life in Christ. Yet, as Taft has noted, "the death and resurrection of Jesus are past events only in their historicity, that is, with respect to us. But they are eternally present in God, who has entered history but is not entrapped in it, and they have brought the presence of God among us to fulfillment in Jesus, and that enduring reality we encounter every moment of our lives."[13] We stand on the very edge of history and Christ is as fully present to us when we gather around word and sacraments as he was ever present among those whom he loved in Galilee or Jerusalem. The presence of the living Christ that we so profoundly encounter when we celebrate the eucharist is not so much a prolongation of the past, but a fleeting present encounter snatched from our tomorrow in Christ. This is what we see so vividly in the post-resurrection encounters of Jesus and his disciples. When Jesus comes and stands among the disciples or travels with them on the Emmaus Road, we do not see prolongations of the past that form a context for the present encounter, but we see self-giving presentations of the Risen Christ which, for the disciples, rendered the past understandable and useful for the living of their lives.

On the matter of church structure and leadership, it is necessary, if we are to escape individualism, to suppress our democratic models of church government, our impossible one office ministry,[14] and at least within some traditions, our powerless episcopacy. Representative assemblies may not always be the best means by which to determine faithfulness to the Gospel. The contemporary parameters of presbyteral ministry are far too broad, and those of the diaconate far too narrow, for effectiveness to be a reasonable expectation. And within those traditions where the problem seems to exist, to charge persons with the responsibilities of *episcope* without risking such an investment of authority in them that will enable them to carry out their responsibilities, is quite simply a bad joke, on us, at their expense.

No matter how much one may theorize to the contrary, or even deny the reality, communities have hierarchies. When there are all leaders and no followers, you have a lifestyle enclave that will be largely handicapped at doing much of anything other than perpetuating its existence. In communities, on the other hand, you will have leaders and followers, thinkers and doers, pastors and priests, bishops and committees, lovers and loved, forgivers and forgiven, healers and healed—looking out not for their personal interests, but for their common life together in the Risen Body of Christ.

On the "pastoral" issue that has been identified, simply a few, brief observations. To be a pastor means to be a symbol bearer of Christ to the faithful and of them to the world. Pastoral ministry should not now nor should it ever have been, a ministry of one person meeting another person's needs. It is the ministry of the community of faith to persons, who for whatever reasons, find themselves in a less-than-whole relationship with God in the Body of Christ. Pastors have spent, and will continue to spend, large quantities of time with individuals, not for the sake of the person, but for the sake of the Body. Because the person is ill or troubled or estranged, the Body is thereby weakened, and the person is healed or restored or forgiven, not for her/his sake alone, but for the upbuilding of the Body. The care of persons must always be with reference to the upbuilding of the Body of Christ if it is to be worthy of the name "pastoral." This implies that all of the corporate means of pastoral care—preaching, eucharist, affirmation of faith, public and private reconciliation, public healing, and prayer—can once again take their place as primary pastoral resources for the care of souls.

Toward the Future

The renewal of the church, not just in liturgy and spirituality, but in every area of her life, depends upon capturing the fullness of a corporate expression of the body of Christ. It is imperative that the future toward which we work and pray be radically conceived as a community in Christ, not as a continuing institutionalization of individualism. That means that we base our life together less on an historicized theology of what God has done for us in the past, but on an eschatological doxology of what God is doing among us now, and how that present illuminates what has been and anticipates what is yet to come. That means in terms of leadership, both lay and ordained, that we will have to raise up and risk following persons whose commitment is less to meeting the needs of individuals and more to building up the Body of Christ, granting of course, that our hand-in-hand, shoulder-to-shoulder ministry in the world may be the exercise by which the body-building is sometimes accomplished.

A former student once argued in a paper that the only hope for the future of the church in our time is to dispense with the present generation, entrust them to the mercy of God, and start over! As the paper continued, it became quite clear that the student did not believe that any more than he expected me to do likewise. The pain, however, that the student was trying to articulate, is still very real. Both our context and the tradition have forced upon us a stiflingly narrow, individualistic, institutionalized collective of saints, with precious few sinners, that is an abundant source of frustration for anyone who may have caught even the most fleeting glimpse of the eschatological Body of the Risen Christ.

What might all of this mean for the pastoral liturgist about the task of liturgical catechesis in parish or seminary? It may mean, particularly in the seminaries, that the instruction may need to focus less on issues of presiding and more on the assembly. It is no longer enough simply to multiply the liturgical roles before the assembly in order that each "order" within the church performs its historic, or not so historic, role. We must develop a deeper sensitivity to that living organism that is the assembly and begin to see that it is something more profound than merely the sum of its parts. It may also mean that rather than teaching liturgical history and theology as means by which our current liturgical books may be understood and properly used, that we must teach the appropriate usage of our liturgical books as the present, and ever evolving, embodiment of liturgical history and theology, the understanding of which illuminates a venerable past and anticipates a yet more faithful future.

Notes

1. Charles Gerkin, *Widening the Horizons: Pastoral Responses to a Fragmented Society* (Philadelphia, 1986).

2. Ibid. 13.

3. Ibid.

4. Ibid. 15.

5. Ibid.

6. Don S. Browning, *The Moral Context of Pastoral Care* (Philadelphia, 1976). Note the use of Browning's work in Gerkin, *Widening* 16.

7. Gerkin, *Widening* 16.

8. Robert Bellah, Richard Madsen, William H. Sullivan, Ann Swidler, and Steven M. Tipton, *Habits of the Heart: Individualism and Commitment in American Life* (Berkeley, 1985).

9. Ibid. 71f.

10. Ibid. 72.

11. Martin Luther, *The Smalcald Articles*, Part III, Article IV, in *The Book of Concord: The Confessions of the Evangelical Lutheran Church*, translated and edited by Theodore G. Tappert (Philadelphia, 1959) 310.

12. Robert Taft, *The Liturgy of the Hours in East and West: The Origins of the Divine Office and Its Meaning for Today* (Collegeville, 1986) 342.

13. Ibid. 343.

14. It is widely recognized that even in those traditions that hold tenaciously to a threefold ministry of bishop, presbyter, and deacon, and in spite of theological affirmations to the contrary, practically speaking many of the proper ministries of each order are subsumed under the presbyterate. For further discussion see, Aidan Kavanagh, "Christian Ministry and Ministries," in D.C. Brockopp, B.L. Helge, and D.G. Truemper, eds. *Church and Ministry: Chosen Race, Royal Priesthood, Holy Nation, God's Own People*, Institute of Liturgical Studies Occasional Papers 2 (Valparaiso, IN, 1982).

A TRIBUTE

19

A Musical Epilogue

David Hurd

Three Fugues

THE FOLLOWING THREE FUGUES ARE FOUNDED ON THE NAME OF THOMAS JU-
lian Talley and composed in his honor. Curiously, each of his three
names has six letters. In each case the six letters have been used to determine the first six pitches of the fugue subject. The practice of deriving
musical themes from the letters which spell names is not new. Although
many of the most famous musical works based upon the spelling of a
name use the letters B A C H, a great variety of composers of many ages
have committed their own and other names to music. Since western musical practice assigns letter names to the seven natural pitch classes, theoretically a musical theme can be derived from any set of letters. The procedure is at its simplest when the letters to be used span the range from
A to G, since these are the standard letter names for pitches in western
music. Problems arise, however, when the letters to be used enter the
range from H to Z. Using the standard German convention, it is possible
to render B and B-flat and H as B-natural, but I through Z still must be
accounted for in some other way. One solution to the problem is to return to A following H and begin again to spell the alphabet to H. The
first eight letters take care of themselves and are read at face value. Successive groups of eight consecutive letters repeatedly assume the identity
of the first eight. The diagram below shows how this identity reassign-
ment works. The top line is the alphabet; the bottom line shows the musical pitches rendered by the letters I through Z.

A B C D E F G H   I J K L M N O P   Q R S T U V W X   Y Z
                  A B C D E F G H   A B C D E F G H   A B

Maurice Duruflé, the recently deceased French composer and organist, used this method to derive the theme for his "Prelude et fugue sur le nom d'Alain," Opus 7. Obviously this system only accounts for eight members of the chromatic scale and makes no provision for C-sharp, D-sharp, F-sharp, or G-sharp. (Only God is perfect.) Nevertheless, it does allow melodic data to emerge from any collection of letters. The primary thematic material for the Three Fugues is derived thus:

T H O M A S   J U L I A N   T A L L E Y
D H G E A C   B E D A A F   D A D D E A

In each of the three fugues the first six pitches, established by the spelling of the name, were freely extended to create a longer and more complete melody for the subject. Issues of register and rhythmic shape also were freely invented by the composer.

Why any of this? It all started on the first Sunday of Lent in 1976 when both the Dean and also the Liturgics Professor of The General Theological Seminary came to worship at the Chapel of the Intercession. They were actually on a fact-finding mission following a lead in their serach for a music instructor for the seminary. Dr. Talley was the liturgy professor, and I was the parish musician to be observed that morning. Although we never spoke that day, the liturgy and music on that occasion constituted my first professional contact with a person who was to become a singular friend, colleague, critic, advocate, teacher, co-conspirator, and any number of other wonderful things to me. A discerning musician himself, and utterly convinced and convincing of the normalcy and fundamental rightness of singing the liturgy, he provided continual stimulation and challenge for this young liturgical musician with a flair for composition. My response then was to compose music. My response now is the same.

Why fugue? In western music there are few compositional procedures more fascinating than fugue. Standard music reference materials contain extensive and detailed entries for this type of composition. Fugue, it seems, does not lend itself to simple characterization. My old undergraduate desktop dictionary makes a reasonable effort at basic description when it says:

> fugue *n.* 1. *Music* **a** A contrapuntal composition in which a theme is introduced by one part, repeated by other parts, and subjected to complex development.[1]

Although this bare-bones definition hardly begins to demythologize the beast, it does at least lead one to the point of recognizing that a mystery exists here; a musical adventure with the fact of "complex development" at its core. The great western composers of the past five hundred years have ventured consciously into this mystery of complex contrapuntal development of essentially simple themes. Generations of listeners have thrilled to trace with their ears the permutations and manipulations which composers have rendered in the name of fugue. Johann Sebastian Bach in his massive *Die Kunst der Fuge*, still incomplete at the time of his death, took this musical procedure to the edge of believability. An extraordinarily and self-consciously learned work, this set of eighteen progressively elaborate fugues is generated from one unassuming melody of twelve pitches. The greatest mystery here is the monumental unfinished final fugue which breaks off abruptly shortly after the composer signed his name, at a point of astonishing complexity, by using the pitches B A C H as a counter-subject. What would J.S. Bach have done next had he lived to finish this piece? Had he stopped here because in fact he had reached the limit of his own incredible ingenuity? Will we all get to hear the consummation of this colossal fugue, as Bach and God would have it, on the last day? Well, after old "Papa" Bach left us dangling in 1750, one would have thought that composers would have left fugue alone. But, no. Haydn, Mozart, Beethoven, Mendelssohn, Schumann, Reger, Hindemith, Shostakovich, and countless others all wrote fugues. Fugue is an inexhaustible and timeless challenge to composer, performer, and listener: logical and mystical, carefully ordered while refreshing and surprising, intellectually rigorous yet emotionally potent, manifest in finite parcels of time yet open to indefinite development, each one a mere temporal suggestion or excerpt of an eternal conversation of musical themes. Every effort to compose a fugue may be likened to the attempt to unlock a piece of truth of natural reality which, from creation, has lain in anticipation of being discovered and shared. For these reasons, because of who he is, my musical tribute to Thomas Julian Talley had to be fugal.

Why three fugues? Obviously because there is one man but three names. For another relevant application of this type of thinking, see Athanasius.

The three fugues presented here are unlike the grandiose contrapuntal explorations of J.S. Bach. In scope they are more closely related to the relatively modest *Magnificat* fugues of Johann Pachelbel. Rather than fully developed sermons, they are more like compact and brief homilies. In them one will find many of the standard devices of fugal writing, including inversion, fragmentation, augmentation, and stretto. No attempt is made, however, to wring ultimate or exhaustive "solutions" from the "problems" posed by the three subjects. The effort here is rather to offer an effective interim commentary on these melodic suggestions. While the conversation potentially is boundless, these three fugues are only brief dialogues. Although they are designed to be played on any keyboard instrument, organ (without pedals) might be considered the preferred medium. The first fugue, "Thomas," is in four voices and should be played in a gentle singing style on flute stops of 8', 4', and perhaps even 2' pitch. The second fugue, "Julian," in three voices, is a more sober piece and might be expressed best by 8' (and 4') foundation tone. The last fugue, "Talley," in four voices, is a gigue. As such, it should sparkle. It may be at its best played on foundations, cornet, and bright reed stops. The clever keyboardist is encouraged to be imaginative.

A New Tune for an Old Hymn

New hymn tunes occur in various ways. The following is a true story. One evening in the fall of 1979, between Evensong and a dinner party at a faculty residence, I found myself walking on the close of the seminary with Dr. Talley. He drew in on his pipe and, as a cloud of fragrant white smoke rose from about his head and dissipated in the crisp early evening air, he inquired as to whether I had ever considered composing an alternative tune to "Let All Mortal Flesh Keep Silence." While, he assured me, he had no problem singing this text to the familiar tune "Picardy," he made clear his conviction that a new tune might be helpful in illuminating this historic hymn text in new and felicitous ways. This was not the first time he had made this particularly unlikely inquiry. In fact, it had never occurred to me that an alternative tune for this hymn might be considered desirable. Yet I took the recurrence of this subject not to be without significance. We parted at the entrance to Lorillard Hall, which I entered, as he continued diagonally left on the path toward Eigenbrodt. The remembrance of Talley's inquiry lingered, however, and transformed itself into powerful suggestion as I proceeded to ready myself for the dinner party. A melody and harmony began forming in my inner ear, and I went to the piano to work them out. A tune in the meter required by the text soon emerged, and I scribbled it on a scrap of manuscript paper. As is my habit when it seems that I might have invented a new hymn tune, I played it again and again and sang the text through repeatedly to see how well the combination of words and music would hold up. The dinner hour soon beckoned me to leave my musical work and go to the party. After an enjoyable evening, it happened that Dr. Talley and I left the dinner party together. On the way to our respective apartments I told him about my new tune and, since he was intrigued, I invited him up to my studio and this music which, it seemed, his suggestion had inflicted upon me. I played it for him on the piano, and he sang it at once in his inimitable and distinctive Texan voice. It was clear to me immediately that the tune should be named "Talley." And thus has it been known since that evening.

Note

1. *Funk & Wagnalls Standard College Dictionary* (New York, 1963) 539.

Three Fugues

1 Andante

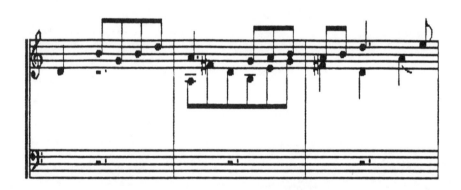

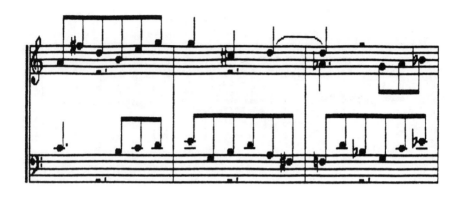

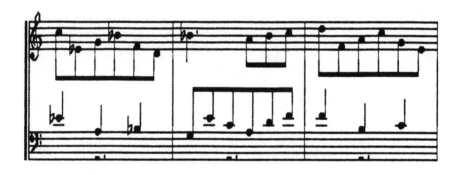

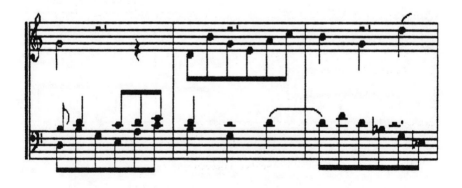

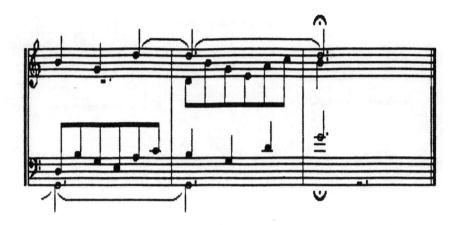

2 Lento

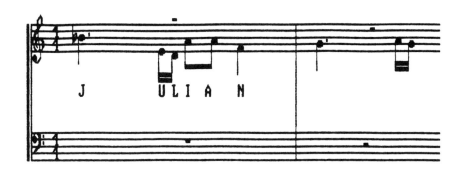

J   U L I A   N

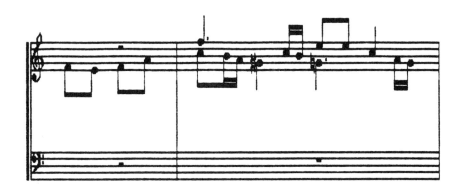

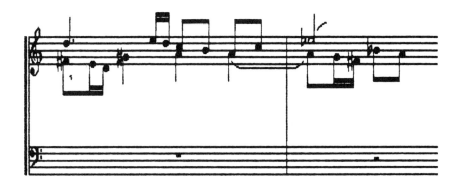

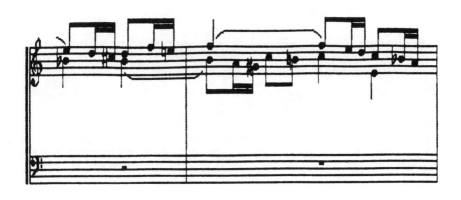

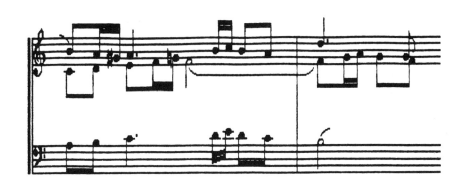

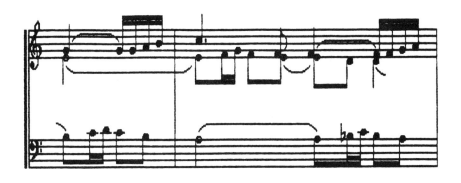

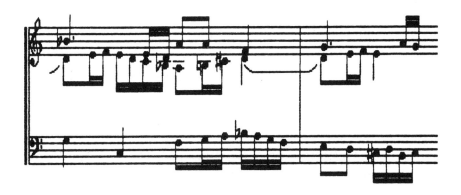

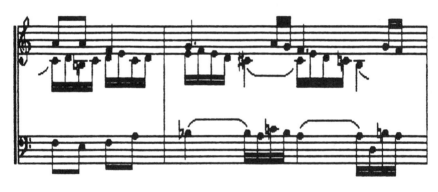

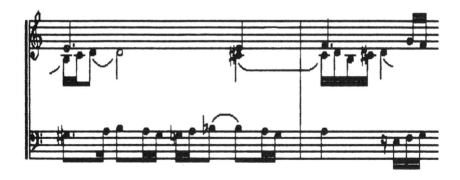

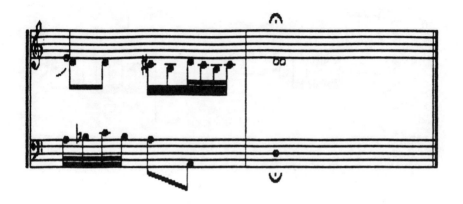

3 Vivace

T ALLEY

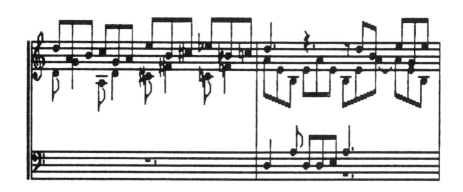

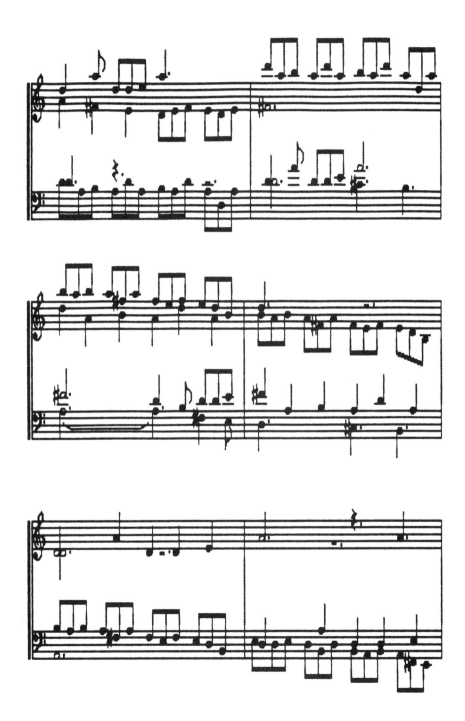

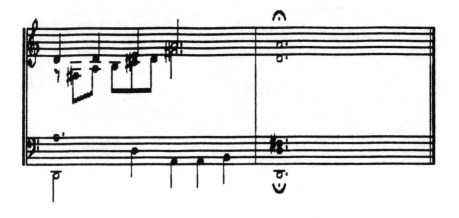

A Hymn Tune

LET ALL MORTAL FLESH KEEP SILENCE

TALLEY 87. 87. 87
David Hurd, 1979

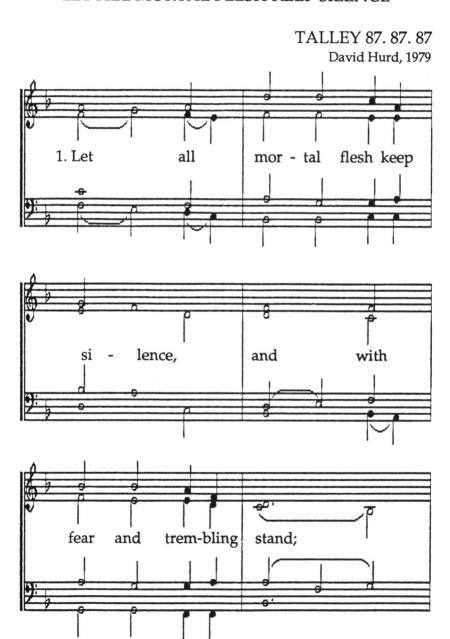

pon - der   no - thing earth-ly

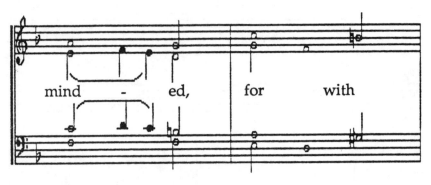

mind - ed,   for   with

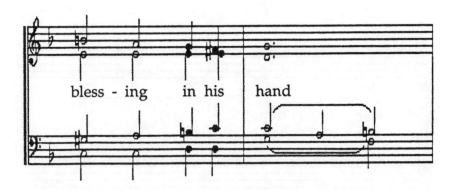

bless - ing   in his   hand

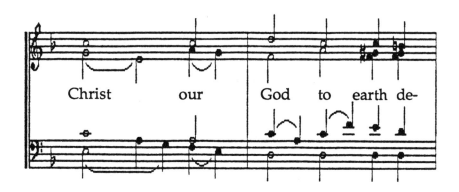

Christ our God to earth de-

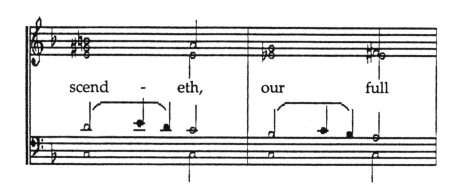

scend - eth, our full

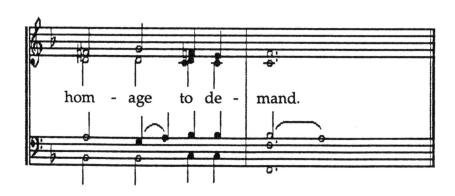

hom - age to de - mand.

2. King of kings, yet born of Mary,
   as of old on earth he stood
   Lord of lords in human vesture,
   in the Body and the Blood
   he will give to all the faithful
   his own self for heav'nly food.

3. Rank on rank the host of heaven
   spreads its vanguard on the way,
   as the Light of Light descendeth
   from the realms of endless day,
   that the powers of hell may vanish
   as the darkness clears away.

4. At his feet the six-winged seraph;
   cherubim with sleepless eye,
   veil their faces to the Presence,
   as with ceaseless voice they cry,
   "Alleluia, alleluia!
   Alleluia, Lord most high!"

Liturgy of St. James, 5th Cent.
Para. Gerard Moultrie, 1864

Contributors

J. Neil Alexander is a priest of the Episcopal Church and teaches liturgics and homiletics in The General Theological Seminary, New York. Previously he taught liturgics and spirituality and was Dean of the Chapel at Waterloo Lutheran Seminary, Wilfrid Laurier University, Waterloo, Ontario, Canada.

John F. Baldovin, S.J. teaches historical theology and liturgy in the Jesuit School of Theology, Berkeley. Before going to Berkeley, he taught in the Department of Theology at Fordham University, New York, and continues to teach in the liturgical studies program at the Univesity of Notre Dame. Dr. Baldovin is the author of *The Urban Character of Christian Worship*, among other studies of the liturgies of the early church.

Paul F. Bradshaw is a priest of the Church of England and is Professor of Liturgy in the Department of Theology at the University of Notre Dame. He is the author of *Daily Prayer in the Early Church* (1981), and *The Anglican Ordinal* (1971), among other works. He currently serves at the Chief Editor of *Studia Liturgica*.

Geoffrey J. Cuming was a priest of the Church of England and lecturer in liturgy at King's College, London, and Ripon College, Cuddesdon. He was the author of numerous liturgical studies concerning both the rites of the early church and those of the Anglican tradition. He died in March 1988.

Emmanuel J. Cutrone is a Professor in the Department of Theology at Spring Hill College, Mobile Alabama. Dr. Cutrone was previously a member of the faculty of Quincy College, Quincy, Illinois, and has taught in the summer liturgy programs of the University of Notre and St. John's University, Collegeville. He has written a variety of studies dealing primarily with the development of eucharistic rites in Syria and Jerusalem.

Balthasar Fischer is a priest of the Roman Catholic Church and was for many years the Professor of Liturgy in the Theological Faculty at Trier where he was also head of the scientific department of the Liturgical Institute. Dr. Fischer is a widely published writer of works on liturgy and spirituality. As a consultant, he played a significant role in preparing for and shaping the liturgical reforms of the Second Vatican Council.

Marion J. Hatchett is a priest of the Episcopal Church and Professor of Liturgics and Church Music in the School of Theology, the University of the South, Sewanee, Tennessee. Dr. Hatchett has written the *Commentary on the American Prayer Book*, 1981, numerous historical studies on the Prayer Book tradition, as well as a variety of supplemental liturgical and musical resources to accompany the *Book of Common Prayer, 1979*, and *The Hymnal, 1982*.

Lawrence A. Hoffman teaches at Hebrew Union College - Jewish Institute of Religion, New York. He has lectured widely in liturgical studies, including the University of Notre Dame. Rabbi Hoffmann is the author of *The Canonization of the Synagogue Service* (1979), *Beyond the Text: A Holistic Approach to Liturgy* (1987), and *The Art of Public Prayer* (1988), among other studies.

David R. Holeton is a priest of the Anglican Church of Canada and presently teaches in the Faculty of Divinity at Trinity College, Toronto, Ontario. Many of his writings concern issues related to Christian Initiation. Dr. Holeton is a member of the Doctrine and Worship Committee of the Anglican Church of Canada and Secretary of the International Anglican Liturgical Consultation.

David J. Hurd is Professor of Church Music, Organist, and Director of

Chapel Music in The General Theological Seminary, New York. Dr. Hurd has performed widely as an organist throughout Europe and North America and has built a distinguished reputation as a composer. His contributions to the development of music in the church have been recognized by the conferral of honorary degrees by three seminaries of the Episcopal Church.

Aidan Kavanagh, O.S.B. is a monk of the Archabbey of St. Meinrad and Professor of Liturgics in the Divinity School, Yale University. A widely published and influential writer on a variety of topics, Dr. Kavanagh has made particular contributions to the study of Christian initiation and liturgical theology.

Paul V. Marshall is a priest of the Episcopal Church and teaches liturgics in the Yale Divinity School and Berkeley Divinity School at Yale. He was previously Rector of Christ Church, Babylon, New York, and Professor of Liturgics and Homiletics at The George Mercer School of Theology, Garden City, New York. Dr. Marshall has published numerous articles in liturgics and homiletics and his research has focussed particularly on seventeenth and eighteenth century English liturgiology.

Leonel L. Mitchell is a priest of the Episcopal Church and Professor of Liturgics in the Seabury-Western Theological Seminary, Evanston, Illinois. Dr. Mitchell has written on a variety of subjects including christian initiation, ritual studies, and liturgical theology. He is the author of *Praying Shapes Believing*, a theological commentary on the *Book of Common Prayer, 1979*.

H. Boone Porter is a priest of the Episcopal Church and Editor of *The Living Church*. He has previously served as a professor of liturgics in The General Theological Seminary and Nashotah House. Dr. Porter is the author of major historical studies on liturgical time, ordination rites, and English liturgiology, in addition to numerous shorter works on liturgical and pastoral subjects.

Bryan D. Spinks is a priest of the Church of England, Chaplain at Churchill College, Cambridge, and lecturer in the Divinity Faculty at

Cambridge. His writings have included major studies of topics related to the sixteenth century reforms of the liturgy as well as studies of the liturgies of the early church, particular those of East Syria. He has recently completed a major study of the *Sanctus* for which he received the degree Doctor of Divinity from the University of Durham.

Kenneth W. Stevenson is a priest of the Church of England and Rector of Holy Trinity and St. Mary's, Guildford. He was previously the Chaplain and Lecturer in Liturgy at Manchester University. Dr. Stevenson has published widely on a variety of liturgical topics including marriage rites, eucharistic offering, and the liturgical year.

Robert Taft, S.J. is Ordinary Professor of Oriental Liturgy and Languages at the Pontifical Oriental Institute and Visiting Professor at the University of Notre Dame. A prolific writer, Dr. Taft has published major historical studies of the oriental rites and the liturgy of the hours as well as major contributions to liturgical theology.

Herman Wegman is a priest of the Roman Catholic Church, Professor of Liturgy, and Dean of the Theological Faculty, University of Utrecht, The Netherlands. Dr. Wegman is the author of a number of liturgical studies as well as the massive study guide to liturgical history, *Christian Worship in East and West*.

Louis Weil is a priest of the Episcopal Church and Professor of Liturgics in the Church Divinity School of the Pacific, Berkeley. He previously served a lengthy tenure on the faculty of Nashotah House. A member of the Standing Liturgical Commission of the Episcopal Church, Dr. Weil is the author of *Sacraments and Liturgy: The Outward Signs* (1983) and *Gathered to Pray* (1986).

DATE DUE